Principalities and Powers

Principalities and Powers

*Revising John Howard Yoder's
Sociological Theology*

Jamie Pitts

The Lutterworth Press

To my parents

The Lutterworth Press
P.O. Box 60
Cambridge
CB1 2NT
United Kingdom

www.lutterworth.com
publishing@lutterworth.com

ISBN: 978 0 7188 9331 6

British Library Cataloguing in Publication Data
A record is available from the British Library

First published by The Lutterworth Press, 2014

Copyright © Jamie Pitts, 2013

Published by arrangement
with Pickwick Publications

Contents

Preface | ix

Acknowledgments | xix

Abbreviations | xxi

Introduction | xxiii

1   Revising Yoder's Theology of Creation | 1

2   Revising Yoder's Theological Anthropology | 36

3   Revising Yoder's Theology of Violence | 61

4   Revising Yoder's Theological Method | 93

5   Revising Yoder's Ecclesial Politics | 133

6   Revising Yoder's Theology of Christian Particularity | 161

Conclusion | 192

Bibliography | 201

Preface

WHAT FOLLOWS IS A light revision of my Edinburgh University doctoral
thesis as submitted in August 2011 and examined by Graham Ward and
Fergus Kerr in October of that year. My examiners had many helpful suggestions as to how the manuscript could be improved and I am grateful
for their sympathetic and sharp readings. Since the examination I have had
fruitful discussions about all or part of the thesis with Tim Jenkins, Derek
Robbins, and John Rempel. I have followed my readers' suggestions when
possible while revising this book, though impending academic employment
narrowed the scope of what I was able to accomplish. Moreover, many of my
readers' comments are worthy of more extended treatment than is appropriate here given the limited aims of the project as a revision of Yoder. Two of
these suggestions are worth discussing briefly, as they point to significant
gaps in the present work.

The first concerns the status of my proposed "sociological theology" as a
viable theological method. As outlined in chapter 4 below, sociological theology is a non-reductive contextual methodology directed toward the church's
mission. But this description only hints at how my proposal may or may not
overlap with other contextual methodologies and forms of "engaged theology" (such as liberation and public theologies). As important as the proposal
is to the present book, I did not feel that I would be able to develop a full-
blown methodology here without detracting significantly from the focus on
Yoder and his legacy. Much more work on this methodology is necessary, and
for that reason I hope to treat it in detail in a subsequent volume.

The second suggestion was that I be more explicit about problems with
Bourdieu's "secularism." Sociological models are not theologically neutral,
and their adaptation for theological purposes should be mindful of how
they are shaped by assumptions about creation and divinity. In contemporary theology, Milbank's *Theology and Social Theory* is the landmark effort
in theological vigilance toward secular sociology, but from a historical perspective the book belongs to a line of theological thought about as old as

sociology itself. In earlier drafts of this manuscript I did include Milbank-style criticisms of Bourdieu, though I was never fully convinced they hit their target. However, some account of the "Christian difference" from secular sociology is necessary. Bourdieu, after all, writes as if God were dead and endorses the classical (French) sociological vision of society as God; his post-liberal anarcho-socialism—in which the defense of the welfare state is a first step toward the redistribution of political and economic power throughout the entire body politic (i.e., "God")—is not precisely the politics of the church; and his Stoical and Spinozistic meditations on the necessity of contingency cannot be separated from his core sociological concepts, which are meant to show how contingency becomes embodied in (and denied by) our bodies and institutions. As I indicate in the introduction, the "revisions" to Yoder—which were written originally as mutual criticisms of Bourdieu and Yoder—hopefully already show clearly how I depart from Bourdieu in articulating a Christian sociological theology. But more work is needed, namely, a detailed and comprehensive theological critique of Bourdieu that also deserves its own volume.

The need to complete the project leaves another set of more recent interlocutors unanswered, and here I have in mind the several books by or about Yoder that have been published since August 2011. While writing my thesis I did not have access to three of the essays contained in *The End of Sacrifice*, a collection of Yoder's writings on capital punishment edited by John Nugent.[1] It will be important for scholars to account for changes over time in Yoder's approach to the topic in light of broader developments in his *oeuvre*, and *The End of Sacrifice* will be indispensable for such efforts. For the purpose of the present book, however, I do not judge that the newly available material would substantially alter my argument. The publication of Yoder's 1966 South American lectures as *Revolutionary Christianity* poses a more difficult problem, as it contains a previously unavailable chapter on the principalities and powers.[2] Since this material mostly made it into *The Politics of Jesus*, I did not feel obliged to include it in the part of each chapter where I review Yoder's other writings on the powers. *Revolutionary Christianity* provides fascinating insight into how Yoder was working toward the arguments of *The Politics of Jesus* and how those arguments hang together with arguments he makes

1. Yoder, "Capital Punishment and the Bible," "Capital Punishment and Our Witness to Government," and "Against the Death Penalty," in *End of Sacrifice*, 29–36, 63–75, 77–152. The other two chapters are "The Christian and Capital Punishment" (37–62) and "You Have It Coming: Good Punishment" (153–238). I had access to earlier publications of these documents and they are referenced below in their original formats. See especially chapter 3 below, on violence.

2. Yoder, "Christ and the Powers," in *Revolutionary Christianity*, 120–34.

elsewhere about ecclesiology and history. But, again, I did not feel like the material was so revolutionary for my own understanding of Yoder that it warranted major revision to the manuscript as it was.

There have been two books published about Yoder that do warrant serious consideration as to how they might change the arguments presented below.[3] In *The Politics of Yahweh: John Howard Yoder, The Old Testament, and the People of God*, John Nugent provides the invaluable service of making sense of Yoder's vast body of writings on the Old Testament. Nugent argues persuasively that, although Yoder's approach to scripture is beset by methodological difficulties, many of his suggestions have been upheld and nuanced by scholarship and others point in fruitful directions even if they do not stand on their own merit. In his own defensive revision of Yoder's "trajectory" approach to the Old Testament—by which Yoder reads the Old Testament critically as pointing forward to the New Testament—Nugent makes an important contribution to discussions about Yoder's treatment of Israelite holy war (or "Yahweh war").[4] Writing in *The Politics of Jesus* and elsewhere, Yoder contends that the holy wars were occasions when Israel learned to trust in God alone, and not military preparedness, for victory. Although God does use these wars to secure Israel's place in the Promised Land, the wars are ultimately a propaedeutic toward the pacifism, i.e., total trust in God, envisioned by Jeremiah and realized by Jesus. This is the basic outline or trajectory that Nugent defends as biblically and theologically adequate.

The reason Nugent must defend Yoder's work is because many of Yoder's readers find an inconsistency between this interpretation of Israelite holy war and the claim that Jesus reveals the character of God and the grain of the universe. If Jesus refuses even the most chastened forms of violence, then why was God directing battles in ancient Palestine? This question is especially troubling from an orthodox Trinitarian perspective, in which the Father and the Son (and the Holy Spirit) share attributes perfectly. If we affirm the trinitarian being of God, then we cannot affirm the violence of the Father and the nonviolence of the Son. The question has ethical implications as well, for if Jesus' nonviolence only reveals God's character partially or provisionally, then perhaps Christians are called to be nonviolent in some

3. Mention should also be made of Daniel Colucciello Barber's *On Diaspora*, which discusses Yoder in the context of a larger, Spinozistic project. Given my own debts to Yoder and, via Bourdieu, Spinoza, I find much of Barber's argument congenial to my own, even though I remain committed to the theological idiom and the faith that produces it. Barber's case for diaspora, instead of theology and philosophy, is powerful and complex, and I am still uncertain how to respond to it. I do wonder if pursuing the theological vision of Nicholas Lash's *Holiness, Speech and Silence* might constitute a beginning.

4. Nugent, *Politics of Yahweh*, 101–2, 110–18, 126–28.

instances and violent in others. H. Richard Niebuhr's trinitarian ethic suggests a possible resolution on these terms, in which each triune person calls for a distinct ecclesial response.[5] A "theocentric" ethic might respect pacifism as a faithful response to the Son and war as a faithful response to the Father; if carried out with integrity, perhaps in the latter case as just war, then both responses can point to the transcendent goodness of God.

Nugent, however, takes a different angle on the issue, depicting the holy wars as a provisional tactic necessary for establishing Israel in the Promised Land. "God must creatively solve the problem of forging a people of peace in a world of war," he argues, and the holy wars are the solution.[6] Holy war serves God well, then, for two reasons: first, because it accomplishes God's purposes in history and, second, because it teaches the Israelites that God is the only security in battle. By forming Israel in such a way, God prepares it for Jesus' later witness of peace. Jesus' witness and God's former use of holy war are in no conflict. Both point to peace as the center and goal of God's purposes. Jesus may reveal the heart of God, but "his actions and teachings were [not] meant to constitute an exhaustive representation of God's responses to evil" (112). Nor is there an ethical dilemma, as Christians are called to be like Jesus and become a people of peace who trust God for their safety. Christians can be nonviolent without having to worship a nonviolent God.

Nugent does not shy away from the difficult implications of his argument, going so far as to explain the total destruction of people and property at Jericho and Ai as ritual sacrifices commanded by God to punish idolatry (116–70). Far from acts of genocide or imperialism, these were purely religious acts whose non-pragmatic nature is evident in the strange military tactics God has the Israelites undertake: marching around a city seven times and blowing a horn is not a blueprint for martial glory. The Israelite holy wars must, therefore, be understood only as a means by which God formed a people whose story culminates in the everlasting peace of Christ. They may not be used to justify genocide or any other act of violence.

This defense is a creative attempt at faithfully extending Yoder's argument while staying true to the apparent shape of the biblical text. Nevertheless, the defense looks a lot like all those expressions of false consciousness by which a people justify their founding acts of violence in order to justify their present political constitution. In this case, the more religiously, spiritually, or morally motivated the violence the better. Although the objective outcome of the Israelite holy wars is the same as any other war—territorial

5. Niebuhr, "Doctrine of the Trinity" and *Christ and Culture*. See chapter 1 below for further discussion.

6. Nugent, *Politics of Yahweh*, 102. Unless otherwise noted, references to *Politics of Yahweh* are hereafter contained in the text.

domination—they belong to a separate class of activities by virtue of God's involvement and purpose. The appeal to Yahweh as the ultimate warrior serves as an ultimate, indisputable form of legitimation: "God gave us this land and disposed of its inhabitants, we only helped out and obeyed God. The integrity of our past and the present it authorizes is beyond dispute."

Of course, God may have given the ancient Israelites Palestine and may have done so by using holy war. Speculative ideological critique cannot tell us what actually happened, it can only warn when our accounts of what happened resemble other accounts used to perpetuate domination. Once the resemblance is acknowledged, moral, historical, and hermeneutical judgments still have to take place. Nugent does his best to separate Israelite holy war from the specter of domination. He downplays questions about their historicity and argues that what matters is how the narratives constituted a people then and can continue to do so today (126–28). The primary arena of judgment, then, is moral, and he regards these texts as righteous because they point to peace and so are consistent with God's overall purpose in redeeming creation. Further, since he insists that Christians, as (spiritual) beneficiaries of Israelite holy war, are called to nonviolence, he denies that Israelite holy war can be used to sanction further violence. The founding act of violence does not, in this case, legitimate a present polity's domination.

Nugent's solution has much to recommend it, insofar as it maintains Jesus' nonviolence as normative for Christians without distorting the holy war passages and their depiction of God as a warrior. I remain troubled, however, by the systematic implication that God's Word and Wisdom, the second person of the Trinity, was apparently uninvolved in the constitution of Israel, surely one of the foundational moments of salvation history. It is one thing to claim that the human Jesus was not leading the Israelites in battle, another thing altogether to say that the divine Christ through whom all things were made and all things hold together was absent from the scene. From a trinitarian perspective, the peace of Christ is not a mere dispensation but definitive of God's being and action in the world from creation to eschaton.[7] If the burden of exegetical proof rests on those of us who seek alternative interpretations of Israelite holy war, then there is an equally

7. See ibid., 188, where Nugent defines his approach as "dispensational*ist* in its attention to various developments in the gradual unfolding of God's plan." As an Anabaptist theologian, I am especially wary of dispensationalist interpretations of scripture given their legacy at Münster, where Bernhard Rothmann told followers the age of Christ's nonresistance had passed and the eschatological age of vengeance had begun. Anabaptist missionary Hans Hut embraced a similar hermeneutic, but, at least after the failure of the Peasants' Revolt, maintained that the end had not yet come and so pacifism was normative for the time being. Nugent would reject such distortions, but dispensational pacifism is always vulnerable to the proclamation of a new, violent era.

weighty theological burden to be borne by Nugent and those who agree with him.[8]

The second book that merits consideration is Paul Martens's *Heterodox Yoder*. Martens, whose earlier essays are discussed throughout the present book, here recapitulates and refines his case that Yoder progressively reduces theology to ethics, politics, and sociology. After dispatching with the shibboleths of the Yoder guild that deny the possibility of a developmental reading of Yoder's *oeuvre*,[9] Martens sets out his argument in four stages: (1) Yoder's core theological commitments, from the very beginning, were oriented to ethics and church practices (19–53); (2) by *The Politics of Jesus*, the ethical and political focus has overtaken Yoder's ecclesiology to the point where he almost exclusively uses governmental language to describe the church (54–86); (3) throughout the 1970s and 80s, he articulates his understanding of the fundamental unity of Judaism and Christianity in ethical terms, such that his primary Jewish interlocutor, Steven Schwarzschild, is unsure why he remains a Christian (87–115); and (4) Yoder's late sociological interpretation of the sacraments makes social practice the only possible point of distinction between church and world (116–40). Yoder, Martens concludes, is "heterodox" in the sense that his sociological theology ignores the substance of historic orthodoxy and presents Jesus as merely an ethical model (143–44). In resisting the forces of theological speculation and idealism, Yoder gives in to "the powerful temptation to turn faith into just another form of ethics or series of practices" (147).

Readers of Martens's earlier essays on Yoder will find much of *The Heterodox Yoder* familiar, although he has considerably restructured the arguments and introduced significant material from Yoder's correspondence and obscure early writings. These changes render Martens's challenge to many of the prevailing interpretations of Yoder more lucid and compelling, supporting the need for the kind of revision I undertake here. That said, my response to Martens remains essentially the same as it was before the publication of *The Heterodox Yoder*. Martens work is valuable insofar as it forces close inspection of Yoder's developing theological practice and of the theological assumptions behind that practice. We are in Martens's debt for his rigorous scholarship and refusal to accept standard presentations of Yoder's

8. The contrast between biblical and theological work should not be overplayed, even when discussing the Trinity. The "systematic" problem arises precisely because of scripture passages like John 1 and Colossians 1 that relate Christ and God in the most intimate of terms. See Hurtado, *God in New Testament Theology*, for a sustained argument that the New Testament authors had a triune understanding of God.

9. Martens, *Heterodox Yoder*, 7–16. Unless otherwise noted, references to *Heterodox Yoder* are hereafter contained in the text.

work. I doubt, however, that the search for a definitive "historical Yoder" will result in a new consensus, as indicated by the lengthy online exchange between Martens and Branson Parler.[10] The unlikeliness of forthcoming consensus does not, of course, render debate irrelevant. But it does suggest that the search for what Yoder "really said" might, if it is to avoid insularity and irrelevance, be subordinated to bold new attempts to move with and beyond Yoder to face the challenges of Christian living in the twenty-first century.

Nevertheless, there is one "historical Yoder" issue that scholars must face squarely, and that concerns the relationship between his sexual misconduct and his writings.[11] This preface is not the place to carry out a comprehensive review of Yoder's theology based on knowledge of his sexual activity, but a few comments must be made. Yoder was a theologian for whom, in theory at least, the consistency between "walk and word" was paramount. Yet his sexual activities clearly contravened his ecclesiology and ethics. By persistently violating physical and emotional boundaries with a large number of women, he failed to exhibit patience as method in moral reasoning and he failed to participate in the dialogue that constitutes the church. Moreover, Yoder used aspects of his theology to justify his actions, as he apparently told several women that he was conducting an avant-garde ecclesial experiment. Anyone familiar with Yoder's ecclesiology will recognize these terms as central to his understanding of the church's role in the world: the church as firstfruits, pioneer, pilot project, and creative transformer of culture. Although Yoder's point about the avant-garde church—it breaks with the world and demonstrates God's coming reign—is theologically sound, perhaps his ability to twist that logic to deviant ends will caution his inheritors from claiming too much for the church and, especially, for themselves as church members. Perhaps we need to say more clearly that the church *might become* avant-garde insofar as it exhibits the integrity-in-discernment that is its calling.

In addition to a more humble ecclesiology, consideration of Yoder's personal failings might lead us to emphasize more strongly than he did that personal spiritual integrity is vital for theological and ecclesial practice. I

10. Parler wrote a thirty-eight page review of *The Heterodox Yoder* that can be downloaded from *The Englewood Review* website (http://erb.kingdomnow.org/the-heterodox-yoder-paul-martens-feature-review/). That page also contains links to a response by Martens and concluding remarks by Parler.

11. For a description of Yoder's sexual misconduct, see Hauerwas, *Hannah's Child*, 242–47, and the articles by Tom Price in *The Elkhart Truth* published in June and July of 1992. Ted Grimsrud has posted these articles on his website, *Peace Theology* (http://peacetheology.net/john-h-yoder/john-howard-yoder%E2%80%99s-sexual-misconduct%E2%80%94part-five-2/).

make this argument throughout the present book in response to critics who think Yoder favors social ethics so much that he occludes the personal and spiritual. Although we should avoid conjecturing personal reasons as to why he did not write much about the spiritual life, it is apparent that his life in this instance stands as a warning not to decouple the personal and the social, the spiritual and the ethical. Heeding that warning will likely involve moving to consider theological labor itself as a spiritual practice.

It goes without saying that no theologian will perfectly embody their stated beliefs, but attempts to grapple with Yoder's legacy that do not reflect on the relationship between his theology and personal life do not take seriously his rejection of idealism. In other words, they assume that his life and words exist on different planes, an assumption he steadfastly resisted when it came to the church's common life. Although the present book is aimed at overcoming idealism without falling into reductive materialism, I acknowledge that I was unsuccessful to the extent that I did not examine Yoder's work in light of his sexual misconduct. Further revision to my revised Yoderian sociological theology is necessary.

As with the other areas of revision, though perhaps somewhat more surprisingly in this case, Pierre Bourdieu's reflexive sociology is a helpful conversation partner. In 1975 Bourdieu published an extended essay on Martin Heidegger, a philosopher whose work was highly influential on his own.[12] Heidegger had been a member of the Nazi party and much ink had been spilled either to expose his Nazi activities and so denounce him personally, or to demonstrate how his Nazism was irrelevant to the interpretation of his "pure philosophy."[13] Bourdieu viewed these opposite biographical and philosophical approaches as unwitting collaborators in protecting Heidegger's writings from criticism: both treated his life and work as separable. By contrast, Bourdieu's essay shows how it is the very ideology and language of "pure philosophy," of ontological inquiry completely removed from politics, that is the philosophical correlate of the Nazi obsession with racial purity. Although this move to link Heidegger's writings and politics would seem to be the strongest form of repudiation, Bourdieu insisted that his essay was "conceived above all as a methodological exercise" and therefore not an effort in "denunciation."[14] "Methodological exercise" perhaps sounds

12. The essay was first published in *Actes de la recherches en science sociales* and then put out in lightly revised form as the book *L'ontologie politique de Martin Heidegger* in 1988, with an English translation appearing in 1991. References to *L'ontologie politique* here are to the 1988 edition.

13. This, anyway, is Bourdieu's understanding of the literature. See *L'ontologie politique*, 9–14.

14. Ibid., 7: "Conçu avant tout comme un exercise de method, il se situe dans une

a bit clinical when dealing with such a sensitive topic, but his point is that the science of understanding how politics and intellectual work intersect is more important than the legacy of this one man. That is because such a science, for Bourdieu, gives its adherents the possibility of understanding, and so of changing, life, work and their often hidden relationship. And so it is for Yoder. Far from denouncing him, we should be concerned to understand him lest we fall into the same trap. There is much to give thanks for in Yoder's legacy, but our thankfulness should not preclude our recognition of the need for repentance.

Yoder eventually did submit to a disciplinary process initiated by the Indiana-Michigan Mennonite Conference, the regional body responsible for his ministerial credentials. Those involved in the process, which lasted over three years, were satisfied to the extent that they publicly "encourage[d] Yoder and the church to use his gifts of writing and teaching."[15] A cautionary reading might suggest that Yoder went through the motions and fooled those tasked with overseeing the process. We now have no way of knowing for sure. What is evident, however, is that his readiness to undergo discipline and offer assurances of repentance were, finally, consistent with his ecclesiology. Sin permeates our world. There is no way of ensuring in advance that Christian leaders will avoid egregious error and live exemplary lives. When error occurs forgiveness and restoration is called for, and Jesus provided an invitation and opportunity for those to be realized. Without downplaying the seriousness of Yoder's failings, we can be grateful that he persistently called Christians to follow Jesus and so to discern and forgive sin. We can best honor Yoder's legacy, in all its complexity, by imitating the politics of Jesus and becoming ministers of reconciliation in church and world.

perspective qui n'est pas celle de la denunciation."

15. This quote is from the Conference's news release "Disciplinary Process with John Howard Yoder Draws to a Close." I am grateful to Sara Wenger Shenk for making available to me this release and other relevant documents about the conclusion of the process.

Acknowledgments

ALTHOUGH THIS BOOK IS a work of my own hands, it is also a product of innumerable friendships in Austin, Houston, Los Angeles, Washington, D.C., St. Andrews, Edinburgh, and elsewhere. My friends have prayed, argued, played music, protested, organized, been silent, taken walks, traveled, and shared food and drink with me over the past few years in ways that have made this book possible. I hope they recognize something of themselves and of our friendships in what follows. I am particularly grateful to Chase Roden, Richard Kentopp, Christina Hirukawa, Richard Davis, Tyler Parks, Wendy Mathison, and Elizabeth White, for their companionship during and beyond the writing period. Patrick Weir and Lois Jones deserve an award for living with me for four years of these preparations. Michael Edwards and Edimpro, Alastair Cole and the Bicycle Thieves, David Metcalf and Bodies of Water, the Badwills, and Diva Abrasiva provided much needed musical nourishment and friendship.

This work is also a product of friendships in several professional and academic networks. At Fuller Seminary, special thanks are owed to Glen Stassen and Nancey Murphy for their early support and guidance. Vincent Bacote was the first to encourage me to do further academic studies, and his summer courses on public theology convinced me that I wanted to. In Washington, D.C., David Ensign, Cindy Lapp, Sojourners, and Church World Service/Immigration and Refugee Program, helped me to connect my academic interests to the church's labor for justice. At St. Andrews, Mario Aguilar shaped my initial thoughts on theology, sociology, and activism, and Michael Partridge and Mark Harris pointed me to Bourdieu. In Edinburgh, I am thankful for Michael Northcott's crucial comments on the first thesis draft and on the first chapter of the present draft. Conversations with Paul Martens, visiting from Baylor, proved decisive for the direction of my arguments. Jolyon Mitchell and the executive board of the Centre for Theology and Public Issues provided tireless support and encouragement. My doctoral supervisor, David Fergusson, is an embodiment of the

Acknowledgments

Scottish intellectual tradition: patiently probing, intellectually rigorous, and slyly humorous. I am honored and grateful to have worked with him. Jeremy Begbie's wisdom guided me through a challenging time. Since moving to Elkhart, Sara Wenger Shenk and Rebecca Slough have helped me sort through some of the darker aspects of Yoder's legacy. In addition, thanks are due to the organizers, respondents, and audiences of the conferences in Durham, Chicago, Edinburgh, St. Andrews, Montreal, and Sydney, where I rehearsed many of the arguments below.

I am truly happy to be able to call my family friends: John, Lesley, the twins, Mom, Dad, Bain, and our extended families. This book would not, in any sense, have been possible without my parents, and I dedicate it to them. They taught me to love God and neighbor, and I hope this work represents a faithful reception of that gift.

Abbreviations

Yoder

ARS   *Anabaptism and Reformation in Switzerland: An Historical and Theological Analysis of the Dialogues between Anabaptists and Reformers*

BP   *Body Politics: Five Practices of the Christian Community before the Watching World*

CA   *Christian Attitudes to War, Peace, and Revolution*

DPR   *Discipleship as Political Responsibility*

FC   *The Fullness of Christ: Paul's Vision of Universal Ministry*

FTN   *For the Nations: Essays Evangelical and Public*

HCPP   *He Came Preaching Peace*

JCSR   *The Jewish-Christian Schism Revisited*

Nevertheless   *Nevertheless: The Varieties and Shortcomings of Religious Pacifism*

"HRN"   *"How H. Richard Niebuhr Reasoned: A Critique of Christ and Culture"*

Nonviolence   *Nonviolence: A Brief History: The Warsaw Lectures*

OR   *The Original Revolution: Essays on Christian Pacifism*

PJ   *The Politics of Jesus: Vicit Agnus Noster*

PK   *The Priestly Kingdom: Social Ethics as Gospel*

Preface   *Preface to Theology: Christological and Theological Method*

Abbreviations

PWK   *A Pacifist Way of Knowing: John Howard Yoder's Nonviolent Epistemology*

RP   *The Royal Priesthood: Essays Ecclesiological and Ecumenical*

"Servant"   *"Behold My Servant Shall Prosper"*

THW   *To Hear the Word*

UNDA   *University of Notre Dame Archive of unpublished writings*

WL   *The War of the Lamb: The Ethics of Nonviolence and Peacemaking*

WWIU   *When War is Unjust: Being Honest in Just-War Thinking*

Berkhof

C&P   *Christ and the Powers*

Bourdieu

CD   *Choses Dites*

CS   *The Craft of Sociology: Epistemological Preliminaries*

Distinction   *Distinction: A Social Critique of the Judgment of Taste*

HA   *Homo Academicus*

IRS   *An Invitation to Reflexive Sociology*

LP   *The Logic of Practice*

MD   *Masculine Domination*

OTP   *Outline of a Theory of Practice*

PM   *Pascalian Meditations*

PR   *Practical Reason: On the Theory of Action*

RA   *The Rules of Art: Genesis and Structure of the Literary Field*

Reproduction   *Reproduction in Education, Society and Culture*

SN   *The State Nobility: Elite Schools in the Field of Power*

SSA   *Sketch for a Self-Analysis*

WW   *The Weight of the World: Social Suffering in Contemporary Society*

Introduction

GLEN STASSEN TELLS A story about the time he approached John Howard Yoder after a session at the Society of Christian Ethics. Noting that many of the papers bore the mark of his friend's thought, Stassen said, "Your influence is really spreading." Yoder's simple response: "Not mine. Jesus.'"[1]

Whatever one thinks about the accuracy, not to mention the humility, of this response, there is little doubt that Yoder's Jesus-centered writings have gained a wide readership. Since 1999, four special journal issues, six monographs, and six collections of essays have focused on his life and thought,[2] and there is a steady market for new collections of his journal articles and unpublished writings.[3] Needless to say, the proliferation of commentary about Yoder has not led to a unified assessment of his legacy, and

---

1. This story is told in Peter Steinfels, "John H. Yoder, Theologian at Notre Dame, is Dead at 70," *The New York Times*, January 7, 1998. The phrasing used above differs slightly from the published account, as I am following an amended version Stassen distributed to a seminar at Fuller Seminary in the fall of 2005.

2. Bergen and Siegrist, eds., *Powers and Practices*; Carter, *Politics of the Cross*; Dula and Huebner, *New Yoder*; Hauerwas et al., eds., *Wisdom of the Cross*; Martens, *Heterodox Yoder*; Nation, *John Howard Yoder*; Nugent, *Politics of Yahweh*; Nugent, ed., *Radical Ecumenicity*; Ollenberger and Koontz, eds., *Mind Patient and Untamed*; Sider, *To See History Doxologically*; Somer, ed., *La sagesse de la croix*; Zimmerman, *Politics of Jesus*. Additionally, see Barber, *On Diaspora*; Bourne, *Seek the Peace of the City*; Doerksen, *Beyond Suspicion*; Park, *Missional Ecclesiologies in Creative Tension*; Shaffer, *Moral Memoranda from John Howard Yoder*. The journal issues are Epp, ed., "John Howard Yoder," special issue, *Conrad Grebel Review*; Holland, ed., "The Jewish-Christian Schism Revisited and Re-Imagined: Reflections on the Work of John Howard Yoder," special issue, *CrossCurrents*; Roth, ed., special issue, *Mennonite Quarterly Review*; Snyder, ed., "John Howard Yoder as Historian," special issue, *Conrad Grebel Review*.

3. In addition to *ARS*, *End of Sacrifice*, *JCSR*, *NV*, *Revolutionary Christianity*, *THW*, and *WL*, see Yoder's essays in Martens and Howell, eds., *John Howard Yoder*; Vogt, ed., *Roots of Concern*; Vogt, ed., *Concern for Education*; Nugent, ed., *Radical Ecumenicity*. New editions of *CA*, *DPR*, *KB* (with previously unpublished essays), *OR*, and *Preface* have been released, and *PWK* gathers his published writings on epistemology and method. See also Yoder's online archive of unpublished writings, *UNDA*.

many dispute the identification of his influence with Jesus'. The present book is an attempt to grapple with Yoder's critics in order to decide how to move forward with a revised "Yoderian" theology. How that revision is accomplished is described in the remainder of this introduction, which is divided into three parts: (1) an overview of the current state of Yoder scholarship and this book's place within it; (2) an argument that Yoder's theology can profitably read as a "sociological theology" that exhibits reductive tendencies, but which can be revised to be non-reductive; and (3) an outline and justification of the proposed method of revision, which involves putting Yoder's theology of the principalities and powers into conversation with the reflexive sociology of Pierre Bourdieu.

The Many Yoders and Yoder's Many Readers

John Howard Yoder (1927–1997) was an American Mennonite theologian whose work centered on the church's mandate to imitate the nonviolent politics of Jesus. Though most of his life was spent in America, he began his career in Europe while enrolled as a doctoral student at the University of Basel in the 1950s.[4] Drawn to questions about the relation of church and state, he organized discussions between the Historic Peace Churches and the established European churches for the World Council of Churches.[5] Many of his early publications emerged from these ecumenical discussions.[6] He was simultaneously involved in a publishing venture, the *Concern* journal, with a few other young American Mennonites who were also based in Europe. Yoder's ecumenical papers and his essays in *Concern* were focused on the correlation between the life of Jesus and the life of the church. They were, in other words, exercises in Christian ethics. For his doctoral dissertation, however, he chose a historical topic: the dialogues between the early Swiss Anabaptists and the Reformers.[7] This choice was necessitated by the resistance Yoder encountered among the European professoriate to work in Anabaptist theology.[8] Researching as a historian, he surmised, would allow him to investigate his theological preoccupations without causing controversy.

By the late 1960s, Yoder had published his dissertation (and some of its findings in historical journals), essays in *Concern*, much of his ecumenical

4. Nation, *John Howard Yoder*, 16–21; Zimmerman, *Politics of Jesus*, 70–100.

5. Ibid., and see Durnbaugh, "John Howard Yoder's Role in 'The Lordship of Christ over Church and State' Conferences."

6. Yoder, *CWS*; *DPR*; *Karl Barth*; "Reinhold Niebuhr."

7. Yoder, *ARS*.

8. Zimmerman, *Politics of Jesus*, 140–141.

material, and a translation of Hendrik Berkhof's *Christ and the Powers*. The main critical response, in print at least, was directed toward his dissertation.[9] Historians accused Yoder of distorting the evidence to serve a romanticized vision of Anabaptist origins. Some of these historians were from rival Reformation or secular historiographical traditions, but some were other Anabaptists concerned that Yoder's reconstruction unfairly limited the heterogeneity of their common beginnings. This fear that his theological preferences served as ideological blinders to historical reality would follow Yoder throughout his career and, indeed, beyond the grave. Although Yoder's historiography has many defenders, and many of his central findings remain plausible, there are serious questions about his methodological approach to scripture and church history.

Yoder did not engage in original historical research again after completing his dissertation, and his attention turned fully to theological ethics. His reputation, too, was made as an ethicist with the publication of *The Politics of Jesus* in 1972.[10] That book presented a powerful reading of the New Testament as a summons to the church to Jesus' radical nonviolent politics. *The Politics of Jesus* was, and is, widely read.[11] Along with other of Yoder's writings, it helped galvanize an emergent "evangelical left" that combined a focus on scripture and the church with social justice activism.[12] Furthermore, it propelled Yoder to the forefront of Anabaptist theology for the remainder of his career.[13] Given the predominance, at the time, of the Niebuhr brothers in American theological ethics, many readers regarded Yoder's pacifistic ecclesiology as an invitation to sectarian withdrawal from political activity.[14] If Christians cannot participate in state violence, the

9. Criticisms of Yoder's historiography, as well as of his general hermeneutic, are detailed in chapters 3 and 4 below.

10. Such is the judgment of, for instance, Dorrien, *Social Ethics in the Making*, 463.

11. See Nation, *John Howard Yoder*, xvi; Zimmerman, *Politics of Jesus*, 23.

12. Yoder's impact was felt especially by the Sojourners community and the Mennonite Central Committee's Washington Office. Cf. Cartwright, "Radical Catholicity," 44, and Graber Miller, *Wise as Serpents*, 175. On the term "evangelical left," see Hunter, *To Change the World*, 136–38. Hunter sees Yoder as a "neo-Anabaptist" separatist (165), underplaying his ties to Jim Wallis and the other evangelical left figures he discusses (150).

13. Gordon Kaufmann is the other twentieth-century Mennonite theologian with a broad ecumenical audience. But "Kaufman does not identify his basic standpoint as Anabaptist" and "challenges all attempts to theologize within any past perspective" (Finger, *Contemporary Anabaptist Theology*, 73). For comparison of Yoder and Kaufman, see Friesen, *Artists, Citizens, Philosophers*, 65–69, and Stoltzfus, "Nonviolent Jesus," 38–41.

14. Criticisms of Yoder's sectarianism are discussed in chapters 5 and 6 below. In *Social Ethics in the Making*, Dorrien presents Reinhold Niebuhr as the major figure in American Christian ethics. Although he acknowledges that Niebuhr's influenced had

critics argued, they must abdicate any claim to political influence. Yoder and his growing number of advocates insisted that the Niebuhrians illegitimately restricted the definition of politics so that a community dedicated to following Jesus could only be considered sectarian and apolitical. By contrast, the New Testament portrays Jesus as a political martyr and the church as an alternative political community based on his politics. To a certain extent, Yoder won the day. His friend and disciple Stanley Hauerwas put his rhetorical and philosophical gifts behind Yoder's project and made it, arguably, one of the leading options in theological ethics.[15] Nevertheless, the chorus of voices clamoring for a more robust and engaged political vision has not quieted. There are many, even among Yoder's own followers, who believe that he unnecessarily limited the scope of Christian political participation and underplayed the significance of the common ethical resources shared by church and world.

The editors of a recent collection of essays entitled *The New Yoder* begin their history of Yoder's reception at this point. "Old Yoder" scholarship, they contend, was concerned with defending or impugning his pacifism and alleged sectarianism.[16] In the intellectual environment in which Yoder's work was first encountered, particularity and difference were frowned upon. After the postmodern revolution, however, those vices became virtues.[17] Important philosophers from various quarters have begun to sound much more like Yoder in their appreciation of historicity, their suspicion of liberal orthodoxy, and their prioritization of dialogue. Now the emphasis shifts from defending Yoder to using him to explore perennial philosophical issues alongside likeminded postmodern travelers. The editors of *The New Yoder* acknowledge Stanley Hauerwas's influence here, as well as that of Radical Orthodoxy, a postmodern theological movement initiated by a trio of British Anglicans.[18] Hauerwas and Radical Orthodoxy, they claim,

---

waned by the 1960s, he views the liberationist ethics that soon became dominant as proper extensions of Niebuhrian realism (271, 447). On H. Richard Niebuhr's legacy, see Werpehowski, *American Protestant Ethics*.

15. See, for instance, the evaluations of Hauerwas's influence in Dorrien, *Social Ethics in the Making*, 474–88, and Stout, *Democracy and Tradition*, 140.

16. Dula and Huebner, "Introduction," ix–xii. They characterize old Yoder scholarship as existing before 1990 and, excepting Hauerwas and James McClendon, mainly being the work of Mennonites. Their primary example is A. James Reimer. This designation of pre-1990 Yoder scholarship as a Mennonite affair is surprising, given the work of Richard J. Mouw, J. Philip Wogaman and many others. All of these figures appear throughout this book.

17. Ibid., xiv.

18. Ibid., xviii.

introduced many Yoder scholars to congenial postmodern voices of both post-analytic and Continental persuasion.

What they do not say, but could, is that Hauerwas and Radical Orthodoxy have also contributed to a theological climate in which traditional metaphysical issues, especially those concerned with the sacraments, are prominent again.[19] Anabaptist theologians have contributed, too, as they have sought to recover their spiritual traditions and emphasize their continuities with creedal orthodoxy.[20] Though differing in important ways, these sacramentally minded theologians draw from patristic and medieval sources in a manner that would have made Yoder uncomfortable, to put it mildly.[21] Whereas Augustine and Aquinas are often their leading lights, Yoder saw those classic theologians as dangerous and unhelpful.[22] Whereas the sacramental thinkers regard Christendom, at least to some degree, as a salutary development, Yoder saw it as the greatest blow to the church's integrity.[23] Whereas they celebrate the interconnections between the spiritual and political dimensions of ecclesial practice, Yoder worried that discussion of the former distracted from commitment to the latter.[24] In each case, the postmodern return to the premodern Catholic and early Anabaptist heritages has led to suspicions about Yoder's typical metaphysical reticence.

19. See, e.g., Hauerwas, *Grain of the Universe*; Hauerwas and Wells, *Christian Ethics*; Milbank, Pickstock, and Ward, "Suspending the Material: The Turn of Radical Orthodoxy," in *Radical Orthodoxy*, eds. Milbank, Pickstock, and Ward, 1–20, and Milbank and Ward, "Radical Orthodoxy Ten Years On," 151–69.

20. E.g., Dintaman, "Spiritual Poverty," and Reimer, *Mennonites and Classical Theology*.

21. On Yoder and Hauerwas see, e.g., Doerksen, "Share the House"; Hovey, "Public Ethics"; G. Schlabach, "Continuity and Sacrament." On Yoder and Radical Orthodoxy, see C. Huebner, *Precarious Peace*, 39–48, and H. Huebner, "Participation, Peace, and Forgiveness."

22. E.g., Brubacher Kaethler, "Practice of Reading the Other," 48–51 (on Yoder and Aquinas); Hauerwas, *Grain of the Universe*, 23–37; Hauerwas, *State of the University*, 136–46; Leithart, *Defending Constantine*, 284–87 (on Yoder and Augustine); Milbank, *Theology and Social Theory*, 382–442; Milbank and Pickstock, *Truth in Aquinas*; Smith, *Radical Orthodoxy*, 116–22; Ward, *Cities of God*, 227–37.

23. See chapter 3 below for Yoder's reading of Christendom. There are various perspectives within Radical Orthodoxy, recent Anabaptist theology, and Hauerwas's work on Christendom. For more positive evaluations, see Hauerwas, *Good Company*, 19–32; Milbank, *Theology and Social Theory*, 410–13; Reimer, "Positive Theology."

24. E.g., Hauerwas, *Grain of the Universe*, 205–41; Kroeker, "Yoder's Voluntariety," 56–58; Milbank, *Being Reconciled*, 162–86. See Yoder's consistently historicist, non-metaphysical treatment of doctrine in *Preface*, 58, 276, 306–7, 318, 371, 393. He identifies historicism as the biblical, "Hebraic" outlook.

In *The Politics of Jesus*, Yoder positioned himself as offering a corrective to metaphysical christologies that bracketed out political questions.[25]
He did not, there or elsewhere, elaborate a trinitarian metaphysics or a doctrine of two natures, considering these topics at best to be doctrinal "fences"
that kept the church's focus on imitating Jesus.[26] There are some indications
that he simply assumed creedal orthodoxy as normative, and some indications that he thought it was dispensable—Yoder has defenders and detractors on both sides of the argument.[27] For his detractors, whether he assumed
orthodoxy or not is beside the point. The problem, they charge, is rather
that a silence about orthodox metaphysics combined with a historicist's zeal
for demonstrating the political and ethical meanings of doctrine leads to
a body of work that is easily assimilable to secular thought. Without some
intelligible framework for speaking of the divinity of Christ, Jesus appears as
just another political hero or wise moral teacher. On this reading, the only
way Yoder's influence is equivalent to Jesus' is if Jesus is the great man of
nineteenth-century liberal Protestant biography.[28]

The editors of *The New Yoder*, therefore, may be correct that a new era
of postmodern, philosophically oriented Yoder scholarship has emerged.
But their sanguine outlook is questionable, as the orientation they celebrate
has raised additional doubts about the validity of Yoder's legacy: the new
Yoder possibly spells the death of Yoder. Furthermore, there is more continuity between old and new Yoders than the editors let on, as familiar criticisms of his method and politics are now heard from "postmodern" readers
as well.[29] A more accurate depiction of the state of Yoder scholarship would
describe the many Yoders that now exist thanks to Yoder's expanding circle
of readers.

David C. Cramer takes this taxonomic route in his review essay on
The New Yoder and two other collections of essays on Yoder, *Powers and
Practices: Engaging the Work of John Howard Yoder* and *Radical Ecumenicity:*

25. Yoder, *PJ*, 11.

26. Yoder, *Preface*, 204, 223.

27. These debates arise throughout the book, but especially in chapters 1 and 2.

28. See esp. Martens, "Universal History," 131–46, where Yoder is compared to
Rauschenbusch.

29. See the essays by Boyarin and Coles in Dula and Huebner, eds., *New Yoder*, and
Sider, *History and Holiness*, 81–117. Dula and Huebner are careful to stipulate that "old"
and "new" are "broad, occasionally clumsy, generalizations" (x), and acknowledge that
"old" readings persist. They do not seem to recognize that many of the "new" essays
in their collection are concerned with "old" questions, even if these are raised by non-
Mennonites and non-Niebuhrians. See esp. the discussion in chapter 5 below.

Pursuing Unity and Continuity after John Howard Yoder.[30] Noting that "a recurring theme in these collections is the question of how to inherit or appropriate Yoder's legacy," he identifies sixteen "distinct, though sometimes overlapping, ways of inheriting Yoder" discussed in the essays.[31] In addition to the "old" and "new" readings of Yoder, he lists the following interpretive possibilities: Yoder as a theological revisionist; an Augustinian; a postmodern theologian; a "radical democrat"; a purveyor of secular Christianity; a Hauerwasian postliberal; an apocalyptic Barthian; an ecumenist; a theological liberal; an evangelical; an advocate of international peacekeeping efforts; an anarchist opponent of international peacekeeping efforts; a sociological reductionist; and an "expansionist" whose sociological emphasis was meant to enlarge, not reject, "personalistic, pietistic and sacramentalistic accounts of the faith."[32] To this catalogue one might append the older readings discussed above, namely, Yoder as a reliable guide to or distorter of scripture and history, and Yoder as political activist or sectarian.

Cramer recognizes that some of these readings are compatible and some are in conflict. The conflicting readings demand attention to the question of what it means to inherit Yoder faithfully, and the three books under review offer different strategies of faithful inheritance.[33] *The New Yoder*, according to Cramer, inherits Yoder by putting his work into dialogue with other thinkers. Its editors acknowledge the dialogical emphasis of their approach, claiming that this emphasis brings a range of new issues to Yoder scholarship.[34] The downside of their approach, as they also acknowledge, is that "the new Yoder" mostly ignores scripture and Anabaptist history in favor of philosophy: "not only is the new Yoder much more philosophical than Yoder himself was, it is more philosophical than he ever would have wanted to be."[35] Cramer, moreover, suggests that this philosophical focus has the tendency to make Yoder's work seem overly theoretical and removed from the concrete ecclesial concerns that were his own focus.[36]

On the other hand, *Powers and Practices* and *Radical Ecumenicity* mostly retain Yoder's idiom and interests. *Powers and Practices* is largely taken up with attempts to resolve criticisms of Yoder's theology through

---

30. Cramer, "Inheriting Yoder." See also Carter, "Liberal Reading of Yoder," and J. D. Weaver, "Yoder Legacy," for less systematic attempts at defining trends in Yoder reception.

31. Cramer, "Inheriting Yoder," 133–34.

32. Ibid., 134–36.

33. Ibid., 137–41.

34. Dula and Huebner, "Introduction," xvi.

35. Ibid., xix.

36. Cramer, "Inheriting Yoder," 138.

clarification of his writings. Cramer finds this strategy helpful, but is wary of attempts to systematize Yoder's thought.[37] Yoder wrote voluminously and for specific contexts; apparent contradictions within his *oeuvre* should be explored patiently in light of the purpose of a given composition. The authors writing in *Radical Ecumenicity* instead use Yoder's thought to explore various dimensions of the Stone-Campbell tradition and its relation to the wider body of Christ. Cramer suggests that this approach of putting Yoder's work into conversation with specific ecclesial traditions is probably the most amenable to Yoder's own conception of theology.[38] Nevertheless, he argues that the approach of each of the three collections is necessary to inherit Yoder faithfully. Although Cramer does not specify the reasoning behind this conclusion, it can be extrapolated from his later definition of faithful inheritance as tending to both the content and the dialogical, unsystematic style of Yoder's writings.[39] This definition is drawn from Yoder's understanding of tradition as a process of "looping back" to resources from the past in order to cope with issues in the present.[40] It is therefore appropriate, and faithful, for scholars of Yoder's thought to take it into new territory, to explore its internal intricacies, and to extend its ecumenical logic.

Cramer's assessment represents the most thorough review of recent scholarship on John Howard Yoder, and is preferable to alternatives that simplify and dichotomize the various viewpoints without thorough examination.[41] The present book is an exercise in faithful inheritance that combines each of the three approaches named by Cramer. Like the new Yoder, Yoder is put into dialogue with an "outsider," Pierre Bourdieu. But unlike the new Yoder, this dialogue does not replace a focus on scripture and Anabaptist history. Yoder's interpretation of the Pauline language of principalities and powers is in view throughout the book. The historical writings are of special interest in chapters 3 and 4, which cover methodological issues, and in chapter 5, which introduces Yoder's politics. Moreover, it is arguable that, as a sociologist, Bourdieu is not quite the outsider that a more philosophical dialogue partner would be. He trained in philosophy, and deals with many philosophical topics, but his sociology was constructed largely as a repudiation of philosophical abstraction.[42] His unremitting focus on

37. Ibid.,139.
38. Ibid.,140–41.
39. Ibid.,142–46.
40. Yoder, *PK*, 69.
41. Cf. Cramer's analysis of Carter's essay, "Liberal Reading," on liberal versus evangelical reception strategies ("Inheriting Yoder," 144–46).
42. See chapter 4 below.

the practical and concrete, his insistence that even the most "pure" theory has (often insidious) political consequences, and his resistance to common sense dualisms in many ways parallel Yoder's own commitments.

Moreover, Cramer's insinuation that Yoder was only interested in ecumenical dialogue is manifestly untrue. Even if he did prioritize ecumenical dialogue, he was engaged in and endorsed dialogue with non-Christian others. Yoder repeatedly referred to social scientific literature to buttress his claims about the political viability of nonviolent action and minority community structures.[43] He was also conversant with the social scientific study of punishment, and made tentative remarks about a nonviolent theology of punishment based on his reading of Durkheim, Girard and others.[44] Besides, in an essay on interfaith dialogue he maintained that there was no real distinction to be made between religious and secular "believing communities."[45] Christians, he argued, should be prepared to dialogue with other believers whether their master is Buddha or Marx. Yoder himself was engaged in a lengthy dialogue with the Jewish neo-Kantian philosopher Steven Schwarzschild.[46] As a sociologist, Bourdieu is perhaps a more fitting dialogue partner than the philosophers treated in *The New Yoder*; but, in principle, there is no reason to limit the range of potential partners.

This book also shares the approaches of *Powers and Practices* and *Radical Ecumenicity*. As in the former collection, there are extended close readings of Yoder's texts in each chapter below. Contradictions are explored and obscurities identified, but there is no attempt to offer a grand Yoderian theological system. Although the book is organized according to the typical creation-fall-redemption pattern, no effort is made to offer a comprehensive Yoderian account of each of the loci. Chapter topics were, rather, chosen by grouping various criticisms of Yoder and organizing them within the framework of his theology of the principalities and powers. At times Yoder's writings are synthesized to avoid redundancy, but more often they are discussed chronologically and contextualized. Yoder's primary context, as explored in *Radical Ecumenicity*, was ecumenical dialogue. This book constantly refers to Yoder's ecumenical context, both when discussing his own writings and those of his critics. Ecumenicity and dialogue are, furthermore, major themes of the book.

43. Yoder's interactions with the social sciences are detailed in chapters 3 and 4 below.

44. Yoder, *You Have It Coming: Good Punishment: The Legitimate Social Function of Punitive Behavior*, in *UNDA*.

45. Yoder, *RP*, 253.

46. Yoder's reflections on Judaism, and comments on Schwarzschild, are contained in his *JCSR*. Martens, *Heterodox Yoder*, 87–115, draws upon their correspondence to examine their relationship in detail.

In conclusion, this book is an attempt to inherit Yoder faithfully without ignoring the serious issues raised by his critics past and present. It acknowledges the methodological, political, and metaphysical problems in his work, and its response at once "loops back" to Yoder's work and seeks new dialogue partners. It dialogues with the work of a secular, arguably "postmodern" sociologist,[47] yet it does not leave behind the ecumenical setting that was dear to Yoder. It does not assume that there is or should be only one Yoder, and it does not pretend to offer the last word on his life and work.

"Sociological Theology," Its Virtues and Vices, and a Possible Solution

Even if Yoder's work cannot be systematized, its different aspects can be emphasized as organizing motifs.[48] For example, Mark Thiessen Nation's introductory book on Yoder is organized around the motif of ecumenism.[49] Chapters explore Yoder's Mennonite heritage, "evangelical witness," and "Catholic convictions." Craig Carter focuses on Yoder's connections to systematic theology, and so his overview includes chapters on Christology, eschatology, and ecclesiology.[50] Chris K. Huebner, on the other hand, highlights Yoder's unsystematic, ad hoc theological method, and his writings typically utilize Yoder's thought to undermine the "theoretical closure" of rival theologies.[51] Such motifs are, of course, the basis for the many readings of Yoder identified by Cramer. As he suggests, the relation between them is complex and there are varying degrees of overlap and tension among them. A given motif may be judged by its faithfulness to the content and method of Yoder's work, but in principle there is no reason why there cannot be multiple faithful motifs. Because Yoder's *oeuvre* is rich and varied, and because his method is resistant to calcification, the flourishing of organizing motifs may be seen as part of the process of faithful inheritance.

On this view, a motif is a practical tool honed to deploy Yoder's thought for some purpose or another. A motif may eventually be deemed unfit for purpose, or the purpose for which it is honed judged as unworthy. Yet the development of a new motif should not in and of itself be dismissed

47. Cf. Lash, "Modernization and Postmodernization."

48. This section foreshadows the discussion of concept construction in chapter 4.

49. Nation, *John Howard Yoder*.

50. Carter, *Politics of the Cross*.

51. See Huebner, *Precarious Peace*, where he brings Yoder into conversation with Mennonite theology, Radical Orthodoxy, narrative theology, Karl Barth, globalization theory, and others.

as a hostile claim to a fixed Yoderian "essence" that defeats all other motifs. A new motif may rather be developed in order to face a new context or to engage a new dialogue partner. In that case, new organizing motifs may be welcomed as potentially faithful co-inheritors of Yoder's legacy. Tension between the various motifs can be acknowledged and explored, and any overlap accepted and welcomed.

The present book is organized around the motif of Yoder's "sociological theology." At its most basic, this motif suggests that Yoder's work offers theological insight into the logic of social being. His writings employ convictions about God to illuminate ideal and actual patterns of social organization. The justification for this motif is mostly contained in the chapters that follow this introduction. In other words, the description of Yoder's work as a sociological theology becomes plausible when his work is displayed as such in the body of the book. The viability of the motif emerges from its use as a heuristic tool in the process of research, and cannot be proven before the fact.

It is, nonetheless, possible to say a few preliminary words about some of the advantages of construing Yoder's theology in terms of a sociological theology—though it must be kept in mind that these "advantages" do not, *prima facie*, entail the rejection of all other motifs. One strong reason for using the motif of sociological theology is that it distances his work somewhat from motifs that portray Yoder as a philosophical theologian. As argued above, there is no clear principle in Yoder's theology that demands separation from philosophy. Yet even the editors of *The New Yoder* admit that highly philosophical treatments tend to displace Yoder's more concrete interests and context. As Cramer puts it, if the authors contained in that volume "err on any side, it is on the side of theory—albeit praxis oriented, anti-theory theorizing."[52]

By contrast, the sociological tradition, at least as it is represented by Pierre Bourdieu, views theoretical construction and empirical inquiry as interdependent.[53] A sociological theology, then, would not err either on the side of theory or on the side of a supposedly theory-free practice. It would marry its propositions about the character of God to scrupulous attention to the history of God's interactions with human society. Further proclamations about social order, whether in the church or at large, would not shy from consideration of specific cases. There are numerous examples of such a sociological theology in Yoder's body of work, from his dissertation on Anabaptist history, to his review of New Testament scholarship in *The Politics of*

---

52. Cramer, "Inheriting Yoder," 138.
53. See chapter 4 below on Bourdieu's method.

Jesus, to his study of the social impact of liturgical practice in *Body Politics*. At its best, Yoder's theology is deeply sociological.

Another reason for using the motif of sociological theology, however, is that Yoder's theology is also deeply sociological at its most troubled. As noted above, a significant current area of concern regards his reduction of metaphysics to issues of social process. This point has been pressed to its furthest extent by Paul Martens in essays on Yoder's view of the sacraments and his conception of history. Martens contends that Yoder's interest in demonstrating the communal, political nature of Christianity to both Christians and non-Christians led him, at least in the 1990s, to speak only of what could be verified empirically. For Yoder, on Martens's view, what is important about Jesus is that he, like the prophet Jeremiah and Gandhi, realized that suffering minority communities change history. What is important about the church is that it is a history changing community. At this point, Yoder seems to exchange theological for sociological claims. No insight into Jesus' status as the second person of the Trinity is necessary to understand his work, nor is any sense of the mystery of sacramental participation in the risen Christ important for describing the church's character. All that is needed is an empirical understanding of social and political processes. All that is needed is sociology, not theology. These arguments raise the possibility that Yoder "is merely presenting a form of Christianity that is but a stepping stone to assimilation into secularism."[54]

Although Martens's arguments might suggest that the second term in "sociological theology" should be left out, Yoder did clearly write in a theological idiom, even in the 1990s. Thomas N. Finger has also written an article critical of Yoder's reduction of theology to social ethics, but he admits that the pneumatological aspects of Yoder's late work *Body Politics* (from 1992) cannot be ignored.[55] It is perhaps better to say, therefore, that Yoder's sociological theology at times emphasized the sociological in a way that obscured its relation to the theological. Whatever he intended, he occasionally makes it too easy to read God out of society. Yoder's is a sociological theology, for better or worse.

If a motif is a tool honed for a specific purpose, what purpose does the sociological theology motif serve? The primary aim of this book is to determine how Yoder's theology might be revised in light of allegations that it does not further the legacy of Jesus, in other words, that it is not fully Christian. In the previous section, Yoder's reception history was traced to highlight three major areas of criticism, each of which may be articulated

54. Martens, "Problematic Development," 73. See also his "Universal History."
55. Finger, "Theology to Ethics," 333.

in terms of a reduction: (1) the methodological reduction of the complexity of church (and other) history; (2) the moral reduction of theologically legitimate socio-political activity; and (3) the sociological reduction of the metaphysical and ontological dimensions of Christian faith. The basic proposal of the book is that the motif of sociological theology allows for Yoder's assumptions about the nature and function of social reality—his "social theory"—to come to the surface. Once surfaced, these social theoretical assumptions can be revised in such a way that his theology ceases either to flirt with or to fall into any of the three named reductions.

This proposal does not assume that Yoder's theological and social theoretical assumptions are neatly separable. One of Yoder's central insights, arguably, is that theological conviction entails a certain vision of social reality.[56] Yet it seems that aspects of Yoder's vision of society limited or distorted his theological convictions. Namely, his attempt to proclaim the gospel in sociological terms appears to have obscured, at times, his theological commitments to methodological patience, faithful politics, and spiritual participation in Christ. A revised Yoderian sociological theology will be willing to revisit each of these commitments and propose an improved, non-reductive social theory.

Outline of the Book

In order to surface Yoder's social theory, the focus of the book is on his theology of the principalities and powers. As detailed in chapter 5 below, Yoder argued repeatedly that the Pauline language of principalities and powers was "roughly analogous" to contemporary social scientific terminology.[57] Drawing principally on Hendrik Berkhof's small book, *Christ and the Powers*, he portrayed the powers as created social structures that fell into sin but are now subject to the redeeming lordship of the risen Christ.

This conception of social structures as created, fallen, and being redeemed, he insists, facilitates a theologically subtle and sociologically realistic mode of moral discernment. Christ is at the center of the theology of the principalities and powers, as firstborn of creation, suffering servant, and risen lord. It is through Christ that anything is known of the "original" shape of the powers, and therefore it is through Christ that a clear understanding is gained of their distorted, fallen shape and of their future state of redemption. By attending closely to Christ's own interactions with the

56. See chapter 4 below on Yoder's view of sociology: he rejected any "closed" vision of society that automatically ruled out servanthood as politically effective.

57. Yoder, "Natural Law," 22.

powers, Christians have a clue as to how they might participate in their ongoing redemption. They will not condemn the powers, which are part of God's good creation, but they will also refuse to identify any fallen power with God's coming reign. They will, rather, carefully review the shape of a given power at a given place and time as they encounter it in the process of imitating the politics of Jesus.

The theology of the principalities and powers is, of course, not the only theme Yoder treated that is laden with social theory. Christian witness to the state, war and peace, the politics of Jesus, body politics, sacrament as social process, the exilic vocation of the church, Jewish-Christian relations, community hermeneutics—all are exemplary of his approach to sociological theology. But these and other themes can easily be seen, and many of them have been seen, as falling prey to the temptation of sociological reduction. Yoder's treatment of the powers has not escaped such criticism, as Marva Dawn suggests that it reduces the complex biblical portrait of social and spiritual structures.[58] Nevertheless, in his theology of the principalities and powers, Yoder commits himself to robust doctrines of creation, providence, the fall, and the church's spiritual participation in the risen Christ's eschatological rule. In no other theme does his commitment to these doctrines—none of which is easily reducible to sociology—emerge as clearly as it does here.

Hence, the decision to focus on Yoder's theology of the principalities and powers brings his social theoretical assumptions to the fore at the point where he is least reductive. For not only does his understanding of the powers include "high" metaphysical commitments, but it also calls for empirical rigor in moral discernment and a broad, cosmic framework for approaching Christian politics. This presentation of the strongest version of Yoder's sociological theology is not meant to shield him from criticism, but rather to provide the most adequate basis for revision once criticisms are considered. Revisions to the social theory contained in his theology of the principalities and powers will be more minimal and, thereby, closer in spirit to Yoder's own work, than if the revision process focused on a more reductive theme.

A final reason for focusing on his theology of the principalities and powers is that it has not been reviewed systematically in its own terms.[59] It is

58. See chapter 1 below.

59. That said, Scott Prather is currently writing a PhD thesis at the University of Aberdeen entitled *Powers and the Power of Mammon*, which draws from Yoder and Barth's theologies of the powers. Other significant treatments of Yoder on the powers include Bourne, *Seek the Peace*, 210–12; Carter, *Politics of the Cross*, 146–47; Dawn, *Ellul*, 59–61; Doerksen, *Beyond Suspicion*, 99–108; Harink, *Paul among the Postliberals*, 114–25; Murphy and Ellis, *Moral Nature*, 179–80; Parler, "Politics of Creation," 69–72; Stassen,

often grouped with Berkhof's *Christ and the Powers* and similar treatments by Karl Barth, Jacques Ellul, and Walter Wink, and is rarely considered to have an integrity of its own in the context of Yoder's wider *oeuvre*. This state of affairs is, perhaps, exacerbated by his self-portrayal as one who merely presented the scholarly consensus summarized by Berkhof. Although it is true that Yoder did not do original exegesis on the relevant Pauline passages, it is also true that, once placed within *Christian Witness to the State*, *The Politics of Jesus* and other works, Berkhof's synthesis became Yoder's own. A subsidiary purpose of this book, therefore, is to articulate a distinctly Yoderian theology of the principalities and powers. This purpose is attained by explicating his writings on the principalities and powers as fully as possible, paying attention to their contextual origins and connections to other of his writings.

There are five primary texts on the powers in Yoder's body of work. His first book, *The Christian Witness to the State*, published in 1963, opens with a discussion of Christ's lordship over the powers as the foundation of the church's witness.[60] Nine years later, the chapter "Christ and Power" in *The Politics of Jesus* summarizes Berkhof's argument to demonstrate that Paul and his followers considered Jesus' relevance in terms of social structure and power.[61] The principalities and powers featured again in two lecture series from the early 1980s. In the third of his Stone Lectures at Princeton Theological Seminary in 1980, he would turn to the powers to indicate that flexible Christian moral discernment can be centered on Jesus rather than the "orders of creation."[62] The eighth of his recently published Warsaw Lectures, from 1983, portrays the powers as part of an early Christian cosmology supportive of nonviolent convictions.[63] Finally, he was asked to revise his unpublished critique of H. Richard Niebuhr's *Christ and Culture* for the 1996 collection *Authentic Transformation*.[64] Yoder, who had recently

---

"New Vision," 211–22; Toole, *Godot in Sarajevo*, 218–25. Cf. N. Kerr, *Christ, History, and Apocalyptic*. See chapter 1 for an overview of scholarship on the principalities and powers.

60. Yoder, *CWS*, 8–11.

61. Yoder, *PJ*, 134–58.

62. Yoder, "Servant."

63. Yoder, *Nonviolence*, 97–106.

64. Yoder, "HRN." Comparison with unpublished drafts of this essay from 1964 and 1976 suggests that the version published in *Authentic Transformation* was an extensive revision. Yoder added a new section on typological analysis (43–52); moved the section on "The Christ of the New Testament"—which contains significant comments on the powers—to highlight how Niebuhr's ethical criteria are unbiblical (67–71); added four new items to the section on "The Social Shape of Moral Judgment in the Church," one of which relates to the powers, (75–77); and added substantial sections treating methodological issues (77–82) and setting forth his alternative understanding of Christian

supervised Marva Dawn's doctoral dissertation on Ellul's treatment of the powers,[65] proposes the theology of the principalities and powers as an alternative framework for cultural criticism.

The exposition of these texts occurs over the course of the entire book, which is organized according to the basic creation-fall-redemption framework Yoder inherited from Berkhof. For each part of the framework, two chapters address different aspects of Yoder's sociological theology and its criticisms. The first two chapters examine the spiritual, personal, and triune context of created life, and the meaning of human freedom in a structured social world. The second two chapters look at violence and theological method after the fall. The third pair is concerned with the redemption of the powers. Church, Spirit, and the relationship between the particular and the universal are the major themes there.

Each chapter itself is made up of three sections. The first section presents material from Yoder's theology of the powers, and then relates it to his broader *oeuvre* and relevant criticisms. This presentation always includes a consideration of the pertinent passages from scripture and Berkhof's *Christ and the Powers* that frame Yoder's discussion. The intent here is to introduce Yoder, not offer original exegesis. Historical-critical insights into scripture are occasionally useful for this purpose, but they are not a focus. Yoder's theology is reviewed through close readings of the powers texts and then of writings from elsewhere in his corpus germane to the topic. The powers texts are most often treated chronologically and, when space allows, so are the other writings. This approach is helpful for showing how Yoder's thought developed, which is a major point of contention in current scholarship. It is also a reminder that Yoder's theology was itself an evolving social practice connected to other events in his life.

The presence of criticisms does not, of course, entail the presence of problems in Yoder's work. The validity of each criticism is judged in light of the prior presentation of Yoder's work and of secondary discussion. But even when a particular criticism appears weak and insubstantial, it often points to a place where Yoder's thought can be revised for greater clarity. The sheer persistence of some of the more obvious misreadings would seem to call for such revision. After identifying valid criticisms of the area of Yoder's sociological theology under review, each chapter moves to a revisionary

---

cultural discernment (82–89). In this final section, part of Yoder's rationale for detailed discernment is drawn from his theology of the principalities and powers (85). The early drafts of "HRN" are held at the library of the Anabaptist Mennonite Biblical Seminary under the titles "Richard Niebuhr—Christ and Culture; Analysis and Critique" and "'Christ and Culture': A Critique of H. Richard Niebuhr."

65. Dawn, *Ellul*.

proposal. The proposals are revisionary in the sense that they are intended as improvements to Yoder's writings. Yoder is neither abandoned, nor is he venerated as infallible. Although it is hoped that these proposals will be judged as "Yoderian," as efforts in faithful inheritance, consideration of criticisms leads to the conclusion that his heritage should not simply be preserved in its original state. Furthermore, Yoder's insistence on the need for continual radical reformation suggests that he did not accept his own word as the last word. An embrace of the *semper reformanda* creed entails turning one's critical sights on Yoder himself.

Each of the proposed revisions aims to correct for the insalubrious reductions present in Yoder's sociological theology. The primary instrument of revision in this book is the reflexive sociology of Pierre Bourdieu. Bourdieu (1930–2002) is perhaps the leading French sociologist after Durkheim and one of France's great public intellectuals.[66] Although there have been waves of resistance to Bourdieu in France and elsewhere, his influence continues to grow around the world.[67] Theologians increasingly appreciate the sophistication of his studies of power and culture, in which exhaustive empirical research is seamlessly interwoven with systematic theoretical reflection.[68] Moreover, he is often praised, though sometimes vilified, as a rare example of a popular intellectual who is as known for his scientific output as he is for his political activity.[69] This combination of theoretical insight, empirical grounding, and political engagement recommends his sociology as a useful resource for approaching the revisionary task.

The respect and popularity currently enjoyed by Bourdieu are, perhaps, sufficient reasons for drawing him in as a conversation partner—though, given Yoder's disregard for popularity, they are also possible reasons for avoiding him. Yet there is, at times, a deep resonance between the two thinkers: both refused to separate theoretical construction from empirical research; both wrote largely for practical, rather than theoretical, purposes; both were engaged in attempts to change the communities that were the subject of their work; both embrace historicity and particularity against what Bourdieu calls a "false universalism"; and both were allergic to common sense dualisms that ruled out their preferred form of politics as impossible. Stronger evidence for the fruitfulness of bringing them together, however, is found in the ways Bourdieu's highly sophisticated writings on

66. See, e.g., Kauppi, *French Intellectual Nobility*; Kauppi, "Sociologist as *Moraliste*."

67. Dubois, Durand, and Winkin, eds., *Réception internationale*.

68. Pilario, *Rough Grounds of Praxis*; Smith, "Redeeming Critique"; Tanner, *Theories of Culture*; Ward, *Cultural Transformation*; Ward, "Postmodernism and Postmodernity." See also Flanagan, "Sociology into Theology."

69. See chapter 5 below on Bourdieu's politics.

social structure and power can be used to prod Yoder's sociological theology in a non-reductive direction. Each of the chapters below provides an overview of some of Bourdieu's major concepts, selected for their relevance to the topic at hand. Although criticisms of those concepts are referenced throughout the book, they are rarely the focus—the purpose, after all, is to revise Yoder, not Bourdieu.

The deployment of a secular sociologist to revise a (possibly secularizing) theologian might seem like a strange, if not impotent, solution. There is no attempt here to hide from the full secular strangeness of Bourdieu's work, yet little effort is made to criticize or correct explicitly this strangeness. The Bourdieusian revisions to Yoder's sociological theology already gesture toward a possible theological transfiguration of reflexive sociology, but a full transfiguration awaits further explication. The presentation of Bourdieu's reflexive sociology, therefore, is mindful of his secularism, as well as its other potential problems, but does not regard them as absolute barriers to constructive appropriation. Throughout the book Bourdieu's concepts are called upon to revise Yoder's social theoretical assumptions in order that they might become non-reductive in terms of method, morals, and metaphysics.

In brief, once Bourdieu's understanding of society as a set of objective relations is incorporated into Yoder's theology of the principalities and powers, society can be regarded as fundamentally related to God, its creator and sustainer. This move opens trinitarian pathways that are followed throughout the book to move beyond Yoder's sociological reductionism. Relational sociology also demands a non-reductive methodology, for claims about any one sociological phenomenon must take into account its full set of relations to other phenomena. The relational approach requires a more intimate dialectic between theoretical construction and empirical research than Yoder's sometimes ideologically charged methods allow for. Finally, Bourdieu's political concepts give sociological clarity and weight to Yoder's ethics, and strengthen his argument that the nonviolent politics of Jesus are a fully responsible, universal, and Christian form of life.

Agreeing with critics that Yoder's legacy is not always identical to Jesus' presumes some understanding of Jesus' legacy that is not derived exclusively from Yoder's writings. For the most part, this book takes Yoder's work as a reliable guide to Jesus and the Christian faith, and the revisions draw as much on that work as possible. As already indicated, the theology of the principalities and powers works well as a focus here precisely because it motions beyond the methodological, moral, and sociological reductions that plague other of Yoder's themes, even if it does not completely overcome them. At times, however, it is necessary to revise Yoder by correcting his theology, not simply by revising the latent social theoretical assumptions in his work. The social theoretical revisions may clear the way for theological revisions that are more clearly Yoderian than alternatives, but they cannot supply the improved theology. In cases where strictly theological questions are at issue, the bias in this book is always to side with the core creedal logic: God is Father, Son and Holy Spirit, and Jesus is fully God and fully human. Although, as mentioned above, there is much debate over whether or not Yoder sided with the creeds, it is questionable if his christocentric sociological theology makes any sense without them. Why base a community on the politics of Jesus unless he uniquely discloses the politics of God? This question is raised both by Yoder's critics who charge him with abandoning the creeds, and by his defenders who argue (or assume) that he remained creedal. Without a more robust affirmation of the creeds, Yoder would seem to be in danger of reducing theological convictions to existential symbols or regulative principles.

In his critique of postliberal regulative accounts of doctrine, John Milbank suggests that exclusively focusing on Christian narratives and practices is like describing a drama without reference to its historical or mythical setting.[70] Just as the drama only makes sense in light of some description of its setting, Christian practice only makes sense in light of an account of the transcendent reality that always exceeds it. Rational debate about the transcendent—Is God triune, or does God only appear that way? Is Jesus God and human, or just one or the other?—cannot be extracted from the "grammar" of the Christian faith. That admission need not lead in a speculative direction or to the search for rational "foundations" external to the faith. From a theological perspective, human knowledge of God emerges from the history of God's self-revelation in creation.[71] Even "natural" knowledge of God, as Paul suggests to the Athenians, is only possible because God created, sustains, and is active in the world (Acts 17:22–31). The process of constructing metaphysical propositions in order to make the faith intelligible, therefore, is a process of faith itself. In other words, adequate statements about God are a possible product of participation in the history of God's self-revelation. Cosmology and the Christian life cannot be separated.[72]

---

70. Milbank, *Theology and Social Theory*, 385. Milbank is criticizing Lindbeck, *Nature of Doctrine*, which attempts to move liberalism beyond "experiential expressive" accounts of doctrine to a regulative view. See also Murphy, *Anglo-American Postmodernity*, 113–30, for constructive criticism of Lindbeck's treatment of conservative propositionalism.

71. This perspective is developed in chapter 1 below as an explication of Yoder's own views, especially as presented in his *Preface*.

72. For sustained philosophical arguments that theological knowledge is rooted

The perspective taken in this book is that the creedal affirmations of the Trinity and the divinity of Christ are faithful developments within Jesus' legacy by communities that participated in the history of God's self-revelation. Where Yoder does not clearly affirm them, his work is revised to do so. Although some readers might regard this move as a work of heretical inheritance of Yoder's legacy, not to mention Jesus', it can be pointed out that there is a considerable textual basis within Yoder's writings for doing so, and, besides, there is no way to satisfy every reader. Nevertheless, it is hoped that the creedal revisions of Yoder's legacy contained herein gain wide assent among his readers, precisely because they are intended as constructive revisions to his sociological theology. Yoder's reluctance to elaborate creedal metaphysics stems from his fear that such elaboration distracts from concrete obedience. The doctrines of the Trinity and the divinity of Christ have indeed been subject to much speculation, but they are developed below through continual attention to the social practices of Jesus and the church. The principalities and powers exist in relation to God, and so the social and the spiritual cannot be neatly separated. The practical is spiritual, and vice versa. Once all the relations that constitute the principalities and powers are admitted, then Yoder's sociological theology can be revised to avoid methodological, moral, and metaphysical reductions, even as it maintains his characteristic focus on imitating the politics of Jesus. Such a revision, it is hoped, will contribute not only to the spread of Yoder's influence, but of Jesus', too.

---

in the life of believing communities, see F. Kerr, *Theology after Wittgenstein*; Murphy, *Anglo-American Postmodernity*; and Westphal, *Overcoming Onto-Theology*.

1

Revising Yoder's Theology of Creation

ONE OF THE PERSISTENT criticisms of John Howard Yoder is the insufficiency of his doctrine of creation. Both friends and foes of his Anabaptist approach worry that he places so much emphasis on the redemptive and eschatological work of Jesus in overcoming the fall that he denies the present goodness of creation. As Yoder himself put it in an early discussion of the powers, after the fall "we have no access to the good creation of God."[1] Others indicate that his exclusive interest in the socio-political dimensions of Jesus' ministry blinds him to personal and spiritual aspects of created humanity. Many blame Yoder's cursory trinitarianism here: a greater appreciation of the work of the Father and Spirit would complete his doctrine of creation. Behind all these factors, critics point to a sociological reductionism that places little value on discussing individuals, metaphysics, or ontological matters.

Yoder, it is true, does not exult the enduring wonders of the "orders of creation" in the manner of a Lutheran or Reformed theologian;[2] nor does he

---

1. Yoder, *PJ*, 141.

2. Yoder, as seen below, uses "orders of creation" as a cipher for Protestant natural theologies. The term is usually traced to the nineteenth-century Lutheran theologian Adolph von Harless, who developed Luther's reflections on the first article of the Apostles' Creed (in the Large and Small Catechisms) to speak of the specific, concrete contexts in which God places us and calls us to obedience. Some Lutheran and Reformed theologians, and—in the twentieth century—their Barthian opponents, interpreted Harless as providing a conservative justification for any given social order. See Schroeder, "Orders of Creation," 5–10, for history and analysis of the concept. Schroeder points out that Harless's term was "Creator's order" (*Schopferordnung*), not "orders of creation" (*Schopfungsordnung*), placing the emphasis on the reality of election and judgment in each present moment. Far from immutable structures, the *Schopferordnung* are the dynamic existential conditions of human life with God: historicity, gendered embodiment, sociality, and so forth. Far from

engage in mystical speculation on the union of the believer with the triune divinity, as might someone from the Anglo-Catholic or Eastern Orthodox tradition. Yet he does promote the theology of the principalities and powers as offering a more adequate understanding of the creational status of social structures than the leading alternatives, and he does attempt to support that theology by stressing the continuities among the members of the Trinity. The crux of Yoder's argument is that the refusal to separate creation from fall and redemption, the Father from the Son and Spirit, enables a far more nuanced view of the present social order than that afforded by a blithe optimism about creation's lasting goodness. By articulating "a doctrine of creation that (like creation itself) coheres with and in Christ,"[3] Yoder places the life and teachings of Jesus Christ as the standard by which Christians judge that which in contemporary society is truly rooted in creation. It is not so much, he clarifies, that we have *no* access to the good creation of God, but that what access we have is through Jesus,[4] and so through the Father whom he reveals and the Spirit whom he sends.

Whether or not Yoder's theology of the powers produces the superior social critique he thinks it does, this fact alone is unlikely to convince those who want, for theological as well as missiological reasons, clarification of how the social dimensions of his account relate to personal spirituality and classic Christian metaphysical claims. The purpose of the present chapter is to formulate a revision of his doctrine of creation that maintains his christocentric ethical emphasis, but is more obviously trinitarian and inclusive of spirituality. Specifically, it will revise his assumption that sociological and historicist discourse must be isolated from spiritual and metaphysical claims. Unlike most other aspects of his theology of the principalities and powers, Yoder treats the doctrine of creation very little elsewhere. Instead of looking at other writings, therefore, the first section of the chapter examines his work on the created powers, its primary influences and theological context, and its critics. In the second section, Pierre Bourdieu's primary sociological concepts—habitus, field, and capital—are introduced as part of his relational philosophy. These concepts are then used to revise Yoder's theology of the powers as created, and implications are drawn for a Yoderian theology of persons, spirituality, and the Trinity. The result is a definition of the "powers" that is clear about their metaphysical status as creatures and their implication in human dispositional structures, yet is nonetheless fully sociological.

---

conservative, the concept includes divine judgment as a fundamental condition of human being: each human is called to obedience in his or her own location.

3. Parler, "Politics of Creation," 76. Cf. Col 1:15–17.

4. Cf. Yoder, "Servant," 163.

Yoder's Theology of Creation

In extolling the virtues of the Son of God, in whom Christians "have redemption, the forgiveness of sins" (1:14), the author of Colossians makes a dramatic statement about Christ's role in creation: "He is the image of the invisible God, the firstborn of all creation; for in him all things in heaven and on earth were created, things visible and invisible, whether thrones or dominions or rulers or powers—all things have been created through him and for him. He himself is before all things, and in him all things hold together" (1:15–17).[5] The same Christ who redeems and guides the church (1:18) is involved in the creation and sustenance of "all things" (*ta panta*). Among these things are thrones (*thronoi*), dominions (*kuriotētes*), rulers (*archai*), and powers (*exousiai*), each of which Yoder regards as representing the constitutive structures of human existence.[6] These structures cannot be understood apart from their status as created, and hence they cannot be understood apart from Jesus Christ.

"We Cannot Live without Them"

In *Christ and the Powers*, Hendrik Berkhof had written of the powers as those "forces which hold together the world and the life of men and preserve them from chaos."[7] They are "the framework of creation, the canvas which invisibly supports the tableau of the life of men and society," the basic "structures of earthly existence" (23). "Creation has a visible foreground, which is bound together with and dependent on an invisible background. This latter comprises the powers" (28). As the author of Colossians puts it, in Christ "all things hold together [*synestēken*]" (Col 1:17). The powers thereby "serve as the invisible weight-bearing substratum of the world, as the underpinnings of creation" (*C&P* 28–29). In other words, physical and social structures are the divinely intended tools by which Christ sustains creation—they are instruments of providence. As such, they may not be considered as fundamentally evil: "They are the linkage between God's love and visible human experience. They are to hold life together, preserving it

5. Cf. John 1:1–3; 1 Cor 8:6; Heb 1:2–3. On the authorship of Colossians and other "disputed" letters, this thesis follows Yoder's lead: "It is not crucial for present purposes whether the same person who wrote to the Romans also wrote to the Ephesians and the Colossians" (*PJ*, 138n3). Unless otherwise noted, all scripture cited in this thesis is from the New Revised Standard Version.

6. Yoder, *PJ*, 140–41, following Berkhof, *C&P*, 27–29. All transliterations follow SBL guidelines.

7. Berkhof, *C&P*, 22. Future references to this work in this paragraph are in the text.

within God's love, serving as aids to bind men fast in His fellowship; intermediaries, not as barriers but as bonds between God and man. As aids and signposts toward the service of God, they form the framework within which such service must needs be carried out" (29). However Christians might view the present fallen powers, they are not to forget that the powers are created, and "therefore the believer's combat is never to strive *against* the Orders, but rather to battle for them, and against their corruption" (29). An interpretation of the powers as fallen and redeemable thus depends crucially on convictions as to their status as created.

John Howard Yoder does not reference the doctrine of creation in his earliest appropriations of Berkhof's theology of the principalities and powers. In "The Anabaptist Dissent," he distinguishes between the subjection of the powers and of the church to Christ.[8] *Christian Witness to the State* contains a strong statement about the powers as God's instruments in "the *order* of providence," where Christ reigns over man's disobedience."[9] This statement, however, is not explicitly related to his later rejection of general revelation as providing norms for social structures.[10] The chapter on "Christ and Power" in *The Politics of Jesus*, however, has a brief section entitled "The Origin of the Powers in the Creative Purpose of God." Reading Col 1:15–17 in similar terms to Berkhof, Yoder insists that, in spite of the New Testament's emphasis on the fallenness of the powers, "it is important . . . to begin with the reminder that they were part of the good creation of God. Society and history, even nature, would be impossible without regularity, system, and order—and God has provided for this need. The universe is not sustained arbitrarily, immediately, and erratically by an unbroken succession of new divine interventions. It was made in an ordered form and 'it was good.' The creative power worked in a mediated form, by means of the Powers that regularized all visible reality."[11] Summarizing the point later, he writes that "there could not be society or history, there could not be humanity without the existence above us of religious, intellectual, moral, and social structures. *We cannot live without them.*"[12] This created indispensability of the powers to humanity is what, for Yoder as for Berkhof, makes them objects of redemption even after their fall.[13] As will be

8. Yoder, "Anabaptist Dissent," in *Roots of Concern*, ed. Vogt, 36.

9. Yoder, *CWS*, 12. Yoder writes "*order*" as such to emphasize that the powers' limited providential role is in mind in Romans 13, where *taxis* ("order") is at the root of several of the words Paul uses, e.g., "Let every soul be sub*ord*inate to the *ord*ained authorities" (Rom. 13:1a, Yoder's translation).

10. Yoder, *CWS*, 33–35; cf. 60–65.

11. Yoder, *PJ*, 141.

12. Ibid., 143.

13. Ibid., *PJ*, 143, 144.

discussed in more detail below, this theology of the created powers became Yoder's alternative to "mainstream" attempts to derive a creational social ethic apart from Christ.[14]

Yoder extends beyond Berkhof's theology of the powers in his mild theoretical preoccupation with the nature of power and structures. Whereas Berkhof does not offer general meanings for those terms at all, in *The Politics of Jesus* Yoder gives common sense definitions of "power" as pointing "in all its modulations to some kind of capacity to make things happen" and of "structure" as "the patterns or regularities that transcend or precede or condition the individual phenomena we can immediately perceive."[15] The latter definition becomes the basis for a holistic or nonreductive social ontology, as "structures are not and never have been a mere sum total of the individuals composing them. The whole is more than the sum of its parts."[16] These transcendent wholes are what Yoder understands the powers to be. He defines the powers in similar structural terms in "Early Christian Cosmology and Nonviolence," even after admitting that Paul is not interested in speculation on "what kinds of entities he is talking about."[17] Yoder is, however, more careful here to clarify that the powers "cannot be *identified* with social structures but are most adequately understood as a larger reality, of which visible . . . structures are the manifestation."[18] Although he does not specify what the "larger reality" is, he does go on to distinguish the powers from personal morality and purpose.

For Yoder, both power and structure are modified by Jesus Christ. Jesus' deployment of nonviolent service is definitive of the "capacity to make things happen" and his creation of a community of nonviolent service is normative for all "patterns or regularities," at least as these involve human social interaction.[19] Although Jesus enters history well into the development of civilization, as the firstborn of creation his life is the primary source of knowledge about creation. According to Yoder, Jesus and the church disclose the original created powers, and are not merely redemptive rejoinders to the fallen powers. In God's providence, we humans do not live with what we cannot live without: structures that provide relative unity and a relatively

14. Ibid., *PJ*, 134–36, 144, 153–55; "Servant," 162–66; "HRN," 68–71.

15. Yoder, *PJ*, 138.

16. Yoder, *PJ*, 143; "Servant," 162. Elsewhere Yoder employs the term "culture" to describe them ("Servant," 157; "HRN," 69–71, 85).

17. Yoder, *Nonviolence*, 100–101.

18. Ibid., 102.

19. Yoder, *CWS*, 9–10; *PJ*, 144–49; "Servant," 155–60, 164; "HRN," 71, 73–76. For an argument that Yoder's kenotic Christology illuminates physical cosmology, see Murphy and Ellis, *Moral Nature*, 202–20.

orderly deployment of power. In Christ, we see an exhibition of the creational goodness of structured existence.

Theology of the Powers in Ecumenical Context

Yoder disclaims any originality in his theology of the powers, preferring instead to speak of "the Berkhof synthesis" that he represents.[20] But Yoder did more than simply repeat Berkhof, and theology of the powers takes a distinctive shape in the context of his own ecumenical theology and practice. This shape can be discerned first by tracing the polemical agenda of Yoder's theology, and then by describing how Yoder drew upon diverse ecumenical resources to construct a theology of the powers that would contribute to his polemic.

The Politics of Jesus results from a commission by a Mennonite think tank for "a 'peace witness' that Mennonites could recognize as their own, yet which would be aimed at non-Mennonite readers."[21] Its argument was meant to counter the assumption of many Christians that Jesus has little to do with practical social ethics.[22] That assumption, for Yoder, reflects a *"theology of the natural"* in which "the nature of things is held to be adequately perceived in their bare givenness; the right is that which respects or tends toward the realization of the essentially given."[23] What "is"—whether that is understood to be creation, the dictates of the state, or the "situation"—is viewed as an unproblematic source for ethical norms. Jesus has nothing to add. Against the theology of the natural, Yoder develops a political reading of Jesus from the Gospel of Luke, and he goes on to demonstrate its continuity with the trajectory of Old Testament political thought, and with the rest of the New Testament. The chapter on "Christ and Power" is part of his effort to demonstrate the consonance between the politics of Jesus and the politics of Paul.

"Christ and Power" opens with Yoder's taking aim at personalistic theologies, especially Lutheran, pietist, and existentialist theologies, which occlude New Testament teachings on social power.[24] The "'pietistic' misunderstanding," in which the path to social transformation runs only through

20. Yoder, "Servant," 161; also *PJ*, 136; "HRN," 280n96, 282n114.

21. Yoder, *"The Politics of Jesus Revisited,"* in *UNDA*. See Nation, *John Howard Yoder*, 110–12.

22. Yoder, *PJ*, 1–20.

23. Ibid., 8.

24. Ibid., 134–36.

redeemed individuals, comes in for specific criticism later.[25] Although not explicitly tied to the theology of the principalities and powers he develops earlier in the book, near the end of *Christian Witness to the State*, Yoder offers an assessment of the politics of pietism as sporadically creative but typically conformist.[26] Although ecumenical theologians like to impugn pietism as the one clearly indefensible Christian social strategy, Yoder sees ecumenists as adopting a pietist position: the state rather than the church is treated as the paradigmatic political community, responsible individuals are seen as the bearers of the Christian social message, and majority opinion (or "natural law") provides ethical standards rather than Christ. In "Christ and Power," Yoder names ecumenical theologian Roger Mehl as an exemplar of this approach.[27] In light of Yoder's theology of the created powers, the error here is ignorance of the powers' creational status: human individuals cannot be isolated from the social structures that give shape to their lives.

Elsewhere in "Christ and Power," theologies of the "orders of creation" are attacked for insufficiently balancing providence with fallenness, omitting religion and ideology from their purview, and negating Jesus as normative ethical source.[28] Although they go beyond pietism to promote a political theology for "responsible" Christian citizenship, their criteria for responsibility are not materially related to Christ. Yoder mentions Lutheran and neo-Calvinist theologies as typical here, but singles out H. Richard Niebuhr as a leading contemporary representative of the theology of the orders.[29] According to Yoder, Niebuhr's fault is to make each person of the Trinity a separate moral source. Niebuhr had argued that Christianity is a loose association of unitarianisms of the Father, Son, and Holy Spirit. Churches tend to derive their theology either from creation, a (mystical or ethical) "Jesus cult," or a mystical spiritualism.[30] Each has validity, and a "synthesized formula in which all the partial insights and convictions are combined" is therefore necessary for Christian unity.[31] Yoder's most expansive critique of Niebuhr's trinitarian theology appears in the essay "How H. Richard Niebuhr Reasoned."[32] There Yoder denies that Niebuhr's argument

25. Ibid., 153–55.

26. Yoder, *CWS*, 84–88.

27. Yoder, *PJ*, 135n1. Mehl searched for a Christian ethic that accepts Jesus' irrelevance. See his "Christian Social Ethics," 44.

28. Yoder, *PJ*, 144.

29. Ibid., 144n7. Yoder focuses on Niebuhr's essay "Doctrine of the Trinity," but see also Niebuhr, *Christ and* Culture, 81–82, 114, and 131.

30. Niebuhr, "Doctrine of the Trinity," 372–78.

31. Ibid., 383.

32. Yoder, "HRN," 61–65.

has any basis in the Bible or in subsequent orthodox theological develop-ment.[33] In fact, given Niebuhr's stated orthodox intentions, it is likely that his modalism is but a screen, "a slogan, symbolizing in a superficial way [his] urbane, pluralistic concern for a balance between Christ and other moral authorities."[34] Yoder opts for what he regards as a more biblical Christology by proclaiming that Christ is the "agent of creation" and "Lord of history."[35] The theology of the powers is then offered as an alternative Christian social vision in which neither creation nor the work of the Spirit is taken to pro-vide independent moral norms.

In his Stone Lectures at Princeton Theological Seminary, many of Yo-der's concerns about Niebuhr are directed toward Reformed theologies of the orders of creation.[36] Yoder does not name specific Reformed theologians in his third lecture, when he discusses the powers, but it is possible that he had his debating partner Richard Mouw in mind there.[37] Mouw advances a neo-Calvinist creational theology, in which the functioning of creational "spheres," such as family and the state, is read as a sign of God's provision of common grace.[38] Excellence within the spheres, as that quality is defined by norms internal to each sovereign sphere, testifies to this grace.[39] Mouw had proposed a neo-Calvinist theology of the powers against Yoder in his early book *Politics and the Biblical Drama*,[40] and they subsequently pub-lished essays together on the Reformed-Anabaptist dialogue.[41] Branson

33. Ibid., 61–62.

34. Ibid., 63.

35. Ibid., 62.

36. Yoder draws the parallel between his critique of Niebuhr and of Reformed the-ology in "Servant," 159.

37. Cf. *PJ*, 144n7, where Yoder names Herman Dooyeweerd, the Reformed theolo-gian and philosopher, and his concept of "sphere sovereignty." Both Dooyeweerd and Abraham Kuyper, the originator of the concept, influenced Mouw. See Dooyeweerd, *New Critique*, 1:101–6, 3:170, 221–22, 629–30; Kuyper, *Calvinism*, 78–109; Kuyper, "Sphere Sovereignty."

38. Mouw, *He Shines*, 31–51; Mouw, *Biblical Drama*, 34–35; Mouw, *Kings Come Marching*.

39. Mouw, *He Shines*, 36: "I think God takes delight in Benjamin Franklin's wit and in Tiger Wood's putts and in some well-crafted narrative paragraphs in a Salman Rushdie novel, even if these accomplishments are in fact achieved by non-Christian people. . . . I think God enjoys these things for their *own* sakes." Cf. Kuyper, "Sphere Sovereignty," 476–77, where he praises Spinoza who "grasped the sovereignty of learn-ing in its own sphere" and refused to compromise his intellectual conclusions, although those conclusions were false.

40. Mouw, *Biblical Drama*, 85–116.

41. Yoder, "Reformed versus Anabaptist Social Strategies"; Mouw, "Reformed As-sist"; Mouw and Yoder, "Anabaptist-Reformed Dialogue."

Parler suggests that Yoder's Anabaptist doctrine of creation, as intimated by his theology of the powers, is complementary to neo-Calvinism, insofar as "both [traditions] are joined by their continued mutual concern to live out the Lordship of Christ in everyday life."[42] Yoder and Mouw indeed agree that they are engaged in an "intra-family" dispute.[43] Nevertheless, insofar as Mouw and other Reformed theologians emphasize the autonomy of a creational from a redemptive ethic, Yoder stands in opposition to them.

Perhaps the weightiest evidence for Yoder's Anabaptist side of the dispute is that his theology of the powers is largely based on the work of Reformed theologians.[44] In addition to Berkhof, other Reformed sources include Oscar Cullmann and Willem Visser 't Hooft. Cullmann, one of Yoder's teachers at Basel,[45] regarded the powers as angels or spirits that act "behind" social structures and leaders to direct the course of world events.[46] These created "angel-powers" are "grounded in Christ from the very beginning."[47] Visser 't Hooft's account of the powers is largely Cullmannian, but he suggests that the impetus for the theology of the powers was born out of Karl Barth's attempt to find an alternative to the traditional "orders" theology during World War II.[48] Yoder does not name Barth as an influence at this point, but Barth is perhaps the most prominent Reformed proponent of theology of the powers—and also happened to teach Yoder at Basel.[49] Barth makes little of the creational status of the powers, though he stresses that they are created (human) potentials gone astray.[50] Barth, of course, famously refuses to separate creation from the revelation of Christ. Yoder's theology

---

42. Parler, "Politics of Creation," 77.

43. Mouw and Yoder, "Anabaptist-Reformed Dialogue," 135.

44. Yoder, "Servant," 161.

45. See Zimmerman, *Politics of Jesus*, 114–30.

46. Cullmann, *Christ and Time*, 190–96. Cf. Schleir, *Principalities and Powers*, 11–39, an early source for Cullmann, Berkhof and others. (Schleir was a Roman Catholic convert from Lutheranism.)

47. Cullmann, "The Kingship of Christ and the Church in the New Testament," in *Early Church*, 130. Cullmann is explicating Colossians 1:16.

48. Visser 't Hooft, *Kingship of Christ*, 28–43. Barth himself was building on work by various New Testament interpreters. See, e.g., the references in Barth, *Church and State*, 23–36.

49. See Carter, *Politcs of the Cross*, 61–90, and Zimmerman, *Politics of Jesus*, 104–14.

50. Barth, *Church and State*, 30, and Barth, *Christian Life*, 214–15. Barth is explicit in the former, which was published after Yoder studied with him, that the powers are "human potentials," though he had earlier referred to them as "angelic powers" (*Church and State*, 10–11). See also Barth, *Against the Stream*, 15–50. On changes in Barth's theology of the powers—he initially rejected Berkhof's interpretation as "mythologizing"—see Berkhof, *C&P*, 9.

of the powers has its own contours, but he agrees with his teachers that the powers originate in creation and that creation originates in Christ.[51]

Yoder's contribution to ecumenical theology was not as an academic spectator, but rather as a lifelong advocate of peace church perspectives in the World Council of Churches and other forums.[52] *Christian Witness to the State* began as a paper for a WCC-sponsored meeting of European peace churches with the established Protestant churches.[53] *The Politics of Jesus* was written as a rejoinder to mainstream ethicists who marginalize Christ, and "Christ and Power" constructively appropriates arguments from ecumenical pioneer J. H. Oldham.[54] Yoder's Stone Lectures were delivered at a Presbyterian seminary, and "Early Christian Cosmology and Nonviolence" was written for the (Protestant) Polish Ecumenical Council as its members struggled to assess a nascent nonviolent movement led by Catholics and secular persons.[55] "How H. Richard Niebuhr Reasoned" was written to counter the pervasive influence of *Christ and Culture* throughout American Christianity, and published within an ecumenical assessment of Niebuhr's theology.[56] The theology of the principalities and powers therefore appears in these works, not merely as an interesting social theory, but also as a key device of Yoder's ecumenical persuasion. By aligning himself with an emerging Reformed theology of creation, Yoder sought to gain a hearing in enemy territory for his christocentric, Anabaptist ethics. Yoder's promulgation of the theology of the principalities and powers, in other words, is a consequence of his conviction that the powers are redeemable in Christ, through whom they are created.[57]

51. Yoder, *PJ*, 157, 159, names the French Reformed theologian Jacques Ellul as modeling social criticism rooted in theology of the powers. Ellul, however, only offers a positive doctrine of the created powers in his early work, *Theological Foundation of Law*, 76–79. Cf. Fasching, *The Thought of Jacques Ellul*, 118. Yoder is more closely aligned with Barth, Cullmann, and Berkhof in underscoring the created goodness of the powers. Along with Berkhof, Yoder considers the British Congregationalist scholar G. B. Caird to have set forth the theology of the powers most "systematically and concisely" (*PJ*, 136). See his *Principalities and Powers*, esp. 25, 46, 78, on creation.

52. See Nation's overview in *John Howard Yoder*.

53. Yoder, *CWS*, 4; Zimmerman, *Politics of Jesus*, 26–27, 55, 114–16. The conference, held in 1955, was titled "The Lordship of Christ over Church and State" and consisted of responses to two papers by Oscar Cullmann, "The Kingship of Christ and the Church in the New Testament" and "The State in the New Testament." These essays are in Cullmann, *The Early Church*, 101–37, and *The State in the New Testament*.

54. Yoder, *PJ*, 4–13, 151–52.

55. Martens, Porter, and Werntz, "Introduction," in Yoder, *Nonviolence*, 1–3.

56. Yoder, "HRN," 31, which is published alongside articles by Glen Stassen (a Baptist) and Diane Yeager (a Lutheran).

57. The present tense here reflects what Parler, "Politics of Creation," 71, rightly

The Created Identity of the Powers

John Howard Yoder understands the created principalities and powers to be those powerful structures that make human life possible. In contrast to other traditional theological options, Yoder stresses that these structures are socio-political in nature and that their creational identity is best seen in the life of Jesus. Put in these terms, Yoder's interpretation is unlikely to encounter much dissent from others working on the Pauline language of the powers. Nevertheless, how he articulates—or in this case, fails to articulate—the created relationship between social structures and spiritual entities has caused some consternation.[58] Yoder disputes any historical evangelical consensus that would secure the identification of the powers with spirits.[59] He counters the alleged consensus with an emerging agreement among biblical scholars that Paul at least had social structures, such as the state "authorities" (*exousiais*) in Rom 13:1, in mind—whatever else might also be meant by "powers" and related words. By focusing on only the agreed upon sociological dimensions of the powers, Yoder puts forth a metaphysically minimalist sociological theology.

Marva Dawn has outlined five typical hermeneutical strategies used by interpreters of the powers passages; an overview of these strategies helps locate Yoder's interpretation. The first strategy is represented by Rudolf Bultmann and Ernst Käsemann, who argue for a thorough demythologization and abandonment of New Testament powers language.[60] Berkhof and Barth go in the opposite direction, and Dawn names this second strategy "the Bible as demythologizer of the powers." Biblical imagery is far more realistic than the modern denuded perspective, and it sees to the core of our political illusions. The third strategy includes Yoder, Cullmann, Visser 't Hooft and others.[61] It treats the Pauline language as analogous to modern

---

notes is Yoder's theology of ongoing creation in which "Christ both restores and perfects creation."

58. Yoder, *PJ*, 160n28, on personal correspondence with John Stott.

59. Ibid.

60. Dawn, *Ellul*, 69. Dawn is critical of this strategy for failing to offer clear standards for determining which modern language or theoretical framework is adequate for translating the old myth. Amos Wilder and G. H. C. MacGregor's demythologization projects illustrate the problem: both affirm demythologization, but Wilder believes something about the New Testament view is real and worth holding onto, and MacGregor rejects Bultmannian existentialism. See Wilder, *Otherworldiness*, and MacGregor, "Principalities and Powers."

61. Dawn, *Ellul*, 71–75, also includes Markus Barth, Gordon Rupp, William Stringfellow, and others in this category.

realities, and these realities are named in functional social terms. Yoder's discussion of the powers as social structures is typical of this strategy.[62]

A more traditional evangelical view is taken up by John Stott and Robert Webber, who both hold a "theory of direct application."[63] Proponents of this fourth hermeneutical strategy argue that the New Testament authors believed personal and intelligent spiritual beings were real, and so Christians today ought to believe likewise. Yoder debated Stott on this point, insisting that the application of the terms "personal," "intelligent," and "real" to the first century is anachronistic.[64] According to Yoder, Stott reads the New Testament through "a worldview which persists uncritically in our popular culture, so that [he] can assume a greater univocality in the evangelical tradition than any scholar has in fact spelled out." Dawn presents Webber as a more nuanced representative of this type; he holds that the New Testament authors had in mind both personal spiritual beings and the social and cultural institutions under their sway. Dawn endorses this view as maintaining the complete, if ambiguous biblical picture.[65] She later contends that Jacques Ellul moved from a view close to Webber's to the functionalist analogies of Yoder, Stringfellow, and the others.[66]

The fifth and final strategy belongs to Walter Wink and his followers. Wink, an American biblical scholar and activist, became convinced in the 1960s that Paul's language was important for "comprehending institutional evil."[67] Developing this conviction led to a trilogy on the powers, a work on the powers in Gnosticism, a popularization of the trilogy, and two books that apply his analysis to contemporary socio-political events.[68] In those works, Wink develops a distinctive interpretation of the powers as at once the "outer," visible dimension of social institutions and their

62. Yoder, *PJ*, 142–43. James McClendon and Nancey Murphy's treatments of the powers are also written in this analogical mode. See McClendon, *Ethics*, 162–76; Murphy, "Social Science, Ethics, and the Powers" and "Traditions, Practices, and the Powers," in *Transforming the Powers*, eds. Gingerich and Grimsrud, 29–38, 84–95.

63. Dawn, *Ellul*, 76–77. See Stott, *Ephesians*, 267–75, and Webber, *Church in the World*, 24–45, 286–90.

64. Yoder, *PJ*, 160n28.

65. Dawn, *Ellul*, 77–78.

66. Ibid., 84–165. Dawn points to Ellul's late *Subversion of Christianity*, 174ff., as the turning point, comparing it to his *Apocalypse* where he repeatedly affirms the existence of independent powers that influence human affairs.

67. Wink, *Naming the Powers*, xi.

68. The "Powers Trilogy" consists of Wink, *Naming the Powers*, *Unmasking the Powers*, and *Engaging the Powers*. These were followed by *Cracking the Gnostic Code*, *Violence and Nonviolence in South Africa*, *When the Powers Fall*, *The Powers That Be* and other works.

"inner," invisible spiritual dimension. Wink's strategy, based as it is on a dense amalgam of Jungian psychology, process theology, modern physics, and biblical criticism, is often difficult to follow and perhaps finally incoherent.[69] But it is currently a leading strategy, recently earning distinction as the only theology of the principalities and powers to be feted with a collection of critical essays.[70]

In summary, Dawn portrays Yoder as pursuing an analogical, functional strategy that rejects demythologization and refrains from speculating on the spiritual dimensions highlighted by the other strategies. For Yoder, the powers may be created with an invisible spiritual dimension, but how to speak of it is far from evident—better, then, to focus on how "this set of passages from the Pauline corpus demonstrates an astoundingly sweeping and coherent 'translation' of the political meaning of Jesus into the worldview of the audience of Paul's missionary witness."[71] The concern to discern a precise metaphysics of the powers actually moves modern interpreters further from the texts, texts that are largely interested in the socio-political meaning of Jesus' ministry.[72] This minimalist sociological interpretation allows Yoder to avoid contentious debates about spirituality, but opens him to charges of reductionism and ignoring what Dawn identifies as the appropriate biblical ambiguity about the powers.

Criticisms

The possibility that Yoder's tactical silence on the spiritual nature of the powers conceals a reduction is linked to questions about the coherence of his doctrine of God. In terms of the present subject, the issue concerns both the identity of creational structures and the identity of their creator. Mennonite theologian A. James Reimer addresses this problem with his suggestion that Yoder's strictly political view "devalues the existentialist-sacramental power [for individuals] of Jesus' message."[73] For Reimer, the human's status *qua* individual before God is irreducible. But Yoder's "sharply-focused ethical glasses" occlude "the mystical, spiritual, and sacramental," as well as the metaphysical and ontological aspects of the

---

69. See Murphy, "Social Science, Ethics, and the Powers," in *Transforming the Powers*, eds. Gingerich and Grimsrud, 33.

70. Gingerich and Grimsrud, eds., *Transforming the Powers*.

71. Yoder, *PJ*, 160.

72. For similar methodological moves, see Yoder, *PK*, 46–62, and *WL*, 165–80.

73. Reimer, *Mennonites and Classical Theology*, 293.

doctrine of God that are the necessary underpinning of Christian ethics.[74] Thomas Finger supports Reimer's interpretation through a close reading of several of Yoder's important works. Finger concludes that "the great majority of [Yoder's] affirmations [about Christ and the church] provide no intrinsic reason to refer to anything beyond" ethics or other disciplines concerned with "exclusively" human realities.[75]

The most stringent criticism of Yoder along these lines has been worked out by Paul Martens in a series of three essays. In the first of these Martens cursorily mentions Yoder as an exemplar of "the spiritual poverty" of contemporary Anabaptist thought, and urges Mennonites to go beyond ethical christocentrism to recover a vigorous biblical and Anabaptist pneumatology.[76] The second and third essays review the development of Yoder's work on the sacraments and on the Hebrew prophet Jeremiah respectively.[77] Martens sees Yoder's thought undergoing three stages of growth. In the first, early stage, Yoder makes clear assertions about the uniqueness of Christ and the church, and his arguments ultimately depend on traditional Christian metaphysical affirmations. During the 1980s, however, Yoder begins to shift his emphasis from God to human activity: there is a blurring of lines between measurable ecclesial practices and God's eschatological and sacramental action. But it is in the texts written in the final years of his life that, according to Martens, "Yoder tirelessly reduces" the life of the church to social processes that, far from being unique, are fully visible to and imitable by the rest of the world.[78] The sacraments are indistinguishable from secular social practices, and there is no difference between the politics of Jesus, Jeremiah, and others who accept "not being in charge."[79]

The allegations of Reimer, Finger, and Martens further indicate that Yoder's theology of the created powers omits important personal and spiritual aspects of the structures of human life. They also raise the possibility that this omission is related to a weak or nonexistent commitment to historic Christian convictions about God, Christ, and the Spirit. As Nigel Goring Wright argues, Yoder lacks the metaphysical or ontological

---

74. Ibid., 12.

75. Finger, "Theology to Ethics?," 332.

76. Martens, "Discipleship," 33–34. He references Dintaman, "Spiritual Poverty," whose argument is that Mennonite theologians writing after Bender's *Anabaptist Vision* tend to focus on ethics rather than the spiritual aspects of sin and redemption. Dintaman does not mention Yoder in his essay, and later defends him as offering an implicit robust theology ("Socio-Ecclesial Brushpile," 33–49).

77. Martens, "Problematic Development," 65–77, and "Universal History," 131–46.

78. Martens, "Problematic Development," 70.

79. Ibid., 70, 74–75, and "Universal History," 140.

resources to develop an adequate trinitarian theology in which God the Father and creator is seen as complementing the redeeming work of Jesus and the Holy Spirit. Yoder holds to a "unitarianism of the Son" that eviscerates his theology of creation.[80] Problems with Yoder's trinitarianism may then explain criticisms by theologians such as Mouw and Gerald Schlabach that Yoder underplays the continuing goodness of the created powers, and so undercuts transformational politics, for example, by advocating limited Christian participation in government.[81] At issue is whether or not Yoder offers cogent replies to the questions of who created the powers and what they were created to be, given that these replies affect his construal of the fall and redemption of the powers. Can satisfactory answers be found in Yoder's minimalistic, sociological theology, or ought Christians look elsewhere?

Yoder apparently found these sorts of questions abstract and distracting, but more recent theologians have found them vital for political discipleship. John Milbank has identified a difference between social theories rooted in a vision of "ontological violence" versus those based on a Christian vision of "ontological peace."[82] Both visions are derived from a narrative of origins that, by necessity, includes some idea of the who and the how of human origins. As David Burrell summarizes, "everything turns on the account we give of 'in the beginning.'"[83] The Christian account of creation does not portray original human being as meaningless or mired in strife, but as the gift of a loving God. Christian politics are, therefore, the pursuit of genuine social harmony, not merely an ever-allusive attempt to manage struggle. Yoder's theology of the created powers ostensibly supplies such a Christian vision of ontological peace based on a narrative of a nonviolent God who wills social structuring as essential to good human life.[84] Yet if Yoder hesitates to endorse the basic convictions about God and creation that make the narrative intelligible, then the nature of his contribution is more difficult to discern. Paul Martens's suggestion that Yoder may assimilate Christianity

---

80. N. G. Wright, *Disavowing Constantine*, 163–64. Wright contrasts Yoder's negative view of the powers with Moltmann's theology of hope. Carter, *Politics of the Cross*, 146, also finds the language of the powers to be unduly negative.

81. Mouw, *Biblical Drama*, 105; Schlabach, "Christian Witness," 234–35, 243n59. See also chapter 5 below. Charles Mathewes, "Culture," 62, proposes against Yoder and others a "Patriological theology of culture": "If God the Father is the Creator and Sustainer of the universe, we might insist that theological discourse—discourse about God—is the most profoundly cultural discourse one can find."

82. Milbank, *Theology and Social Theory*, 278–326, 429–40.

83. Burrell, "Introduction," 329.

84. Cf. chapter 3 below.

to a secular ethos indicates that he may rather embrace, wittingly or not, ontological violence and its attendant politics.[85]

This suggestion is strengthened by recent worries about Yoder's partial endorsement of the Israelite holy war tradition. Yoder regards the biblical holy war passages as demonstrating Israel's reliance on God in battle rather than on than their own military strength.[86] The relativization of military preparedness is said to prefigure Jewish and Christian pacifism. But if the hallmark of Jesus' revelatory politics is nonviolence, then a tension exists between Jesus and the fighting God of Israel. "Yoder has left us with the biblical and theological problem of a warrior God—of a moral Son and, if measured by the same criteria, an immoral Father."[87] If the Father is violent, then it is difficult to see how his creation is fundamentally, "ontologically" peaceable. Clarification is required around Yoder's theology of the Trinity and its relation to his theology of creation.

There are a number of possible internal defenses of Yoder's understanding of God and creation. Glen Stassen uncovers hints in Yoder's late writings that "the experiential dimension and spiritual commitment crucial for peace church traditions cannot be reduced to ethical argument."[88] Craig Carter and Stephen Dintaman highlight the "orthodox" assumptions that would seem to undergird Yoder's entire project—but even they admit that more constructive doctrinal work is necessary.[89] One could also point to recent writings on Yoder's work on the powers that puts it into an apocalyptic context that always includes politics.[90] Likewise, biblical scholarship tends to affirm the validity of a political interpretation of the powers.[91] Even if Yoder only gets part of the picture, perhaps his work can be developed fruitfully with a recognition of its limitations and need for supplementation.

85. It would be ironic if Yoder embraced a kind of secular pacifism, given his criticism of Niebuhr for doing just that ("Reinhold Niebuhr," 101–17).

86. Yoder, *PJ*, 76–88.

87. Gingerich, "Yoder's God," 418. See also Stoltzfus, "Nonviolent Jesus." Here the irony would be if Yoder were to be guilty of the critique he leveled at H. Richard Niebuhr's doctrine of the Trinity.

88. Stassen, "Introduction," in Yoder, *WL*, 15.

89. Carter, *Politics of the Cross*, 236–37; Dintaman, "Socio-Ecclesial Brushpile," 45, 48.

90. Bourne, *Seek the Peace*, 210–16; N. Kerr, *Christ, History, and Apocalyptic*, 137–39.

91. See Harink's evaluation in *Paul among the Postliberals*, 146–49. For a more critical perspective, see Forbes, "Demythologizing Apocalyptic?," and "Pauline Demonology and/or Cosmology?" Although Forbes contests the apocalyptic and "demythologizing" interpretations that follow after Berkhof, he argues that Paul saw a continuity between physical (e.g., political) and spiritual realities.

But hints, assumptions, and restricted claims do not get to the heart of the criticisms of Yoder's project. Those criticisms suggest that his sociologically reductive theology of the created powers neglects personal spirituality and makes his account of the Trinity incoherent—problems that have rather negative implications for the theological and political recommendations based on them. A revision of Yoder's theology of creation will need to attend to the larger spiritual reality in which the powers exist. Such a non-reductive sociological theology will acknowledge that social structures only exist in relation to God and persons.

Bourdieu on Society

During his more than forty years of sociological and anthropological research, Pierre Bourdieu formulated and refined a handful of concepts for practical analysis of the social world. Under the influence of the philosopher of symbolic forms Ernst Cassirer, psychologist and field theorist Kurt Lewin, and others, Bourdieu sought to move sociological science beyond an understanding of society as a grouping of substances, of objects with intrinsic identities outside of social relations—"the real is relational."[92] On this model, agents and institutions, as well as society itself, are viewed as relatively dense ensembles or nodes of relations to other ensembles or nodes. Relations are never static or neutral, but always more or less intensely "charged," pushing or pulling toward some node or another. Lines of relation are lines of force, shaping groups of ensembles dynamically. Hence, Bourdieu's approach to sociological description consists in identifying and exploring the objective relations determinative of a given agent or institution. As Lahouari Addi writes, Bourdieu works against substantialism and "privileges rather the structural and relational approach, because, for him, society is a flux and not an organ."[93] He accordingly creates "concepts that express movement and relations, not substance or a system exterior to the individual."[94] Three concepts are at the basis of this relational sociology: habitus, capital, and field.

92. Bourdieu, *IRS*, 96–98; *PR*, vii. In addition to Cassirer and Lewin, Bourdieu names Georges Dumézil, Norbert Elias, Claude Lévi-Strauss, Edward Sapir, and the Russian Formalists (such as Roman Jakobsen) as precedents. Bourdieu's book *IRS* was co-authored with Loïc Wacquant. Aside from an introductory essay, which will be referenced under Wacquant's name, the rest of the book consists of two interviews with Bourdieu. When the reference is to Bourdieu's responses in those interviews, it simply reads Bourdieu, *IRS*.

93. Addi, *Bourdieu*, 25–26: Bourdieu "privilégie plutôt l'approche structurale et relationnelle, car, pour lui, la société est un flux et non un organe." See also Schinkel, "Sociological Discourses of the Relational"; Vandenberghe, "'The Real is Relational.'"

94. Ibid.: He creates "concepts qui expriment un mouvement et des relations et non

Habitus

Relegated to Algeria in 1955 as a disobedient soldier, Bourdieu slowly left behind academic philosophy, including his incomplete doctoral thesis on "The Temporal Structures of the Affective Life."[95] Upon his exit from the military, in 1958, he learned ethnographic and sociological techniques in order to represent the struggles of Algerian peasants to a French public ignorant of the consequences of war and colonialism. The rigors of empirical research satisfied his scientific epistemology and, before long, his ethnographic work provided material for reflection on his earlier philosophical preoccupation with the social experience of agents.[96] Whereas Bourdieu's early studies betray the strong influence of the structuralist emphasis on the determination of social practice by external structures,[97] his later reflections demanded attention to agents. At the time, however, philosophical respect for the agent was typically expressed as existentialist exultation of the self-determining individual.[98] Habitus is the concept Bourdieu formulated to transcend or dissolve the antinomy between deterministic structuralism and ahistorical subjectivism.[99]

Bourdieu claims, perhaps immodestly,[100] to work within an ancient philosophical tradition in which "habitus" has been used in various ways to denote the historical, embodied nature of human dispositions.[101] More

une substance ou un système extérieur à l'individu."

95. Bourdieu, CD, 16; SSA, 38–44.

96. Bourdieu's doctoral investigations formed the basis of OTP (SSA, 33). See the many works on Algeria listed in the bibliography below.

97. Marlène Benquet, "Détermination," in Abécédaire, ed. Cazier, 42–43. Bourdieu attended the structuralist anthropologist Claude Lévi-Strauss's research seminars in the early 1960s (Robbins, Bourdieu and Culture, 22). Bourdieu writes on structuralism in OTP, 1–71; LP, 30–41; CD, 19–28. On this period of French intellectual activity, see Bourdieu, CD, 13–38; HA; SSA, 4–43; and Kauppi, French Intellectual Nobility.

98. Bourdieu opposes as ahistorical all subjectivisms and intellectualisms, including existentialism, phenomenology, ethnomethodology, rational action theory, and (Christian) humanism and personalism (OTP, 72–95; LP, 42–51; CD, 22; CS, 251). Cf. Throop and Murphy, "Bourdieu and Phenomenology."

99. Bourdieu often notes his debt to Ludwig Wittgenstein's efforts in "dissolving" debates between objectivists and subjectivists, especially his understanding of rule following. See Bourdieu OTP, 29; CD, 19; LP, 18, 25, 39; PM, 1, 31. Cf. e.g., Wittgenstein, Philosophical Investigations, §82, 197–202. For critical accounts of Bourdieu's relationship to Wittgenstein, see Schatzki, "Practice and Actions," and Stirk, "Wittgenstein and Social Practices."

100. Sterne, "Bourdieu, Technique and Technology," 377. Sterne sees Norbert Elias and Marcel Mauss as the relevant antecedents of Bourdieu's "habitus."

101. Bourdieu, CD, 20, 22–23, calls habitus a "vieux concept artistotélicien-thomiste"

immediately, Bourdieu first employed the term in discussions of art historian Erwin Panofsky's *Gothic Architecture and Scholasticism*.[102] Panofsky wrote to demonstrate that high scholasticism's "monopoly on education" endowed cultured persons with shared "mental habits" unconsciously formative of the *modus operandi* of artistic production.[103] Using "habitus" as an *a propos* translation of "mental habits," Bourdieu elaborated his understanding of historically endowed habits dynamically generative of innovative cultural practices of production. The concept would soon appear in his writings on education and religion as the primary means through which societies reproduce their norms and structures.[104] Inculcation of a habitus, of determinate and durable ways of seeing and acting in the world that are effective even in unforeseen circumstances, is the central task of families, schools, and cultural institutions.[105]

In the 1970s Bourdieu returned to his earlier ethnological research in order to conceive a general theory of practice as non-intentional strategy. *Outline of a Theory of Practice* and *The Logic of Practice* represent major leaps from Panofsky's "mental habits" insofar as habitus now includes "bodily hexis," dispositions that are written into the shape, movement, and use of the body, for instance, by the differential use of the family household space by the mother and father.[106] Bourdieu notes a connection between

---

either used by or similar to other concepts in Hegel (*Habitualität, Sittlichkeit*), Heidegger, Husserl, Merleau-Ponty, Weber, Durkheim, Mauss (*hexis*), and others to reintroduce dispositions and embodied practices into philosophy and sociology (cf. Bourdieu, *IRS*, 121). Bourdieu, *OTP*, 214n1, defines "disposition" as "the *result of an organizing action*, with a meaning close to that of words such as structure; it also designates a *way of being*, a *habitual state* (especially of the body) and, in particular, a *predisposition, tendency, propensity*, or, *inclination*" (emphasis original).

102. Panofsky, *Gothic Architecture and Scholasticism*. Bourdieu, "Creative Project and Intellectual Field," 118–19, and "Postface" to *Architecture gothique et pensée scholastique* by Panofsky.

103. Panofsky, *Gothic Architecture*, 22, 27–28. Bourdieu later contrasts his focus on *modus operandi* with structuralist emphasis on the *opus operatum* (*OTP*, 18, 36, 72, 90, 111; "Sur le pouvoir symbolique," 407; *Distinction*, 172–73; *LP*, 12; *RA*, 340).

104. Bourdieu and Passeron, *Reproduction*, 31, 40, 43, 46–48, 179, 205; Bourdieu, "Legitimation and Structured Interest," in *Max Weber*, eds. Lash and Whimster, 126, 131.

105. Bourdieu and Passeron, *Reproduction*, 43. As such, "habitus" can be seen as the inheritor to Émile Durkheim's attempt to sociologize the *a priori* categories of Kantian epistemology through an exposition of religious "collective representations" functional for social stability. Durkheim, *Elementary Forms*, 8–18. Cf. Champagne and Christin, *Bourdieu*, 89.

106. On bodily hexis, see *OTP*, 88–95; *Distinction*, 173–74; *LP*, 66–79; *MD*, 64. On the household, see *OTP*, 90, 93; *LP*, 271–83. Mauss, Merleau-Ponty, and Goffman are influential in his discussion of bodily hexis (*OTP*, 94–95; *CD*, 20, 23; *IRS*, 121). On Bourdieu's departure from Panofsky's intellectualism, see Bourdieu, *CD*, 23, and

"traditional"[107] peasant habitus and that which is designated in modern societies as "personal style."[108] Through surveys assessed in *Distinction*, he proposes judgments of cultural "taste" as highly significant categories in the stakes of French cultural reproduction.[109] Preferences in music, theatre, newspapers, fashion, and other areas are both indicative and constitutive of social class. Habitus is both a "structured structure" of embodied dispositions, and a "structuring structure" of new practices and modes of cultural production[110]—though for the most part "new" does not entail the interruption of social reproduction. In social theory, habitus thus replaces the determining rules of structuralism, as well as the conscious calculations of subjectivists. The ends of practice are given by the objective possibilities of a given social situation, and are only available to agents insofar as they possess the perceptual schema, the habitus, to see and use them.[111] Because the logic of practice is inscribed into bodies and brains through education, its exercise requires no "logic" in the academic sense but rather a "feel for the game."[112] As Bourdieu would put it in a late work, the human body is a "memory pad" that both registers the effects of history, and strategically deploys them to make new history.[113] The experience of human being in the world is historical, social, and embodied.

Capital

As in a Darwinian account of biological evolution, in which certain evolved physical traits result in a species advantage in a given context, for Bourdieu each habitus or, more accurately, each group of similar habitus has features that are more or less valuable in a given setting.[114] In particular,

Hanks, "Practices of Language," 70–72.

107. Martín-Criado, *Les deux Algéries*, 91–95, rejects Bourdieu's description of postcolonial Kabylia as traditional. This debate would not seem to affect Bourdieu's account of the collision between relatively undifferentiated societies and complex capitalist societies.

108. Bourdieu, *OTP*, 85; *LP*, 60. The connection Bourdieu makes here undermines, at least somewhat, the complaint that he used Algeria as a pre-modern foil for modern French society. See, e.g,. Engler, "Modern Times"; Martín-Criado, *Les deux Algéries*, 110–111. See further discussion in Reed-Danahay, *Locating Bourdieu*, 84, 90.

109. Bourdieu, *Distinction*, 6, 11, 18, 56.

110. Bourdieu, *OTP*, 72; *Distinction*, 170; *LP*, 53.

111. Bourdieu, *OTP*, 96–158; "Avenir de classe"; *LP*, 80–97.

112. On the "feel for the game," see Bourdieu, *LP*, 66–67, 81, 104; *PR*, 23.

113. Bourdieu, *PM*, 141.

114. On Bourdieu's Darwinian sociology, see Bennett, "Historical Universal." Cf. Bourdieu and Passeron, *Reproduction*, 32, on the analogy between cultural and genetic

it is vital that agents recognize what is and is not valuable for their material and social well-being—and such perceptual ability depends on habitus. Bourdieu's theory of capital is far more expansive than the Marxist focus on material property.[115] It is, indeed, less a "theory of capital" than an attempt to enumerate all that has value for humans. "Capital," for Bourdieu, includes aspects of the agent herself and her relations, as well as material holdings. Whatever else it may be, capital is always symbolic, its value always derived from perceptions that differentiate the world into hierarchies of worth.[116]

Bourdieu's influential early work on the French education system, *Les Héritiers*, with Jean-Claude Passeron, portrays a series of correlations existent between the "cultural heritage" of university students, their socio-economic background, and their chances of academic success. The authors repudiate any reduction of success to social origin, instead positing a complex relationship between class, setting, and practice.[117] But "cultural heritage," as a stable deposit of dispositions toward specific cultural products and practices, is soon replaced in Bourdieu's work by capital as value arising situationally from a set of relations.[118] Already in *Reproduction*, what counts as "cultural capital" emerges in the *process* of school selection.[119] In *Outline of a Theory of Practice*, Bourdieu writes on the "matrimonial game" as involving both "symbolic" and material capital, as well as the "capital of alliances."[120] As in a card game, success is always a combination of the hand dealt and the strategic skill of the player vis-à-vis the other hands and players. The value of skill, hand, and relation to the other players only arises insofar as the game is underway. Bourdieu also emphasizes the relative interconvertibility of different kinds of capital, as when strategic skill compensates for a poor hand, e.g., in a bluff.[121]

capital.

115. On Bourdieu's relation to Marx and Marxism, see Bourdieu, *PM*, 9; *IRS*, 126, 250; Champagne and Christin, *Bourdieu*, 89–95, 117; Grenfell, *Education and Training*, 184–87; Heinich, *Pourquoi Bourdieu*, 102–5; Robbins, *Bourdieu and Culture*, 44–49, 61, 123–24.

116. Bourdieu, *PR*, 47. This is a late definition of symbolic capital, and earlier Bourdieu often contrasted symbolic with economic capital (e.g., *OTP*, 178). As detailed in chapter 4 below, Bourdieu used functional, "open concepts" that he constantly refined through research (Bourdieu, *IRS*, 95–96). See Anheir, Gerhards, and Romo, "Forms of Capital," 862n2, for a critique of Bourdieu's ambiguous use of "capital."

117. Bourdieu and Passeron, *Les Héritiers*, 61.

118. Champagne and Christin, *Bourdieu*, 109. See also Bourdieu, *LP*, 41, on capital and his other concepts as relations rather than "entelechies."

119. Bourdieu and Passeron, *Reproduction*, 87.

120. Bourdieu, *OTP*, 58, 70.

121. Bourdieu, *OTP*, 178–79, 193; *Distinction*, 310; *LP*, 121–34; "Forms of Capital," 252–54.

Bourdieu's understanding of capital receives further refinement in *Distinction* and other works written around the same time. Capital is now defined explicitly as a "social relation" or "energy" that functions within the setting of its production.[122] It is at once power itself, and the means of gaining greater power.[123] The formation of habitus within "social spaces"[124] structured by differential capital distribution tends to lead to perceptions of those structures as "natural."[125] Agents' particular dispositions toward their social spaces are, however, inextricable from their own locations, from the opportunities afforded them by their dynamic capital holdings.[126] In "Forms of Capital," Bourdieu delineates possible holdings as economic,[127] social (relationships),[128] and cultural capital. Cultural capital is found in an *embodied state*, as habitus; in an *objectified state*, as a *culturally* valuable accumulation of objects, e.g., a "tasteful" private literary archive, rather than one assembled by those with economic but no cultural means; and in an *institutionalized state*, as formal cultural recognition such as an academic degree or an award for artistic achievement.[129] Each of these forms of capital represents a relative potential for different forms of social existence, a more or less limited opportunity to explore various kinds of social practice.

122. Bourdieu, *Distinction*, 113; *LP*, 122.

123. Bourdieu, *Distinction*, 315–16, cf. 228; Bourdieu and Saint-Martin, "La Sainte Famille," 28–29.

124. Bourdieu, *Distinction*, 114, defines "social space" as "a space whose three fundamental dimensions are defined by volume of capital, composition of capital, and change in these two properties over time (manifested by past and potential trajectory in social space." It is essentially Bourdieu's conception of social class (see Champagne and Christin, *Bourdieu*, 124–27).

125. Bourdieu, *Distinction*, 172. This process is central to Bourdieu's concept of symbolic violence, discussed below in chapter 3.

126. Bourdieu, *Distinction*, 13, 53–54, 110; *LP*, 63; Fowler, "Autonomy, Reciprocity and Science," 102.

127. Bourdieu, "Forms of Capital," 252, maintains that economic capital is at the root of the other forms, yet the other forms are not reducible to economics. In this he opposes both Marxist "economism," as reducing practice to market activity, and postmodern "semiologism," as ignoring the economic context of cultural products. Bourdieu is somewhat confusingly accused of both vices (e.g., for failing to engage economics, by Callinicos, "Social Theory," 94–95, and Guillory, "Bourdieu's Refusal," 372–74; and for economism by Addi, *Bourdieu*, 142–48; Certeau, *Everyday Life*, 55; Fine, *Social Capital*, 17, 55).

128. "Social capital" is a term used by a variety of academics from various theoretical perspectives. On Bourdieu and Robert Putnam, see Swartz, "Pierre Bourdieu and North American Political Sociology," 89. For a critique of the concept as used by Bourdieu, Gary Becker, and John Coleman, see Fine, *Social Capital*. Bourdieu criticizes Becker's "human capital" in "Avenir de classe," 36.

129. Bourdieu, "Forms of Capital," 241–49.

Field

Throughout the preceding discussion of habitus and capital has been constant reference to the importance of historical and social context in understanding the dispositions, practices, and values of agents. Bourdieu specifies
this context with the concept "field," dynamic networks of determinate,
objective relationships. His first significant treatment of the concept was
in 1966, with "Champ intellectuel et projet créateur."[130] There Bourdieu reviews the development of "the creative project" in western art and literature
as occurring within a nexus of relations between producers, distributors,
and audiences. The concern is to refute reductions of cultural production
to either economics or aesthetics. As he would put it later, fields of cultural production mediate between individual producers and the economic
sphere by providing internal, semi-autonomous production standards.[131]
A field emerges as those standards are constructed and enabled progressively to regulate production, product distribution, and product reception.
Increasing allegiance to a set of field standards results in the legitimation
of the field, a situation that agents in the field will typically seek to prolong
through reproductive institutions (schools). Concomitant with the elaboration of the field, there is a gradual creation of individuals who are disposed
to participate within it—the birth of a field births habitus.

Derek Robbins notes that, as Bourdieu distanced himself from structuralism in the late 1960s, his interest in fields turned to their practical
construction.[132] In *Reproduction* and "Legitimation and Structured Interests in Weber's Sociology of Religion," Bourdieu begins to unfold an account of fields as existing through a practical logic of competing interests.[133]
Legitimation of an area of interest is equivalent to power for the interest
holders,[134] who establish their interests as an orthodoxy.[135] But as allegiance
to a single interest is never uniform, heterodoxies arise, and so a field is both
a power structure and a struggle to transform it. Bourdieu soon begins to
refer to belief in the prevailing orthodoxies as a "doxa."[136] He also specifies

130. As Addi, *Bourdieu*, 26, and Engler, "Modern Times," 455, point out, Bourdieu
constructed the concept "field" only after returning to complex modern French society
from Algeria.

131. Bourdieu, *Les usages sociaux de la science*, 14.

132. Robbins, *Bourdieu and Culture*, 37–38.

133. Bourdieu and Passeron, *Reproduction*, 18–19, 203–4; Bourdieu, "Structured
Interests," 121–22, 126.

134. Bourdieu, "Structured Interests," 127.

135. Bourdieu and Passeron, *Reproduction*, 19.

136. Bourdieu, *OTP*, 165–66, 168; *LP*, 36, 68; *IRS*, 98–100; *PR*, 66–67. For Bourdieu,

"illusio" as the investment in the "game" of a field, an investment shared even by those who seek to break the doxa ("heresiarchs").[137]

Implicit in Bourdieu's understanding of fields is an appropriation of the classic sociological depiction of societal development from a simple unity to modern differentiation.[138] From *Outline of a Theory of Practice* onward, Bourdieu employs the terminology of temporal differentiation to represent both the complexification of structures and interests.[139] Capital is introduced into field theory, and a key difference between traditional and modern societies is said to be the relative unity and ease of conversion of the forms of capital in the former.[140] In *Distinction*, Bourdieu reworks "social class" as three dimensional groupings of certain volumes and types of capital as these are flexibly held by groups and individuals over time.[141] At this point, a field is defined as a dynamic class hierarchy specific to a given form of capital. Agents are thus involved in the construction and attempted legitimation of capital, and the force of other forms of capital is more or less blunted, or "refracted," insofar as a complex, autonomous field is built up around it.[142] In highly complex societies, a "field of power" exists in which large-scale holders of particularly valuable capital vie for the ascendancy of their own type.[143] Fields as "microcosms" of the social "macrocosm" are the results of agents' efforts to distinguish themselves and gain power.[144] As with habitus and capital, these areas of social possibility are ineluctably tied to economics, but they are not reducible to economics. They are driven by personal interests, yet they shape interests through the collective weight of the embodied and institutionalized historical structures that constitute them.

---

doxa is closely associated with "common sense." See Holton, "Common Sense."

137. Bourdieu, *IRS*, 98–100; *PR*, 77–79; *RA*, 333. On orthodoxy and heterodoxy in Bourdieu's sociology of religion, see Rey, *Bourdieu and Religion*, 96.

138. Lash, "Modernization and Postmodernization," 248–49. Lash also sees Durkheim's "collective consciousness" behind Bourdieu's understanding of an unbroken doxa in traditional societies. See also Rey, *Bourdieu and Religion*, 76–77, 104.

139. Bourdieu, *OTP*, 176–78, 183–84; *Distinction*, 228; *HA*, 174–75; *IRS*, 97–98. See chapters 3 (on reproduction) and 4 (on traditional and modern "modes of domination") below.

140. Bourdieu, "Forms of Capital," 243, 246.

141. Bourdieu, *Distinction*, 112–13; 170–72; 208–9, 230.

142. Bourdieu, *Les usages sociaux de la science*, 15–16.

143. Bourdieu, *Distinction*, 315–16; *IRS*, 76n16; *PR*, 16, 30–34, 41–42.

144. Bourdieu, *Propos sur le champ politique*, 5, and *Firing Back*, 66–67.

Revising Yoder's Theology of Creation

Bourdieu's concepts of habitus, capital, and field provide a richer interpretation of power and structure than Yoder's common sense definitions.[145] Beyond Yoder's definition of power as "some kind of capacity to make things happen," Bourdieu points to how capacities arise as determinate relational nodes or, more precisely, as accumulations of various dispositions and goods recognized by participants in a field as valuable (capital). The conviction that power is created by God thus involves, in this construal, an anthropological claim about the centrality of practical value judgments to created human being and, further, that such judgments always exist as structured by particular historical and social contexts. Power is a function of structure, but it is also constitutive and generative of structure: power is always an interested act, a practice of capital maintenance or investment, in and for a given structural configuration. Yoder's definition of structure as "the patterns or regularities that transcend or precede or condition the individual phenomena we can immediately perceive"[146] is therefore not wrong but incomplete. It underestimates how patterns and regularities are products of a dialectical encounter between agents and structures or, in Bourdieu's terminology, between capital-endowed habitus and fields (structures of capital). Structures both transcend individual practices, and are contained within them. Interest is a personal and systemic phenomenon and, on Bourdieu's account, must be viewed in action to be comprehended. The powers exist as habitus, capital, and field, independent but interpenetrating realities lived as relatively durable ensembles of structured practices (institutions and agents). "We cannot live without them" indeed, for we are them.

The Bourdieusian reading of the powers may give conceptual depth and clarity to Yoder's understanding of what it means that human existence is innately socially structured. The issue for many of Yoder's critics, however, is how to deal with the omission of personal and spiritual dimensions of reality from his sociological theology of creation—how can Bourdieu help here?

145. One can accept aid from Bourdieu without accepting that all reality is "relational." Willem Schinkel, for instance, accepts much of Bourdieu's sociology, but insists on the need for "substantive" definitions of social concepts. See note 93 above and chapter 4 below. As discussed in chapter 4, Bourdieu himself sometimes wrote of his relational perspective as only a useful heuristic, and not an ontological claim.

146. Ibid., 138.

Recovering the Personal

It should be apparent, first of all, that Bourdieu gives considerable attention to personal practice and affect. Bourdieu's dispositional sociology[147] privileges the examination of agents insofar as their *modus operandi* reveals the conditions of their practice more accurately than a decontextualized analysis of their products (their *opus operatum*). This move toward agents is not a veiled repristination of structuralism, but an insistence that society, as a human phenomenon, is only understood with reference to emotional, intellectual, and bodily ways of being. Each of these overlapping ways of being is irreducibly personal and irreducibly social: the personal is social, and the social is personal.[148] Theological interpretation of the powers ought to include the personal, not as an alternative to the social, but because society is lived and experienced personally. "The powers are created" is as much a statement about social structures as it is about the structured nature of personal existence. Because the theology of the principalities and powers concerns the powers as a whole, its area of inquiry includes persons and structures as interlocking realities.

Critics who wish Yoderian theology to consider an asocial soul or "subject" will undoubtedly be disappointed by this solution, but to do so would be to abandon Yoder's sociological theology altogether.[149] From a sociological perspective, Yoder may be faulted for choosing the structuralist or objectivist extreme in his rejection of pietistic subjectivism. Although, as previously noted, Yoder's definition of structure in the *Politics of Jesus* is non-technical, and most of his other examples are unexceptionable, he does write of "the way words function following unwritten laws located somewhere in the common mental process of the race."[150] This line, perhaps, is only accidentally reminiscent of structuralist linguistics, but the resemblance strengthens the point made by critics, such as Reimer or Finger, who see no room for the personal in Yoder's theology. On the other hand, in the context of a critique of "the pacifism of redemptive personalism," Yoder reviews the practical and philosophical inadequacies of personalism and states, "nevertheless, there is no alternative to personalism. What cannot be done by persons will not be done. Overarching structures and institutions

147. For this phrase see Bourdieu, *PR*, vii.

148. Cf. Bourdieu, *IRS*, 202–15.

149. See Neufeld, "Realism," 44–57, for a criticism of Yoder's "objectivism," and Kroeker, "Yoder's Voluntariety," 56, for an argument that Yoder needs to embrace a Platonic-Augustinian conception of God's invisible rule over the soul. These criticisms are considered in chapter 2 below.

150. Yoder, *PJ*, 138.

may amplify or dampen, twist or straighten what people do, but still people will do it."[151] Yoder may not have capitalized greatly on this insight in his own work, but it could be taken as the cornerstone of a Yoderian sociological theology integrative of personal and social analysis.

Recovering the Spiritual

On one level, this Bourdieusian restoration of the personal to the powers is already indicative of how spirituality, too, might be secured as a legitimate social query. As a dimension of both personal and collective being, spirituality is simply another of the dispositions upon which a theologian attentive to the powers might focus.[152] The powers are spiritual inasmuch as their identity is inextricable from practices and structures experienced as "spiritual," whatever that may mean in a given time and place. To fail to discuss the spirituality of the powers is to ignore an important aspect of their objective being.

Such a minimalistic definition may recover spirituality in some sense, but it is unlikely to satisfy many of Yoder's critics. Critics of his theology of the powers, such as Dawn or Stott, seek ontological affirmation of an objective spiritual being (personal or otherwise) behind, accompanying, or in lieu of those social structures Yoder names as powers. Critics of his broader work wish, at the very least, for attention to spirituality as an integral component of created humanity's relation to the triune God. For Finger, there is also a missional dimension here, since "interest in transcendent reality is strong today, and [the] inability to speak of it will often hinder mission."[153] The challenge is to meet these criticisms without surrendering to individualism or asocial metaphysical speculation. Ostensibly, Bourdieusian sociology can add little to ontological claims about invisible spiritual realities. Yet it is possible to deploy Bourdieu's relationalism within Yoder's theological framework in order to account for the God-relatedness of social practice, and for the trinitarian shape of that relationship.

Christians have long drawn upon relational terminology to account for God's identity and interactions with humans. Jesus, after all, speaks

151. Yoder, *Nevertheless*, 94.

152. Cf. Verter, "Spiritual Capital." References in this and the following "revision" sections will tend (a) to show how proposed revisions are in continuity with Yoder's thought, and (b) to highlight possible overlap with other scholarly resources. Because of the importance of the present revision section to the rest of the thesis, references here are far more extensive than in later chapters.

153. Finger, "Theology to Ethics," 333.

throughout the Gospels of his intimacy with his Father[154] and prays "as you, Father, are in me and I am in you, may they [those who will believe in Jesus] also be in us."[155] Paul frequently meditates on the work of the Spirit of Christ[156] or, especially, the Spirit of God[157] to incorporate believers into God in Christ. Early Christian theologians drew extensively upon biblical relational language in formulating the doctrine of the Trinity and in writing about Christian spirituality.[158] In more recent years, theologians have integrated various philosophical and scientific accounts of relations into their doctrines of God and creation.[159]

Yoder himself gestures to such a move in *Preface to Theology*, where he writes that "to be in Christ is to have one's identity derived from a relation to Christ."[160] He goes on to write of faith as "commitment to the faith-union of obedience made available to us through the perfect and triumphant obedience of Christ."[161] Salvation is participation in and solidarity with Christ through obedient faith.[162] He extends these reflections near the end of *The Politics of Jesus*. The biblical apocalyptic vision of the universe is of a system in which "God acts and we act, with our respective actions relating to another. The spiritual and providential laws which we expect to see at work in this system are as solid for the believer as are the laws of dialectical materialism for the Marxist."[163] Although there are shades of determinism in this statement, it at least envisions society as intrinsically related to God.[164]

For Yoder, social structure is integral to the way God creates and sustains humanity, and its paradigmatic form has been revealed in history by Jesus. Adopting Bourdieu's sociological concepts, created society can be construed as a highly differentiable, dynamic relational structure. From a theological

154. E.g., Matt 11:27; John 13–17.

155. John 17:21. For an overview of "expressions of the inherently relational life of God in Scripture," see Shults, *Doctrine of God*, 60–65.

156. Rom 8:9; cf. 1 Pet 1:11.

157. Rom 8:9; 8:14; 1 Cor 2:11; 12:3; Phil 3:3; cf. 1 Pet 4:14; 1 John 4:2.

158. Shults, *Doctrine of God*, 135–38.

159. Prominent accounts are associated with open and process theisms, Barth, Moltmann, Pannenberg, and Zizioulas. For overviews, see Holtzen, *Relational Theology*, 29–64, and Shults, *Doctrine of God*, 143–65. For critiques with general relevance to the relational approach, see Coakley, "'Social' Doctrine of the Trinity"; Harris, "Personhood"; Otto, "Perichoresis."

160. Yoder, *Preface*, 306.

161. Ibid., 313.

162. Ibid., 96, 109, 118, 120, 123, and *PJ*, 112–33.

163. Yoder, *PJ*, 242.

164. See chapter 2 below on freedom in Yoder's anthropology.

perspective, created society therefore exists as an ensemble of objective relations that are simultaneously the various interactions between agents and institutions that characterize it, and interactions with God who creates and sustains it. The ground of social being is thus inherently spiritual in the sense that it subsists in God, who is spirit (Jn 4:24) and in whom "we live and move and have our being" (Acts 17:28).[165] Every human person and every institution is spiritual for none has reality outside of the constitutive relation to spirit: God is part of the relational structure of society, even as God transcends it.[166] Social practice is unintelligible without including its relatedness to God who, on Yoder's account, provides humanity with an awareness of its purpose through interaction with Israel, Jesus, and the church.[167]

Although this discussion of "spiritual relations" may sound speculative and detached from historical reality, it is rooted in the material objectivity of creation *qua* creation.[168] Furthermore, the biblical witness to a God who is active among human social practices, though not reducible to them, lends theological credence to the claim that God is a structuring force within and upon society. Examples of this divine social structuring include the covenant with Abraham, the Law of Moses, the teachings and practices of Jesus, the scriptures, and the ministry of the church. Each of these examples is a specific structured product of the relation between God and human beings—structures that are at once spiritual and material. The spiritual nature of society as a whole may be seen in the relative lack of chaos that affects social practice, in the continued ordering of life that makes it possible.[169] A spirituality rooted in the relation of society to God thus remains part of a sociological theology, and is not a speculative departure.

Such a spirituality also has the feature of considering persons as relationally structured, making a purely individual spirituality impossible.

165. For perspectives on the subsistence of creation within God, see Clayton, "God and World," in *Postmodern Theology*, ed. Vanhoozer; Holtzen, *Relational Theology*, 47–50; Shults, *Doctrine of God*, 146; Stramara, "Trinitarian Perichoresis," 262–63.

166. It is axiomatic even for panentheists like Clayton that God transcends the world ("God and World," 208, 212). See also Milbank's postmodern relational trinitarianism, which maintains the classic ontological division between creator and creature (*Theology and Social Theory*, 429–38).

167. See esp. Yoder's essay "But We Do See Jesus" in *PK*, 46–62. If Stott, Webber, and Dawn are correct that intermediary beings are at work "behind" the powers, then their spiritual influence might be cast in similar relational terms.

168. On the dependence of genuine materialism on the transcendent, see Milbank, "Materialism and Transcendence," in *Theology and the Political*, eds. Davis, Milbank, Žižek. See also Murphy's non-reductive physicalist construal of spirituality as practical participation in the reign of God (*Bodies and Souls*, 30–36).

169. Cf. Pannenberg, *Anthropology*, 409, on cultural order as an experience of the kingdom of God.

Relationships, in Bourdieu's view, consist of capital-laden social practices. The spirituality of agents and institutions may be discerned as a degree of intensification or diminishment of the basic divine-human relation established in creation. In other words, the extent to which the social practices of agents and institutions deny or embrace relationship with God determines their spiritual quality.[170] Traditional language of "spiritual practice" may, on this model, be taken to refer to habitual intensifications of a person or group's relation to God, evinced by a correspondence to the social patterns revealed through the aforementioned spiritual structures (e.g., Israel, Jesus). Maintaining Yoder's emphasis, the standard spiritual structure by which all practices are judged is Jesus Christ. Correspondence to the social activity of Jesus Christ determines whether or not something is a spiritual practice in the special, intense sense. Although they are always personal, such practices are in no way individual, if by that is meant some form of relation to God that escapes society. Prayer, worship, activism—all may be spiritual so long as they are patterned after Christ.

Recovering the Trinity

The facts of Christ's earthly obedience, i.e., his own practical relation to God, allow for the construction of a trinitarian theology "from below."[171] Drawing on the account of spiritual practices above, it is possible to see Jesus' life as a single spiritual practice, a continuously intense practical relationship to God. Further reflection on Jesus' spiritual practice by his Jewish and later Gentile followers, in light of the history of God's interactions with humanity, especially with Israel, suggested that the particular intensity of that practice pointed to a relationship of significant identity between God and Jesus.[172] This identity is seen especially in Jesus' fulfillment of a singular Jewish habitus. Embodying the structured dispositions of a first-century Galilean Jewish male, his structuring social practice corresponds with maximum intensity to the God of Israel's structuring practices and with the products of those practices: the one who fulfills the law is the one in

170. Cf. Shults, *Doctrine of God*, 65, on "intensification" of life in the Spirit.

171. This account follows Yoder's in *Preface*, 180–209, though it tries to resolve the antimony between the "*historical* trinitarian structure," which he identifies as more amenable to biblical perspectives, except that it struggles to affirm Christ's pre-existence, and "*philosophical/ontological*" trinitarianism, which makes it difficult to speak of the Father's action in the world (emphases original).

172. Ibid. Yoder depicts this process as a series of attempts to protect the authority of Christ.

whom all things hold together.[173] Similar reflection on the church's practical experience with the Holy Spirit indicates that it, too, enjoys an identity with God and Jesus, the three forming an integral and distinct divine relational node.[174] The Trinity is defined then from an anthropological perspective by the manner in which the practical interactions with human society by the Father, Son, and Holy Spirit are unified in their intense correspondence to each other. Insofar as Christians trust that God's activity with humanity is not deceptive, that it is revelatory in some way of God's identity, it is possible to say on the basis of the unity of these practical interactions that God *is* triune.[175] Triune unity on this model is not undifferentiated. Christian reflection has typically regarded the quality of humanity's interactions with Father, Son, and Holy Spirit as suggestive of three distinct divine "persons" or centers of interaction—the proposal here is not modalist.

This understanding of the Trinity, rooted in the human experience of God's action as witnessed to by Israel and the church, maintains Yoder's sociological orientation yet unambiguously affirms the tri-unity of God. Important aspects of God's being may be hidden from humans, but the history of revelation points to a triune divinity. Yoder is right: "the doctrine of the Trinity is a test of whether your commitments to Jesus and God are biblical enough that you have the problem that the doctrine of the Trinity solves."[176] Practical commitment to Jesus and God, to Jesus as God, gives rise to trinitarian language.

The major problem identified by critics of Yoder's minimalist trinitarianism is that it underspecifies the unity of the work of the Father and the Son, resulting in an assimilation of creation to redemption, and a disjuncture between violent providence and nonviolent atonement. It might be objected that the relational trinitarianism outlined above exacerbates the problem, as Bourdieu's understanding of relations is conflictual: relations

173. See Yoder, *OR*, 91–111, and *JCSR* on the deep continuity between Jesus and Judaism.

174. Yoder, *Preface*, traces the development of pneumatology from the early Christian assumption that the Spirit is present in the church to witness to Jesus (100–101, 126, 152), to the first developed statements in the Apostles' Creed (159), to Nicea ("this is the way to say 'love' in the language of ontology," 202) and the filioque controversy (211–12). He states that "the truth of the Nicene-Constantinopalitan doctrine of the Spirit is its affirmation of the true deity of God's working through our obedience" to Christ (312).

175. As Yoder, *Preface*, 195, points out in regards to Sabellius, any theology that leaves God "shapeless" except in relation to humanity "does not provide a real revelation of God coming into the world to save it." Some affirmation of trinitarian ontology is necessary for the New Testament to make sense.

176. Ibid., 204.

exist as objective interactions between competing forces. But for Bourdieu "competition" is a relative term, and he insists that he does not posit a Hobbesean war of each against all as the basis of social reality.[177] Social differentiation is indeed only possible within fields that, by definition, are more or less coherent and unified. It would be possible then to speak from a human perspective of the Trinity as a field of three forces that are distinguished from each other by the particular relational mode taken by each toward creation.[178] To draw from traditional terminology, the Father's primary mode of relating is as creator and sustainer, the Son's as redeemer and lord, and the Spirit's as advocate and guide.[179] These relations are not antagonistic, as if one member were vying for supremacy over the others, but complementary in their distinctiveness.[180] Traditional theological language of the mutual indwelling of each member in the other (*perichoresis*) is suggested by what, above, has been described as the intense correspondence of each of these modes of practical relating with the other.[181] Biblical language that speaks of the Father's role in redemption, or Jesus and the Spirit's place in creation, is not confused, but rather is a coherent expression of the unified trinitarian force toward creation.[182]

These considerations strengthen Yoder's contention that there is an essential unity between the social practices of Jesus and creational structures, that Jesus reveals "the grain of the universe."[183] Against H. Richard Niebuhr and Nigel Goring Wright, it is possible to speak christologically

177. Bourdieu repudiates "the logic of competition of everyone against everyone" as a capitalist strategy (*PR*, 27). See Fowler, "Autonomy, Reciprocity, and Science," 106, contra Addi, *Bourdieu*, 198.

178. Cf. Pannenberg's conception of the Spirit as a field of force that pervades creation and "releases event after event into finite existence" (*Systematic Theology*, 44–52).

179. One could argue on Thomistic grounds that these descriptions "from below" are consistent with the "internal" or "essential" identities of the persons of the Trinity, insofar as the persons "are constituted in the *actions* of being mutually related" (F. Kerr, *After Aquinas*, 199). Given the reliability of revelation, it would be strange if there were not at least some continuity between descriptions of each person of the Trinity's relation to creation (as these descriptions are developed from practical interaction with God) and adequate descriptions of the relations between Father, Son, and Holy Spirit.

180. Aquinas, *Summa Theologica* Ia28, Article 3: "So as in God there is a real relation, there must also be a real opposition. The very nature of relative opposition includes distinction. Hence, there must be real distinction in God, not, indeed according to that which is absolute—namely, essence, wherein there is supreme unity and simplicity—but according to that which is relative."

181. Stramara, "Trinitarian Perichoresis."

182. Cf. Lewin, "Field Theory," 39–40, on "goal" as "a force field where all forces point toward the same region."

183. Yoder, "Armaments and Eschatology," 58; *PJ*, 246.

of God without thereby falling into a monotheism of the Son. Christians, indeed, must attend to and celebrate God's action in creation, providence, redemption, and mystical union with the believer, but not in such a way that any of these actions is viewed as conflicting with the others. Moreover, a minimalistic, sociologically oriented trinitarianism can be articulated without denigrating creation. The created powers may not be autonomous sources of moral authority apart from the instruction of Christ, but they do have integrity as ongoing agents of providence.

What, then, to make of Yoder's acceptance of Old Testament imagery of God as divine warrior? It seems that Gingerich and Stoltzfus are correct that a critical hermeneutic influenced by a constructive doctrine of God is necessary if Yoder's theology is to be coherent. The outlines of such a doctrine of God should be evident from the foregoing discussion of creation and Trinity. This doctrine might be elaborated by a trinitarian interpretation of Yoder's metaphor of God as a "librarian" who, at this point in history, simply puts the errant books (powers) in order rather than forcibly correct or destroy them.[184] Instead of suggesting complicity with the powers' violence, this imagery could suggest a providential practice of nonviolent patience that is complimented by God's more "activist" activity in resisting violence through the work of Jesus and the Holy Spirit.[185] To extend Yoder's metaphor, God runs a library whose books have been effaced such that a reader is more likely to become ignorant than wise from reading them; reading is liable to incite further textual effacement, as well as a disordering of the library. But God continually reorganizes the library to optimize the possibility of enriching reading, and God's Son has in fact demonstrated how to read for true knowledge. God's Spirit leads readers to the right reading revealed by Jesus, who is found to be the subject of the books. Jesus' forbearance—he neither effaces nor disorders, but rather enables understanding—is echoed by the forbearance of the providing God and the empowering Spirit.[186]

The doctrine of the Trinity developed here emphasizes that triune unity is visible in the unity of the structuring practices of each divine person within human society. The single purpose of the trinitarian force in human society is to (re)produce the social structures seen in Jesus, which

184. Yoder, *PJ*, 201–2.

185. Patience has become a significant theme in scholarship on Yoder. See chapter 4 below.

186. It is outside the scope of this thesis to evaluate whether or not this doctrine of God can make sense of the Old Testament holy war narratives. One possible reading of them, however, is that they exhibit God's patience both with Israel's (limited) war-making and with their construction of a bellicose image of God. Jesus' nonviolence then repudiates both war-making and the bellicose divine image.

are in continuity with those from creation and with those that the Spirit labors to bring about in the church. Spiritual practices are activities that align with or participate in the spiritual structures, especially the structured dispositions and practices of Jesus Christ. In other words, to be spiritual is to identify, in the specific ways highlighted by the New Testament authors, with Christ's bodily hexis, to be his body by imitating his cruciform practices. God's providential use of the powers and invitation to a different set of power structures can therefore not be reduced to an intellectual or individual metaphor, but are fully social phenomena. Because providence is a trinitarian activity, the specters of intra-divine antagonism and ontological violence dissipate. Insofar as the created powers continue after the fall to provide a relative ordering enabling the possibility of human social life, they continue to witness to God, albeit for the most part in an extremely limited manner. The structures seen in and produced by Christ are no less "created powers" for being structures of redemption; they emerge from the long labor of God's interaction with humanity through creation and Israel. There is no substantial rift between creational and redemptive structures: Christ is the firstborn of creation.

Conclusion

Bourdieu's relational concepts allow for the following revisions to Yoder's theology of creation: First, the concepts depict personal existence as socially structured, thereby dissolving the antinomy between social and personal theology created by Yoder's emphasis on the former. The theology of the principalities and powers necessarily includes personal dispositions and practices, for structures are personally mediated, and habitus are socially structured. This recovery of the personal already allows for a recovery of the spiritual, though only in the sociological sense that theologians must examine those dispositions, practices, and structures regarded as spiritual by agents. Second, a more metaphysical recovery of the spiritual is enabled by extending Bourdieu's relationalism analogically to God's creative and providential activity. If society only exists in relation to God, who is spirit, then spirit is constitutive of society itself. This spiritual constitution is displayed both in the general cohesion of society and in the specific structures resulting from God's interactions with Abraham, Israel, Jesus and the church. Spirituality is thus metaphysical, rooted in the spiritual being of God, yet at once fully practical, a matter of structuring social practices in accord with the revealed will of God. Third, Bourdieu's practical relationalism can be opened toward a trinitarian theology robust enough to escape the charge of ontological violence, but sociological enough to maintain focus on the social practices or politics of Jesus. God's trinitarian identity is revealed in the high degree of consistency or correspondence between the activities of the Father, Son, and Holy Spirit as witnessed to by Israel and the church. These three revisions result in a sociological theology of creation as personal and social, spiritual and material, and as a work of the triune God.

This construal of creation brings up a further question about the status of human beings: are humans free in any sense if their lives are structurally constituted by relations to God and the powers? Yoder would seem to err on the side of determinism, yet he upholds a traditional Anabaptist "free church" ecclesiology. For all the worry that he favors the social to the exclusion of the personal, there is a strong case that his ecclesiology rests on a (secular) view of persons as autonomous wills. In the following chapter, the revisions made to his theology of creation are extended to his anthropology in order to articulate a conception of personhood as freedom for relationship with God.

2

Revising Yoder's Theological Anthropology

JOHN HOWARD YODER FREQUENTLY described his basic outlook as that of a "free church" theologian.[1] Anabaptist convictions about the meaning of Christian discipleship led to the rejection of infant baptism, the separation of church and state, and the elevation of a scripture-centered community ethic above doctrine as a principle of unity.[2] In each case, the impetus to free the church from identification with the civil community was derived from a command of Christ as recorded in the New Testament: baptize believers (Matt 18; Mark 16); do not take up the sword or otherwise resist evil (Matt 5:39); order your community through disciplinary discernment (Matt 18).[3] Freedom from civil control meant freedom for obedience to Christ's commands. Ecclesial membership was no longer a cultural given, but a radical commitment to discipleship. Stated in this form, Yoder's free church theology is just that: theological. A christological premise about the authority of the risen lord Christ leads to a clear ecclesiological conclusion. This ecclesiological conclusion furthermore yields an anthropological conclusion, namely, that persons who encounter the disciplined, Christ-centered

---

1. At various points Yoder employs other descriptions of his perspective as belonging to a "believers' church," "peace chuch," "radical reformation," or "baptist" vision. In *RP*, 279 he states his preference for "free church." See also Yoder, *PK*, 26, 105; *RP*, 221–41, 262–88, 338–41; *JCSR*, 105–19.

2. Yoder, *RP*, 279.

3. See Yoder, ed. and trans., *Schleitheim Confession*. The author (probably Michael Sattler) also points to Jesus' example, e.g., in refusing to stone the adulteress (John 8:11) or to settle an inheritance dispute (Luke 12:13), and to early church teaching, e.g., to the association of baptism with belief (Acts 2, 18, 16, 19), or the exemplarity of Christ's suffering (Rom 8:29; 1 Pet 2:21). See also Yoder's discussion of the Christocentrism of early Anabaptist ethics in *ARS*, 285–99.

church possess the freedom to respond to it positively or negatively. Stated evangelically, persons have a choice whether or not to repent and believe the gospel. The governing logic of this anthropology is theological, as Jesus' nonviolence reveals the God-given freedom for belief that constitutes human being as such.

Recent writings on the role of voluntarism in the rise of secular modernity have, however, brought Yoder's valuation of voluntary membership into critical perspective. According to Oliver O'Donovan, voluntarism involves the prioritization of the will in descriptions of human action, and has restrictive implications for divine grace and for the institutional mediation of personhood.[4] Voluntarism assigns ultimate authority in decision-making to the individual will, thereby reducing the influence of the church to that of the many optional social clubs littering the late-modern landscape: "Join if you feel like it" becomes the heart of the gospel proclamation. Although Yoder's ostensibly theological account of the free church would seem to escape such criticisms, O'Donovan rather sees it as a conformist expression of this secular anthropological "heresy." The desire to avoid implicating the church in coercion may be laudable, but not when it comes at the expense of the church's authoritative witness to and mediation of the power of grace. Given the portrait of Yoder's free church theology sketched above, it is unsurprising that its defenders draw attention to its theological context. Yet almost all of them confess that it is unnuanced and susceptible to O'Donovan's critique to some degree. At the same time, neither its defenders nor its critics offer an anthropology that does justice to the meaningfulness of non-coerced church membership. The requirement that faith be free is repeatedly affirmed, but the accent then shifts to divine and human influence in eliciting faith—as if specifying the conditions for human choice is already to be guilty of voluntarism.

The present chapter risks a revision of Yoder's theological anthropology that holds together his emphases on "voluntariety" and structure. In the first section, his free church theology and its critics are examined in the context of his writings on the powers. Although his overall perspective goes a long way to answering the critics, it is finally difficult to see how it can be reconciled with some of his more troubling affirmations about the freedom of the will. The suspicion that Yoder's anthropology requires clarification is thus confirmed, and to that end the next section introduces Pierre Bourdieu's sociological attempt to dissolve the philosophical dualism between freedom and determinism. Although Bourdieu argues for a strong theory of social reproduction, he maintains that freedom is a possible product of social activity. On Bourdieu's anthropology, genuine choice never escapes

---

4. O'Donovan, *Desire of the Nations*, 274.

social structuring, but can be its result. These moves lead to a revision of Yoder's theological anthropology in the final section that draws from the previous chapter's conclusions. Because human beings only exist in relation to social structures and to God, choice as a social product can be conceived of as a divine gift that is received through human labor for freedom. Freedom, moreover, is not merely the ability to choose anything, but a freedom for intense relationship with God and others—it is a freedom for obedience to God. The possibility of free choice is socially and spiritually mediated. From the perspective of this revised theological anthropology, church membership can be viewed as a voluntary response to the extension of God's grace through the witness of the church in the world.

Yoder's Theological Anthropology

Issues of human freedom and its limitations run throughout the central biblical texts on the powers. In Romans, Paul rhapsodizes about the vastness and finality of Christian freedom: "For I am convinced that neither death, nor life, nor angels, nor rulers [*archai*], nor things present, nor things to come, nor powers [*dynameis*], nor height nor depth, nor anything else in all creation, will be able to separate us from the love of God in Christ Jesus our Lord" (Rom 8:38–39; cf. 1 Cor 15:24–28). Yet a little later he recommends subjection to "governing authorities" (*exousiais hyperechousais*) as a necessary form of subjection to God (Rom 13:1–3). In other passages, a state of enslavement or death is contrasted with the enlivening freedom of being God's children in Christ (Gal 4:1–11; Eph 2:1–10; Col 2:8–23). Although freedom is achieved through Christ's ongoing defeat of the powers, Christians are called to join the battle by resisting the coercive powers with God's strength and armor (Eph 6:10–18).

Within the biblical portrait, there are tensions between a general determination by the enslaving powers and Christian freedom from the powers; between Christian freedom and the duties of Christian commitment; and between the gift of freedom and the labor of its reception. These tensions are mediated in Yoder's theology by the concept of voluntariety: escape from determination occurs with the choice to follow Jesus and join the church, and that choice commits one to an ecclesial mode of life patterned after Jesus. This construal of choice, with its voluntaristic anthropological implications, raises problems for Yoder's theology. As a first step toward revising his theological anthropology, summaries are offered here of Yoder's views of structure and freedom in the powers and of the free church. The section concludes with an analysis of the criticisms of Yoder's account.

The Powers: Structure and Freedom

Yoder's theology of the created powers suggests that he does not perceive the structured nature of human existence as an impediment to the exercise of human capabilities. If "society and history . . . would be impossible without regularity, system, [and] order,"[5] then freedom and choice are structured phenomena. This freedom is restricted, though not completely eliminated, once disobedience is chosen. After the fall, the powers continue to provide an essential order. As Paul preached to the Gentiles, the general structures of the world still offer a glimpse of God.[6] Yet they also "have enslaved humanity and our history" and become "our masters and our guardians."[7] The powers "exercise dominion over men and women"[8] and are "invisibly determining human events."[9] By contrast, the "genuinely free and human existence" of Jesus Christ breaks with this determinism: "Here we have for the first time to do with someone who is not the slave of any power, of any law or custom, community or institution, value or theory."[10] As a human being, Jesus' freedom is not of course from the powers as such, but from collaboration with their rebellious "self-glorification." Freedom and structure are not basically opposed, but rather determinism is defined by the inhabitation of structures denigrative of divine-human and interhuman relations. Humans are created for freedom, for an ordered mode of being with God and others. It is this freedom that the church witnesses to when it proclaims Christ's redemption of the powers.[11]

At various points in his writings on the powers and elsewhere, Yoder deepens his description of freedom as a created and intrinsic aspect of human being. In *Preface to Theology* he argues that, because "God is *agape* and *agape respects the freedom of the beloved*," the choice between obedience and

---

5. Yoder, *PJ*, 141.

6. Ibid., 141–42, and *BP*, 39, on Acts 14:15–17 and 17:22–31. The latter verses are especially interesting as Paul includes the "times" and "boundaries" of the nations in the order of providence. In *BP*, Yoder stresses that "it was by *naming* the risen Jesus that Paul ended his description of the providential plurality of peoples" (emphasis original). The universality of revelation through the providentially-maintained fallen powers is consonant with the particular lordship of Jesus. Cf. *FTN*, 63, where he explains this "providential plurality" as the gracious intent of the scattering at Babel (Gen 11). These themes are treated in detail in chapter six below.

7. Yoder, *PJ*, 141–42.

8. Yoder, "HRN," 68.

9. Yoder, *CWS*, 8. Cf. Berkhof, *C&P*, 30–33.

10. Yoder, *PJ*, 145. Cf. Berkhof, *C&P*, 36–39.

11. Yoder, *PJ*, 147–53; *CWS*, 16–22. Cf. Berkhof, *C&P*, 44–52.

disobedience has existed from the beginning.[12] Freedom is, therefore, "the context of choice before God, which is our condition" as humans. It is built, as it were, into the powers, part of the structural make-up of the cosmos. Humanity is thus fundamentally free from divine coercion, but always free to choose obedience—and both of these freedoms are rooted in God's love. This situation does not change after the fall. The providential ordering of the powers, and the existence of Israel and the church, continue to hold open the possibility of obedience. The Jewish and Christian communities proclaim God's love in word and deed and, in fact, are constituted in response to it. As Yoder puts it, "the gospel is not a mere message; it is a continuum of loving relationship extending in a chain—imperfect, to be sure, but historically real—from Christ to those who today become recipients and givers of love. The church is not an end in itself; it exists for the sake of the world."[13] Evangelism cannot be separated from social witness, because repentance occurs as a response to the church's witness to love.[14] The proclamation of the gospel, moreover, is not ahistorical or otherworldly, but always "translated" into terms understandable by its hearers.[15] Yoder regards his sociological theology of the principalities and powers as just such a translation.[16] This translated proclamation invites persons not only to a new communal structure, but also to enjoy a transformation of their dispositions or "heart" by entering "a whole new world."[17] The reality of gospel proclamation, of baptism as the transition into the new community of love, and of the community itself means that change is a real possibility within history.[18] Change is possible, but not required. Its possibility emerges most clearly as an encounter with a community formed in free response to God's love.

Free Church and Free Choice

Yoder considers voluntary membership to be a basic trait of the "free church" tradition to which he belongs as a Mennonite. In the Schleitheim

12. Yoder, *Preface*, 309.

13. Yoder, "Review: *The Context of Decision*," 135.

14. Yoder, *CWS*, 22–25; *OR*, 76; *RP*, 90–91.

15. Yoder, "Natural Law," 21–22; *CWS*, 25; *PK*, 46–62; *HCPP*, 69–88.

16. Yoder, *PJ*, 136, 138.

17. This is Yoder's interpretation of 2 Cor 5:17 and the "new creation." See *PJ*, 218–23; *THW*, 13–24. Cf. Yoder's discussion of "cosmological conversion" in *WL*, 56; *Nonviolence*, 23.

18. See Yoder, *BP*, 41–42, on baptism as the possibility for change (and so for nonviolent reconciliation).

Brotherly Union, arguably the founding document of Swiss Anabaptism, the first article, after all, reserves baptism for those who "wish to be with Him [Jesus Christ] in death, so that they may be resurrected with Him and to all those who with this significance request it (baptism) of us and demand it for themselves."[19] This "requested" baptism then becomes the principle on which the other articles are based, in particular church discipline and the Lord's Supper.[20] Harold S. Bender, the Mennonite historian who was Yoder's early mentor, saw voluntary membership as one of three "essential" features of the "Anabaptist Vision."[21] For Bender, the choice of discipleship entailed separation from the world, readiness for persecution, and commitment to a community of goods. Yoder inherits this emphasis, and from early on highlights the role of voluntary membership as the basis for Christian moral discipline and distinction from the world.[22] It would soon become a central concept in his ecumenical and interreligious efforts.[23]

In order to synthesize Yoder's writings on voluntary membership, it is possible to divide his concerns into groups of negative and positive freedoms.[24] The practice of choosing to join the church, according to Yoder, involves freedom from "the givenness of the social order"[25] and from the tyranny of human sovereignty. The latter of these negative freedoms founds the separation of church and state, which Yoder interprets as the sovereign's admission of finitude in matters divine.[26] Yoder links freedom from "inherited faith" with the "genuineness of choice" implicit in Jesus' admonition to count the costs of discipleship in Luke 14:25–33.[27] Discipleship is difficult. Those who enter it without consideration of the hardships they will undergo do so unadvisedly.

This point elucidates the primary positive freedom involved in voluntary church membership, namely, the freedom to obey the commands of God as these are revealed in the biblical testimonies. Yoder tellingly titles

19. Yoder, ed. and trans., *Schleitheim Confession*, 10. On the debatable influence of the *Brotherly Union*, see Snyder, "Influence of the Schleitheim Articles."

20. Yoder, ed. and trans., *Schleitheim Confession*, 10–13. Cf. Yoder, *JCSR*, 124–29.

21. Bender, *Anabaptist Vision*, 26–31. On the legacy of Bender's *Anabaptist Vision*, see Biesecker-Mast, "Anabaptism as a Vision"; Hauerwas, *Good Company*, 65–78; Hershberger, ed., *Anabaptist Vision*; Nolt, "Anabaptist Visions."

22. Yoder, "Anabaptist Dissent," in *Roots of Concern*, ed. Vogt, 31; *ARS*, 273–77.

23. Yoder, *PK*, 105–22; *RP*, 221–320; *JCSR*, 103–43.

24. Cf. Yoder, *JCSR*, 136.

25. Ibid., 136, cf. 126; *PK*, 25; *RP*, 254–57.

26. Yoder, "Amateur Historian," and "Religious Liberty and the Prior Loyalty of the People of God," in *UNDA*. Cf. *PK*, 172–95; *RP*, 265–66, 273; *JCSR*, 136.

27. Yoder, *JCSR*, 255.

a section of his theological study of Swiss Anabaptism "Commandment as Freedom"[28]—to choose the church is to choose the way of Jesus. "'Freedom' in this sense is not only a descriptive trait but also a theological value. Behind those formal ways in which it has been tested or stated in the past lie deeper concerns regarding the faithfulness of the individual and the Body, their mission and their renewal."[29] As such, freedom for obedience provides the soil in which the other positive freedoms are rooted. Because the voluntary church is founded on personal choice, it is more likely to maintain a distinctive identity and is thus more capable of fulfilling its missional mandate.[30] Choice grounds practices of accountability, making ethical performance and awareness of defectibility more likely.[31] This awareness provides the humility necessary for missionary work.[32] The constitution of the church through baptismal mission gives it the knowledge that differences can be resolved through dialogue, thereby reinforcing its commitment to nonviolence.[33] Further, focusing Christian identity on ecclesial obedience has the potential to move ecumenical discussions onto the (ostensibly) common ground of the life of Jesus as portrayed in scripture.[34] From freedom for obedience therefore spring freedoms for peaceful mission and growth, communal cohesion and Christian unity. Those freedoms are unthinkable, according to Yoder, without the corresponding negative freedoms. But the negative freedoms are intelligible only in light of the material commitments they enable. Repentance is only the "shadow side of the new beginning, its face is reconciliation."[35]

Criticisms

This review of Yoder's writings on the structured nature of human being and on the free church indicate that he has a rich account of choice as a response to God's love mediated through social structures. To put it in a Heideggerian register, human being is "being-with-God." Because we are with God,

28. Yoder, *ARS*, 295–99.

29. Yoder, *RP*, 264.

30. Ibid., 270–72; *FTN*, 153–55; *JCSR*, 136.

31. Yoder, "Review: *The Context of Decision*," 135; *PK*, 25; *RP*, 265; *JCSR*, 126, 140–41.

32. Yoder, *RP*, 254–57; *FTN*, 157.

33. Yoder, *PK*, 110–11. Cf. *BP*, 28–46, on baptism as the creation of a new community out of previously opposed groups.

34. Yoder, *PK*, 119–20; *RP*, 225–30, 238, 274–76.

35. Yoder, *HCPP*, 138.

always faced by God, the option of loving obedience is always present—but never forced. Far from being reducible to autonomous wills, humans are rather constituted by their concrete relation to God and to those structures that make God's love visible in the world. Moreover, God does not simply appeal to the will, but invites the whole person into deeper relationship. What, then, are Oliver O'Donovan and other critics concerned about?

For his part, O'Donovan points to Yoder's essay "Radical Reformation Ethics," where Yoder distinguishes between free church and established Protestant views on baptism, the relation between church and state, compulsory church membership, and violence.[36] O'Donovan finds it "disconcerting that such a heterogeneous collection of issues should be so drained of theological distinctiveness as to serve the general cause of voluntariety." It becomes unclear, moreover, what "this all-important act of will" has to do with the broader faith, especially with convictions about the prevenience of grace and "the testimony of community faith in awakening individual faith." Although O'Donovan admits that "a church defined by the faith it confesses will be free, for 'coerced faith' is a contradiction in terms," he worries that emphasizing voluntariety is a capitulation to the modern scenario in which various non-essential "voluntary societies" constitute the civic marketplace. Yoder's free church fits a little too easily alongside political parties and social clubs. In the end he appears to be "championing a great conformism."[37]

The problem for O'Donovan clearly lies with Yoder's anthropology, which he regards as reducing persons to individual decision-makers devoid of grace and unable to trust others. It is easy to reply to O'Donovan by pointing to the writings reviewed above, or even just to the wider context of the quote he lifts out of "Radical Reformation Ethics." That essay was delivered at a symposium on "Christian Ethics in Ecumenical Perspective."[38] Given the setting, Yoder explicitly limits his discussion to ethics as the obvious original point of disagreement between the established and radical Protestant churches.[39] This is not to say that related theological and metaphysical issues are unimportant, but that the rupture was over issues such as violence and the organization of the church. His focus is therefore on the ethics of a missionary, scripture-centered community that subordinates itself to the lordship of Christ.[40] Once again, free membership is a response to God's

36. O'Donovan, *Desire of the Nations*, 223, on Yoder, *PK*, 106–7.

37. O'Donovan, *Desire of the Nations*, 224.

38. Yoder, *PK*, 202n1.

39. Ibid., 108.

40. Ibid., 116–18.

love encountered through the church's mission. The human will is not isolated, but confronted with concrete grace.[41]

Similar arguments can be raised against other criticisms of Yoder's anthropology. Stanley Hauerwas, usually among Yoder's most stalwart defenders, confesses that Yoder's voluntarism "can too easily, particularly in modernity, underwrite rationalistic accounts of the faith."[42] It further "puts too much stress on process separate from the material convictions [Yoder] wants the process to serve."[43] In other essays on Anabaptism and Protestantism, Hauerwas spells out his fear that such voluntarism leaves the church without resources for a thick identity after Christendom, which at least maintained that social norms were above the will of its citizens. The accent on voluntary commitment "cannot help but appear as a legitimation of the secular commitment to autonomy,"[44] one that "nicely underwrites patterns of domination characteristic of capitalist social orders with much less basis for critique than was provided by the Catholic church."[45] Hauerwas instead articulates a "non-voluntary" ecclesiology in which, with special reference to conversion and baptism, "Christians discover that what they thought they had done voluntarily has in fact been done to them."[46]

Not only is it difficult to see how this non-voluntary ecclesiology respects human freedom,[47] but it also fails to see the context of Yoder's writings on the free church. Indeed, if rationalism is the fear, then Hauerwas might have looked at Yoder's prioritization of community life—which has both intellectual and affective dimensions—over individualistic "intellectualism."[48] If formalism is the problem, then he might have at-

41. A similar reading of Yoder's essay "Hermeneutics of Peoplehood" is possible (*PK*, 15–45). The essay contains his strongest language of negative freedom (25), but only in light of the church's *"missionary ethic of incarnation"* (44–45; emphasis original).

42. Hauerwas and Fodor, "Remaining in Babylon: Oliver O'Donovan's Defense of Christendom," in Hauerwas, *Wilderness Wanderings*, 224n15.

43. Hauerwas in Milbank and Hauerwas, "Christian Peace," 215.

44. Hauerwas, *Good Company*, 73. See also his "Confessions."

45. Hauerwas, *Sanctify Them*, 166. It is perhaps ironic that he does not capitalize "church" in this sentence. See also Hauerwas, *Good Company*, 19–31, esp. 228n2, for his attempt to find, beyond Yoder, "traditioned practices or disciplines where imposed will and total freedom are not assumed to be the only alternatives."

46. Hauerwas, *Sanctify Them*, 166; cf. 93.

47. Hauerwas claims to dissolve the freedom-determinism dualism with the recognition that our decisions are only made intelligible in retrospect (*Sanctify Them*, 93). For example, it is impossible for a couple to "know" in advance precisely what the commitment entailed by their marriage vows means (102). That may be true, but it does not negate the importance of *relatively* informed decision-making.

48. Yoder, *PK*, 38–40.

tended to Yoder's comments on the positive freedoms, and especially to his identification of nonviolence as the "substance" of Christian ethics made possible by the "form" of voluntary membership.[49] Similarly, those theologians who worry about Yoder's "almost Pelagian denial of the prevenience of grace" overlook his account of grace as mediated through the powers, Israel, and the church.[50]

Although these criticisms can be refuted through careful readings of Yoder's *oeuvre*, it is notable that they occur at all—especially among readers as sympathetic as Hauerwas. Internal defense is legitimate and important but, in this case, it does not fully explain why Yoder is subject to distorted interpretations. The reading of Yoder's theological anthropology given above is textually plausible, but it must be admitted that he often left the connections between the negative and positive freedoms vague and implicit. He may see theology and metaphysics as intrinsically related to ethics, but it is the ethics that always gets his attention.[51] The new community may be graced and affective, but his focus is on the socio-logical rationale for joining. Nonviolence may be the substance of his ethics, but he mainly treats it as a dialogical procedure.[52] If this is the case, then how should Yoder's project be revised? Hauerwas's non-voluntary ecclesiology dispenses altogether with the emphasis on choice, as God does something to us we only thought we were doing ourselves.[53] O'Donovan offers a quite

49. Ibid., 110.

50. Bourne, *Seek the Peace*, 257. Cf. Bourne, "Governmentality, Witness, and the State," 110–11; Doerksen, *Beyond Suspicion*, 183–85; Doerksen, "Share the House," *MPU*, 194; Kroeker, "Messianic Political Ethic," 156; Kroeker, "War of the Lamb," 82–83; Kroeker, "Yoder's Voluntariety," 55–58, 63n63; Harink, *Paul among the Postliberals*, 283–84. Each of these critics seeks to repudiate O'Donovan's reading of Yoder as caricatured, but each wants a stronger, more consistent and explicit account of grace and election. Carter, *Politics of the Cross*, 187–88, 199, also repudiates O'Donovan, but still wants a better description of the experience of the believer in baptism.

51. Cf. Yoder, *PK*, 101, where he says that "the imperatives of dialogue with majority mentalities have skewed description toward the problematics of weakness and effectiveness. An authentic portrayal of 'the peace church vision' from the inside would have spoken more of worship and servanthood, reconciliation and creativity, *Gelassenheit* and the Power of the Light, 'heart-felt religion' and transforming hope, and the person of Jesus Christ." It may be, as Gerald Schlabach maintains, that these lines speak for Yoder's entire career and show that he "would have come across as *more* orthodox and pious" if he were not constantly fighting majority views ("Christian Witness," 241n41). But it is striking that Yoder never does consider many of these "pious" themes, even when speaking in peace church settings.

52. Chapters five and six below are especially concerned with an attempt to articulate a dialogicism that overcomes substance-form dualism.

53. Hauerwas, *Sanctify Them*, 102: "At most, 'agency' names the skills correlative of a truthful narrative that enables us to make what happens to us our own, which

remarkable account of freedom that is in many respects similar to Yoder's;[54] yet this freedom is articulated within the horizon set by Christendom political theologies.[55] Another proposal is from P. Travis Kroeker, who suggests that Yoder incorporate a Platonic and Augustinian conception of the inner soul ruled invisibly by God.[56] This spiritual invisibility supposedly allows for an accounting of the movement of grace in spite of an imperfect church. But Yoder's church is merely real, not sinless—and its reality, like the reality of the fallen powers and Israel, is what mediates grace in the world. Taking these criticisms and their shortcomings into consideration, the question then becomes how to revise Yoder's theological anthropology in such a way that better integrates his emphasis on voluntariety with his attention to the spiritual and social context of freedom. That remains the task of this chapter.

Bourdieu on Freedom and Structure

Pierre Bourdieu sought to overcome classical debates about freedom and determination by demonstrating how freedom, as a concept and state of being, is socially produced. "Freedom" does not describe normal social functioning, but may be created through strenuous intellectual and practical

---

includes 'decisions' we made when we thought we knew what we were doing but in retrospect seem more like something that happened to us."

54. See also O'Donovan's pneumatological account of freedom in *Resurrection and Moral Order*, 106–9.

55. O'Donovan, *Desire of the Nations*, 252–56. As will be seen in chapter five below, Yoder worries that Christendom betrays the politics of Jesus and proper Christian mission when it uses state power to promote the faith. It should be noted that, unlike many Christendom apologists, O'Donovan advocates a theology of international law rather than of empire (267–68). Either way, he wants a legal framework conducive to Christian political judgment. The fate of religious freedom under a Christian legal framework is unclear, and its omission from O'Donovan's theological "redemption" of liberal freedom is troubling. In his book *Defending Constantine*, Peter J. Leithart contrasts Constantine's religious toleration with Yoder's claim that "Constantinianism" is corrosive of religious freedom (112). But he then goes on to demonstrate approvingly how Constantine's policies encouraged and enforced Christian beliefs and practices, since a religiously neutral public space is impossible (112–46). With reference to O'Donovan, it is difficult to see how any theology of religious freedom he could offer would be different from Leithart's Constantianian theology of enforced religious "concord." It then becomes unclear how faith is free in any sense. See O'Donovan's "Response to Skillen" for a defense of his Christendom theology in light of concerns about religious "pluralism." For a Yoderian critique of O'Donovan's non-christological ontology, see Neufeld, "Just War Theory."

56. See note 50 above.

labor. Bourdieu developed two analytical concepts relevant to this conception of freedom, "reproduction," and "margins of freedom."

Reproduction

In the 1960s and early 1970s Bourdieu collaborated with Jean-Claude Passeron to produce two seminal works of disenchantment, *Les Héritiers* and *Reproduction*.[57] Against a prevalent communist "Jacobin" ideology that cast the French education system as a perfect meritocracy,[58] Bourdieu and Passeron set out to demonstrate that, "the formal equality of chances being realized, the school can place all the appearances of legitimacy at the service of the legitimation of privileges."[59] French law guarantees equal access to the education system, making that system appear to be neutral. But a student's chances of success are inextricably linked to the confluence of their class of origin, social status, and academic practices.[60] Legal neutrality thus masks the subservience of the system to elites.

Pedagogical practice, according to Bourdieu and Passeron, generally depends on the education system's legitimacy being as broadly unquestioned as one's native language.[61] In this context the system is free to inculcate whatever "cultural arbitrary" it is entrusted with.[62] Teachers are granted pedagogical authority by the system to shape student habitus, and their authority is validated by the "truth" or correspondence of their decrees to the system.[63] The authors support these claims with evidence from their research into the function of cultural capital, especially linguistic capital, in the French school system.[64] Students whose family life prepares them to speak more or less like their professors almost always exceed their peers from different backgrounds—and these successful students are almost always from relatively privileged families.

57. See Kauppi, *French Intellectual Nobility,* 50, on their impact.

58. Law, "Unredeemed Marxism," 679; Wacquant in Bourdieu and Wacquant, *IRS,* 80n24.

59. Bourdieu and Passeron, *Les Héritiers,* 44: "l'égalité formelle des chances étant réalisé, l'Ecole pourrait mettre toutes les apparences de la légitimité au service de la légitimation des privilèges."

60. Ibid., 61.

61. Bourdieu and Passeron, *Reproduction,* 13–14.

62. Ibid., 31–54.

63. Ibid., 67, 186–206. The authors name this process "dependence through independence." See chapter five below on the "circuits of legitimation."

64. Ibid., 72–161.

The role of the habitus in reproducing social order receives even more treatment in *Outline of a Theory of Practice* and subsequent works. Whereas the Bourdieu of *Reproduction* is still indebted to structuralism[65]—which views practices as mere epiphenomena of social structures—*Outline* presents what has come to be known as a "constructive"[66] or "genetic structuralism."[67] On this view, "structural distinctions are the construction of social agents who are struggling to reconcile their indigenous cultures (their *habitus*) with those objectified cultures which carry value and power."[68] Social reproduction is thus not a matter of static systems implanting ideology into passive agents, but a product of ongoing contest between agents for power. Marriage is for Bourdieu a typical example of "the system of reproduction practices," as it tends to preserve capital holdings through a matrix of uncoordinated strategies.[69] The reproductive outcome of these strategies requires no explicit planning, because the principles of and for reproduction are already embedded in the habitus of participating agents: "The habitus, the durably installed generative principle of regulated improvisations, produces practices which tend to reproduce the regularities immanent in the objective conditions of the production of their generative principle, while adjusting to the demands inscribed as objective potentialities in the situation, as defined by the cognitive and motivating structures making up the habitus."[70] Reproduction occurs across changes in "objective potentialities" because agents have learned, consciously or not, to recognize and respond to these changes in ways that perpetuate their class position. As habitus is formed in conditions laden with specific expectations of success and failure, it is difficult for agents to conceive of strategies that would truly disrupt the social order. Reproduction is thus a generative product of agents throughout society whose often agonistic practices maintain field structures over time.

65. Robbins, "'Cultural Capital,'" 25–26. In *Le bal des célibataires*, 12, Bourdieu names his essay, "Le stratégies matrimoniales dans le système des stratégies de reproduction," (from 1972) as signaling a clear break from structuralism. Some are unconvinced that the break was complete: Dillon, "Pierre Bourdieu," 426; Heinich, *Pourquoi Bourdieu*, 142; Martín-Criado, *Les deux Algéries*, 119–21; Schinkel, "Bourdieu's Political Turn?," 83.

66. Bourdieu, *CD*, 147; Accardo, *Lire Bourdieu*, 259.

67. Accardo, *Lire Bourdieu*, 259; Addi, *Bourdieu*, 141; Fowler, *Bourdieu and Cultural Theory*, 35, 85–89. Cf. Grenfell and James, eds., *Bourdieu and Education*, 155–56, on Bourdieu's "phenomenological structuralism." Fowler, *Bourdieu and Cultural Theory*, 85–89, and Robbins, *Bourdieu and Culture*, 44–47, relate Bourdieu's understanding of reproduction to Marx and Marxism.

68. Robbins, "'Cultural Capital,'" 25.

69. Bourdieu, *OTP*, 59; cf. *LP*, 160–161.

70. Bourdieu, *OTP*, 78.

During the 1970s and 80s, Bourdieu expanded his generative structuralism through a number of essays on education,[71] culture,[72] and religion.[73] Intellectual interests, cultural "tastes," and religious convictions are all ways agents distinguish themselves from one another and, in doing so, help reproduce the order of society. A particular interest, taste, or conviction may gain or lose value over time, but the capital "rich" and "poor," dominant and dominated, tend to stay the same due to habitus-shaped acquisition strategies. *The State Nobility*, originally published in 1989, is perhaps Bourdieu's most elaborate attempt to show how reproduction strategies adapt to constantly changing structures.[74] Among other topics, the book examines a shift in France from the family to the school as the basis of social reproduction. Although this shift could have occasioned a transfer of power from family dynasties to intellectuals, in fact school-based reproduction became a strategy employed selectively by dominant families.[75] Reproduction in this case occurred as a battle within the field of power, as "a struggle to dictate *the dominant principle of domination*."[76] As a result of this struggle, academic credentials replaced family titles as the most valuable form of symbolic capital, but continuities of habitus across the field prohibited this from drastically affecting French class structures.[77] Dominant habitus is simply better equipped than dominated habitus to take advantage of and gain from social transformation—most change is therefore reproductive.

Bourdieu returns to these themes in his exploration of the most enduring of social structures, gender. In *Masculine Domination* he writes of gender as an "eternalized arbitrary,"[78] a product of "the history of the continuous (re) creation of the objective and subjective structures of masculine domination, which has gone on permanently so long as there have been men and women, and through which the masculine order has been continuously reproduced from age to age."[79] Family, church, and state have all played important roles in

71. E.g., Bourdieu and Boltanski, "Demand for Education"; Bourdieu, *HA*, esp. 84–89, 176, 183, 217.

72. Esp. Bourdieu, *Distinction*, 164–65, 193, 414, 480; "Forms of Capital," 241–42, 246, 249, 253–54.

73. Bourdieu and Saint Martin, "La Sainte Famille," 30, 44.

74. Bourdieu, *IRS*, 140, names *SN* as his best response to the question of social change. See *IRS*, 80–81, 131–40, on habitus and change.

75. Bourdieu, *SN*, 278–99.

76. Ibid., 265.

77. As explored in chapter five below, Bourdieu believes this development had positive political effects that may still be utilized.

78. Bourdieu, *MD*, vii–ix.

79. Ibid., 82–83.

perpetuating gender structures over eras of considerable social upheaval, and today the neoliberal economic order serves the same function.[80] The association of women with "symbolic goods" (art, fashion, etc.), for example, may provide women with "professional emancipation," but only by consigning them to the bottom rung of cultural production.[81] Reproduction strategies can thus be so successful as to appear to transcend the flow of time, even if they only occur through continual labor on fields, capital, and habitus.

Margins of Freedom

Bourdieu's emphasis on reproduction has led many commentators to accuse him of deterministically underplaying the possibility of change.[82] If perceptions of social possibility are rooted in the habitus, and the habitus is formed by the possibilities available during agents' primary formation, then structural transformation seems unlikely, if not impossible: agents will only see the limited possibilities of their field positions. Bourdieu, however, saw his conception as transcending a binary construal of freedom and determinism. With Luc Boltanski he called for an end to the "academic polarity between stability and change" in favor of the recognition that reproduction "can be realised in and through the translation of the structure whenever the members of the dominated classes enter separately, through statistical actions and reactions, in the free play of competition, i.e., in that form of class struggle which is imposed on them by the dominant class."[83] Far from being antithetical to change, stability on this model is achieved through constant change—even through competitive struggles waged by the dominated, given that the dominant dictate the terms of the struggle.

But this alleged resolution of the stability-change antinomy seems actually to add weight to the criticisms; for the overcoming of the antinomy accepts micro-change only as a mechanism of macro-stability.[84] Neverthe-

80. Ibid., 85–87, 92–95; cf. *PR*, 19, 66–71, 108, on the family. See Mitrovic, "Neoliberal Philosophy."

81. Bourdieu, *MD*, 102.

82. E.g., Bennett, "Habitus Clivé," 221–25; Certeau, *Everyday Life*, 53–60; Crossley, *Social Body*, 115–18; Fowler, *Bourdieu and Cultural Theory*, 4–5, 66; Heinich, *Pourqoui Bourdieu*, 145–51; Marginson, "Global Field," 308–13; Skeggs, "Bourdieu and the 'Self,'" 87–90. Cf. Hobsbawm, "Sociologie critique," 286–89.

83. Bourdieu and Boltanski, "Changes in Social Structures," 221. Cf. Bourdieu, *OTP*, 95.

84. But see Addi, *Sociologie*, 32; Grenfell and James, "Theory, Practice and Pedagogic Research," in *Bourdieu and Education*, eds. Grenfell and James, 25; Passeron, "Le sociologue en politique," 99–100.

less, Bourdieu elaborates a concept of "margins of freedom" in and from which to challenge unfettered reproduction. This concept is treated in detail in Bourdieu's late work, *Pascalian Meditations*, but its lineaments may be perceived throughout his *oeuvre*. These lineaments may be described in terms of the freedoms of knowledge, practice, and symbols.

For all its interest in revealing the closed circle of educational success, *Les Héritiers* concludes with an appeal for a democratizing "rational pedagogy."[85] Rational pedagogy consists of constant assessment of pedagogical forms in light of the differential social backgrounds of the students in question. Rather than demonstrating their high cultural capital, teachers should make their material as comprehensible as possible to all members of a class. This pedagogy would have the effect of leveling academic opportunities, especially if practiced on the youngest schoolchildren. It is not clear if Bourdieu continued throughout his career to believe that rational pedagogy was possible or desirable,[86] but he remained convinced of the emancipatory potential of knowledge. No positive proposal ends *Reproduction*, yet Bourdieu and Passeron do position themselves as exposing the "illusion of freedom and universality" that makes agents "prisoners of their limitations."[87] Presumably their sociological disenchantment of French educational ideology would break the illusion and allow for some freedom of action. This conception of sociology and intellectual production as liberating becomes a major theme of Bourdieu's work in the 1980s and 90s. During these years, which unsurprisingly coincide with his own increased political activity, he argued for a "corporatism of the universal" which would use the tools of scientific reflexivity to defend the autonomy of cultural fields. This "*Realpolitik* of reason" will be discussed in detail in chapter 5 below, but here it is important to note it as a contribution to his understanding of human freedom. Knowledge, especially of one's illusions and limitations, births at least the possibility of freedom.[88]

Knowledge, nevertheless, cannot fully capture the logic of reproduction or, for that matter of any practice. Practice obeys what Bourdieu calls

---

85. Bourdieu and Passeron, *Les Héritiers*, 111–15.

86. Grenfell, *Education and Training*, 77, 93, 109–10, 115–16; Zanten, "Education Policy Analyst," 671–86.

87. Bourdieu and Passeron, *Reproduction*, 40.

88. Touraine, "Le sociologue du people," 111, sees Bourdieu as a successor to Norbert Elias on this point. On knowledge and freedom in Bourdieu's thought, see Marlène Benquet, "Determination" in *Abécédaire*, ed. Cazier, 43–44; Castel, "Entre la contrainte sociale et le volontarisme politique," 303–31; Fowler, "Autonomy, Reciprocity and Science," 113–14; Reed-Danahay, *Locating Bourdieu*, 153; Francisco Vázquez García, *Pierre Bourdieu*, 219–20; Wacquant, *IRS*, 49–52.

"polythetic" logic; put more colloquially, the logic of practice is "fuzzy."[89] Scientists too easily accept "the synoptic illusion" which imposes the rigor of academic logic onto human practices.[90] But the interpretive schemes of the habitus are "practical operators." Academicism misses "the unceasing dynamism of units which are constantly forming and reforming" and the "fuzziness" that allows non-academic "native notions" to work.[91] This fuzziness results from the extreme efficiency by which a multitude of practical relations are formed by analogy with a small set of oppositions.[92]

The "poverty" of practical logic is expressed, for instance, in bodily motion. The body does not rely on geometrical calculations to navigate space, but on a small set of dualisms: up/down, forward/back, left/right, east/west, and so on.[93] Such "practical geometry" can be observed in ritual, where spatial inversions provide symbolic order: the eucharistic host is raised, then brought down to the lips of the faithful; bread is broken, while water and wine are mixed; the cross is processed into and then out of the sanctuary; and so on.[94] These oppositions provide a wealth of combinations of bodily movements that may be imitated and innovated upon in ritual practice. Similarly, distinctions of "taste" take a few adjective pairs and categorize the entire social world: heavy/light, hot/cold, dull/brilliant, etc.[95] Agents do not apply these adjectives in the logical or systematic sense demanded by academics, but in an open manner whose coherence is that of lived experience. A "heavy" conversation can be clunky or intimate, while a "light" one may be fun or frivolous. Meaning is not supplied by semantic rigor, but by fluid, often contradictory usage pertaining to specific contexts.

Because the habitus is, therefore, an "open system of dispositions,"[96] the fuzzy practical logic it embraces does not *necessarily* lead to the reproduction

89. Bourdieu, *OTP*, 106–7, 109, 110, 112, 123, 221n25; cf. parallels in *LP*, 80–97. Bourdieu cites Husserl on "polythesis" and George Lakoff on "fuzziness." See Pilario, *Rough Grounds of Praxis*, 205–8, for summary.

90. Bourdieu, *OTP*, 98–109.

91. Ibid., 109. Bourdieu regards Edmund Leech as sensitive to the gap between academic and practical classification, whereas Durkheim and many others confound the two. Chapter four below returns to the issue of scientific knowledge and practice.

92. Ibid., 109–13.

93. Ibid., 117–19.

94. Ibid., 120; *LP*, 92. The liturgical example is supplied by the present author.

95. Bourdieu, *OTP*, 120–23; cf. *Distinction*.

96. Bourdieu, *IRS*, 133. The openness of the habitus counters the critique of Bennett, "Habitus Clivé," 201–28, that Bourdieu overemphasized the unity of the habitus until late in his career.

of field structure. Freedom is latent within practice.[97] Habitus may be extremely durable, but even the most "eternal" dispositions are susceptible to transformation.[98] As dispositions are formed in specific contexts, habitus is only "activated" by similar contexts, and significant contextual change may result in unexpected practical outcomes.[99] In normal circumstances, habitus is characterized by "conatus," a desire for reproduction.[100] But the disjunction of field and habitus can give rise to "hysteresis," a disorientation full of both opportunity and peril.[101]

Bourdieu explores the possibilities of hysteresis in the context of crises such as the May 1968 student demonstrations in France.[102] Changes in the French economy during preceding decades resulted in the disappointment of a generation of students' career expectations. This "break in the *chain of anticipated identifications*" produces "agents who, excluded from the race for future prospects which until then had been programmed into their position, are now led to call into question the race itself."[103] When this questioning leads enough of the less-dominated agents, e.g., teachers, to disrupt the race, a "critical situation" occurs. This critical situation involves "the intrusion of the possibility of novelty, in short, [an] open time where all futures appear possible, and are indeed so to a certain extent, for that very reason."[104] If the crisis is trans-sectoral—as in May 1968, when it included both workers and students—agents inhabiting homologous positions in different fields may find that their disruptive interests and practices overlap.[105] In this moment of solidarity the typical flow of time as reproduction is halted, and new modes of production may be imagined.[106] Belief in such alternative futures

97. Passeron, "Le sociologue en politique," 99–100, describes freedom in Bourdieu's sociology in terms of Democritus's clinamen: a "flick of obliqueness" that ripples through "the river of necessity."

98. See Bourdieu, *MD*, 102.

99. Bourdieu, *Distinction*, 99–168; *IRS*, 135.

100. Bourdieu, *HA*, 176; *WW*, 508; *PR*, 19. See Fuller, "Conatus," 171–81. Bourdieu names Spinoza as the antecedent here, and Fuller traces the term back to John Philoponus in the sixth century. Bourdieu's book *Weight of the World* has several co-authors but, since every reference to the work in this thesis is to Bourdieu's own contribution, it will simply be referenced as Bourdieu, *WW*.

101. Bourdieu, *OTP*, 83; *LP*, 62; *PM*, 162. In *PM* Bourdieu calls this "the Don Quixote effect." See Hardy, "Hysteresis."

102. Bourdieu, *HA*, 160–86.

103. Ibid., 172.

104. Ibid., 162.

105. Cf. Ross, *May '68*, 11: "The principle idea of May was the union of intellectual contestation with workers' struggle."

106. Bourdieu, *HA*, 182–83.

may inspire alternative practices and structures, the institutionalization of revolution.[107] The crisis may therefore draw out the liberating potential of practice, enabling the creation of free structures.

In *Pascalian Meditations* Bourdieu draws together the rational and practical dimensions of freedom under the concept of "margins of freedom."[108] The generalization of crisis under neoliberalism paradoxically results in the omnipresence of the conditions for revolution. In this context the "relative autonomy of the symbolic order" may become the source of those alternative imaginations that facilitate social change: "Symbolic power, which can manipulate hopes and expectations, especially through a more or less inspired and uplifting performative evocation of the future—prophesy, forecast or prediction—can introduce a degree of play into the correspondence between expectations and chances and open up a space of freedom through the more or less voluntarist positing of more or less improbable possibles—utopia, project, programme or plan—which the pure logic of probabilities would lead one to regard as practically excluded."[109] To be successful, these symbolic actions would need to account for the dispositions of targeted agents, and for the limitations of those dispositions.[110] Freedom is thus produced through realistic assessment of possibilities for creating a space within the habitus, which separates unconscious expectations from the "*explicit aspirations*" elicited by visions of alternate futures.[111] This margin of freedom is "a site of twofold uncertainty" encompassing an openness in the symbolic and material structure of fields and of agents. Their existence, whether possible or real, belies the "fatalism" of all orthodoxies, including that of "a sociologism which constitutes sociological laws as quasi-iron laws or an essentialist pessimism based on belief in an immutable human nature."[112] Reproductive transformations may be the norm, but within the margins of freedom, new beliefs and practices may be produced that take society in a new, freer direction.

107. Bourdieu regards this situation as "a general model of the revolutionary process" (ibid., 172). Bourdieu's understanding of revolution is generally indebted to Weber's sociology of religion. See esp. Bourdieu, "Structured Interests."

108. Bourdieu, *PM*, 234–36.

109. Ibid., 234

110. Ibid., 234–35.

111. Ibid., 235.

112. Ibid.

Revising Yoder's Theological Anthropology

Bourdieu interprets reproduction and freedom in light of his basic anthropological concept habitus. Human being as habitus is structured by fields oriented toward certain forms of capital. Personal dispositions, including dispositions to choose, are therefore formed publicly. "Choice" is always a selection among given options and never the creation *ex nihilo* of an autonomous subject. Humans most often choose to accept their social order, since that is what they were formed to do. But freedom to break from the social order is also a possibility; albeit one that is realized only by taking advantage of specific challenges that arise in the reproductive cycle. This kind of freedom is produced by an imaginative act of collective will, yet neither the imagination nor the will are drawn from nowhere. Voluntariety is essential, but can only be understood in its social context.

At one level, Bourdieu's anthropological insights mirror Stanley Hauerwas's "non-voluntary" construal of human agency. Bourdieu's sociological reading of May 1968 would seem to confirm Hauerwas's contention that decisions can later be narrated as having happened to the decider. The 1968 protests only happened because contradictions in the mode of reproduction caused a trans-sectoral crisis. Dominated members of various fields were given the opportunity to work together for a new order. But Bourdieu's anthropology cannot be called non-voluntary; the will cannot be subtracted from his account. The labor of freedom is rational, for people need to know that alternatives are available. The labor of freedom is emotional, for people need to value the goals set forth by any freedom program if they are going to work for them. But the labor of freedom is inevitably voluntary too, for people need to choose the available opportunity. Indeed, Bourdieu's anthropology complicates the division of persons into reason, emotions, and will or, for that matter, into any other collection of discrete "organs" that could be exulted with an "-ism" or rejected with a "non-."[113] Bourdieu's willing agent is an intellectual and affective agent; and in every respect this agent is socially structured.

Incorporating Bourdieu's integrated sociological anthropology into Yoder's revised theology of creation enables a further step to be made: willing, intellectual, and affective agents are also spiritual. As Yoder at his

---

113. As quoted above, Bourdieu does identify his politics as "more or less voluntarist" (*PM*, 234). See also Kauppi, "Sociologist as *Moraliste*," 17. But, given Bourdieu's commitment to collective intellectual political intervention (see chapter five below), he could hardly be accused of reductive "voluntarism." Consistent with his overall sociological perspective, the formation of the will is an historical process, an outcome of historical struggle.

best maintains, human being is being-with-God. Although this point was made in a general way in the previous chapter, it can now be given greater specificity. The spiritual constitution of humans is such that reason, affect, and will only exist in relation to God. No idea or feeling or choice ever occurs outside of structures created and sustained by God, namely, the human body and other powers.[114] If human bodies are part of the powers, then bodies themselves are providential instruments holding open the possibility of freedom for obedience. On this account, there is no reason to downplay voluntariety, but rather to portray embodied volitional structures as a gift from God, as part of the gift of human being. Choice is a product of grace; choice is mediated and, after the fall, deformed by social structures.

In light of these comments, it is clear that the voluntary church cannot be defined by a series of acontextual choices made by autonomous individuals. There are no acontextual choices, and "individuals" are constituted by social relations. Yoder's occasional language of escape from the social order to join the church is sociologically implausible. Nevertheless, the concept of a voluntary church remains theologically defensible. Hauerwas makes an important theological point that God is the primary agent in conversion and baptism.[115] Yet unless this conviction is to devolve into an ahistorical spiritualism, an account must be given of the social context of conversion.[116] Yoder is right to insist on voluntary membership as a mark of the church, not because, as O'Donovan fears he believes, voluntarism is an adequate anthropology, but because God calls humans to discipleship within their varied social realms. "Voluntary" membership here should be understood as a social, rather than an "inner" psychic achievement.

Conversion involves, for example, a person whose initial habitus is formed within a context that is not well oriented to the activity of God; his dispositions and practices are not in continuity with those structures

---

114. Cf. Milbank, *Theology and Social Theory*, 417–21, on Augustine's treatment of the soul, in which reason, passions, and will overlap as embodied "movements of desire" toward some goal or another in a spiritual context (421). Milbank summarizes the anthropology and its implications for ethics: "It is the whole desiring person who sins or does right, and the measure of right desire is not the rule of reason over the body, but the external relation of person to person in the community of peace, under God" (421). See also Smith, *Desiring the Kingdom*.

115. Flinn, "Conversion," 52, notes that Paul uses the language of "call," not conversion, to describe what happened on the road to Damascus (see Rom 1:1; 1 Cor 1:1). Flinn suggests that Paul patterned his account after the Old Testament prophets (Isa 49:1; Jer 1:5).

116. Recent studies of conversion insist that it is a contextually locatable social process. See, e.g., Flinn, "Conversion," 52–61, Peace, *Conversion in the New Testament*, and Rambo, *Religious Conversion*.

that result from intense interactions between humans and God. In *Christian Witness to the State*, Yoder argues that the primary difference between those belonging to the "present aeon" and those belonging to the "coming aeon" is "a matter of direction" toward or away from concrete obedience to the will of God.[117] This difference is not temporal, for the Holy Spirit is present in the church "as a foretaste of the eventual consummation of God's kingdom."[118] Transfer from one age to another thus involves a sociological shift from mild to intense interaction with God, namely, through participation in the Holy Spirit through the church.[119]

From a Bourdieusian perspective, this shift is only precipitated by a gradual or sudden change of the person's *interest* such that they now ascribe value to Christian identity. Presumably there could be any number of reasons for this change of interest: Christian identity guarantees citizenship or survival, as it did for some Jews in the middle ages; it is the identity of the rich and powerful, as it was in Protestant America; one's primary social group or family adopts it, as in missionary settings; it offers intellectual or emotional resources that are distinct from those offered by other available identities, as it may in today's increasingly post-secular society. Whatever the reason, Christian identity only appears as valuable capital to anyone for reasons related to their habitus, to the structure of his or her interests.[120] The adoption of Christian identity may be judged as superficial, i.e., it does not accompany participation in dispositional or institutional structures that are intensely related to God. But it may rather involve such participation and be deemed an "authentic" conversion.[121] Authentic conversion may come about because of the proximity between one's original habitus and the new Christian habitus, or because a margin of freedom is found within the dispositional structure such that the church appears to offer a desirable and interesting alternative future. Regardless, God has interacted with the person through the visibility of ecclesial structures to shift that person's interested practice in such a way that he is now in solidarity with the church, that is, he belongs to the body of Christ. The only adequate human way to

117. Yoder, *CWS*, 9. See chapter five below.

118. Yoder, *CWS*, 9.

119. Cf. Rambo, *Religious Conversion*, 66–141, on the potential progression from initial encounter with a religious "advocate" to initial participation to commitment.

120. Cf. Rambo, *Religious Conversion*, 56–65, on the various personal motivations and "availabilities" (structural, emotional, intellectual, religious) that encourage conversion.

121. Cf. Rambo and Farhadian, "Converting," 32: "For converting to be authentic (as judged by particular religious traditions), converts must change aspects of their life according to the prescriptions and proscriptions of specific religious communities. These dimensions include affective, intellectual, ethical, religious, and social/political domains."

describe his response to God is as a voluntary conversion enabled not by an autonomous will, but by a divine appeal to his context-formed interests via the church. Inasmuch as it is constituted by such conversions, the church is rightly called voluntary.

There are, of course, many persons whose initial habitus are formed within a context that is well oriented to the activity of God; discipleship provides the only way of being they know.[122] Yoder's arguments are not denigrative of such "cradle Christianity." But his connection of voluntary membership to church discipline suggests that, if accountability is a constitutive practice of ecclesial being, then reliable readiness to give and receive correction is a condition of full membership, i.e., of baptism.[123] This reliable readiness need not presume an omniscient self, only the ability to give an account of oneself as reliably ready that is comprehensible by the community. The voluntary membership of a Christian reared in the church, therefore, is at once a recognition by the church of her reliable readiness to give and receive correction, and a personal affirmation of this reliable readiness. The disposition to affirm, to choose, ecclesial belonging is inculcated by the church itself. Choosing the church from within the church gives assent to the church-shaped habitus. This assent is necessary from a theological perspective as it signals the maturation of a habitus that is able to give and receive correction. The decision to assent to church membership is an invitation to receive correction and an announcement of one's intention and (ecclesially recognized) ability to give it. Insofar as the church is constituted by persons who are reared within it, it is still rightly called voluntary.

This account of the voluntary church responds to O'Donovan, Hauerwas, and the others' worries about Yoder's rationalism and lack of attention to the prevenience of grace in decision. The latter point can be stated more strongly. If the practices of created society are intrinsically related to the activity of the triune God, then practices of freedom are produced with God. Freedom is at once a divine gift and divine-human co-production. There can be no separation of the work of freedom from the gift of

122. Anabaptists have typically included their children in the church, assuming that children's salvation is assured until they begin to choose sin—which they inevitably will, thus leading to the necessity of conversion even within the church. See Finger, *Anabaptist Theology*, 168–69.

123. Cf. Finger, *Anabaptist Theology*, 179: "Believers' baptism also portrays membership not only as submission to or reception into an institution—but also, since it involves, inward, conscious choice, as taking an active role. Infant baptism can hardly express that interplay between individual freedom and corporate identity central to ecclesial existence. Neither does it symbolize that interaction of divine grace and human response woven through all Christian life." Finger correctly notes (180) that Yoder (*BP*, 28–35) rejects a view of baptism as the result of "inward believing."

freedom—Christians engage in the labor of receiving freedom.[124] Because this labor responds to God, it is necessarily involved in those structured structures that in different ways result from God's intense structuring activity. The production of Christian freedom is thus centered on the practices of Israel, Jesus, and the church, especially as these are given normative shape in scripture. One of these practices is the inclusion through baptism of outsiders who respond to God's call through the church by committing themselves to discipleship. Another practice is the baptism of children who assent to the church's recognition of their capacity to participate in accountability practices. These practices contribute to the labor of receiving the gift of freedom for discipleship. As they are central to the being of the church, the church is rightly called voluntary.

The Bourdieusian revision of Yoder's theological anthropology further allows for a cogent response to Kroeker's call for a return to Augustinian inwardness and invisibility. Because decisions and choices are products of interested practices, the "inner" and "outer" dimensions of Christian commitment cannot be separated.[125] Decisions and choices are powerful practices, and God relates to them creatively by drawing them toward those structures resulting from intense divine-human interaction. God therefore relates to personal decisions and choices, not by bypassing their visible social context, but through the practical presence of the body of Christ. God's personal relating to personal interests is intertwined with the church's labor of receiving the gift of freedom. Richard Bourne is thus correct to suggest election as the theological locus for a revision of Yoder's understanding of the voluntary church: God has chosen a people on earth through their voluntary identification with Jesus Christ. The body of Christ is formed over time by a series of decisions that are the gifts and products of socially structured personal interests interacting with God through Christ.

Conclusion

This chapter began with an examination of John Howard Yoder's theological anthropology as seen in his writings on the powers and the free church. Those writings yield an anthropology centered on the constitutive encounter between humans and God. Because human being is being-with-God, the freedom for obedience is always and everywhere available to some degree.

124. This language is indebted to Walzer's discussion of the Jews' free self-bondage to divine law as achievement of God's promise (*Exodus and Revolution*, 52–53, 77–97, 108).

125. Cf. Murphy, *Bodies and Souls*, and F. Kerr, *Theology after Wittgenstein*, for theological critiques of anthropologies that separate an "inner" and "outer" person.

The powers provide the basic order that makes freedom possible, and Israel and the church make it a reality through their response to and proclamation of divine love. Although this anthropology would seem to strike a fine balance between the priority of grace and the importance of choice, several critics indicate that Yoder's emphasis lands squarely on choice. He thereby comes dangerously close to modern voluntarism, and thus to downgrading the church to the status of other optional societies.

The remainder of the chapter pursued a revision of Yoder's theological anthropology that drew from Bourdieu's sociological anthropology. Bourdieu's concepts of reproduction and margins of freedom place choice fully within a sociological context. Choice is a product of social forces, but cannot be reduced to social forces—any account of action has to include the process through which agents come to accept a decision as their own. The irreducibility of choice is perhaps best seen in crisis situations, where agents may be swayed in multiple directions. Appeals to their embodied wills (and intellects and emotions) must attend to their formation, but the habitus can become more flexible when fields collapse into each other.

A theological interpretation of these sociological concepts led to a discussion of conversion and baptism as part of the labor of receiving freedom as a gift from God. This language returns to Yoder's most coherent depictions of voluntariety, but more clearly shows how choice can be emphasized without undermining the priority of grace and its social mediation. Conversion is a labor, both of the church that extends grace abroad and of the new believer who affirms and participates in that grace. But the laborious reception of grace is irreducibly a responsive labor. Grace is structurally part of creation, but it does not have to be chosen. It is often not chosen—sin and violence are the result.

3

Revising Yoder's Theology of Violence

THE SOCIAL AND SPIRITUAL context of human beings suggests that the refusal of grace, as much as its acceptance, is not just an inner or individual phenomenon. Yoder's sociological theology unsurprisingly casts sin in broad structural and cosmic terms. The powers are fallen, meaning, the created social structures are now badly malformed. God's intended peaceful order has been disrupted and violence is the norm. As a Christian pacifist, Yoder was concerned to expose how violence is implicated in the everyday language and practices of Christians. Some critics argue that he was so focused on violence that he lost sight of the goodness that is still present in the world—goodness that is so precious that at times it requires protection by violent means. These critics insist that the possibility of protecting the good with violence casts doubt over unilateral assessments of violence as an evil. It even raises questions about the nature of violence itself, especially if mind-body and spirit-matter dualisms are destabilized. The barrier between violent and supposedly nonviolent modes of persuasion weakens. From here one can moot the possibility that violence is inescapable and simply part of being. The best humanity can do is to play off lesser versus greater forms of violence.

This chapter responds to similar criticisms of Yoder's pacifism by revising his theological conception of violence. There are strong resources within Yoder's work for countering such criticisms, and none stronger than his theology of the fallen principalities and powers. After investigating the latter, it is possible to see violence as part of a wider reorientation of the powers away from their created role in binding humans to God. Prideful rebellion is now built into our social structures, as their own autonomy as state, family, or market is now valued higher than their service to human flourishing. When humans give primary allegiance to these structures instead of to God, it then becomes possible to violate, or to do violence to, the freedom of others in the names of those structures. Nowhere is this violation more obvious than in the decision to take another's life. For Yoder, as suggested by the previous chapter, the freedom that is violated is the freedom to obey God. Taking life is the ultimate refusal of the other's freedom for obedience. Yoder thus focuses his polemical energies against physical violence, especially war, but his vision is by no means limited to the physical, and he discusses a wide range of "violences."

Although these moves go a long way to answering Yoder's critics, they are not sufficient in the end. More analytical clarity is desirable around the term "violence," such that it includes the panorama of "violences," while still validating a special moral imperative against killing. Pierre Bourdieu is helpful at this point, for he articulates the relationship between physical, symbolic, and other forms of violence in such a way that clear moral distinctions can be made between them, at least at the extremes. These distinctions enable revisions to Yoder's theology of violence useful for a robust Christian pacifism.

Yoder's Theology of Violence

The focus of this section is Yoder's substantive identification of violence: what does he consider to be the primary features of violence, what distinctions does he make between types of violence, and how does violence relate to other fallen realities? Methodological questions as to how Yoder diagnoses violence are addressed in the following chapter, and his redemptive remedy is discussed in chapters 5 and 6. This presentation of Yoder's views on violence begins by outlining his theology of the fallen powers, in the context of the Pauline texts and Berkhof's influential interpretation. A definition of violence emerges as a symptom of the rebellion of the powers against their divine ordering in creation. This definition is confirmed and significantly deepened through a study of Yoder's writings on violence. An analysis of criticisms of Yoder's understanding of violence follows, with suggestions as to necessary revisions.

"We Cannot Live with Them"

Yoder's understanding of the fallen powers is drawn from Berkhof and his own exegesis of a variety of Pauline texts that link the powers with oppression, violence, and death. In Rom 12–13, Paul urges Christians not to avenge themselves, but to allow God to maintain order through the sword of the "governing authorities" (*exousiais hyperechousais*).[1] Yoder understands the reference to *exousiais* here to indicate, not simply government, but tyranny.[2] The tyrannical dimension of the powers is also visible in Ephesians, where the author writes of the death "through trespasses and sins" experienced by those who followed "the ruler of the power of the air [*ton archonta tēs exousias tou aeros*], the spirit that is now at work among those who are disobedient" (2:1–2).[3] At the end of the letter, the author warns of ongoing struggle "not against enemies of blood and flesh, but against the rulers [*archas*], against the authorities [*exousiais*], against the cosmic powers [*kosmokratoras*] of this present darkness, against the spiritual forces [*pneumatika*] of evil in the heavenly places" (6:12). Christians are to take up "the whole armor of God" (6:13) to withstand the onslaught of the powers.[4] In language that is less overtly violent, Paul also writes to the Galatians about their erstwhile enslavement "to the elemental spirits [*stoicheia*] of the world" (4:3).[5] The author of Colossians similarly admonishes his readers to beware of captivity to the deceitful *stoicheia* (2:8, 20).[6]

Berkhof notes that, if the powers were created for human flourishing, then their fall represents a "demonic reversal" of their intended purpose.[7] It is not just human individuals who are fallen, but "the invisible side of the cosmos functions in diametric opposition to its divinely fixed purpose."[8] This situation means that human relations with each other, the rest of creation, and God are now deeply disordered. Thus when Paul relays his conviction that the powers cannot separate us from Christ (Rom. 8:38–39), "he presupposes that the nature of the Powers is to do just that, to separate us from love."[9] God's providential oversight means the powers are not wholly given over to chaos, but now the order they provide separates us from rather

---

1. Yoder, *CWS*, 74–83, and *PJ*, 193–211. The exegetes cited by Yoder devoted much time to these verses. See Berkhof, *C&P*, 66; Caird, *Principalities and Powers*, 22–30; Cullman, *State in the New Testament*, 50–70; MacGregor, "Principalities and Powers," 24–25; Morrison, *Powers That Be*; Visser 't Hooft, *Kingship of Christ*, 94–95; Wink, *Naming the Powers*, 47–50. Hays, *Moral Vision*, 247–48, supports Yoder's reading.

2. Yoder, *PJ*, 141.

3. Ibid. This living death is later characterized as the hopelessness and desolation of Gentiles excluded from God's covenant with Israel, practically experienced as "hostility" and a "dividing wall" between Jews and Gentiles (2:11–14). On this passage, see Yoder, *HCPP*, 108–15.

4. Yoder, *PJ*, 149, on Berkhof, *C&P*, 51–52.

5. Yoder, *PJ*, 141, and Berkhof, *C&P*, 21–24, 33.

6. Yoder, *PJ*, 141.

7. Berkhof, *C&P*, 30.

8. Ibid.

9. Ibid. Cf. Yoder, *PJ*, 141.

than unites us to God.[10] Citing Gal 4:8, Berkhof suggests that the problem is our enslavement to "beings that by nature are not gods."[11] It is their pretension to divinity that makes the powers' reign tyrannical.

Berkhof then gives extended attention to the imagery of the powers as existing in the "air" (cf. Eph 2:2; 6:12).[12] For first-century Christians, "air" united the earth to the heavens, but the central point in the powers passages—according to Berkhof—is that something or someone more powerful than humans directs terrestrial affairs. Berkhof observes that we still use this language when we say a mood or idea is "in the air." He draws from recent experience to speak of the "Powers of *Volk*, race, and state" that seemingly dominated German life "from above" during Nazi rule: "these powers intruded as a barrier between God's Word and men. They acted as if they were ultimate values, calling for loyalty as if they were the gods of the cosmos."[13] But it is not just obvious tyrannies that are at fault. All the various powers—state, opinion, morality, etc.—that dominate everyday human life unite by separating us from God.

In *Christian Witness to the State*, Yoder considers the state's "universal temptation" to abuse its divine mandate to provide basic social order by instead using violence to bring about a supposed "ideal world."[14] Yoder goes beyond Berkhof to suggest that the problem is deeper than the state's self-deification; that deeper problem is "pride, the one sin that most surely leads to a fall, even already within history."[15] Pride, according to Yoder, is behind every use of violence, and "the sword is itself . . . part of the Fall"—it would not be legitimated if somehow the state were more humble.[16] This analysis corresponds to his portrait of the powers earlier in the book. As seen in previous chapters, Yoder introduces his discussion of the state with a review of New Testament language of the powers. He then relates this language to his teacher Oscar Cullmann's eschatology, in which Christ inaugurates an "aeon" different from the present one.[17] Yoder summarizes: "The present aeon is characterized by sin and centered on man. . . . The present age, by rejecting obedience, has rejected the only possible ground for man's own

---

10. Cf. Yoder, *HCPP*, 30–36, 108–15.

11. Berkhof, *C&P*, 30.

12. Ibid., 31–33.

13. Ibid., *C&P*, 32. See also Rupp, *Principalities and Powers*, 15.

14. Yoder, *CWS*, 37.

15. Ibid. Cf. *HCPP*, 89–95.

16. Yoder, *CWS*, 38. Yoder is distinguishing his approach from Cullmann, *State in the New Testament*, 78, and Barth, *Church and State*, 24–30. They suggest that a humble, non-idolatrous state could wield the sword without sin.

17. Cf. Cullmann, *Early Church*, 109–20.

well-being."[18] Disobedience and self-centeredness are definitive of the fallen powers. Like Berkhof, Yoder does not identify the fall with absolute evil. Rather, Christ "channels" violence through a "vengeance-upon-vengeance mechanism" that discourages violence through the selective and restrained use of violence, thereby maintaining the minimal order necessary for human life.[19] The state, at least "in its judicial and police functions," is therefore throughout fallen history "the major incarnation of this channeled evil."[20] It is also a major force behind the exclusion of widows, orphans, strangers, and enemies.[21] Pride turns humans against each other and God; this pride is at the heart of our most basic social institutions.

Throughout *Christian Witness to the State*, Yoder criticizes theological modes of approaching the moral status of the state that use standards not rooted in revelation. He counters, for example, ethics rooted in natural law or in readings of Romans 13 that assign moral autonomy to the state.[22] Autonomy from Christ, as will soon be evident, is Yoder's primary way of describing the fallenness of the powers. The pride that wields violence and oppresses the poor is a conviction that one possesses standards for living that derive elsewhere than God's revelation in Jesus Christ. This pride is the major target of Yoder's *The Politics of Jesus*. As discussed in chapter 1 above, that book argues against "mainstream" Christian ethics that Jesus is politically normative.[23] Some say Jesus' ethics were meant only for an eschatological interim, or for a powerless sect; others that his message was purely spiritual, or that his purpose purely one of metaphysical atonement. Whatever the reason, what mainstream ethics have in common is their ethical methodology: they hold that it is "by studying the realities around us, not by hearing a proclamation from God, that we discern the right."[24]

The chapter on "Jesus and Power" in *The Politics of Jesus* has the particular role of showing that Paul thought about the reign of Christ in terms related to social structure and power.[25] The theology of the powers is then offered as an alternative both to personalism, which denies Christian social

18. Yoder, *CWS*, 9.

19. Ibid., 11.

20. Ibid., 12–13.

21. Ibid., 41–42.

22. Ibid., 33–35, 74–83.

23. Yoder, *PJ*, 4–8, 15–20, 99–109. Yoder further updates his account of mainstream ethics in "Confessing Jesus in Mission," in *UNDA*, 1996. Cf. his *DPR*, 38–43; *FTN*, 99; *THW*, 61.

24. Yoder, *PJ*, 9.

25. Ibid., 134–36.

teaching as such,[26] and to "orders of creation" theologies that hold that fundamental social institutions have "an autonomous value unrelated to redemption and church, by virtue of their being the product of a divine act of creation."[27] Yoder, intentionally or not, is giving examples of fallen powers here, as evident from his characterization of the fallen powers as abandoning their created purpose to enslave and dominate humanity:[28]

> These [created] powers have rebelled and are fallen. They did not accept the modesty that would have permitted them to remain conformed to the creative purpose, but rather they claimed for themselves an absolute value. They thereby enslaved humanity and our history. We are bound to them; "slavery" is in fact one of the fundamental terms used in the New Testament to describe the lost condition of men and women outside of Christ. To what are we subject? Precisely to those values and structures which are necessary to life and society, but which have claimed the status of idols and have succeeded in making us serve them as if they were of absolute value.[29]

If the powers are constitutive of human being to the extent that "*we cannot live without them*," the disastrous effect of their rebellion means "*we cannot live with them*."[30] There is now no obvious path to human freedom; all is circumscribed by the prideful powers. Therefore, those ethical systems that propose some set of standards independent of Christ are, following Yoder's biblical interpretation, themselves fallen and idolatrous. "Creation" now cannot provide moral insight, for creation is fallen and in need of redemption. Remaining chapters in *The Politics of Jesus* discuss cultural and state power, warning, finally, against the temptation to "handle history."[31] The chapter on the state is concerned with physical violence, but the broader treatment underscores the prevalence of prideful autonomy throughout the social order.

These themes are expanded and given greater specificity in Yoder's remaining discussions of the powers. In his third Stone Lecture, "Behold My Servant Shall Prosper," he insists that the powers participate in the fall.[32] Their fallenness is constitutive of the fall itself, and not merely a byproduct

26. Ibid., 153–55.
27. Ibid., 144.
28. Ibid., 141–44.
29. Ibid., 142.
30. Ibid., 143.
31. Ibid., 162–92 (on culture), 193–211 (on the state), 228–47 (on "handling history").
32. Yoder, "Servant," 163.

of human fallenness. He suggests that this formulation acknowledges the effects of sin in a way that trumps the Reformed doctrine of "total depravity"—for even the orders of creation offer only ambiguous moral testimony. Nevertheless, he is careful again to maintain that the fall does not totally negate the goodness of the powers. Fallenness means that power is never neutral, but it also means that it is not uniformly good or bad. "'Undetermined'? 'Malleable'?," he asks, "Paul's picture is more finely nuanced than any one word we can find."[33]

In his lecture on "Early Christian Cosmology and Nonviolence" in Warsaw, he returns to the language of autonomy, now suggesting an intrinsic relation between autonomy and tyranny.[34] In becoming separate from God, the powers also become separate from humans, allowing their existence over and against us. The fall, therefore, cannot be limited to strictly personal matters: "It is also that the structures which surround us have become instruments of our subjugation, not of our empowerment." This structural reality is revealed clearly in the cross of Jesus Christ, which Yoder interprets as "the product of the consistent outworking of the nature of things in the fallen cosmos operating according to their own character." Because the powers are their own ends,[35] they must do violence to any challenger. The violence of the powers against Jesus unveils their true grain.[36]

Yoder gives no examples of fallen powers in either his third Stone Lecture or his Warsaw lecture, but he does discuss "the fundamental wrongness of the vision of Christendom" in his first Stone Lecture, "Why Ecclesiology is Social Ethics."[37] What is wrong with Christendom is "its ascription of a Christian loyalty or duty to those who have made no confession," thereby restricting the freedom of unbelief. This restriction rejects God's nonviolent patience with non-Christians and, by implication, denies any possible process of legitimate Christian conversion. It is, once again, the prideful act of a power separated from God. At the same time, the Christendom arrangement encourages a number of institutional developments that reinforce its basic error: it searches for a generalized morality that gives special license to

---

33. Ibid., 164.

34. Yoder, *Nonviolence*, 99.

35. Cf. Yoder, *OR*, 149.

36. Cf. Yoder, *HCPP*, 32, where he draws an analogy between the fallen powers, or "the world," and the grain of a piece of wood. E.g., the arms race and nationalism expose the deep structures that run through the world. Yoder regards "the world" as the Johannine equivalent to the principalities and powers. See also his "Prophetic Dissent," 101; *ARS*, 265; *RP*, 55–56; and "Review: *The Context of Decision*," 136.

37. Yoder, *RP*, 109.

the ruler as the "privileged actor of history";[38] it supports a clericalism that assigns "a privileged handle on the social decision process" to the institutional church;[39] and it allows quietist communities to flourish—which "are interested only in their own intensity and integrity"—thus refusing the missionary imperative.[40] As a model fallen power, Christendom illustrates the breadth of Yoder's vision of the fall. He returns to it throughout his writings, most famously in his frequent references to the "Constantinian" temptation to unite church and state that characterizes subsequent church history.[41]

Another example of a fallen power is in the essay on H. Richard Niebuhr. Yoder regards Niebuhr's *Christ and Culture* as itself "deceptive" or "in the technical sense demonic, a structure that gets in the way of wholeness and understanding rather than serving those goals.[42] At issue is the descriptive adequacy of Niebuhr's five types of relating Christ to culture. Yoder claims that few readers find their tradition accurately represented by the types, and many find their forebears' positions to be grossly distorted.[43] The typology is thus "more convincing to the naïve than it is true when examined," casting serious doubts on its pedagogical or normative helpfulness. Furthermore, Yoder accuses Niebuhr of using the objectivity of the typology to cloak an argument for his own preferred "transformationalist" option.[44] This option, as Yoder tendentiously summarizes it, states that "Jesus would have us turn away from all culture, but we prefer not to do this because of our more balanced vision of the values of nature and history. Yet in our affirmative attitude to 'culture' we do want to continue to show some respect for the criticism (or the 'transformation') which flows from Christ's critical attitude toward it."[45] *Christ and Culture* is thus also "demonic," a fallen power that unifies readers around an option that leads them away from Jesus. This judgment is especially clear in light of Yoder's exegesis of Niebuhr's use of the term "culture."[46] According to Yoder, Niebuhr portrays

38. Ibid., 117.

39. Ibid., 118.

40. Ibid., 119.

41. Yoder saw the "Constantinian" (Christendom) temptation as present in all ages of church history (*OR*, 149–55; *PK*, 135–41; *RP*, 57–60; *CA*, 42–73). The same logic he uses to discuss Constantinianism is evident in his criticisms of violent movements within ancient Judaism (*OR*, 13–33; *JCSR*, 72–75, 107–8, 152, 187–88).

42. Yoder, "HRN," 47. For a recent defense of *Christ and Culture* in light of Yoder's criticisms, see Stackhouse, *Making the Best of It*, 31–41.

43. Ibid., 45, 51.

44. Ibid., 42.

45. Ibid., 42–43.

46. Ibid., 54–55.

culture as a monolithic unity that is autonomous from Christ. The question for Niebuhr is how Christians are to relate to this autonomous monolith. Unity that autonomously forms a people apart from Christ, however, is what the New Testament calls a fallen power.[47] Yet the New Testament does not portray the powers as monolithically evil, but as at once created and fallen. Discernment of evil is, therefore, a "dialectical challenge" requiring careful real-time judgments, not a timeless typology.[48] *Christ and Culture*, consequently, ill-prepares its readers for the real task they face. The book, like other fallen powers, undermines genuine freedom.

Violence

Between 1969 and 1996, Yoder explored the meaning of violence in a variety of contexts. In "Conflict from the Perspective of Anabaptist History and Theology," Yoder investigates the nuances of the term "nonviolence."[49] This term is inadequate, he alleges, as a way of defining what Christians are against, for "there is real difficulty in defining how far the word violence goes." In itself, "violence" offers no clarity in distinguishing between physical and other injustices—and Christians are concerned with the breadth of injustices. Jesus, for example, suggests that hatred of another is to an important degree morally equivalent to murder (Matt 5:21–22). But it is also right to insist that "the act of intent of taking life . . . is qualitatively one serious step worse than physical force that shocks, insults, or wounds, but does not kill."[50] There is thus a basis for discrimination between, on the one hand, the violence of murder and other types of physical force and between, on the other hand, physical violence and other injustices.

The essay "Jesus and Power," an evaluation of a 1972 World Council of Churches consultation on violence, sees Yoder return to the question of the meaning of violence.[51] He notes that the consultation documents vary between definitions of violence as something "discrete, identifiable, avoidable" and as something built into the fabric of human being, i.e., "interference with the fulfillment of human potential."[52] To some extent this ambiguity

47. Ibid., 68–69.

48. Ibid., 85.

49. Yoder, *WL*, 145. On Mennonite debates about the proper description of their stance against violence, see Yoder, *CA*, 297, 305–6, 356–57, and *Nevertheless*, 107–14.

50. Yoder, *WL*, 146.

51. Yoder, "Jesus and Power," 453–54.

52. Ibid., 453n15.

is unavoidable, as violence is not "a univocal, unidimensional something varying only in terms of more or less; each varies in quality, in depth, in direction, in wholeness."[53] Refinement of the definition is desirable, but it should not distract from Jesus' love of enemies and rejection of domination. For the Christian, these imperatives cannot be slighted by analytical sophistication.

Over a decade later, Yoder makes a first attempt at refining his definition of violence in a brief but important comment in his ecumenical essay, "A 'Peace' Church Perspective on Covenanting."[54] There he insists that the identifications of "social authority" or effectiveness with violence are "denials of the gospel."[55] There must be, in other words, a peace that is beyond or deeper than violence. Whatever violence is, it is not fundamental to reality.[56]

This view of the limited ontological status of violence receives further specification in Yoder's "A Theological Critique of Violence." Yoder begins by rejecting the "dominant view" that violence must be defined before it can be assessed morally.[57] He therefore turns to the Cain and Able story (Gen 4:1–16), observing that the first biblical reference to people outside of Adam and Eve's family occurs just after Able's murder.[58] When God tells Cain he is condemned to be "a fugitive and wanderer on the earth," Cain protests that "anyone who meets me may kill me" (4:12, 14). According to Yoder, "this is the primeval definition of *violence* for our present purposes: that there are people out there whose response to Cain's deed is *mimetic*. They will quasi-automatically, as by reflex, want to do to him what he had done to Abel. It will not occur to them not to do so. It will seem self-evident to them that that is what he has asked for by what he did."[59] God swears an oath of "sevenfold vengeance" upon anyone who would harm Cain (4:15), an oath so powerful as to deter would-be assailants. But as the subsequent story of Lamech demonstrates—Lamech brags of wreaking "seventy-sevenfold"

---

53. Ibid., 454. Cf. Hauerwas, *Performing the Faith*, 169–75, where he argues that Yoder is not actually a pacifist, if by that is meant someone who always knows in advance what violence is.

54. Yoder, "Covenanting," 318–21.

55. Ibid., 320.

56. But see Blum, "Ontology of Violence," for a challenging argument that "the deconstructionist insistence on the ubiquity of violence might actually imply that nonviolence is made possible by its very impossibility" (26).

57. Yoder, *WL*, 27.

58. On Cain, see also Yoder, *HCPP*, 57–68.

59. Yoder, *WL*, 28.

vengeance on anyone who challenges his murders (4:23–24)—"the retalia-
tory reflex, by its very nature, runs amok."[60]

French anthropologist René Girard has argued that civic control is
introduced as a means of placing a limit on mimetic vengeance.[61] Although
Yoder identifies a number of problems with Girard's theory, he agrees that
it describes the objectivity of ancient violence—its basis in the fallen order
of things—better than rationalizations that view violence as restorative of
social or cosmic order.[62] The problem with rationalizations is that violence
is not ultimately rational. In short, "there is a destructive reflex at work,
which will not go away and whereby violence propagates itself."[63] Yoder next
reviews several leading ways of defining violence, concluding that there is
no obvious way to judge between them.[64] He therefore turns to "ordinary
language" analysis of the term, beginning with the observation that "violence" is a verbal noun from the transitive verb "to violate."[65] Hence violence
is always directed toward an object. "To evaluate violence, morally, then, is
to evaluate the worth of the value violated." Violence appears to be unavoidable, and this raises the possibility of weighing greater and lesser evils. But
Yoder warns that this mode of moral analysis assumes we have high level of
accuracy about the facts of the case, that we can easily judge who has the
legitimacy to wield violence, and that we can quantify the various values
weighed against each other.

Yoder does not develop these arguments, but the implication is that,
while violence may be unavoidable in many circumstances, not everything
humans do is violent. There may be a moral scale of "violences," but unless
some violations can be judged as more or less nonviolent, and others as so
violent as to be off limits, then evaluation lacks hard criteria. For Yoder,
theological commitments provide the evaluative criteria for the critique of
violence. Turning to the ancient creeds, he suggests that the affirmation of
God as creator provides a clear standard: "What is wrong with violence is
that what is violated is a creature of the sovereign God."[66] Humans, in par-

60. Yoder, *WL*, 29.

61. Cf. Girard, *Violence and the Sacred*.

62. Yoder, *WL*, 29–31. See also Yoder, *You Have It Coming: Good Punishment. The
Legitimate Social Function of Punitive Behavior*, in *UNDA*, where Yoder explores how
punishment and coercion are "in the order of things" and therefore must be dealt with
and not simply opposed. He looks at mothering as a necessary agonistic discipline, governmental justice as constitutive of public order, and the victim's need for vindication.

63. Yoder, *WL*, 30.

64. Ibid., 33–35.

65. Ibid., 36.

66. Ibid., 38.

ticular, are bearers of God's image, meaning that violence against humans is an attack on *"the majesty of the creator God."*[67] Yoder notes that in the Bible the only sin linked to the image of God is the shedding of human blood (Gen 9:6). Although some kinds of "violation" may be unavoidable after the fall, killing another human cannot be one of them. Killing is the grossest violence against God and fellow humans.[68]

The fall of the powers is their prideful rebellion against the God-human relationship. As an assault on the image of God in humanity, killing, more than any other offense, attempts to negate that relationship. It represents an absolute threat against human freedom. Elsewhere on the spectrum there is room to weigh violences; and on the far end from killing lies the possibility of nonviolence.

Criticisms

Yoder's theology of Christian pacifism has been criticized from a number of angles. These can be grouped into four areas: Yoder insufficiently recognizes that violence requires discernment; Yoder's focus on violence misses out on the broader meaning of the fall; Yoder fails to relate his critique of violence to the judgment of God; and Yoder is ambiguous as to the legitimacy of state violence in the order of providence.

Violence and Discernment

In an essay titled "Violence: Double Passivity," Anglican theologian John Milbank claims that "violence is never simply *evident*, because we have to *judge* whether a substantive good has been impaired."[69] A "phenomenological pacifism" that simply condemns all "apparent" violence skips over the necessary discernment process. Moreover, although the ultimate good is invulnerable to violence, our fragile approximations do require appropri-

---

67. Ibid.

68. See also Yoder, *Preface*, 311. Cf. his *Capital Punishment*, 4–6, on the absolute prohibition against killing. Yoder never discusses the various ambiguities that exist for human life in the womb or at old age. Although it is possible to question the language of "killing" at these stages, Yoder's distinction would seem to apply at all other times. Arner, *Consistently Pro-Life*, contends that Yoderian pacifism should extend to opposition to elective abortions.

69. Milbank, *Being Reconciled*, 28. His argument, which rests on an interpretation of evil and violence as convertible "anti-transcendentals," is not entirely clear. Presumably he means to say that violence is evil when it impairs a substantive good, and not evil when it does not.

ate defensive measures.[70] The status of an action as violent or not, then, is judged in light of both the goods it threatens and the goods it protects.[71]

Milbank directs his general critique of pacifism toward Yoder in a recent essay, "Power is Necessary for Peace: In Defence of Constantine."[72] After portraying the church as a "realm of non-violence which proclaims the power of weakness," Milbank restates his claim that such a realm needs defense from communities that refuse weakness. He praises Mennonites who, refusing apolitical and compromised stances, posit the church as the true polity that lives "beyond the law." But the Mennonite solution, especially in the "avowed anti-Constantinianism" of Yoder and Hauerwas, is "politically disingenuous and theologically dangerous" in its refusal to admit minimal coercion.

Yoder's "absolute purity,"[73] according to Milbank, fails in two respects.[74] First, it does not see how a close church-state relation can benefit both parties: the church can and sometimes has redeemed the state, and the state can and sometimes has protected the church from extinction.[75] Second, it does not appreciate the fragility of churches and (Christian) bodies as physical realities requiring defense if "the offer of the sacred" is to be made at all. Yoder may protest that "coercive resistance to evil does more

70. Ibid., 39–40.

71. Milbank also argues that the passive gaze upon violence is actually more violent than "defensive counter-violence," because surviving victims can only interpret such non-interventionist voyeurism as a further act of violence (*Being Reconciled*, 29). Mennonite theologians object to this binary division between passive pacifism and active defensive violence, e.g., Blum, "Ontology of Violence" and Derksen, "Milbank and Violence." Nevertheless, in a conversation with Stanley Hauerwas about "Violence," Milbank states that his target was not the "christological pacifism" that Hauerwas represents ("Christian Peace," 209). His critique of passive, non-christological pacifism thus will not be pursued here.

72. Milbank, "Defence of Constantine." A modified version of this essay is the foreword to *Gift of Difference*, xi–xviii. Milbank had earlier interacted with several theologians who used Yoder's work to dispute his portrayal of pacifism. In addition to the conversation with Hauerwas in "Christian Peace," see Snyder, ed., "Radical Orthodoxy and Radical Reformation," special issue, *Conrad Grebel Review*.

73. Cf. Milbank, "Forum with John Milbank," 48, on "pure pacifism" as falling prey to "Kantian formalism." See also Donahue, "Review of *The Politics of Jesus*," 180: Yoder is in danger of "proclaiming a formal ethic of suffering, where pacifistic suffering is self-justifying."

74. Milbank also suggests that Yoder denies the Old Testament political pattern as normative, and so risks Marcionism. This charge, made also by Leithart and others, is treated in the following chapter on methodology.

75. Here Milbank names the positive effects on the state of the Justinian code, and the dependence of the church for survival on medieval kings. One does not have to refute the former claim to be confused by the latter. It is not clear when the church's existence per se has ever been threatened, especially in the Christendom era.

damage than original evil itself," but surely there are enough examples to the contrary to suggest that defensive violence can be salutary.[76] Violence, as Milbank suggested in his earlier essay, must be weighed in perspective of the goods it sacrifices and the goods it protects. It is possible to distinguish between "a Christian acceptance of legitimate uses of force" and "its brutal, altogether idolatrous manifestations."[77] Just wars are possible, and Christians can endorse killing.

Milbank's concerns are echoed by a number of Yoder's critics, and are valuable precisely because they put the question so clearly: is Yoder's pacifist ethic fully Christian, or does it overlook a properly Christian outlook on the ambiguity of violence? Peter Ochs raises a similar question from a Jewish perspective, asking if Yoder's "pure pacifism" owes more to the absolutizing logic of "the colonialist philosophies of western civilization" than to his ancient sources.[78] These issues, of course, have long been raised by Christian defenders of just war theory against Yoder. Richard J. Mouw, for example, insists that a valid moral distinction exists between coercive activities that emerge from a desire to coerce and those that emerge as unintended effects of just actions.[79] To refuse to make this distinction is to refuse "significant political activity."

Other critics defend just war as an appropriate response to the Christian call to "neighbor love,"[80] "justice,"[81] the "common obligation to just institutions,"[82] and to engage "the dilemma of civilization."[83] In each case, the rationale offered for war is rooted in a Christian ethic that the critic regards as ruling out an absolute prohibition of lethal violence. In an interesting twist, there is now a group of Yoder-influenced "pacifists" who support armed international peacekeeping efforts under the rubric of "just

76. It is uncertain why Milbank attributes this view to Yoder. Yoder's argument is rather that nonviolence runs "with the grain of the cosmos" as revealed by Jesus, and so it is unsurprising when it works—this argument depends on no claims about the success of violent methods in resolving specific conflicts. See, e.g., Yoder, *PJ*, 228–47.

77. Milbank adds this as a "footnote" to his article in a comment made on November 1, 2010. As an example, he imagines a British foreign policy aligned with France, Russia, and Commonwealth nations instead of, primarily, America. Milbank believes "that the UK can start to take an imaginative lead in pursuit of an international order based on more balanced alliances and compatible with genuine Christian principles."

78. Ochs in Yoder, *JCSR*, 4. Ochs remark about Yoder's potential "colonialism" relates to the concern that Yoder distorts rabbinic Judaism to fit his pacifist theological agenda.

79. Mouw, *Politics and the Biblical Drama*, 110.

80. Lutz, "Foreword to the First Edition," in Yoder, *WWIU*, xix.

81. N. G. Wright, *Disavowing Constantine*, 91–92.

82. Beckley, "Rawls's Idea of Justice as Fairness—Part I," 219.

83. Wogaman, *Christian Method of Moral Judgment*, 192. See also Wogaman, *Christian Perspectives on Politics*, 46, and *Christian Moral Judgment*, 111–15.

policing."[84] Like the just warriors, advocates of just policing insist that minimal violence in defense of the innocent is justified on Christian grounds. The critics agree: the morality of violence must be discerned, and Yoder's absolute pacifism evades this task.

Violence and the Fall

Earl Zimmerman and P. Travis Kroeker both lament Yoder's almost exclusive focus on war. For Zimmerman, Christians ought to confront "other equally pressing social and economic problems."[85] War exists in a web of issues, and cannot be adequately addressed without attending to them all. Kroeker concurs, adding personal moral and psychic matters to the list.[86] By neglecting these, Yoder "has lost sight of certain aspects of moral discernment that would allow for a better account of idolatrous 'Roman' (or Constantinian) politics and how such temptations might be agonistically engaged also in the Church and the academy." Although Cynthia Hess is more generous to Yoder's approach, she too seeks to supplement his work on external physical violence with a look at "violence that has injured persons from the outside and then moved into their bodies, minds, and souls (internal violence)."[87] If all the powers are implicated in the fall, then Yoder's concentration on physical violence misses the wider reality of which it is just a part.

A Violent God?

As discussed in chapter 1 above, several critics doubt if Yoder's commitment to nonviolence can be reconciled with the traditional conception of God as a holy warrior. In the present context, these same criticisms raise the possibility that Yoder's interpretation of violence as a mode of autonomization from God cannot be sustained.[88] If God's judgment takes the form of violence, then Yoder's definition collapses.

---

84. Reimer, *Christians and War*, 167–70; Schlabach, ed., *Just Policing*. Reimer and Schlabach note that Yoder raised the question of Christian participation in policing (in *CWS*, 56–57), and then argue that international crises call for a non-militaristic police force that retains lethal force as an option. See A. Alexis-Baker, "Unbinding Yoder from Just Policing," for a response.

85. Zimmerman, *Politics of Jesus*, 122.

86. Kroeker, "War of the Lamb," 82–83.

87. Hess, "Traumatic," 202.

88. See, e.g, Boersma, *Violence, Hospitality, and the Cross*, for an argument that God's redemptive hospitality includes the use of violence.

Violent Providence?

A similar question can be raised as to the role of violence in providence. Even if state violence is simply permitted, and not condoned, by God as a means of maintaining relative order, it seems that Christians are required to validate the legitimacy of state violence. What is the shape of this legitimation? Does it include political endorsement of certain wars? Chaplaincy? Qualified military service? Craig A. Carter suggests that this issue demands far more clarification than Yoder gave it.[89]

The third and fourth criticisms can be dealt with using material from previous chapters of this thesis. As for divine violence, chapter 1 discussed God's permissive providence as a practice of nonviolent patience. This practice is complementary rather than antithetical to Jesus' nonviolence. Whatever the shape of God's judgment, it need not include violence. A similar argument can be advanced in relation to the fourth criticism, about Christian legitimation of state violence that God permits. If Christians are meant to participate concretely in the structures that result from intensive interactions with the triune God, then there is no reason Christians should do more than imitate God's permissiveness in this area. Christians accept that states will use violence to bring about order, but refuse to endorse violence as such. Christian nonviolence models an alternative politics that, through dialogical witness, calls the state to chasten its violence.[90] Neither of these criticisms fundamentally challenges Yoder's conception of violence.

A response to the first and second criticisms, however, is more difficult. To a significant degree, concerns about a limited definition of violence and a too narrow focus on violence were addressed by the presentation of Yoder's theology of violence. Yoder does recognize a wide spectrum of violences, even if he draws an absolute line between killing and the rest.[91] He likewise places violence within a much broader interpretation of the fall of the powers as prideful autonomization from created structures.[92] It should also be mentioned that none of the advocates of just war or policing engage Yoder's theological arguments as to why human life is a good that cannot be

89. Carter, "Liberal Reading of Yoder," 99.

90. The Christian response to violence is treated extensively in chapters five and six, below.

91. Cf. Bourne, *Seek the Peace*, 203–6, who argues that, although Yoder's terms could have been clearer, his support for nonviolent protest indicates a willingness to identify forms of coercion that stop short of violence.

92. Cf. N. Kerr, *Christ, History and Apocalyptic*, 138, for an excellent formulation of how the political dominion of the powers is predicated upon an "immanently determined nexus of causality" that closes history's divine horizons. State violence and the autonomy of the powers cannot be separated.

taken in exchange for other goods.[93] Yoder's writings on punishment suggest that he does not refuse the need for justice as a correction or deterrent for injustice. As later chapters will explore, neither does he pose responsible political engagement and nonviolent practice as alternatives. To Milbank's statement that "we have to *judge* whether a substantive good has been impaired," Yoder would reply that each time a human life is taken a substantive good is impaired. None of the other legitimately Christian goods can be played off against the value of human life.

Nevertheless, Yoder offers few analytical clues about how violent and nonviolent coercion can be parsed, or about how to assess the moral status of modes of coercion that do not seek, but still risk, lethal violence. It can be asked, moreover, how (or if) Yoder's view allows for the separation of violence from other forms of prideful rebellion, such as that lodged within human dispositional structures. Yoder's Christian pacifism, therefore, needs a definition of violence that is at once more capacious and more precise: one that distinguishes, on the one hand, between physical and other forms of violence and, on the other hand, between violent and nonviolent coercion. Pierre Bourdieu's sociological concept of "symbolic violence" offers just such an understanding of violence.

Bourdieu on Violence and Domination

Loïc Wacquant suggests that "the whole of Bourdieu's work may be interpreted as a materialist anthropology of the specific contribution that various forms of symbolic violence make to the reproduction and transformation of structures of domination."[94] It is therefore unsurprising to find that the principles of Bourdieu's interpretations of violence and domination are embedded in his general theories of practice and social reproduction. Those theories were honed on research into the disintegration of rural traditions in Algeria and France, and the erosion of French democracy by dominant

93. Presumably Yoder would say that human life can only be given freely in suffering service.

94. Wacquant, "Social Praxeology," 14–15. See also Wacquant, "'State Nobility,'" 134: Bourdieu's "sociology of 'culture'" is "a *political economy of symbolic violence*, of the imposition and inculcation of instruments of knowledge and construction of reality that are socially biased but unseen as such." Cf. Heinich, *Pourquoi Bourdieu*, 87. There is considerably less secondary literature on symbolic violence than on Bourdieu's other concepts. For summaries, see Addi, *Sociologie et anthropologie*, chapter seven; Champagne and Christin, *Pierre Bourdieu*, 135–37; Fernández, "La noción de violencia simbólica"; Lakomski, "Symbolic Violence"; Rey, *Bourdieu and Religion*, 52, 156; Schubert, "Suffering"; Webb, Shirato, and Danaher, *Understanding Bourdieu*, 24–26, 117–19.

political, intellectual, and economic forces. Like Yoder, Bourdieu does not offer a "prelapsarian" social theory that then can be contrasted with developments in this postlapsarian world. Rather, he begins his social criticism in the midst of efforts to expose and overcome injustice in the present.[95]

Bourdieu conceptualized domination as a particular kind of relation made possible by inequalities in capital holdings. As the following review demonstrates, the sorts of relational practices that warrant the label "domination" involve the use of superior, in quantity and/or type, capital holdings to bring about the acceptance of inequality by those with inferior capital holdings. He does not decry inequality as such, but the symbolic, structural, and physical forces used to maintain it. His special emphasis is on "symbolic violence," a concept he uses to describe the complicity of the dominated in their domination. In the following, this concept is described alongside his account of the transition from traditional to modern modes of domination. It is then fleshed out in greater detail through an engagement of Willem Schinkel's recent criticisms of Bourdieu, criticisms that are taken here as elucidating rather than weakening Bourdieu's treatment of violence.

Symbolic Violence and the Modes of Domination

Bourdieu first systematically outlines his theory of symbolic violence in *Reproduction*, with Jean-Claude Passeron, but its features may be discerned in his earlier work as well. After a brief overview of the theory as presented in *Reproduction*, the rest of Bourdieu's work on domination comes into view.

Book One of *Reproduction* is titled "Foundations of a Theory of Symbolic Violence," and its central concept is defined at the start: "*Every power to exert symbolic violence, i.e. every power which manages to impose meanings and to impose them as legitimate by concealing the power relations which are the basis of its force, adds its own specifically symbolic force to those power relations.*"[96] The imposition of meaning may therefore be violent, in the first place, when its legitimacy is obtained by hiding the power imbalance that makes the imposition possible. But concealment is not the only problem. It is also that concealment *obtains* legitimacy. The dominated's recognition of the imposition as legitimate can only be described as illegitimate, as co-

---

95. See chapter five below on Bourdieu's political activity.

96. Bourdieu and Passeron, *Reproduction*, 4. The authors portray themselves at this point as having resolved tensions between Marx, Weber, and Durkheim on the social theory of domination (4–5). See Addi, *Sociologie et anthropologie*, 16; Fernández, "La noción de violencia simbólica," 8; Hobsbawm, "Sociologie critique," 290; Poupeau, "Reasons for Domination," 70–71.

erced. Further, because the content of the imposition is "meanings," and not primarily a physical or structural restraint, the particular character of such violence is symbolic. Symbolic violence is a deceitful, coercive use of symbolic power.

In *Reproduction*, these themes are shaped around an account of pedagogical activities and institutions as means of imposing dominant culture. The symbolic violence of pedagogical activity as a whole is revealed, according to Bourdieu and Passeron, in its "arbitrary" nature. Neither the power structure that sees one group instructing another, nor the meanings that have been selected by the instructing group can be *"deduced from any universal principle, whether physical, biological or spiritual, not being linked by any sort of internal relation to 'the nature of things' or any 'human nature.'"*[97]

Neither the pedagogical structure nor its cultural meanings, however, are open for dispute. Indeed, the central task of "pedagogical work" is the formation of a habitus that accepts the legitimacy of the pedagogical imposition or, more broadly, of the culture which that particular form of pedagogy maintains.[98] Bourdieu and Passeron describe the resulting habitus as suffering "genesis amnesia," a forgetting of the origins of culture and of cultural learning.[99] For example, academic success is often attributed to "innate gifts," but strong correlations can be found between success and the cultural habits and social class of the pupil's family of origin.[100] The supposed objectivity of the education system, guaranteed by initial conditions of equal access, enables the source of differences in intellectual capacity to be cloaked under the rhetoric of natural ability. Agents who go through the system are educated to recognize its objectivity, but this recognition is in fact a misrecognition (*méconnaissance*) of the objective power relations that facilitate the cultural reproduction of symbolic violence.[101]

The concealment of imposition, therefore, is buried deep within the embodied dispositions and perceptions of agents. When students explain their failure as a simple lack of talent, neglecting to consider the sociocultural bases of academic success, they legitimate the system's symbolic schema for rationalizing reproduction. Agents' own practices contribute to

97. Bourdieu and Passeron, *Reproduction*, 8.

98. Ibid., 31–54.

99. Ibid., 38–39.

100. This is the main argument of Book Two of *Reproduction*. It is also a case the authors made in their earlier *Les Héritiers*. Another example they discuss in *Reproduction* is the attribution of aesthetic taste to "innate gifts," when there is really a strong correlation between taste and early museum frequentation (38–39). This case is made in detail in Bourdieu and Darbel, *Love of Art*.

101. Bourdieu and Passeron, *Reproduction*, 25–26, 38, 40, 51, 206.

the reproduction of their power holdings, of their status as more or less dominant. The ultimate, most pernicious effect of symbolic violence is this ability to co-opt the dominated into supporting their own domination.[102]

Bourdieu does not employ the vocabulary of symbolic violence in his earliest ethnographic writings. Its nascent logic is nonetheless evident in his concern over how, for example, aging peasant men explain their perpetual bachelorhood in terms of financial prudence or lack of romantic interest— even when their systematic exclusion from marriage (and so from biological reproduction) can be traced to the shift in cultural power from rural to urban ways of life.[103] Bourdieu's later reflections on his ethnographic work, *Outline of a Theory of Practice* and *The Logic of Practice*, do classify such explanations as effects of symbolic violence and its misrecognition of the objective reality of social inequalities.[104] Beyond that, however, they propose two distinct "modes of domination" that correspond to relative uses of symbolic violence in traditional, undifferentiated societies and in modern, differentiated societies.[105]

The lack of social differentiation in "pre-capitalist" societies such as Kabylia or the Béarn means the mediation of power relations is primarily personal.[106] The "archaic economy" functions not through abstract money, financial instruments, or banking institutions, but through informal exchanges of goods and services, often under the guise of a gift. In traditional societies, Bourdieu observes, gifts are given and received as gratuitous, disinterested capital distributions.[107] But, on an objective level, a gift

---

102. Many critics, especially feminists, complain that Bourdieu underplays the ability of the dominated to challenge domination. See, e.g., Fowler, *Bourdieu and Cultural Theory*, 4, 173; Krais, "Gender," 123; Reed-Danahay, *Locating Bourdieu*, 59. Castel, "Entre la contrainte social et le volantarisme politique," 110, nevertheless suggests that, because Bourdieu's account of domination is constructivist, it allows for the reconstruction of social relations.

103. Bourdieu, *Bachelors' Ball*. Addi, *Sociologie et anthropologie*, chap. 7, argues that Bourdieu developed the concept of "symbolic violence" while studying traditional societies, and that it does not function well when applied to modern societies. But Fernández, "La noción de violencia simbólica," uses close exegetical readings of texts from the early anthropological works to *Masculine Domination* to portray the dynamic development of the concept, especially in the 1970s and 80s when Bourdieu drew from classical sociological resources to contruct a theory of the autonomy of the symbolic object. This theory, Fernández contends, is a flexible research tool rather than a systematic, timeless statement.

104. Bourdieu, *OTP*, 183–97; *LP*, 112–34.

105. See also Bourdieu, "Les modes de domination," and "Stratégies de reproduction et modes de domination."

106. Bourdieu, *OTP*, 183–84, 189, 190–97; *LP*, 122–31.

107. Bourdieu, *OTP*, 171–98; *LP*, 98–111.

always calls forth a counter-gift. The relative amounts of capital exchanged and the timing of the counter-gift establish and maintain material and symbolic hierarchies. A livestock- and honor-poor family risks much of its holdings when it offers a gift that is too large or too small, too late or too fast, to a richer family.

Yet Bourdieu emphasizes that this work of euphemizing the maintenance of capital inequalities, of domination, as gift exchange is costly for the dominant as well. A gift has to be received as a gift. Given the personal interdependence of the dominant and dominated, a gift cannot appear as overt exploitation and must contain a significant downward distribution of capital. This redistribution is what qualifies a gift as a gift, what calls forth its recognition from the receiver as gratuitous. But the gift's subjective, symbolic reality does not negate the objective reality of the exchange cycle, which is reproductive. Because it hides the power relation to legitimate its imposition of meaning, Bourdieu views this first, traditional mode of domination as reliant on symbolic violence.

The second mode of domination he describes is characteristic of the modern period. Gradual accumulation of capital allows for its objectification as institutions and their mechanisms. Relations between dominant and dominated are mediated by institutions, reducing the need for euphemism and symbolic violence. A capitalist needs no other reason to justify the exploitation of workers than the systemic requirements of the pursuit of profit. A teacher needs no other reason for failing students than the systemic requirements of the pursuit of a degree. The legitimacy of domination is thereby shifted from the interpersonal to the objective institution. A more "naked" and brutal form of structural violence arises. Inequalities are kept stable through coercion, and coercion is now visible in the structure of the institutions. But brutality has its own price: resistance. As the dominated become aware of and react to their domination, the dominant have to construct new forms of symbolic violence. Gifts return as donations to foundations, charities, hospitals, and academic and cultural institutions.[108] The consumption of luxury goods is euphemized as a product of "taste," not self-interested accumulation. Although the structural framework of domination is still present, its legitimacy has to be won again at some mild but impressive expense to the dominant.

Aside from his ethnographic writings, the bulk of Bourdieu's *oeuvre* is concerned with exposing the symbolic violence at work in modern capitalist cultures. Studies of the education system, such as *Reproduction*, *Homo Academicus*, and *The State Nobility*, show how the French Republican

108. Bourdieu, *LP*, 133.

ethos of equal access to education masks vast inequalities of educational opportunity. *Distinction* extends earlier comments into a lengthy account of how all classes accept the symbolism of cultural taste. When the dominated insist on the superiority of spartan aesthetics or common cultural sensibilities, they make a "virtue out of necessity" and inadvertently legitimate the material conditions that restrict their cultivation.[109] The pursuit of cultural distinction is a universal strategy within modernity that, for the most part, only affirms the material composition of society. Similar conclusions are drawn from various works on photography, museums, and literature.

In *Masculine Domination*, Bourdieu identifies the symbolic violence at work in upholding the most basic and stable of inequalities, that which exists on the basis of gender. This book advances the quite controversial arguments that (1) expanded opportunities for women in the workplace continue to confine women to subordinate aesthetic and symbolic realms; and (2) that most iterations of feminism fail to break with a masculinist vision of the world and so contribute to the reproduction of gender inequality.[110] Following the general logic of symbolic violence, masculine domination is internalized in and as the female habitus and legitimated, however unwittingly, through female practice.

Other investigations of symbolic violence and domination include the function of "media intellectuals" in providing legitimation for neoliberal economics;[111] of the appeal to the private home as a model of domesticity in justifying the end of welfare housing;[112] of the rhetoric of formal universal suffrage in concealing links between education, class, and political participation;[113] and of the many, many social scientific and philosophical methodologies that distract from the material bases of social practice.[114] In each case, symbolic resources are deployed to activate the self-evidences built into the habitus: academics know what is best; having my own home is better than social housing; times may be bad, but at least this is a free country; and so on. By activating the self-evidences, what Bourdieu calls

109. Bourdieu, *Distinction*, 174. See Kauppi, "Sociologist as *Moraliste*," 12, for an excellent summary.

110. Bourdieu, *MD*, 41–42, 62–63, 98–102. These arguments, needless to say, have been highly controversial. See Adkins and Skeggs, eds., *Feminism after Bourdieu*; Fowler, "Gender, Culture and Class"; Heinich, *Pourqoui Bourdieu*, 94–96; Krais, "Gender."

111. Bourdieu, *Sur la télévision*. See also Chartier and Champagne, eds., *Bourdieu et les médias*.

112. Bourdieu, *Les structures sociales de l'économie*.

113. Bourdieu, "Mystery of Ministry," 57–59.

114. See esp. Bourdieu, *CS*; *OTP*, 1–30, 72–78; *LP*, 31–51; *PM*.

doxa or common sense,[115] the dominant conceal the underlying unequal power relations and coerce consent to the reproduction of the dominant, dominating order.

Perhaps the most sinister implication of Bourdieu's depiction of symbolic violence is that, for the most part, it is not exercised intentionally: symbolic violence is not a conspiracy theory of domination. The dominant rarely need to scheme to guard their exalted positions or to maintain capital inequalities. Domination structures tend to reproduce themselves regardless of anyone's intent. Symbolic violence is such an effective means of perpetuating domination because it is almost impossible to assign blame or to escape the cycle.

Symbolic, Physical, and Other Violences

Symbolic violence involves the formation of dominated habitus to misrecognize domination as the legitimate, "natural" social order. It coerces by shaping people who will not and, likely, cannot challenge capital inequalities. Bourdieu does not systematically investigate the links between symbolic and physical violence, portraying the latter as either a last resort when symbolic violence fails to elicit the desired legitimation, or as the more efficient path to domination when legitimation is not necessary.[116] These two possibilities are inscribed in both modes of domination, explaining, on the one hand, the personal brutality of traditional societies and, on the other hand, the structural and state brutality of modern societies. On Bourdieu's interpretation, physical violence is an exception to the symbolic violence that constitutes daily human interactions. If the rise of modernity coincided with an outbreak of brutality, then the return of symbolic violence signals a return to a more typical situation.

However, Bourdieu's discussion of physical and symbolic violences is more complex than these statements let on. His comments assume a distinction between physical and symbolic violence based on the distinction between external force and internal force. Physical violence coerces agents from without, by dominating their bodies; symbolic violence coerces

115. See chapter one above.

116. Bourdieu and Passeron, *Reproduction*, 36; *OTP*, 191; *MD*, 34. Some critics charge Bourdieu with ignoring the material objectivity of violence (Addi, *Sociologie et anthropologie*, 166–73; Hobsbawm, "Sociologie critique," 290; and Lakomski, "Symbolic Violence," 155). But, as Webb, Shirato, and Danaher, *Understanding Bourdieu*, 118, rightly maintain, the point of "symbolic violence" is not that some violence is subjective and non-material, but that symbols are effective means of maintaining objective material hierarchies.

agents from within, by dominating their habitus. But of course the habitus is not merely an intellectual aspect of human being; it is embodied. Insofar as symbolic violence is formative of embodied habitus, it too is a kind of violence against the body.[117] The primary difference between physical and symbolic violence cannot be the object of violence. Nor can the spatial location (internal or external) of the force on the object be the main distinction, since there can be no clear demarcation here where the body is concerned—poison works internally; words may elicit tears. It is, then, the means of violence, its *modus operandi*, which allows for differentiation between physical and symbolic violence: whether violence includes the action of a physical instrument (a fist, a knife, a bullet) on a body, or only the action of symbols (words, images) on a body, symbols that specifically call forth a legitimation of the (physical or symbolic) violence.

These considerations allow for a response to Willem Schinkel, who argues that Bourdieu inadequately relates symbolic violence to other forms of violence and, more generally, fails to give a proper definition of violence at all.[118] Evaluating these criticisms is helpful for expanding Bourdieu's conception of violence to its furthest extent, so that it might better serve the revision of Yoder. Schinkel, in his book *Aspects of Violence*, worries that definitions of violence based exclusively on "personal" forms of violence (e.g., murder, rape, arson) are not capable of comprehending structural or state forms of violence. The problem is not just analytical, but political: narrow definitions of violence legitimate, and so potentially excuse and encourage, the violence they refuse to name as violence—and by the very act of not naming it violence.[119] In the Bourdieusian terms Schinkel uses explicitly, narrow definitions of violence misrecognize much violence by calling it something else. Bourdieu is thus correct (and less violent) to develop symbolic violence as an "extended theory" of violence.

Yet Schinkel is not satisfied with Bourdieu's lack of definitional work around the concept of "violence" itself. He goes on to develop his own definition, via an engagement of Heideggerian ontology, as "reduction of being."[120]

---

117. Symbolic violence can even result in "permanent" transformations of the embodied habitus, i.e., the long-term hereditary, formation of bodies, as with the smaller, weaker, and more frail female body produced by millennia of masculine domination (Bourdieu, *MD*, 7–33). This observation contradicts Schinkel, *Aspects of Violence*, 183, who argues that habitus explains how violence is internalized through socialization, but not how it may become a biological disposition.

118. Schinkel, *Violence*, 191, 193–94.

119. Ibid., 33. Schinkel identifies Randall Collins's "micro-sociological theory of violence" as featuring such a narrow definition. See Collins, *Violence*, esp. 24, where he distances his approach from Bourdieu's.

120. Schinkel, *Violence*, 45–83. This definition is meant to "radicalize" Enlightenment

Being as such is pure potential, but actual being, ontic being, is always being with others; interactions with other humans restrict certain potentials and so reduce being.[121] Violence is inscribed in and, as "an ontological condition of ontic being," productive of (human) being—only fear of life (*biaphobia*) causes us to deny this.[122] There is, of course, a difference between quotidian productive violence—a reduction that produces the possibility of life—and those cases typically called violence. The difference is one of degree, as some interactions are more reductive than others of another's potential. Schinkel proposes a "sliding scale" of violence, with the reduction to matter—killing—at the far extremity from productive violence.[123]

Although Schinkel presents his definition of violence as more basic than Bourdieu's theory, it is possible to see it rather as a helpful extension thereof. Bourdieu is admittedly not explicit about his broad definition of violence, but the account given above indicates that he, too, regards the problem as a limitation of being, understood as power or capital. As has been pointed out, the issue for Bourdieu is not with capital inequalities as such, but with efforts to maintain or increase capital inequalities through concealment and coercion. Coercion does not necessarily entail symbolic legitimation through concealment of power relations, but the latter is usually present in traditional and modern societies, at least after the latter pass through the initial period of brutality enabled by institutional objectification.

It is confusing, therefore, when Schinkel attempts to fit Bourdieu's theory of symbolic violence into his classification of ideal-typical forms of violence, specifically as a form of structural violence.[124] Schinkel usefully distinguishes between three forms of violence: state, private, and structural. State violence is built into and exercised primarily by state institutions as a means of confirming the legitimacy of its use of violence.[125] The legitimacy of state violence is derived from the state's own definition of legitimate violence as a reaction to violent infractions of its juridical code, in other words, to illegitimate violence.[126] "State violence is, in the end, a reduction of [its] subjects to legitimate subjects," subjects who legitimate state violence by re-

anthropology and symbolic interactionism (45).

121. Ibid., 48–53.

122. Ibid., 45.

123. Ibid., 48.

124. Ibid., 191.

125. Ibid., 166–70.

126. Ibid., 173. Schinkel argues that this definition of state legitimacy is necessarily tautologous, as the state has to deny the active, extra-statal, and so technically illegitimate violence which lies at its foundations. State violence is therefore an unending attempt to "detautologize" itself through legitimate violence.

fraining from illegitimate violence.[127] Within a state, any violence exercised primarily by individuals or groups not legitimated by and as the state is considered illegitimate. Schinkel names such individual or group violence as private violence, which reduces being through non-state agency.[128]

In contrast to state and private forms of violence, structural violence, on Schinkel's definition, is the reduction of being that occurs as society as a whole undergoes a process of differentiation.[129] The agency of structural violence is neither the state nor a single individual or institution, but the variously fracturing and fusing relations between agents. Agents' beings are reduced as they are increasingly confined to a social position (class). They are further reduced as differentiating social subsystems fracture subjects, and as "structural coupling" brings together subsystems that were formerly separate.[130] It is only at this point that Schinkel identifies symbolic violence, "as a form of incorporated or embodied structural violence, in which subjects are violated but accept the legitimacy of the structure from which this violence emanates."[131]

He then goes on to adapt Bourdieu's conception of "the law of the conservation of violence" in which, e.g., structural violence leads to private violence.[132] Bourdieu did not specify three ideal-typical forms of violence, so Schinkel sets forth clearly how the three forms may translate into one another. In doing so, he complains that Bourdieu's account reduces private to structural violence, and ignores state violence completely.[133] Although Schinkel has a point in reference to the specific passages in which Bourdieu proposes his "law," his critique is less convincing when examined in light of his broader understanding of violence. The traditional violence of the first mode of domination is, by Schinkel's definition, almost entirely "private," since traditional society is mostly undifferentiated and does not include the state. Schinkel also overlooks Bourdieu's extensive discussion of the creation of the state as the simultaneous monopolization of physical and symbolic violence.[134] But to accept Bourdieu's analysis of private and state violence is to admit symbolic violence into those forms of violence.

127. Ibid., 173.

128. Ibid., *Violence*, 175–76.

129. Ibid., 185.

130. Ibid. As an example Schinkel mentions the effects of economics and labor relations on gender identities, which bring up tension and often violence in the domestic sphere.

131. Ibid., 191.

132. Ibid., on Bourdieu, *Acts of Reistance*, 40; *PM*, 233.

133. Schinkel, *Violence*, 193–94.

134. Bourdieu, *SN*, 373–89; *PR*, 36–56; "Reason of State"; *PM*, 5.

At this point, one might plausibly amend Bourdieu's history of violence—which tells of symbolic violence's retraction under modernity and subsequent (postmodern?) return—to argue that overt forms of violence are almost always accompanied by efforts to conceal the underlying power relation and coerce the (mis)recognition of violence as legitimate.[135] Symbolic violence is present in interpersonal relationships and institutions, in ancient and modern societies.

In conclusion, Schinkel's arguments against Bourdieu's theory of symbolic violence appear more plausible as useful explications of the same. Schinkel's definition of violence as reduction of being coheres with Bourdieu's focus on the reproduction of capital inequalities. But Schinkel fruitfully proposes that this definition allows for a sliding scale of violence that measures the degree to which being is reduced. Bourdieu does not affirm that killing is the most extreme form of violence, but his logic leads to the same conclusion: killing eliminates personal capital by eliminating the person, and is an ultimate refusal of the possibility of an adjustment in levels of capital inequality. Moreover, Schinkel's delineation of three convertible forms of violence is helpful for drawing out themes in Bourdieu's theory that are mostly left unstated. In light of Schinkel's elaboration of structural violence, which is characteristic of the second mode of domination, it is appropriate to add to the earlier discussion that objective conditions can be a means of violence as well as symbolic and physical means. Bourdieu's theory and research suggest that structural and physical violence are most often accompanied by symbolic violence. One means may be prompted by another, and each is rarely exercised independently.

Revising Yoder's Theology of Violence

One of the criticisms of Yoder's pacifism is that he does not attend suitably to the ambiguous nature of violence: it may be mostly reprehensible, but it is sometimes a morally justifiable way to attain or protect otherwise out of reach or threatened goods. Violence is justifiable when the good it seeks is theologically mandated, such as political responsibility or the preservation of the church. This criticism features a strong "realist" component that casts doubt on the sociological possibility of attaining those theologically

135. Bourdieu's claim that the modern objectification of capital enables overt violence and the withering away of symbolic violence is not backed up with any research. Schinkel, *Violence*, 167, contends that modern theories of the "state of nature" are always attempts to justify the legitimacy of state violence vis-à-vis this earlier mythical chaos. This account suggests that symbolic violence was foundational for the modern period.

mandated goods without the use of violence. Because nonviolence is unrealistic, it is unfaithful, and thus violence is theologically and sociologically legitimated. Given that this argument typically concerns just war (or policing), the violence so legitimated is killing. Theological and moral reasoning may treat violence as undesirable, but sociological considerations rehabilitate it as a tragic necessity for the sake of the broader Christian mission. The other major criticism of Yoder's theology of violence and the fall concerned its breadth and depth. As a leading Christian pacifist, Yoder directed much of his theological energy to issues of war and peace. But economic oppression, racism, sexism, and psychological maladies are also effects of the fall. Yoder captures neither the sociological width, nor the psychological depth of violence and the fall.

Both criticisms suggest that Yoder requires a new sociology of violence, one that more clearly states why killing is the extreme form of violence he thinks it is, and how it relates to other violences. Bourdieu's contribution to such a repair is readily apparent. Killing is the most extreme form of violence because it is a final negation of the person's capital or power. Whereas other forms of violence devalue, distort, or deny the dynamism of a person's capital, killing destroys what is arguably her most valuable capital, that which she embodies in and as habitus. Interpreted theologically, this destruction of capital is a refusal—for another or, in the case of suicide, for oneself—of the divine gift of freedom insofar as it takes away the basic sociological, not to mention biological, conditions for obedience.[136] When Christian defenders of just war and policing argue that the demands of discipleship in a fallen world require killing, they pit their own obedience against that of their enemies. They favor their own obedience to the extent that they are willing to employ a means (killing) they admit is, at best, tangentially related to obedience, in order to take away the enemies' possibility for obedience. On this account, just war is a classic example of symbolic violence: a legitimation of violence through the concealment of the power relation, in this case a relation of differential powers for obedience.[137] Put in Yoder's theologi-

---

136. See further Ellul, *Violence*, 130, on Christian freedom as freedom from the sinful cycle of violence. This point is a reminder that violence not only affects the victim, but the victim's community, often leading to violent retaliation—that is, to further bondage to sin. Christian violence is therefore a failure of mission both to the victim and to the victim's community. These reflections strengthen the theological case against Milbank's justification of violence because of the (supposedly negative) effects of refusing violence. See also Yoder's comments on disobedience, murder, and freedom in *Preface*, 310–11.

137. The symbolic violence of just war is not directed to enemies—whose assent is of course not sought—but to the mass of society that supplies soldiers and goods for war. They have to be convinced of the worthiness of their sacrifices, and just war is the preeminent way that has been accomplished in Christian societies.

cal terminology, the Christian justification of killing is paradigmatic of the church's Constantinian compromise with the fallen powers.

Bourdieu's theory of violence furthermore indicates how killing can be integrated at the far extreme of a theological scale or spectrum of violences. Each institutional or personal practice of symbolic, structural, and physical violence denies the possibility of obedience to some degree. Structural violence makes obedience difficult by restricting or denying access to the capital necessary for obedience. For instance, chapters 5 and 6 below discuss dialogue before scripture as a form of obedience. Structural differences in access to quality education, however, make meaningful dialogue difficult— though of course not impossible—for those with less access, given that education can enhance dialogical skills and textual interpretation. Similar conclusions can be drawn about the dialogical abilities of those whose emotional make-up has been denigrated by structural violence. At its extreme, of course, structural violence kills, whether through the violence that tends to accompany those whose access to capital has been systematically and severely restricted (e.g., gang warfare, suicide), or through "natural" deaths resulting from, for example, lack of access to medical care or money for winter heating. Symbolic violence can also kill—as when it is "mixed" with physical violence[138]—and may be implicated in a range of "lesser violences," such as those Bourdieu describes as at work in pedagogy. And of course physical violence runs from killing to the betrayer's kiss.[139]

In addition to its usefulness for conceiving of a spectrum of violences with killing at the far extreme, Bourdieu's theory of violence also enables a look at "internal violence."[140] Violence is not simply embedded in social structures, nor is it exhausted by specific acts of physical violation. Although Bourdieu's construal of the state as the monopolizer of physical and symbolic violence somewhat vindicates Yoder's focus on war and peace,[141] state,

138. Schinkel, *Violence*, 197–202, writes of forms of violence "mixing" when they fulfill Bourdieu's law of the conservation of violence. Yoder, *PK*, 111, intriguing hints at such a mixing when he states, without further explanation, that "behind" different understandings of violence are varying convictions about truth telling and oaths, ownership and accumulation, and the selfish use of nonviolent civil power. It would be intriguing to work out, in Yoderian terms, the relation between each of these practices and physical violence.

139. Judas' kiss can be read as an interesting mix of symbolic and physical violences: physical, because it involves touch, and symbolic, because it draws on the legitimacy of familiarity to approach Jesus and signal his captors.

140. As is evident, the use of the phrase "internal violence" here includes but extends beyond Hess's concern for the psychological effects of physical violence.

141. Nevertheless, as explored in the following chapter, Bourdieu's attention to relations and symbols adds much to Yoder's approach.

structural, and private violence are all inscribed in minds and bodies. Symbolic violence is an especially precise conceptual tool for describing how violence becomes part of persons' basic dispositions and outlook. To accept a view of the world as legitimate, when the purveyors of that view hide the power that structures the pedagogical relation, is to have one's existential being shaped by violence. Physical and structural means of violence also affect the habitus insofar as they restructure the specific capital available to it, whether that capital is a certain bodily unity—without scar or mutilation—or includes other material and symbolic goods. Because available capital forms personal and group expectations, all types of violence exact psychological and emotional tolls. Moreover, because the habitus suggests a basic unity, or at least a permeability, between a person's body, intellect, and emotions, a violation of one is sure to have implications for the others— there is a kind of "subjective" law of conversion of violence. The powers are not just "out there." They are "inside" us and are us, and the fall restructures every aspect of our humanity. Our autonomization from God is spiritual, intellectual, emotional and, in each case, social.

As a theologian of Christian pacifism, Yoder does not accept that humans merely are separated from God. Obedience is a possibility, and so nonviolence is a possibility. From this theological perspective, the spectrum of violences has to give way to a spectrum of nonviolences. But Bourdieu's sociology would not seem to allow for the description of any action as nonviolent. Or would it? Bourdieu does refer positively to nonviolence at various points,[142] and his definition of symbolic violence seems to allow for reversal. One could seek legitimacy, ostensibly, without concealing the sources of his or her power. Power relations could be subject to open scrutiny, and those with more power could be genuinely receptive to those with less—a world without domination is possible. As a social practice, violence is never necessary and power can be deployed otherwise. The reversibility and non-necessity of violence gives a strong sociological warrant for accepting what Yoder proposes on christological grounds. For Yoder, the possibility of a world without domination derives from the reality of the human Jesus Christ.[143] Christ embodies nonviolent servanthood, as foreshadowed by Israel and witnessed to haltingly by the church. Even if what constitutes nonviolent practice is not always obvious, its existence is not wishful thinking.

These reflections do not yet constitute an adequate response to Schinkel's argument that violence, understood as reduction of being, is inherent in

142. These references are discussed in chapter six below.

143. See Yoder, WL, 106, 121, on the basis of nonviolence in spirituality and faith.

being itself. If human being is finite, then we have always and only ever been violated. If human practice fulfills some potential modes of being by denying others, then everything we do violates others, if not ourselves. This is the bleak and nihilistic vision that seems to be the only end of the sociological trail. Yoder denied this vision, even if he grappled with how destructive forces, such as aggression, are also productive forces.[144] Moreover, whatever one makes of the coherency of non-Christian attempts to articulate a genuine peace, Bourdieu and Schinkel at least implicitly point to a mode of being beyond violence—their sociological critiques of violence make little sense otherwise.[145] Schinkel drew a distinction between the minimal, quotidian violence that enables being and the violence that reduces and destroys it unnecessarily. Bourdieu's theory of symbolic violence implies a distinction between violent and nonviolent modes of deploying power. The distinctions are far from clear cut: they can only be made on moral grounds. As Milbank had it, "violence" must be judged in light of the goods it impairs or preserves. That admission is, however, only the beginning of a process of moral discernment in which Christians look to the social practices of Jesus as definitive of nonviolent being and, by implication, its other.

Bourdieu's theory of violence and domination therefore facilitates a revision of Yoder's theology of violence and the fall that responds to critics of its allegedly too strict proscription of killing, the lack of clarity around its positioning of killing vis-à-vis other violences, and its silence on those dimensions of the fall that affect human dispositions. Violence restricts the possibility of obedience; killing definitively eliminates it. Violence transcends any neat boundaries between internal and external personhood, realigning both social and dispositional structures. These deformed fallen structures indeed hold persons and society together. But in doing so, they hold persons and society away from God. Nevertheless, the violence of the fallen powers is not absolute. Social practices fall on a moral spectrum, with killing at one extreme and nonviolence at the other. The boundary between violence and nonviolence must always be discerned, but the boundary is real. And at the boundary we see Christ crucified, victim and nonviolent victor.

144. Yoder, *Nonviolence*, 69–72. See also his *You Have It Coming: Good Punishment: The Legitimate Social Function of Punitive Behavior*, in *UNDA*.

145. See Sayer, "Disinterested Judgment," 412–13, 415, for an argument that Bourdieu's language of "domination" requires a moral framework. On the other hand, Hobsbawm, "Sociologie critique," 290, suggests that Bourdieu's use of the moral term "violence" interferes with his objective explanation of domination.

Conclusion

This chapter has reviewed John Howard Yoder's theology of violence and the fall, with special attention to its basis in his theology of the principalities and powers. Yoder, following the New Testament and Berkhof, depicts the fall of the powers in terms of an autonomization of human social structures from God, and specifically from the process of development intended in their creation. This broad understanding of the fall is also visible in his analysis of violence. Yet critics of his thought are rightly concerned with the ambiguities in his presentation of violence, focused as it is on war and peace. Is violence simply killing, or does it, in every instance, need to be discerned anew? If killing is especially violent, how does it relate to other forms of violence, especially those experienced in thoughts, emotion, and spirituality? Bourdieu's theories of violence and domination enable responses to these questions that are in continuity with Yoder's project. As an especially definitive form of the reduction of capital—of the person him or herself—killing is indeed, in every instance, the most extreme form of violence. But there exists a range of less extreme forms of violence, and these include state, structural, and private forms, all mediated through physical, symbolic, and structural means. In each case, the "inner" person is affected alongside the social structure. These revisions clarify Yoder's Christian pacifism by specifying that which it censures, violence. This clarity is not gained at the expense of a complementary definition of nonviolence. Nevertheless, as a form of Christian theology and practice, the clarity of Yoder's pacifism is ultimately provided by the light of Christ.

At this point, a question arises as to humans' ability to perceive the light of Christ. The habitus shaped by violence is unlikely to recognize nonviolence. One might even regard the fall itself an ultimate "act" of symbolic violence, one that universally inculcates habitus to recognize the legitimacy of the fallen powers. Such a habitus is liable to reject Christ as a pretender and, of course, that is exactly what the Gospels depict as happening. The Christian tradition insists, nonetheless, and Yoder is no exception, that God reveals Godself authentically in the order of the powers, in the descendants of Abraham and their scriptures, and especially in Jesus Christ and his Spirit-empowered body and its scriptures. These modes of revelation have been described above as structures produced through intense spiritual relationship to God. As of yet, little has been said to indicate how humans can and do relate to God intensely. The following chapter begins that task by examining Yoder's theological method, his proposal for how Christians discern between violence and nonviolence in light of Christ. This discernment is already political, already involved in God's redemption of the powers, an argument that is spelled out in detail in the final two chapters.

4

Revising Yoder's Theological Method

THE POWERS' DYNAMIC AUTONOMIZATION never escapes the grip of providence. The fallen powers are created powers. As neither wholly good, nor wholly evil, the shape of the powers must be discerned. Yoder's theological method privileges a form of discernment rooted in the practical encounter between specific Christian communities and specific powers. Discernment is ultimately a function of mission. Theologians' contribution to this mission is limited, according to Yoder, yet indispensable for the discernment process. The theologian's gifts of linguistic analysis and scriptural and historical memory are useful because they facilitate a comparison of the powers with the way of Jesus. For Yoder, critical discernment of the powers is a comparative task.

Yoder's own work, therefore, concentrates on illuminating the way of Jesus as portrayed in scripture and comparing it to various points in Christian history. If the portrayal of the pacifist Jesus in *The Politics of Jesus* holds true, then a church that justifies war is obviously a fallen power. Christian discernment relies on accurate memories of Jesus, but it also relies on memories of how Christians in the past attempted to be faithful in their diverse settings. If the early church, St. Francis, the Anabaptists, and Martin Luther King Jr., could find ways to imitate Jesus' nonviolence in their times, then churches today can, too. Linguistic analysis is helpful at this point to expose the faulty logic behind justifications of deviance from the way of Jesus.

This work of discerning history and language is always contestable, and many critics are dissatisfied with Yoder's attempts. Several critics point to the insufficiency of his own theological language, given that he ignores both the need for metaphysical language to support the normativity of his ethics and the need for theological construction to specify his theological concepts. In other words, the metaphysical and constructive aspects of language cannot be overlooked in the discernment process. Other critics charge Yoder with a faulty memory: his interpretations of scripture and (church) history are tendentious, skewed to fit his theological agenda. Self-seeking and impatient, Yoder is an example of a fallen theological power, not a guide to discernment.

The present chapter suggests that Yoder can be a guide for discernment if aspects of his method are revised by Pierre Bourdieu's reflexive sociology. The chapter opens with an overview of Yoder's theological method and its critics, with special emphasis on his understanding of how to discern the powers. Next, resources in Bourdieu's sociology are examined, specifically his concepts of the epistemological break, relational object construction and confirmation, and reflexivity. The chapter concludes with a proposal for a Yoderian theology of the powers that is sociologically reflexive, perceptive of the symbolic, material, and spiritual dimensions of the powers, and inclusive of a rigorous empirical component.

Yoder's Theological Method

The first part of this section is a study of Yoder's comments on discerning the powers. He envisages the theology of the principalities and powers as a subtle mode of social criticism useful for the church's mission. Although he does not say how the powers are to be discerned, already in these writings it is clear that the basic methodology is comparative: contemporary powers, including the church, are judged by comparison to the way of Jesus as portrayed in scripture. This comparative method is elaborated in the second part of this section, through an overview of Yoder's understanding of theology as service to the church. The final part of this section examines the many complaints about Yoder's allegedly poor theological service.

Discerning the Powers: A Comparative Theology

Yoder regards the Pauline language of the principalities and powers as supplying the basic framework for Christian social discernment and critique. The Pauline authors continually correlate God's redemption of the world through Christ with the exposure of the continuing rebellion of the powers. Christian social criticism is based on the lordship of Christ over the powers, since this lordship requires a qualification of every competing claim to ultimacy. The structure of Christian criticism is therefore comparative: immanent claims to ultimacy are compared with Christ's ultimate status.

For Yoder, "discerning the spirits" (1 Cor 12:10) always involves close attention to who Jesus is. Although some Christians may be especially gifted hermeneuticists, the entire witness of the gifted congregation is necessary for an accurate perception of Christ (1 Cor 12, 14).[1] Scripture, moreover, is the primary witness to the congregation of Jesus' identity. Yoder often takes Phil 2:1–11 as an adequate summary: Christ's suffering humility results in his divine exaltation and reception of "the name that is above every name" (2:9).[2] The church that sees the humble Jesus is equipped to see the prideful powers. It is the powers' failure to conform to Christ that gives away their fallenness.

This comparative logic is also evident in Berkhof's *Christ and the Powers*. Of particular interest here is Berkhof's exegesis of Col 2:15. Through the cross and resurrection Christ "disarmed the rulers [*archas*] and authorities [*exousias*] and made a public example of them, triumphing over them in it." According to Berkhof, "it is precisely in the crucifixion that the true nature of the Powers has come to light."[3] Before the advent of Christ, the powers "were accepted as the most basic and ultimate realities, as the gods of the world." But after the powers turn against God-in-Christ at the cross, there can be no illusions: "they are unmasked as false gods by their encounter with very God." The shape of the fallen powers becomes clear in the light of Christ. Present discernment of the powers is then grounded in consideration of Christ's life and work.[4]

Yoder makes the connection between Jesus and discernment explicit in *The Christian Witness to the State*. The "ground of Christian witness" and the "criteria for political judgment" have the same source. Christian witness has its purpose, form, and content in the lordship of the crucified and risen Christ.[5] Moreover, "the Christian social critique finds its standards in the kingdom of God—for there are no other standards."[6] The state's fallenness is apparent through the many ways in which it is not the kingdom, as seen especially in its use of violence to bring about order.[7] At the same time, "the judgments of Christians who are well informed will often differ little in substance from the

---

1. See, e.g., Yoder, *FC*; *BP*, 47–70.

2. E.g., Yoder, *Preface*, 80–88, 104; *PJ*, 121–22; *PK*, 52; *HCPP*, 83, 89–95.

3. Berkhof, *C&P*, 38. The meaning of Christ's "triumph" is the subject of chapters 5 and 6 below.

4. Cf. Berkhof, *C&P*, 47–64, on the church and the powers.

5. Yoder, *CWS*, 8–28, 35–44.

6. Ibid., 39; see also his "Natural Law," 22.

7. Yoder, *CWS*, 36–38, 74–83.

intelligent judgment of other social critics."[8] Apart from his typical censure of state violence, Yoder's focus in this work is on the positive political alternatives Christians might offer as part of their witness.[9]

Subsequent writings on the powers indicate a shift in Yoder's understanding of Christian social critique. From "Jesus and Power" in *The Politics of Jesus* onwards, he highlights not just positive Christian alternatives, but also the uniqueness of Christian moral judgment. The theology of the principalities and powers aids in discerning both what is wrong with society, and what Christians should do about it. Although the latter is the topic of the following chapter below, it is worth noting again that, for Yoder, Jesus Christ is the criterion of political critique and construction. In *The Politics of Jesus*, Yoder argues that a critically informed review of the canonical text of Luke's gospel shows the distinctiveness of Jesus' teachings on violence, economics, and power.[10] If the gospels communicate the "substance" of Christ's politics, the theology of the principalities and powers convey its "form" by directing readers to issues of power and structure "in the sense in which these terms are used by modern thinkers in the social and political sciences" (136). Yoder therefore begins his treatment of the powers with a common sense analysis of the different ways modern people use the terms power and structure, and then asks if Paul's language is "translatable into the concepts of modern social science" (138).

To answer this question, Yoder turns to recent European historical-critical studies of the Pauline texts, observing that these arose from a need to understand the "power of evil" during Nazism and the Cold War (139). Yet what marks the recent criticism is not an eisegetical leap to see modern problems in ancient texts, but careful attention to the meaning of the texts in the authors' own age. Modern evils are illuminated by ancient insights. After detailing Berkhof's exegesis of the powers passages, Yoder concludes that, "far from being archaic or meaningless, the 'exousiology' of the apostle, that is, his doctrine of the Powers, reveals itself to be a very refined analysis of the problems of society and history, far more refined than the other ways in which theologians have sought to describe the same realities in terms

---

8. Ibid., 35.

9. These alternatives are discussed in the following chapter, below.

10. Yoder, *PJ*, 11–13, defends his decision to attend mostly to the canonical shape of the New Testament, as his concern is precisely with the distance between the canon and current Christian ethics. He does not reject historical criticism, which he sees as providing confirmation for his arguments (e.g., 12n17, 41n35, 54–58, 72–75, 87–88, 139–49, 158–61). This overall approach is consistent with Yoder's "biblical realism" (vii, x, 136), as explained below. Subsquent references to *PJ* in this and the following two paragraphs are in the text.

only of 'creation' or 'personality'" (143–44). Yoder now sees the theology of the powers as offering insight into social problems, not just alternatives. It is, he believes, superior to other theological options for social interpretation that, like Reformed "orders of creation" theology, do not "combine with such clarity and precision the simultaneous recognition of humankind's fallen condition and the simultaneous providential control." Nor do these other options account for the pervasiveness of religion and ideology in perpetuating the fall. Nor, crucially, are they focused on Jesus Christ—and, as mentioned, Philippians 2 provides a clear contrast between the dominion-seeking powers and Christ's voluntary subordination (145).

Because the Pauline language of the powers indicates an interpretation of all these elements (fall, providence, Christ) along social lines, Yoder sees it as affirming that "the New Testament provides [a] concept with which it would be possible to interpret the structures and the history of a secular society" (149–50). Secular criticism does not have the last word, as it does not account for the church as a community with special insight into social ills and their remedy.[11] This insight is rooted in the biblical cosmology as "a more adequate intellectual framework of the task of *social* discernment."[12] A similar argument appears at the end of *The Politics of Jesus*, where Yoder argues that the apocalyptic depiction of the victory of the suffering lamb has implications for our understandings of causation, community, and conflict.[13] The risen Christ sheds his light on all things. For those with eyes to see, evil is unveiled as is good.[14]

In the Stone Lecture "Behold My Servant Shall Prosper," Yoder calls for discernment of the powers, since "some may be more fallen than others."[15] The church does not possess *a priori* knowledge of the shape of the powers; its engagement of each hangs on the outcome of a discernment process. "The community," therefore, "will not ask whether to enter or to escape the realm of power, but what kinds of power are in conformity with the

---

11. Ibid., 152–53. Yoder is criticizing World Council of Churches studies that leave social analysis to secular critics.

12. Ibid., 156. Yoder mentions the extremely critical studies of French sociologist and theologian Jacques Ellul as exemplary modern appropriations of the powers language (157). He specifically names Ellul's studies of "money, the law, violence, and technology." By 1972 those studies would have included Ellul, *Money and Power*; *Technological Society*; *Theological Foundation of Law*; and *Violence*.

13. Yoder, *PJ*, 245–46.

14. Cf. Anderson, "Original Sin," for a Barthian account of sin as only intelligible in light of redemption.

15. Yoder, "Servant," 165.

victory of the lamb."[16] Moral judgment of the powers involves a community focused on imitating Jesus. In Yoder's first Stone Lecture he suggests that this focus—which he terms doxology—automatically places "any claim to glory or authority made on behalf of alternative value definitions" under question.[17] This doxological hermeneutic is expanded in the essays derived from Yoder's second lecture as an "apocalyptic critique" or "apocalyptic consciousness."[18] Biblical apocalyptic literature has been subjected to a variety of fanciful interpretations, but Yoder is convinced that, if readers let the texts speak for themselves, they can "help us to see things 'as they really are.'"[19] Christ's lordship means that no human ruler "is the primary agent of divine movement in history."[20] It means that the identification of moral righteousness with popularity or power is erroneous.[21] It means that conceptions of society as a closed causal system that can be known (and manipulated) with certainty are fallacious.[22] The fallenness of the powers is revealed in their resistance to the slain lamb who is risen as cosmic lord.

In this perspective, Yoder's writings on the powers in his Warsaw Lectures and in "How H. Richard Niebuhr Reasoned" can be viewed as confrontations with competing modes of social criticism. The purpose of the lecture on "Early Christian Cosmology and Nonviolence" is to uncover "specific points at which we can see how [early Christian] thought was different from ours, and how this can help us to make sense of their witness and way in the world."[23] The Pauline powers passages and, more generally, New Testament apocalyptic affirm the socio-political nature of redemption and the lack of correlation between social control and moral progress.[24] These insights help make sense of an earlier lecture, "The Science of Conflict," in which Yoder critically engages social scientific accounts

16. Ibid., 167.

17. Yoder, RP, 123. He moves to critique the "realist" exchange of means for ends along these lines (124–25).

18. Yoder, "Armaments and Eschatology," 53–54.

19. Ibid., 48, 52.

20. Ibid., 53.

21. Ibid., 54, 56, and "Ethics and Eschatology," 123–24.

22. Yoder, "Armaments," 54–55; "Ethics," 122–23, 125–26. Cf. his essay on the sacraments in RP, 359–73, which is a significantly revised version of material from his fourth and fifth Stone Lectures. There Yoder depicts the sacramental community as internally and externally defined by dialogue—i.e., it does not accept a view of society as a closed causal system, but is constantly open to the future. This argument is a major theme of chapters 5 and 6 below.

23. Yoder, Nonviolence, 97.

24. Ibid., 102–3.

of human nature and social process.[25] Accounts that deny the possibility of faithfulness to the way of Jesus, or the efficacy of that way, are cast in doubt. For example, when psychological findings on the detrimental effects of passivity are used to argue against pacifism, Yoder counters that there is no reason nonviolence should be passive.[26] Studies of human aggression are sometimes read as justifications of the innateness of violence; but they can also be interpreted as highlighting the importance of direct conflict resolution in maintaining peaceable community.[27] In sum, faith in the lordship of Christ over the powers requires suspicion toward and reformulation of social scientific frameworks that overlook the power of suffering service.

Yoder takes a similar approach toward H. Richard Niebuhr's theological understanding of cultural transformation. Niebuhr dismisses interpretations of Jesus as the exemplary human or as cosmic lord as "radical."[28] His own Christology is moderated by a trinitarianism that views the Father and Holy Spirit as alternative moral sources.[29] Although this move appears to be faithfully "theocentric," Yoder views Niebuhr as surrendering Christian discernment to the ethical definitions of a given cultural mainstream.[30] Whatever this mainstream says is wrong with culture is wrong, and whatever it says is right is right—Jesus has nothing to contribute. The Pauline theology of the principalities and powers, on the other hand, encourages communal discernment of the powers in light of scripture's testimony to the work of Christ.[31]

Community, Language, and Memory

Yoder eschews methodological discussion that is not directly subordinate to the life of the church. In his essay "Walk and Word: The Alternatives to Methodologism," he argues that "the life of the community is prior to all possible methodological distillations."[32] Ethical methods are pragmatic tools for moral discernment. There is no need for a unified methodology, but rather for "skills of mixing and matching [methods] according to the

25. Ibid., 63–72.

26. Ibid., 71–72.

27. Ibid., 67–68, 71.

28. Yoder, "HRN," 58–61 (on Niebuhr, *Christ and Culture*, 45–82).

29. Yoder, "HRN," 61–65.

30. Ibid., 66–67. Yoder later identifies theologies of cultural autonomy and relativism as similar moves that deny Christ as norm, and so disable discernment (77–82).

31. Ibid., 68–69, 71–77, 82–89 (esp. 85).

32. Yoder, *PWK*, 87.

shape of a particular debate."[33] Some debates call for a focus on duties, some on consequences, and others on virtues—and some on all three. The "wholeness of community culture" as it encounters concrete situations has priority over "the appetite for intellectual thoroughness," and this goes for ethics as well as other theological disciplines.[34]

Theologians are, consequentially, only relevant contributors to Christian mission insofar as they participate in the church's encounter with the powers.[35] They are a resource in the discernment process, not the primary executives of that process.[36] In his essay "The Hermeneutics of Peoplehood: A Protestant Perspective," Yoder writes of theologians ("scribes" and "teachers") as being "agents" of the church's practical reasoning. Among these he mentions "agents of direction" who prophetically "state and reinforce a vision of the place of the believing community in history, which vision locates moral reasoning."[37] There are also "agents of linguistic self-consciousness" who help the church untangle itself from linguistic thickets that impede practice.[38] "Agents of memory" surface aspects of scripture and church history relevant to a problem at hand. Theologians thus have the linguistic tasks of cosmological construction and logical criticism, and the mnemonic tasks of recalling the church's stories and scriptures. The following paragraphs outline Yoder's own approach to each of these tasks.

Language: Cosmology and Critique

Little needs to be said here about Yoder's prophetic cosmology given the focus of this thesis. Nevertheless, it is worth noting that he sees the purpose of cosmological constructions such as the theology of the principalities and powers as "locating" the church's moral discernment.[39] Yoder does not seek

33. Ibid., 93.

34. Ibid., 92.

35. Although see Yoder, *PK*, 45, where he asks open-endedly about the prospects of an individual "internalizing" the discernment process in the absence of a functioning Christian community.

36. Yoder, *THW*, 121: "The ethicist is a servant of the communal identity, not its founder or its ruler."

37. Yoder, *PK*, 29.

38. Ibid., 30–33. In addition to these three roles, Yoder discusses "agents of order or due process" (33–34). As Yoder describes this role in terms of an organizational facilitator, it will not be discussed here. Although there is no reason to think a theologian would be ineligible for such a role, it is not intrinsically linked to theological work, as the other agencies are to some degree.

39. Cf. Yoder's comment that, biblically speaking, the audience of the prophet is

a systematic biblical "worldview," but rather a general framework that can help churches understand their place in history as they go about interacting with various powers. Biblical cosmology is not speculative, but practical. Theologians imaginatively reconstruct contemporary language forms in order to convey the biblical cosmology, with full awareness of the theological risks involved.[40] The risk enables cultural transformation.

Yoder observes that the New Testament authors repeatedly adopted cosmological categories from their surrounding cultures, but "seized the categories, hammered them into other shapes, and turned the cosmology on its head, with Jesus both at the bottom, crucified as a common criminal, and at the top, preexistent Son and creator, and the church his instrument in today's battle."[41] The Pauline use of powers language is one example, along with the logos Christology of the Johannine Prologue (John 1:1–14); the angelology of the book of Hebrews (2:8–9); the apocalypticism of Revelation (4:1—5:4); and the kenotic Christology of Philippians 2.[42] Yoder writes of the process of cosmological adoption as a search for an "interworld transformational grammar" that faithfully translates the gospel into contemporary idioms.[43] Church history can be read as a catalogue of more or less faithful attempts at imitating the biblical model of gospel translation.[44] Even a non-Christian like Gandhi can be viewed as rearticulating the gospel within a Hindu cosmology.[45] The theology of the principalities and powers is, as seen above, an effort in translating the gospel into a secular social scientific cosmology. Such cosmological translation is central to the theologian's linguistic task.

Yoder recognizes that technical aspects of theological practice require "professional" training and oversight.[46] But for him theology is more than a profession, it is a way of serving the body of Christ—of which most members are not professional theologians. Technical theological vocabulary then has its place, but theologians "must make sense in ordinary language." Translating the gospel into contemporary cosmologies is one way to make sense.

---

the people of God, and not primarily the nations (*CWS*, 36).

40. Yoder, *PK* ; *THW*, 109, 123.

41. Yoder, *PK*, 54.

42. Ibid., 50–52. See also his *HCPP*, 69–88 (on John 1) and 89–95 (on Phil 2).

43. Yoder, *PK*, 56; cf. 54–59; *CWS*, 25; *PWK* 110–112.

44. E.g., the Anabaptists used Reformation-era biblicism, the Quakers used Enlightenment spirituality, and so on (Yoder, *CA*, 161–252).

45. Yoder, *Nonviolence*, 22–26; *WL*, 56–57. See also his *RP*, 260.

46. Yoder, *THW*, 125.

Comprehensible prose and well-distributed publications is another.[47] Nevertheless, Yoder envisions the theological encounter with ordinary language as critical and not merely affirmative. Hence one of the theological agencies described above is that of "linguistic self-consciousness." At the same time as theologians are to be sensitive to common language that communicates the gospel, they are to be alert for words and concepts that obscure it. As a theologian, Yoder is especially alert to "professional" theological language that enters the common parlance of the church with distorting effect—thus, his attack on Niebuhr's *Christ and Culture*.

At the end of *Christian Witness to the State*, Yoder offers a formulation that could serve as the job description for an agent of linguistic self-consciousness: "It is normal for a newcomer to a debate which is already in process to accept the prevailing definitions of terms and choose one of the existing sides, whereas the wiser approach is to question the definitions."[48] Yoder refers there to a debate current among American Mennonites in the 1950s over the implications of Reinhold Niebuhr's thought.[49] Many Mennonites accepted Niebuhr's designation of them as apolitical, arguing that the doctrine of nonresistance entails political and cultural "withdrawal." Yoder's response in *Christian Witness to the State* and elsewhere is to cast doubt on definitions of politics that exclude obedience to Christ as a possible political stance. Such definitional labor permeates his writings, for instance in treatments of "pacifism,"[50] "imago dei,"[51] "responsibility,"[52] "Trinity,"[53] "evangelical,"[54] "democracy,"[55] and so on. Yoder is also suspicious of dualisms that preclude obedience as an option, such as "inner versus outer,"[56] "grace versus works,"[57] or "Reformed versus Anabaptist social strategies."[58] In each case the point is to uncover how common word usage can deceive

---

47. Yoder published numerous small church pamphlets, such as *Capital Punishment*, and spoke at church meetings around the world (see, e.g., the essays in *Revolutionary Christianity* and *OR*, and the "bible lectures" in *HCPP*).

48. Yoder, *CWS*, 90.

49. See Yoder, *Nevertheless*, 107–14.

50. Ibid.

51. Yoder, *WL*, 165–80.

52. E.g., Yoder, "Reinhold Niebuhr," 112.

53. Yoder, "HRN," 61–65; *Preface*, 203–4, 297–98.

54. Yoder, "Evangelical Dualism," 450; *PK*, 54–55.

55. Yoder, *PK*, 151–55.

56. Yoder, "Evangelical Dualism," 449–59.

57. Yoder, *PJ*, 212–27; see 103–9 for a further list of unhelpful dualisms.

58. Yoder, "Inadequate Typology."

Christians into thinking that the way of Jesus is irrelevant or impossible.[59] Both transformative cosmological construction and definitional critique are central to Yoder's understanding of theological practice.

Memory: Scripture and History

In "Hermeneutics of Peoplehood," Yoder observes that there is only one time a Gospel writer depicts Jesus using the term "scribe" positively: "every scribe who becomes a disciple of the kingdom of heaven is like a householder who brings out from his storeroom things both new and old" (Matt 13:52).[60] The faithful scribe therefore "does not speak on his own, but as the servant of a community and of the communal memory." Moreover, the existence of a storehouse of memories indicates that the scribe's job is to select a memory or set of memories appropriate to a given issue. The community's memories are diverse, not univocal or interchangeable, and require regular review. "The scribe as practical moral reasoner does not judge or decide anything, but he (or she) remembers expertly, charismatically the store of memorable, identity-confirming acts of faithfulness praised and of failure repented."[61] Yoder is again concerned with practical mixing and matching, not with a systematic framework for discernment.

For the scribe of the kingdom, Yoder suggests, "scripture is the collective scribal memory, the store *par excellence* of treasures new and old."[62] In other writings, he designates his approach to recalling the treasures of scripture as "biblical realism."[63] This approach has its roots in a loose movement of biblical scholars from the 1950s and 1960s who pioneered a form of post-critical hermeneutics.[64] Biblical realists utilize all the tools of historical

---

59. Yoder's reliance on lists for investigating the various ways words are used bears further examination. See Belknap, *The List*, 8–11, for a brief history of lists, and Eco, *Infinity of Lists*, for a partial list of lists. Eco's ruminations on definition by a list of properties (versus definition by essence) are especially relevant to Yoder's method (200–243).

60. Yoder, *PK*, 30 (the translation is Yoder's).

61. Ibid.

62. Ibid., 31.

63. Yoder, *PJ*, viii, x; "The Politics of Jesus Revisited," in *UNDA*; *THW*, 61, 100–101, 155–77, 178–91.

64. In his various references to the movement, Yoder names Markus Barth, John W. Bowman, John Bright, Oscar Cullmann, Edmund La B. Cherbonnier, Suzanne de Dietrich, Walter Eichrodt, Floyd Filson, Hendrik Kraemer, George Eldon Ladd, Paul Minear, Otto Piper, Gerhard von Rad, Adolf Schlatter, Claude Tresmontant, Hans-Reudi Weber, and G. Ernest Wright as the major figures. Yoder distinguishes it from the concurrent "biblical theology" movement (*THW*, 181–84). The eighteenth- and nineteenth-century German *heilsgeschichtlich* school, including the work of Johann

criticism, but refuse the cynicism toward the texts with which those tools are often wielded.[65] Yoder takes the title and content of Paul S. Minear's book *The Eyes of Faith: A Study in the Biblical Point of View* as indicative of the main features of biblical realism.[66] Biblical realists search for "the biblical point of view," but without the assumption that a single timeless biblical theology or worldview exists. The unity of the biblical perspective is resistant to systematization, and to any other effort to domesticate it by shaping it to modern categories. Yoder reports that Minear imagined the biblical scholar as an archeologist opening a sarcophagus and finding a mummy, when suddenly the mummy reaches out and bends the tools of the archeologist.[67] The goal of biblical realism is similarly to let the Bible shape exegesis, in order to find "the message of the Bible on its own terms."[68]

The "realism" of this approach is therefore its methodological conviction that critical tools can uncover the real message of the Bible.[69] Yoder accordingly accepts historical, literary, and sociological methods of biblical interpretation.[70] These methods, of course, have their origins in Enlightenment skepticism about biblical authority. Yoder praises skepticism as a corollary of Radical Reformation biblicism, which denies the presupposition of an "identity between what [the Bible] says and what we believe."[71] Biblical realism nonetheless goes beyond Enlightenment objectivity with its realization that biblical authority is derivative of its ongoing function of constituting believing communities.[72] Rather than drawing its authority from propositional infallibility or a pre- or proto-canonical history, the

---

Tobias Beck, Johann Georg Hamann, and Johann Christian Konrad van Hofmann, is an antecedent (159). More recent interpreters in the same spirit include Brevard Childs, Paul Ricoeur, and James Sanders (189).

65. Yoder, *THW*, 158.

66. Ibid., 160–67.

67. Yoder, *THW*, 176. Minear does not use this image in *Eyes of Faith*, and Yoder does not report its source, but see *Eyes of Faith*, 3–5, on the impossibility of systematic objectivity in biblical studies, and 206–14, on how the biblical authors remember history as events of encounter with God.

68. This is the title of a lecture Yoder gave in 1964 to Mennonite students on biblical realism (*THW*, 155–77).

69. Ibid., 167.

70. Ibid., 124, 147. In the 1980s and 90s Yoder critically embraced aspects of René Girard's socio-anthropological interpretations of scripture. See Yoder, "Review: *The Scapegoat*"; "Twenty Years Later" in UNDA; *WL*, 29–41, 176–78; *You Have It Coming: Good Punishment. The Legitimate Social Function of Punitive Behavior*, in UNDA. These studies are anticipated by *HCPP*, 58–65.

71. Yoder, *THW*, 130.

72. Ibid., 131, 153; see 94–119 on the canon.

scriptural canon is normative as a paradigmatic record of authentic norming efforts—a record that can "reach out" and judge contemporary efforts.[73]
True hermeneutical objectivity enables the objectivity of the Bible to stand
over against Christians today.

Biblical realism is also "realistic" in its (biblical) focus on historical
events.[74] Yoder, following Minear, argues that the biblical point of view begins with the practical activities of God in creation, and so is unconcerned
with questions of philosophical (mono)theism. "The Bible is not interested
in this kind of truth, but only in those things which truly were done in a
particular time and place by a particular divine initiative."[75] The unity of
the biblical point of view thus emerges from meditation on the disparate
narratives, not from conceptual systematization.[76] Hence Yoder privileges
an inductive hermeneutic that identifies structural homologies within the
diverse biblical literature.[77] Inductive inquiry is complemented by an in-
terpretative bias toward a "straightforward" reading of the biblical texts.[78]
The events that matter are portrayed in the text as it stands, not in a history
that allegedly exists prior to the texts.[79] Again, this confidence in the text is
not primarily from an *a priori* faith in biblical authority—though that faith
may be present too—but from observation of the way scripture works in the
church.[80] The events recorded in scripture are the events that continue to
form the church. Attention to these events takes priority for a hermeneutic
sensitive to the real encounter between Bible and congregation.

The biblical realist scribe of the kingdom remembers God's interactions with humanity as reported in the Bible, recalling them as appropriate
for a given situation and in such a way that their normative force is not
blunted by modern concerns. As with the agent of linguistic self-consciousness, the purpose of this mnemonic task is largely critical. "The theologians'

73. Yoder, *THW*, 107–8, follows through on the logical implications of this view, and
argues that the canon can never be closed. He mentions the *Didache* as a text that might
be included in the canon. That said, he does not view the canon as totally flexible and
open-ended: the records of Jesus' participation in the norming process, and of those of his
closest followers, have priority. It is against those records that later norming processes are
judged, and it is this paradigmatic nature of the canon that makes it a canon.

74. Yoder, *THW*, 167.

75. Ibid., 167.

76. Ibid., 145.

77. Ibid., 142–47.

78. Ibid., 145–47, 178–91.

79. Ibid., 145; see 155–57 for Yoder's account of the failed search for the "Christ of
history" behind the "Christ of faith" presented in the gospels.

80. Ibid., 146–47. Yoder mentions Brevard Childs, George Lindbeck, and Alasdair
MacIntyre as supporting a similar view on scriptural authority.

task is more often to defend the text against a wrong claim to its authority than to affirm in some timeless and case-free way that it has authority."[81] All Christians have the ability to interpret scripture; the theologian's special job is to make sure that in each instance scripture is allowed to speak for itself.

According to Yoder the church's memories are of two kinds: "faithfulness praised and failure repented."[82] Within the Bible he discerns memories of both faithfulness and failure. These memories include the faithfulness of Abraham, the prophets, Jesus, and the apostles; and the failures of the Israelite monarchs, Ezra, and the opponents of Jesus and the prophets and apostles. This list suggests the inventiveness of Yoder's own memory, as he goes against traditional readings to see a continuous lineage of failure that begins with the Israelites' request for "a king to govern us, like other nations" (1 Sam 8:5).[83] Ezra did not restore the monarchy, but he adopted their logic of top-down, centralized administration backed by force, as did the powerful Jewish factions in Jesus' day. Although antithetical to the way of Jesus, that logic grew within the church until it captured mainstream Christianity from Constantine until the present day.[84] Here as elsewhere, it is the way of Jesus that matters—events, even biblical events, are remembered as faithful or failures insofar as they align with Jesus Christ.[85]

To recall these memories of post-apostolic "failure" suggests that the storehouse of the scribe of the kingdom is not limited to scripture, but includes the entirety of Jewish and Christian history. Yoder's doctoral training was in Anabaptist church history and, although he quickly turned to theology and ethics, he remained active in historical scholarship through much of his life.[86] His approach to history is much the same as his approach to scripture, and he proposes a "doxological" historiography that "discern[s], down through the centuries, which historical developments can be welcomed as progress in light of the Rule of the Lamb and which as setbacks."[87] Doxologi-

---

81. Yoder, *THW*, 84.

82. Yoder, *PK*, 30.

83. See Leithart, *A Son to Me*, for a "traditional," typological reading of King David.

84. See chapter 3 above on Yoder's critique of Christendom.

85. Yoder, *PK*, 37. Cf. Hays, *Moral Vision*, 248, on Yoder's exemplary Christocentric hermeneutic. Yoder did not take the complement well (*THW*, 207–16).

86. Yoder's contributions to historical scholarship mostly cease after the late 1970s, and by 1989 he considered himself only an "amateur" historian (see his essay "Amateur Historian"). Although it is true that he did not again embark on the kind of original historical research that characterized his dissertation, in 1989 he co-edited a collection of the writings of the sixteenth-century Anabaptist Balthasar Hubmaier (Pipkin and Yoder, eds. and trans., *Balthasar Hubmaier*). In the early 1990s he began to assemble a "History of Religiously Rooted Nonviolence" (in *UNDA*).

87. Yoder, *RP*, 132. See also his "Historiography as a Ministry to Renewal."

cal historiography is regulated by the prophetic-apocalyptic cosmology of the lordship of Christ, and so interprets historical events, movements, and persons as more or less coherent with the way of Jesus. Elsewhere Yoder emphasizes that the critical perspective on history enabled by this cosmology is a particular gift of the Anabaptist and, more broadly, "restitutionist" or Free Church movements.[88] These groups refuse to assume that the way things are is the way things are meant to be, and offer a variety of narratives of how the church deviated from authentic discipleship. The purpose of these narratives is not primarily to stoke academic interest, but to offer insight into the church's present options for renewal. Free Church historiography is thus an exemplary mode of remembering for the sake of Christian mission.

Yoder's own contributions to such a doxological, Free Church historiography are numerous. His doctoral dissertation examines the formation of the Swiss Brethren—one of the first Anabaptist groups—as a process of differentiation from Huldrych Zwingli after he deferred the pace and form of reformation to the town council of Basel.[89] The existence of the Swiss Brethren indicates that the Reformation as a whole could have been otherwise. Yoder's narrative of Constantinianism as a gradual compromise with imperial power similarly suggests that discipleship was not impossible for third- and fourth-century Christians, but a lifestyle they willingly abandoned.[90] He states the underlying historiographical principle explicitly in the title of an essay on the Jewish-Christian schism: "It Did Not Have to Be."[91] Historians should therefore become as familiar as possible with the options facing historical agents, as experienced by the agents themselves. Without denying the objectivity of causation, understanding the first-person experience of history as an open future achieved by real decisions is indispensable. Because the Christian doctrine of sin implies the freedom of choice for or against obedience, history cannot be wholly determined. If not, then it always could be different. Yoder's readings of history aim to demonstrate that discipleship is a latent possibility in every present—including our

88. Yoder, *PK*, 123–34; *JCSR*, 133–42.

89. Yoder, *ARSS*.

90. Yoder, *CA*, 42–74.

91. Yoder, *JCSR*, 43–44. Other examples of Yoder's doxological historiography include his readings of Jeremiah, Jesus, the early church, the Quakers, Tolstoy, Martin Luther King Jr., Gandhi, and the nonviolent people power movements of the 1980s. Each of these persons and movements affirm the possibility of discipleship and the contingency of disobedience. In the 1980s and 90s Yoder was especially interested in the sociologies of nonviolence and conflict resolution as contributions to this historiography. See *BP*, 8, 12; *CA*, 355–68; *Nonviolence*, 63–72; "The 'Power' of 'Nonviolence'" in UNDA; and the writings on René Girard listed in note 69 above.

own. As a scribe of the kingdom, Yoder sought treasures new and old in the storehouse of scripture and church history.

Cosmological construction, linguistic self-awareness, biblical realist scripture interpretation, and doxological historiography are tasks of the church's process of moral discernment. Theology is a practical aid for the church as it responds to the good news of the life, death, and resurrection of Jesus Christ. Because Christian mission is responsive across time and place, theology is an ad hoc affair. Theologians mix and match conceptual tools in order to supply the church with the right words and memories it needs to discern the path of discipleship in its diverse contexts. Often finding the right word or memory arises only after recognizing the wrong ones. Theology is an eminently critical practice, albeit one aimed at the positive goal of Christian faithfulness.

Yoder is under no illusion that theological insight and critique will be received by the church, much less by those outside the church. For the church, this is partially because theologians are not dominant and must yield to the other members of a congregation. Non-Christians are likewise discerning creatures whose decisions for or against Christ must be respected. In both cases Yoder counsels patience. However convinced a theologian, or any other Christian for that matter, may be of the rightness of his or her belief, the proper response to disagreement is never haste. In his essay "'Patience' as Method in Moral Reasoning: Is an Ethic of Discipleship 'Absolute'?," Yoder outlines nineteen different forms patience might take.[92] These include pedagogical patience with someone in a learning process; ecumenical and multicultural patience for persons formed differently than oneself; patience with one's own epistemological finitude; the patience of apocalyptic hope; and the patience of an outvoted minority. Practicing these and other forms of patience does not necessitate moral compromise or a weakening of conviction, but rather involves "accepting willingly and not just grudgingly" the differences of our conversation partners from ourselves.[93] Theologians guided by the conviction that Christ is lord of the cosmos can have the confidence to tarry with dissenting interlocutors within and without the ecclesial community. Theological patience enables and enlivens the discernment process. Patience is Yoder's method in moral reasoning.

92. Yoder, *PWK*, 114–19.

93. Ibid., 117; cf. 125–30 for Yoder's response to those who charge him with ethical "absolutism."

Criticisms

Nevertheless, Yoder reports that an early reader of his essay on patience saw it as a self-justificatory apologia, as a claim that his position is "right."[94] To this criticism Yoder objects, first of all, that the critic obviously thought she was "right" in her evaluation of his work. There is no escape from the making of moral and intellectual judgments. More than that, however, Yoder insists that "the authorial 'I' here speaks for the coherence of a mode of moral discourse, a position, not for a person. I as the person John Yoder am not generous, or consistent, or transparent, or adequate."[95] He accepts, in other words, his personal failings as a patient theological servant of ecclesial moral discernment. A host of critics concur and point to several cases in which Yoder's language and memory evidence failure not faithfulness, haste not patience.

Language: Reductive Cosmology, Hasty Words

Other chapters of this thesis examine how Yoder's metaphysical reticence reduces spiritual, personal, and theological dimensions of human being. Yoder's reduction can be seen as at least in part a methodological error, and specifically as an overly restricted understanding of the linguistic aspects of theological labor. Although he develops a prophetic-apocalyptic cosmology centered on the principalities and powers, he does not investigate its metaphysical dimensions. No attempt is made at locating the powers within the activity of the triune God, and therefore the usefulness of this cosmology for "locating" ecclesial moral discernment is limited. Yoder connects cosmological vision to Christian worship, yet he leaves unaddressed "the task of investigating and clarifying the ontological grounds for the practice of doxology."[96] By failing to make his theological convictions clear, Yoder leaves the rationale behind his call to worship ambiguous. Cosmology and metaphysics are inseparable.

The effects of this cosmological problem are best seen in the confusion caused by Yoder's use of the word "God." When Yoder writes God, what

---

94. Ibid., 131.

95. Ibid., 131–32. "'Patience' as Method in Moral Reasoning" was first printed in Hauweras et al., eds., *WC*, 24–42. An editorial note states that it was edited several times between 1982 and 1997 (24n1). It is difficult to read the above cited personal confession without recalling Yoder's own moral failings, and the public process of reconciliation he underwent in the 1990s. See Hauerwas, *Hannah's Child*, 242–47, for the most complete published report of these events.

96. Dintaman, "Socio-Ecclesial Brushpile," 43.

or who does he mean? How precisely is this God related to Jesus Christ? Because he did not explore the assumptions behind some of his basic theological terms, he muddles the process of moral discernment—do we follow the nonviolent Jesus, or the warrior God? Philip E. Stoltzfus suggests that Yoder's followers need to adopt a "theologically robust" form of conceptual construction to avoid internal contradictions that undermine faithful practice.[97] In other words, those who join debates over Yoder's cosmological pacifism must begin by questioning his definitions. They must begin by being more patient agents of linguistic self-awareness.

Memory: Slanted Scripture, Cynical Historiography

The results of Yoder's reduced cosmology and hasty words are on full display in his hermeneutical and historiographical practices. Ray Gingerich accuses Yoder of bringing an unexamined agenda to his interpretation of Old Testament holy war passages.[98] The need for those passages to cohere with the gospels overrules any critical appreciation of the frailty of the authors of the Torah. In the end, Torah and incarnation are left as competing sources of moral truth.[99] Gingerich sees Yoder's biblical realism as at fault here, for it "did not allow sufficient freedom to view scripture more dialogically, as the product of a fallible and faltering people of God—writings produced and preserved by communities in which power politics was at times more determinative than faithful prophecy and servanthood."[100] A constructive doctrine of God rooted in the nonviolence of Christ would allow for an alternative, critical reading of Israelite holy war. Other scholars raise similar concerns about Yoder's hermeneutical method. Richard B. Hays regards Yoder's reading of the New Testament *Haustafeln* passages in terms of "revolutionary subordination" as "apologetic wishful thinking."[101] According to Earl Zimmerman, Yoder displays "an inordinate confidence in his ability to read the Bible straight, without paying too much attention to historical and hermeneutical issues.[102] Mark Thiessen Nation furthermore wishes for deeper engagement with biblical scholarship.[103] It is notable that, aside

97. Stoltzfus, "Nonviolent Jesus," 41. See also Gingerich, "Yoder's God."

98. Gingerich, "Yoder's God," 427.

99. Ibid., 429.

100. Ibid., 432.

101. Hays, *Moral Vision*, 246. Cf. DeFerrari, "Review: *The Politics of Jesus.*" Like Gingerich, DeFerrari faults biblical realism here.

102. Zimmerman, *Politics of Jesus*, 200.

103. Nation, *John Howard Yoder*, 198–99.

from a few references in the second edition of *The Politics of Jesus*, Yoder's interaction with contemporary biblical scholarship seems to have ceased in the 1960s. Perhaps Yoder considered his post-critical turn as an excuse to neglect rigorous hermeneutical and exegetical labor; but this is not the purpose of biblical realism as he presents it. Yet biblical realism or some other source seems to have encouraged him toward a less critical, even eisegetical interpretive practice.[104] Such practice is neither biblically realistic, nor does it serve the church in truth.

Gingerich also worries that "Yoder seems to have had an innate urge to sacralize the Hebrew worldview."[105] For Gingerich, this urge is evident in his unwillingness to criticize Israelite holy wars. Gingerich does not consider that Yoder is consistently critical of Israelite kingship, as well as of Ezra's post-exilic restoration of Temple authority. But he does point to a recurring theme in criticisms of Yoder's position: a split between a positive "Hebrew" and a negative "Greek" worldview. A. James Reimer first raised this issue in his essay "The Nature and Possibility of Mennonite Theology."[106] Reimer contends that Yoder, especially in *Preface to Theology*, accepts an Enlightenment bifurcation between the ethically-focused Hebrews and the speculative Greeks. This interpretation actually reads modern historicism into the Hebraic—but in contrast to moderns, both the ancient Hebrews and Greeks believed in "an absolutely transcendent spiritual reality."[107] Yoder excises the spiritual from the Bible and so misses what Reimer later calls the "existential-sacramental" aspects of Jesus' message.[108] Stanley Hauerwas and Alex Sider make a similar point in their editorial introduction to Yoder's *Preface to Theology*, as does P. Travis Kroeker in a 2005 essay.[109] Yoder's avoidance of philosophical inquiry haunts him, as he uncritically embraces an outdated dualism that distorts his reading of scripture.

---

104. Gingerich, "Yoder's God," 431–32, further blames Yoder's loyalty to the Mennonite church as causing him to skew scripture. For similar arguments, see Leithart, *Defending Constantine*, 317–19; Reimer, *Mennonites and Classical Theology*, 178.

105. Gingerich, "Yoder's God," 432.

106. Reimer, *Mennonites and Classical Theology*, 171–72.

107. Ibid., 585n39.

108. Reimer, *Mennonites and Classical Theology*, 293. See also Swartley, "Jesus and Jubilee," 297, on Yoder's reading of Jesus' Jubilee proclamation in Luke 4. Swartley praises Yoder for recovering the ethical significance of this passage, but thinks he "short-changes" its personal and communal dimensions. Hays, *Moral Vision*, 246, and J. Zimmerman, "Yoder's Jesus and Economics," raise further questions about Yoder and Jubilee.

109. Hauerwas and Sider, "Introduction," in Yoder, *Preface*, 23–24; Kroeker, "Messianic Political Ethic," 147–48. Cf. Bourne, *Seek the Peace*, 93n54.

A related concern for Reimer is that Yoder seems to exclude in advance any reading of scripture that supports church institutions.[110] Reimer as well as Peter J. Leithart insist that Jesus' fulfillment of the Jewish law includes the civil law.[111] These critics and many others draw special attention to Yoder's interpretation of Jeremiah's call for the exiled Jews in Babylon to "seek the peace of the city" (Jer 29:7).[112] In spite of the vision of return to the land that immediately follows (29:10),[113] Yoder regards this call as definitively establishing landless diaspora as the normative political shape of Judaism and Christianity. John C. Nugent, who defends the general features of Yoder's interpretation, still admits that it rests on a "needlessly pejorative reading of palestinocentric existence, the city of Jerusalem, and the return from exile."[114] As mentioned, Yoder dismisses Israelite kingship and Ezra's restoration as distortions of the faithful politics of Abraham, the judges and prophets, and Jesus. Peter Ochs argues, however, that Yoder can only do so because he has generalized his reading of the gospels and is deaf to additional biblical themes. In doing so he draws "Jews and non-Anabaptist Christians into a sphere of already completed interpretive conclusions."[115] As a scribe of the kingdom, Yoder's cursory inspection of the storehouse leads him to pass over many of its treasures. This is not a mere "methodological" problem. Hermeneutical haste precludes dialogue and does violence to the interlocutor.

Yoder's historiography has been subjected to a similar range of criticisms. Reimer warns his Mennonite readers against Yoder's example of "selectively . . . read[ing] the Bible and history and undervalu[ing] the positive mandate for institutional life found in the biblical narrative as well as in our own Anabaptist-Mennonite heritage."[116] Critics have struggled with Yoder's reconstruction of Anabaptist origins since the publication of his dissertation in the 1960s. One influential response is from historian James M. Stayer. Although he acknowledges that Yoder's "writings establish him as the most effective polemicist among contemporary Mennonite thinkers,"

110. Reimer, "Positive Theology," 270.

111. Ibid., 245–73; Leithart, *Defending Constantine*, 133–36. See also Miller, "Footsteps of Marcion," 89–90.

112. Cartwright and Ochs in Yoder, *JCSR*, 29n68, 39–40, 158–59, 179, 203, 219, 222; Doerksen, *Beyond Suspicion*, 27, 46–50; Goldingay, *Israel's Gospel*, 764; Kissling, "Old Testament," 135–44; Leithart, *Defending Constantine*, 250n61, 293–97; Reimer, *Mennonites and Classical Theology*, 294; Schlabach, "Deuteronomic or Constantinian," 449–71.

113. Kissling suggests Daniel 9 as a more fitting support for Yoder's argument.

114. Nugent, "Biblical Warfare," 174.

115. Ochs in Yoder, *JCSR*, 159.

116. Reimer, "Positive Theology," 247.

he fears that the equation of the pacifist Swiss Brethren with normative Anabaptism "imposes on the disparate Anabaptist sects a consistency and a system which do not correspond to sixteenth-century realities."[117] Stayer identifies diversity among early Anabaptists in regards to the use of violence and civic authority to bring about reform. Even some of the Swiss Brethren were initially open to a "top down" reform given their alliance with Zwingli, who always saw reform as a cooperative effort with the Basel town council.[118] Pacifism only became a broad Anabaptist imperative when survival was at stake.[119] Yoder and other proponents of "Evangelical Anabaptism" read their theological ideals into the past at the expense of historical truthfulness.

For Yoder it is Stayer, rather, who fits the unsystematic "logic of events" into predetermined conceptual categories.[120] Stayer can only see two possible political stances, apolitical separatism and realpolitik—and the early Anabaptists were either one or the other. This framework precludes him from considering the possibility that sixteenth-century Anabaptists were mostly unconcerned with systematic political ethics, and were instead involved in a dialogical negotiation of their convictions. The seeds of normative Anabaptism are present from the start. But Hans-Jürgen Goertz responds that Yoder "appears to have missed the main point"—Stayer's categories are based on rigorous empirical research. It is Yoder's "systematized theological history which tends to abstract historical reality."[121] Anabaptist theologians do better to reflect on the objective findings of historians than to produce their own tendentious interpretations. Later Mennonite historians like C. Arnold

---

117. Stayer, *Anabaptists and the Sword*, 12–13. See also Stayer, Packull, and Deppermann, "Monogenesis to Polygenesis"; Stayer, "Reflections and Retractions"; Stayer, "Separatist Church of the Majority."

118. Stayer, *Anabaptists and the Sword*, 93. Stayer judges Yoder's reading of Zwingli's theology and politics as "willfully perverse," with "brilliant polemic" masking serious historiographical distortion (61n35, 65n44, 101n18). On the Zwingli debate see, in order of appearance, Yoder, "Turning Point in the Zwinglian Reformation"; Hillerbrand, "'Turning Point'"; Walton, *Zwingli's Theocracy*; Walton, "Was There a Turning Point of the Zwinglian Reformation?"; Yoder, "Evolution of the Zwinglian Reformation"; Harder, "Zwingli's Reaction to the Schleitheim Confession"; Snyder, "Birth and Evolution of Swiss Anabaptism," 503–37.

119. Stayer, *Anabaptists and the Sword*, 117–29. He acknowledges that Conrad Grebel and Felix Mantz were opposed to the sword and government from an early date (95, 102–5, 111), but denies that their position was representative of Swiss Anabaptism before Schleitheim.

120. Yoder, "'Anabaptists and the Sword' Revisited." Yoder is more sympathetic to Stayer here than to Clarence Bauman and Hans Hillerbrand, but still sees him as "theoretically committed to the systematic dualist definition of the question" (132).

121. Goertz, "History and Theology," 183.

Snyder are less convinced that history and theology can be so divided,[122] but still see Yoder as unduly twisting the former for the sake of the latter.[123] Analogous criticisms have been raised about Yoder's readings of the Jewish-Christian schism,[124] Constantine,[125] the creeds,[126] just war theory,[127] and scholasticism.[128] As Paul G. Doerksen argues, Yoder has a tendency toward "lumping" movements together that leads him to ignore historical subtleties for sweeping themes.[129] Others observe that Yoder's historiography favors dualistic, "essentialized" alternatives that do no justice to complex positions: positions Yoder likes are equated with his idealized Anabaptism, and those he dislikes with Constantinianism. For instance, Jewish theologians Daniel Boyarin and Peter Ochs receive no compliment from Yoder's construal of a single normative line of pacifistic, diasporic Judaism stretching from Jeremiah through Jesus to Theodore Herzl. Yoder inadvertently adopts a form of supersessionism by eliminating those aspects of Judaism that do not conform to his understanding of Jesus and Anabaptism. Paul Martens worries that a similar logic is at work in Yoder's writings on Hindu, Protestant, and Roman Catholic nonviolent movements.[130]

---

122. Recent attempts to synthesize a coherent Anabaptist theology in light of diverse origins include Finger, *Contemporary Anabaptist Theology*; Snyder, "Beyond Polygenesis"; and J. D. Weaver, *Becoming Anabaptist*. See also Paul Toews, "Mennonite Search for a Useable Past."

123. Snyder's contention is with Yoder's reading of Schleitheim as a broadly normative, non-separatist Anabaptist document. Snyder, "Editor's Preface," in Yoder *ARSS*, xxxviii; "Influence of the Schleitheim Articles," 323–44 ; "Revolution of the Common Man," 429.

124. Boyarin, "Judaism as a Free Church"; Cartwright and Ochs in Yoder, *JCSR*; A. E. Weaver, *States of Exile*, 25–40.

125. Leithart's arguments are discussed below. See also Doerksen, *Beyond Suspicion*, 141–48; Reimer, *Mennonites and Classical Theology*, 259–71; Sider, *History and Holiness*, 81–117.

126. Reimer, *Mennonites and Classical Theology*, 259–71; Kroeker, "Messianic Political Ethic," 152.

127. Doerksen, *Beyond Suspicion*, 206; Wiebe, "Evangelical Recognitions of Christ," 304–5.

128. Brubacher Kaethler, "Practice of Reading the Other," 47–54.

129. Doerksen, *Beyond Suspicion*, 27. Cf. Cartwright, "Sharing the House of God," 605, on Yoder's purely synchronic historiography.

130. Martens, Porter, and Werntz, "Introduction," in Yoder, *Nonviolence*, 11–12. Martens also suggests that Yoder threatens the integrity of the academic disciplines of biology, history, politics, and sociology by co-opting them for support of his particular reading of nonviolence. One assumes that Marten objects less to Yoder's use of various disciplines and figures to make an argument, and more to the reified way in which they are deployed.

Yoder's enemies fare no better. Peter J. Leithart has written an extensive defense of Constantine against Yoder, and his concerns resonate with the greater chorus of critics. On Leithart's reading, Constantine is an exemplar of Yoder's own theology of good governance.[131] He ended Roman sacrificial practice; banned gladiatorial games; extended justice to the poor; increased religious tolerance; promoted Christian unity over his personal theological preferences; and (sometimes) subordinated imperial warmongering to ecclesial mission.[132] Constantine was far from perfect, but he was a man like all of us slowly working out the implications of his salvation. Just before he died he laid aside the imperial purple, received baptism, and prepared to dedicate himself to the church.[133] Yoder is oblivious to all of this. His Anabaptist "fall of the church" narrative ahistorically reaches back to the early church and disavows the possibility of faithful contextual development.[134] He repudiates the primary historical source on Constantine, Eusebius of Caesarea, as captive to a "univocal" interpretation of history, but then sees that trait reproduced throughout the west up to Hegel—as if the reduction of fifteen hundred years of intellectual history to one word is not itself univocal.[135] This homogenizing historiography is quintessentially "Constantinian," as is Yoder's apparent conviction that rulers indeed do direct history: if Christ and the church are at the center of history, then why is Yoder so obsessed with Constantine?[136] His historiography is controlled neither by a proper apocalyptic vision, nor by a corresponding patience. The faithfulness and effectiveness of his contributions to Christian moral discernment are questionable.

Acknowledging criticism does not mean abandoning Yoder altogether, and his readings of Jesus, exile, church history, and Paul and the powers are still widely accepted as important, if incomplete, contributions.[137] His

131. Leithart, *Constantine*, 200–201.

132. Ibid., 97–254.

133. Ibid., 297–300.

134. Ibid., 181–83, 315n20, 317–19. Leithart is also unconvinced by Yoder's reading of a "pacifist consensus" in the early church (256–78, 265–67). Leithart's outlines his own hermeneutical approach in *Deep Exegesis*.

135. Leithart, *Constantine*, 316n22, on Yoder, *FTN*, 70.

136. Leithart, *Constantine*, 317–21. Leithart also argues that Anabaptist primitivism is *literally* Constantinian insofar as it was Eusebius who generated the myth of the pristine church in order to call post-Constantinian Christians to obedience (319).

137. Blough, "Historical Roots"; Boyarin, "Judaism as a Free Church"; Cartwright and Ochs, "Editors' Introduction," in Yoder, *JCSR*, 1–29; Harink, "The Anabaptist and the Apostle"; Harink, *Paul among the Postliberals*, 105–49; Heilke, "Theological and Secular"; Hays, *Moral Vision*, 239–53; Kissling, "Old Testament," 130–35; Klassen, "Jesus and the Zealot Option"; Nugent, "Biblical Warfare Revisited"; Nugent, "'Trial and Error'"; Smith-Christopher, *Biblical Theology of Exile*, 6–15; Stassen, "Sermon on the

legendary "patience," moreover, has become the focus of a growing body of literature.[138] Yet the criticisms cannot be ignored: Yoder's linguistic omissions and faulty memory raise serious questions about his sociological theology. Several of Yoder's critics maintain that Yoder's theology continues to be a powerful tool for the church, but it needs to be made more consistent, if not subjected to constructive systematization.[139] As seen above, even the friendliest of critics call for greater cosmological, linguistic, hermeneutical, and historiographical coherence. Nonetheless, both its proponents and its critics see the lack of a grand system as central to Yoder's legacy. Writing against Nancey Murphy's systematic account of Yoder's pacifism, Chris K. Huebner argues that it "fails to appreciate that Yoder's ad hoc, nonsystematic way of operating is crucial to the very substance of his pacifist theological position."[140] Murphy "cancels Yoder's understanding of the priority of ecclesiology to epistemology by reasserting the Enlightenment dogma of epistemological primacy."[141] Instead of systems, we should accept Yoder's nonsystematic approach and read his *oeuvre* "as a series of thick descriptions of social practices . . . that collectively define a particular stance or way of life called church."[142]

Whether or not Huebner is fair to Murphy's effort,[143] some methodological adjustment is called for if the distorting infelicities of Yoder's ap-

---

Plain"; Swartley, "Smelting for Gold"; A. E. Weaver, *States of Exile*; N. T. Wright, *Jesus and the Victory of God*, 294.

138. Blum, "Yoder's Patience"; Brubacher Kaethler, "Practice of Reading the Other," 57–60; Coles, *Beyond Gated Politics*, 109–38; Huebner, *Precarious Peace*, 115–32; Ollenburger and Koontz, eds., *Mind Patient and Untamed*.

139. Doerksen, *Beyond Suspicion*, 26–27; Schlabach, "Anthology in Lieu of System"; Stoltzfus, "Nonviolent Jesus," 38–42; Zimmerman, *Politics of Jesus*, 198.

140. Huebner, *Precarious Peace*, 107. See Murphy, "Yoder's Systematic Defence of Christian Pacifism," 45–68. Murphy endorses Yoder's view that theology should not "be driven by any philosophical or systematic motivations," but suggests that others can draw out the systematic implications of his thought to better defend it (45). She argues that the "hard core" of Yoder's research project is: "the moral character of God is revealed in Jesus' vulnerable enemy love and renunciation of dominion. Imitation of Jesus in this regard constitutes a *social* ethic" (48).

141. Huebner, *Precarious Peace*, 107.

142. Ibid., 108.

143. For Murphy, viable intellectual systems are developing products of living communities. Internal to their structures as "research projects" is continuing flexibility and indeed vulnerability to the vicissitudes of lived ecclesial reality. Huebner's objection may be that it is wrong to specify a hard core for Yoder's project, but it is difficult not to see something like Murphy's account operating behind the various "thick descriptions." Murphy's Lakatosian systemization of Yoder's thought should be read in light of her appreciation of Alasdair MacIntyre's epistemology. See her *Anglo-American Postmodernity*, 52–62. See also Schlabach's argument that the effect of anti-foundationalism is not

proach are to be avoided. Put more bluntly, if Yoder's work is to continue to serve the church in the way he envisioned, its defects will have to be resolved, and that resolution entails some form of intellectual coherence. Huebner rightly demands that extensions of Yoder's thought take his (a)methodology seriously. For Yoder methodological mixing and matching is intrinsic to the vocation of the theologian, which is to privilege the demands of concrete moral situations faced by the church over intellectual systems. The issue is once again between adequate theological construction and faithful ethical service. The present chapter places Pierre Bourdieu's reflexive sociology in the methodological mix. Bourdieu offers resources for a more coherent and nuanced theological methodology that is rigorously attentive to concrete ecclesial realities.

Bourdieu's Reflexive Sociology

Like Yoder, Bourdieu is suspicious of methodological discussion and theoretical systemization that does not serve practical ends. "Those who push methodological concern to the point of obsession," he suggests, "are like Freud's patient who spent all his time cleaning his spectacles and never put them on."[144] Bourdieu's early methodological treatise, written with Jean-Claude Chamboredon and Jean-Claude Passeron for classes in sociological epistemology in the mid-1960s, is accordingly entitled *Le métier du sociologue* (translated as *The Craft of Sociology*).[145] The words *métier* and craft are meant to evoke a set of creative habits oriented toward production—a research habitus rather than a theory of research.[146] The sociological habitus Bourdieu and his co-authors propose requires, in short, a break from common sense language and concepts, systematic theoretical construction, and testing and revision of these constructions through empirical research. This "applied rationalism" is offered as an alternative to regnant positivist and theoreticist epistemologies and methodologies. The benefits of applied rationalism are identified for statistical and ethnographic methods, as well as for sociological science as a whole.

---

to rule out systems as such, but to point out their historical embeddedness. In that case systematizers and nonsystematizers are on a level playing field ("Anthology in Lieu of System," 308–9).

144. Bourdieu, Chamboredon, and Passeron, *CS*, 5.

145. For information on the production and context of *CS*, see Bourdieu's interview from 1988 that closes the English edition (247–59).

146. Bourdieu, *IRS*, 139, 222.

Excerpts from exemplary philosophical and sociological texts are included in *The Craft of Sociology*, but Bourdieu later came to regret not simply offering a number of "master works" in the style of a medieval crafts-man.[147] It was too easy for readers to treat the book as a new master theory instead of a prompt to masterful practice.[148] Even so, Bourdieu consistently affirms the arguments of *Craft*,[149] and it remains useful as a presentation of his methodology. The first part of this section accordingly summarizes *Craft*, taking note of later elaborations and modifications. Bourdieu does suggest that, were he to write the book again, he would place much greater emphasis on the closing comments on "the sociology of sociology."[150] As this sociological reflexivity became a major preoccupation of Bourdieu's later years, the second part of this section treats it in detail.

Applied Rationalism: The Epistemological Break

In *The Craft of Sociology*, Bourdieu and his co-authors describe their epistemology as falling between the extremes of idealism and realism: it is an "applied rationalism."[151] This middle ground "alone can yield the full truth of scientific practice by closely associating the 'values of coherence' and 'fidelity to the real.'"[152] The values of coherence are associated with idealists. In the sociological tradition, idealism is associated with the great theoretical system builders such as Talcott Parsons and Robert K. Merton.[153] For Bourdieu, their problem is precisely that they treat sociology as a tradition. They see their task as integrating past sociological theories into a whole, not

147. Bourdieu, *CS*, 256.

148. Cf. also the 1972 preface to the second French edition, where the authors note their refusal to turn the book into a programmatic pedagogical text, lest it be confused with a new, eternal methodological alternative.

149. See Schinkel, "Bourdieu's Political Turn?," 70. The most sustained accusation of methodological inconsistency comes from Mayer, "L'entretien selon Pierre Bourdieu," who sees Bourdieu, *WW*, as a betrayal of the approach outlined in *CS*.

150. Bourdieu in Bourdieu, Chamboredon, and Passeron, *CS*, 257.

151. Ibid., part 3.

152. Ibid., 66. In Wittgensteinian fashion, the authors name realism and idealism as a co-dependent "epistemological couple" which must be broken (66–67). However, there are several critics who suggest that he should embrace (critical) realism: Evens, "Logic of Practice"; Maton, "Epistemic Conditions"; Sayer, "Disinterested Judgment", Vandenbergh, "'The Real is Relational.'" And there are some who say he already does: Fowler, "Bourdieu's 'Understanding,'" 7–11; Outwaithe, "Myth of Modernist Method." As previously stated, the (Wittgensteinian) perspective taken in this thesis is that such debates are ultimately interminable and unhelpful.

153. Ibid., 15, 27.

performing detailed empirical studies that could give substance to their theories.[154] On the other side are the positivist realists, like Paul Lazerfeld, who likewise treat sociological theory as a tradition, but one to be rejected as a whole in favor of quantitative analysis. Yet without some coherent theory to make sense of their data—not to mention their research practices—there is no way to verify their findings.[155] As Bourdieu would put it later, "plagiarizing" Kant, "theory without empirical research is empty, empirical research without theory is blind."[156]

Applied rationalism, by contrast, is a dialectical approach that includes both theory construction and its testing through empirical research. The purpose of both sides of the dialectic is to effect an "epistemological break" from everyday, common sense knowledge of the social world.[157] Without the break, sociology simply affirms common sense—thereby putting its status as a social science in doubt. Scientific practice consists neither in the organization of theoretical speculations, nor in the compilation of random facts. For Bourdieu, tutored in the Bachelardian philosophy of science by Georges Canguilhem, the logic of science is a "logic of error."[158] Scientific discovery occurs after the recognition that a phenomenon is not adequately accounted for by received understandings. A new hypothesis is formulated to account for the phenomenon, and that hypothesis is tested experimentally. If that hypothesis is found to account better for the phenomenon, it replaces the old understanding—but only until errors are identified in it and another hypothesis constructed to replace it. There can therefore never be a single timeless scientific method.[159] There can only be provisionally confirmed theories awaiting disconfirmation and supersession. Theories are heuristic tools that allow for a more or less adequate conception of the aspect of reality for which they were constructed. Theoretical construction, methodological review, and empirical research are not ends in themselves, but part of an epistemological break that

154. Ibid., *CS*, 26–29. In his interview on *CS*, Bourdieu says his primary "theoreticist" target was the Frankfurt school and its French epigone Lucien Goldmann (248). See also Bourdieu, *IRS*, 69.

155. Bourdieu, Chamboredon, and Passeron, *CS*, 29, 35–38, 63–64, 70–72. See also Bourdieu, *HA*, 31; *IRS*, 235–36.

156. Bourdieu, "Vive la crise!," 774–75.

157. Bourdieu, Chamboredon, and Passeron, *CS*, 13.

158. Ibid., 3. This epistemological tradition was widely introduced into the English-speaking world by Kuhn's *Structure of Scientific Revolutions*, which drew from Alexandre Koyré in constructing the concept of a paradigm shift. On Bourdieu's relationship to Kuhn and the philosophy of science, see Callewaert, "Bourdieu, Critic of Foucault," 85, and Fowler, "Autonomy, Reciprocity, and Science," 105–6. The influence of Bachelard on Bourdieu's reflexive sociology cannot be overestimated.

159. Bourdieu, Chamboredon, and Passeron, *CS*, 4.

aims to increase human knowledge of the real. Fidelity to the real is not realized without the values of coherence.

"*The preconstructed is everywhere*," as Bourdieu would put it in a later writing.[160] A Cartesian method of radically doubting common sense is necessary if sociology is to make the epistemological break consistently. In *The Craft of Sociology* and through his empirical studies, Bourdieu advocates for a unified social anthropology that would critically employ the best statistical and observational techniques to achieve the break and scientifically construct social facts.[161] This language of social facts recalls Durkheim's "first and most basic rule" of sociological method: "*to consider social facts as things*."[162] Considering social facts as things means considering them as independent of the individual human will; they in fact determine the will.[163] To identify them, the sociologist must discard her preconceptions of the social and investigate isolated, rigorously defined groups of phenomena.[164] Bourdieu and his co-authors interpret Durkheim as describing a scientifically productive way of seeing social phenomena and not as making an ontological statement.[165] Just as Galileo's view of physical entities as "a system of quantifiable relationships" birthed modern physics, and Saussure's distinction between *langue* and *parole* made the discipline of linguistics possible, so Durkheim's turn to constructed social facts is the sociological revolution.

Seeing the social world as a collection of social facts is to begin to see it as a system of relations. In *The Craft of Sociology*, Bourdieu describes analogical reasoning as the "principle of construction of the relations between relations."[166] The manner in which related scientific disciplines, such as linguistics, anthropology or biology, depict the relations between the objects they study is a useful starting point for developing sociological hypotheses. Analogically constructed hypothetical systems of relations can be developed into generalized models, and each model acts as a "miniature theory" that can be tested scientifically (52–55). Empirical sociological research is then a form of experimentation, "a permanent reminder of the reality principle"

160. Bourdieu, *IRS*, 235.

161. Bourdieu, Chamboredon, and Passeron, *CS*, 45; Bourdieu, "Participant Objectivation," 293. The original French title of *Invitation to Reflexive Sociology* is *Réponses: Pour une anthropologie réflexive*.

162. Durkheim, *Rules of Sociological Method*, 60.

163. Ibid., 70. As discussed in chapter 2 above, Bourdieu's acceptance of the formation of the habitus by social fields does not lead him to embrace a total determinism.

164. Durkheim, *Rules of Sociological Method*, 75–85.

165. Bourdieu, Chamboredon, and Passeron, *CS*, 33–34.

166. Bourdieu, Chamboredon, and Passeron, *CS*, 50. In this and the following paragraph references to *CS* are in the text.

(61). The attempt to confirm a theory with data reveals flaws in the theory, which then allows for theoretical revision. The method is deductive (54) or, in the terms of Anglo-American philosophers of science, hypothetico-deductive.[167] Theory is important because only a systematic, coherent body of concepts can be falsified by experimentation; and experimentation is important, because only it can falsify theory (63–64).

Bourdieu recognizes that the view of the social world as a set of objective relations is not agreeable to those who see society primarily as a set of individuals consciously choosing their actions *de novo* at each moment. The "principle of non-consciousness" is indeed at the root of sociology, a methodological determinism that enables the construction of sociological objects (16). Because relations are fundamental, the sociologist must "reject all attempts to define the truth of a cultural phenomenon independently of the system of historical and social relations in which it is located" (19).

In order to construct the systems of relations, a number of research tools are helpful. Statistics, field observation, and questionnaires all contribute to the break from a common sense understanding of a phenomenon and its scientific reconstruction as a system of relations. But Bourdieu and his co-authors caution that each tool carries a theory about the nature of the social world and the way in which it can be known. In other words, each tool is more or less successful in effecting the break. Random statistical sampling, for instance, treats the social world as a group of acontextual individuals.[168] Bourdieu, who worked extensively with leading French mathematicians and statisticians in his research, prefers multivariate analysis, and especially multiple correspondence analysis, as it allows for the modeling of statistical relationships between all the relevant variables in complex social ecologies.[169] Likewise, Bourdieu recommends conversational interviews based on extensive prior observation over the dominant practice of non-directive interviews.[170] The artificiality of non-directive interviews can only produce "artefacts," showing only how interviewees respond to questions and questioners foreign to their

167. See Murphy and Ellis, *Moral Nature*, 8–10, on Carl Hempel's hypothetico-deductive method.

168. Bourdieu, Chamboredon, and Passeron, *CS*, 39–40.

169. Ibid., 14, 40, 45n27, 46–47, 65, 254; Bourdieu, *IRS*, 96. Correspondence and multiple correspondence analyses are types of multivariate analysis that developed out of Jean-Paul Benzecri's work in the late 1960s. On Bourdieu's statistics, see Griller, "Return of the Subject?," 8–10; Heinich, *Pourquoi Bourdieu*, 45–47; Lebaron, "Economic Models," 555–58; Rouanet, Ackerman, and Le Roux, "L'analyse géométrique"; Sanders and Robson, "Quantifying Bourdieu"; Seibel, "Bourdieu et les statisticians."

170. Bourdieu, Chamboredon, and Passeron, *CS*, 41–46. On Bourdieu's interview method, see Griller, "Return of the Subject?," 10–12; Mayer, "L'entretien selon Pierre Bourdieu."

social contexts. Encounters rooted in familiarity have a better chance of elicit-ing useful knowledge of interviewees' practices. Questionnaires suffer from similar problems, and the implications of each question, and especially the taxonomy of questions, should be carefully controlled.

Although the tools just discussed are highly technical, Bourdieu lo-cates their foundations in the logical and lexical critique of common lan-guage analysis.[171] Common sense understandings are expressed in words, and technical sociological tools are sophisticated means for exposing their assumptions and offering alternative constructions. Historical analysis of words and concepts likewise brings their theoretical resonances to the sur-face. Bourdieu did not emphasize historical tools in *Craft*, but they later became prominent in his research. "There is no more potent tool for rup-ture," he would write in the 1990s, "than the reconstruction of genesis."[172] Words have histories. Forgetting them is to treat them as expressions of an unquestionable grasp on the world. For Bourdieu, the discipline of philoso-phy is the exemplar *par excellence* of the "forgetting or denial of history."[173] Sociologists are to break from philosophy with their radically doubting ap-plied rationalism.

Reflexivity: Radical Doubt Radicalized

The Craft of Sociology concludes with a call for the "sociology of sociology": the path to a reliably preconception-free sociology is only through the appli-cation of sociological tools to sociology itself.[174] Over twenty years later, in Bourdieu's other sustained methodological reflection, *Invitation to Reflexive Sociology*, he would identify reflexivity as the hallmark of his sociology: "I believe that if the sociology I propose differs in any significant way from the other sociologies of the past and of the present, it is above all in that it *continually turns back onto itself the scientific weapons it produces*."[175] Des-cartes' radical doubt was insufficient, as it failed to question the social basis of the philosophical mode of thought.[176] As Bourdieu put it in *Pascalian*

171. Bourdieu, Chamboredon, and Passeron, CS, 14, 21–24.

172. Bourdieu, PR, 40. In CS, Bourdieu, Chamboredon, and Passeron do offer a brief history of positivism in French sociology (70–72).

173. Bourdieu, PM, 30–31.

174. Bourdieu, Chamboredon, and Passeron, CS, 69.

175. Bourdieu, IRS, 214.

176. Bourdieu, IRS, 241.

Meditations, his final review of and break from philosophical categories for the social world, radical doubt must be radicalized.[177]

Even before *The Craft of Sociology*, Bourdieu had already begun to practice a kind of reflexivity. During his Algerian fieldwork he recognized that many of his basic intuitions about Kabyle culture had their origins in his rural upbringing in Béarn, in southwest France.[178] He therefore began to carry out simultaneous research in Béarn in order to convert those intuitions into disciplined tools for research. *The Logic of Practice*, perhaps Bourdieu's most advanced theoretical statement, reworks the conclusions of his Algerian studies, from *Outline of a Theory of Practice*, in view of his work in Béarn. It offers a reflexive theory of practice that accounts for its author's predisposition to conceive of practice in certain ways rather than others.

After leaving Algeria in the early 1960s, Bourdieu's reflexive discipline was turned to the education system that produced him. *Les Héritiers*, *The State Nobility* and his other educational studies all examine socio-economic and cultural forces behind academic success. The high point of this reflexivity came in *Homo Academicus*, where he studied correlations between the social and cultural backgrounds of French professors and their political views on the May 1968 student rebellion.[179] Although *The Inheritors* contributed to the student unrest, and he was in broad sympathy with Foucault and the other professors who supported the protests, Bourdieu himself did not man the barricades.[180] As Derek Robbins points out, Bourdieu well inhabits the category of an "oblate," defined in *Homo Academicus* as a career academic who, due to his low social origins, owes everything to the system.[181] He was only "able to resist conservatism as a result of his capacity to understand his situation," i.e., through the reflexivity of works like *Homo Academicus*. Bourdieu states that the purpose of that book is "to trap *Homo Academicus*, supreme classifier among classifiers in the net of his own classifications."[182] In doing so, he of course traps himself, and so increases his awareness of and control over the academic common sense that shapes his research.

A few years before writing *Homo Academicus*, Bourdieu published a short essay entitled "Sur la objectivation participante."[183] There he expands

177. Bourdieu, *PM*, 28–32.

178. Bourdieu, "Participant Objectification," 288.

179. Bourdieu, *HA*, xi, portrays the book as the culmination of a reflexive project that began with his Béarn studies.

180. Schinkel, "Bourdieu's Political Turn?," 81; Swartz, "Critical Sociology," 792.

181. Robbins, "Epistemological 'Break,'" 39, on Bourdieu, *HA*, 291.

182. Bourdieu, *HA*, xi.

183. Bourdieu, "Sur l'objectivation participante," 67–69. See also his "Vive la crise!" 74; *IRS*, 260; "Participant Objectification," 281–94.

upon the comments in *The Craft of Sociology* about a form of ethnographic research that would account for the social gap between observer and observed better than the supposed neutrality of participant observation. The success of the effort to objectify the observed, he argued, depended on a parallel objectivation of the point of view of the observer.[184] Only participant objectivation can escape the false choice between the "mystified immersion" of participant observation and a mythic all-seeing objectivism. Although he does not use the phrase there, Bourdieu would return to participant objectivation as an interview methodology in *The Weight of the World*. In his closing essay on "Understanding," he describes his research team's construction of a method of *"active and methodical listening"* that evades symbolic violence as much as possible by employing interviewers who share a similar background to interviewees and who have studied that background thoroughly.[185] A "double socioanalysis" is made possible, as the researcher is implicated in her interviewees' responses.[186] Although this method may seem highly subjective, distortions can be avoided so long as the sociologist is willing to practice the "permanent control of the point of view."[187] Reflexive knowledge of the self is a condition of adequate knowledge of the other.

Elsewhere, Bourdieu discusses the history of sociology as another necessary component of the sociology of sociology.[188] Although he did not write an extensive history, at various points he addressed critically the origins of French sociology in philosophy and Christian humanism.[189] As mentioned, *Pascalian Meditations* is an especially trenchant break from sociology's philosophical past.

Disciplinary history, participant objectivation, and study of one's own familial and academic context, therefore, all serve as tools for sociological reflexivity. Each is a means for sociologists to break from the common sense that inhabits their research practices. Bourdieu's identification of his sociology with this type of reflexivity, and his zealous advocacy for it, have struck some

184. Bourdieu, "Sur l'objectivation participante," 67.

185. Bourdieu, *WW*, 609–10.

186. Ibid., 612. Bourdieu often discussed his sociology, and especially sociological reflexivity, in therapeutic terms. See, e.g., Bourdieu, "Introduction à la socioanalyse"; *IRS*, 49–50, 62–74; *SSA*.

187. Bourdieu, *WW*, 625–26. Bourdieu is partly inspired and partly forewarned by the linguistic studies of William Labov, who used black Harlem youths as interviewers in his study of black Harlem dialect. According to Bourdieu, Labov did not subject his interviewers to rigorous training, nor had they objectified their context, leading to highly subjective interviews.

188. Bourdieu, *PR*, 39.

189. Bourdieu, Chamboredon, and Passeron, *CS*, 70–72, 251.

observers as beside the point. Reflexive review of one's practices is a built-in feature of human consciousness, some argue, and does not require special sociological tools.[190] Others maintain that Bourdieu is simply describing the basic research competence taught to every sociologist.[191] Whatever the case may be, Bourdieu nowhere reviews systematically alternative conceptions of reflexivity in order to distinguish his own.[192] He is not altogether reflexive about his concept of reflexivity. Nevertheless, he is clear about the sources of his passion for reflexivity: the special vulnerability of the sociologist and the potential fruitfulness of rigorous scientific reflexivity.

In *The Craft of Sociology*, Bourdieu and his co-authors warn that "the sociologist . . . is vulnerable to the illusion of immediate self-evidence or the temptation to unconsciously universalize particular experience when he forgets that he is the cultivated subject of a particular culture and fails to subordinate his practice to a continuous questioning of this relationship."[193] In particular, sociologists often overlook how their "class *ethos*" shapes their understanding of social reality, and how academic fads direct their research interests.[194] Because the object of sociology, society, is a constant subject of common debate, it is often very difficult for sociologists to separate themselves from spurious modes of social thought. But because sociology does, at times, carry scientific prestige, it becomes doubly difficult to escape common social sense when an audience demands "prophetic" vision about weighty topics such as "the future of civilization."[195] Sociologists must fortify themselves and refuse the social essences offered up by popular debates—even when these debates are supplied by past sociology. Concepts like "multiculturalism," "race," "globalization,"[196] "pure

---

190. Crossley, *Social Body*, 117; Lynch, "Against Reflexivity."

191. Griller, "Return of the Subject?," 12–14; Lynch, "Against Reflexivity," 34–35.

192. Jenkins, *Pierre Bourdieu*, 109. Typologies of reflexivity are offered by Holland, "Reflexivity"; Lash, "Modernization and Postmodernization," 258–59; Lynch, "Against Reflexivity," 27–34.

193. Bourdieu, Chamboredon, and Passeron, *CS*, 72.

194. Ibid., 73–74. The authors want "to encourage a systematic prejudice against all fashionable ideas and to make an allergy to modishness a rule for the direction of the sociological mind."

195. Ibid., 24–25,

196. These terms are disputed in Bourdieu, *Acts of Resistance*, 29–44; Bourdieu and Wacquant, "Cunning of Imperialist Reason." See Hanchard, "Acts of Misrecognition," for a vitriolic response to the latter.

art,"[197] and even "reason"[198] and "the state"[199] must be subjected to socio-historical review.

Bourdieu notes that sociologists who supply and/or rely on official state statistics are especially prone to accepting official categories without criticism: "thought on the state (*pensée de l'État*) is always liable to be a state thought (*pensée d'État*)."[200] This problem can be seen for instance with legally accepted definitions of "the family."[201] Sociologists who do not at least question the identification of a family with heterosexual marriage, childbearing, and a shared domicile are blind to the various moral and practical issues raised by homosexuality, divorce, and cohabitation. Moreover, any sociological treatment of the state must be willing to ask, "*what if the state was nothing but a word, upheld by collective belief?* A word which contributes to making us believe in the existence and unity of this scattered and divided ensemble of organs of rule which cabinets, ministries, departments, administrative directions, bureaus of this and that are."[202] The reflexive sociologist gives up the certainties of the "illusory quest for an ontological foundation" and constructively explores the relational constitution of reality.[203]

Bourdieu promises great reward for those who endure on the path of reflexivity. Rather than being prey to the state and common sense, the reflexive sociologist has the opportunity to become "the *subject* of the problems she can pose about the social world"[204] She can begin to think the social world for herself, instead of allowing the social world to think through her.[205] Yet she cannot do it alone. "The gains from epistemological reflection cannot be really embodied in practice until the social conditions are established for epistemological control," that is, for a fully reflexive scientific field.[206] The sociology of sociology and of other disciplines enables a generalized conflict of the faculties to reign. Institutional inertia gives way and the scientific community moves "closer to the ideal city of scientists, in which, ideally, all the scientific communications required by science and

197. Bourdieu, "Pure Aesthetic."

198. Bourdieu, *PM*, 93–127. The historicity of reason is treated further in the following two chapters below.

199. Bourdieu, *PR*, 36–56; "Reason of State."

200. Bourdieu in Wacquant, "Ruling Class," 40. Bourdieu names Durkheim as an obvious example of a "civil-servant sociologist (*sociologue-fonctionnaire*)."

201. Bourdieu, "Des familles sans nom"; "On the Family."

202. Bourdieu in Wacquant, "Ruling Class," 41.

203. Bourdieu, *PM*, 121.

204. Bourdieu, *IRS*, 240.

205. Bourdieu in Wacquant, "From Ruling Class," 40.

206. Bourdieu, Chamboredon, and Passeron, *CS*, 74.

the progress of science, and only those, would be able to take place."[207] Reflexivity does not offer an absolute, position-less view of the social world, but it can produce scientific knowledge.[208] The freedom gained by reflexive sociologists to know themselves and know the world is a kind of "collective conversion."[209] The liberated scientific community can act as a model for and goad to a free and rational political community—and this political goal, ultimately, is the purpose of Bourdieu's reflexive sociology.[210]

Revising Yoder's Theological Method

Bourdieu's reflexive sociology is premised on the break from the common sense of and about the social world. Everyday practical reason is to be objectified and so purified by social science—especially when it is the scientist's own practical reason.[211] One possible summary of the problems with Yoder's theological method is that he does not make the objectifying break. His language and memory are too indebted to Anabaptist common sense and he fails to question preconceived essences such as "Constantinianism," "ethics," "metaphysics," and "the state." Yet Yoder's theology is explicitly a servant of ecclesial processes of practical moral reasoning. Does this focus not put him and Bourdieu at irreconcilable odds?

The previous section concluded with the observation that the purpose of Bourdieu's reflexive sociology is political. Its goal is practical, but an improved practice stripped as far as possible of its tendencies to reproduce domination. Reflexive sociology aims to bring about a purified reason, but not a reason that escapes history and the realm of empirical practice: a pure practical reason. To the extent that Yoder's doxological theology is oriented toward a more faithful discipleship, it too can be viewed as a kind of purifying practical reason. The theologian's task within the church is not to leave it as it is, nor to affirm ecclesial common sense as always already adequate. As an agent of prophecy, linguistic self-consciousness, and memory, the theologian breaks from preconstructed theological concepts and critically constructs new ones suitable for a situation. Some of Yoder's corrective

207. Ibid., 76.

208. Bourdieu, *HA*, 31; *PM*, 118–22.

209. Bourdieu, *Les usages sociaux de la science*, 58. See also his *HA*, 15–16; *IRS*, 251–52; *WW*, 612–15; "Participant Objectivation," 292.

210. The title of the second part of *IRS* is "The Purpose of Reflexivity," and it contains a call for a "*Realpolitik* of reason" directed by reflexivity (174–201). The political nature of reflexivity is treated in the following two chapters below.

211. Bourdieu, *IRS*, 247.

theological constructions are "the politics of Jesus," "body politics," and "the war of the lamb." In each case, Yoder takes familiar ecclesial texts, language, history, and practices, and identifies new relations among them. These relations are not constructed haphazardly or without guiding hypotheses.

Although Yoder labels his approach as inductive, his explanation of his research process is deductive, as theological patterns arise in response to specific questions brought to texts and other theological data. When discussing, for instance, his discovery of a pattern among New Testament authors' translated contemporary cosmological concepts, he does not say that the pattern occurred to him as he was combing through the scriptures at random. Rather, the pattern "fell into place as I was reading the New Testament *with a view to standard questions about how a small faith community can claim that its message is pertinent to a wider world*."[212] His interpretation of the Gospel of Luke in *The Politics of Jesus*, likewise, is not the result of a presuppositionless scouring of the text: "I propose to read the Gospel narrative with the constantly pressing question, 'Is there here a social ethic?' I shall, in other words, be testing a hypothesis that runs counter to the prevalent assumptions: the hypothesis that the ministry and the claims of Jesus are best understood as presenting to hearers and readers not the avoidance of political options, but one particular socio-political-ethical option."[213] This method is not inductive. Yoder breaks from theological common sense by testing alternative hypotheses against scripture. He is engaged in a deductive process of "theory" construction, whether he likes it or not.[214]

Recognition of the deductive process at work in Yoder's research practice opens avenues for dialogue with Bourdieu's reflexive sociology. Yoder's break from common ecclesial reasoning mostly occurs through common language analysis and broad alternative readings of ecclesial history. As Leithart and many others contend, Yoder's historiography requires far more precision if it is to be convincing. Sometimes his dualistic logical analysis seems to get in the way of textured interpretations of events. At this point

212. Yoder, *THW*, 143, emphasis added.

213. Yoder, *PJ*, 11.

214. One obvious point of divergence between Yoder and Bourdieu is their primary audience and object—the church for Yoder, the state for Bourdieu. This makes a difference insofar as Yoder is committed to the entire church, as is, having methodological input (in the "open meeting"), whereas Bourdieu's democratic secular politics requires a process of education to prepare citizens for critical participation. Several of Bourdieu's critics have accused him of sociological elitism at this point: Geldof, "Bourdieu and the Aesthetic Judgment of Kant," 37; Griller, "Return of the Subject?," 19–20; Lapeyronnie, "L'académisme radical"; Verdès-Leroux, *Le savant et la politique*. However, any alternative political program requires training and, as will be discussed in chapter 5 below, it is possible to see Yoder's "ecclesial practices" as such a training program.

Bourdieu's dense, focused sociological investigations of various phenomena are a helpful model. The careful social histories he produced at the end of his life are likewise exemplary. Adopting the relational thinking at the heart of these studies would, furthermore, encourage the kind of multivocal logic sought by Peter Ochs and those concerned with Yoder's tendency to essentialize pluralistic movements as faithful or unfaithful to Jesus.

Relational thinking is, for Bourdieu, at once the principle of the break and of object construction. Yoder's primary concepts are often underconstructed. When he fails to break from Anabaptist common sense about Constantine, he fails to construct an historical object, "Constantinianism," that could be useful for his theological purposes. To critique the powers is to construct the powers. But what would such construction look like in light of Yoder's theology of the powers? The basic hypothesis of this theology is that the powers can be identified by contrast to the life of Jesus. This hypothesis postulates a relation between Jesus and the powers that is only made intelligible by postulating a further, unique relation between Jesus, God and God's Spirit. If Jesus does not have a unique relation to God and the Spirit, then it makes little sense to make him the standard against which the powers are judged. The God-Jesus-Spirit relation then has critical priority over the Jesus-powers relation, and cannot be dismissed as mere metaphysical speculation. Some minimal construction of trinitarian relations is necessary to ground a critique of the powers.[215] The God-Jesus-Spirit relation is social, but also more than social. It may not be possible to say much about ontological relations "within" the Trinity, but some acknowledgment of those relations is required if language about the powers is going to be theologically adequate. From a theological view, a power is incompletely constructed if its constituting relation to the triune God is left out. Moreover, recognition of that constituting relation enables genuine criticism of the powers, since it raises Jesus above them. The fallen powers are visible in light of the God-human Jesus Christ, not just the life of a first-century Jewish martyr.

Relational construction of the powers therefore must include all their dimensions: material, symbolic and spiritual. Yoder's approach to cosmological construction might be labeled as "prophetic materialism." He regards cosmology as fulfilling a prophetic function by offering a vision of a possible state of affairs that contrasts with a present state of affairs. In each case, the state of affairs identified is a material and a social reality, and not a spiritual plane or realm. Like early Marxism, Yoder's prophetic materialism pays little attention to the affective and cultural aspects of the present

---

215. See the first chapter of this thesis for one attempt at such a minimal construction.

or anticipated state of affairs.[216] Like atheistic social theory in general, it pays little attention to actual or possible spiritual relations to the triune God. Bourdieu's symbolic materialism can only respond directly to the first problem; but preceding chapters have argued that it can nonetheless help theologians comprehend spiritual relations in such a way that enriches, not denigrates, an appreciation of material sociality.

Applied rationalism calls for empirical "testing" of the object—but how could this revised Yoderian methodology test its objects if they include metaphysical relations? For Yoder the majority of theological statements are about God's interactions with human beings within history. Metaphysical statements about God's trinitarian being may be necessary, but only as fences to keep us from saying the wrong things about Jesus.[217] Yoder may have underestimated the need for constructive description of those fences, namely, of the relationship between Jesus, the Father and the Spirit. But his ethico-political theology supplies later theologians with a large number of empirical statements that can be confirmed or disconfirmed through empirical study.[218]

A nonreductive study of the principalities and powers might go as follows. First, construct the metaphysical "object," the unique relation between Jesus, the Father, and the Spirit. This construction demands further construction of the historical life of Jesus of Nazareth, such as Yoder provides in *The Politics of Jesus*. That construction can then be used to investigate the relations between the Father, creation, and Israel; the Spirit and the church; and so on. Further, the human Jesus exists in relation to fallen creation, which must be constructed in all its complexity—each variance in time and place, each power, is constructed in its particular relation to Jesus. Constructions of the historical Jesus and specific powers can of course be subjected to empirical scrutiny. With rare exceptions, Yoder's handling of empirical data is far from rigorous. Nor does he clarify the central metaphysical hypothesis required for his research project to make sense: Jesus enjoys a unique relation to the Father and the Spirit. That theory can only be partially tested by investigating the coherence between Jesus' life and interactions between YHWH and Israel, and the Spirit and the church—although systematic examination of the historical data in each case is crucial. At the heart of the

216. On early Marxism and its critics, see Hawthorn, *Enlightenment and Despair*, chapter 3, and Hughes, *Consciousness and Society*, 67–104.

217. Yoder, *Preface*, 223.

218. Cf. Murphy, *Anglo-American Postmodernity*, 159–65, on ecclesial discernment as equivalent to scientific theories of instrumentation. She argues that theological claims can be "tested" by communities for their consistency with scripture and their practical effects (164).

theory is just that, a theoretical statement about the being of God that is only indirectly testable by its coherence with associated objects. A realist constructivist theology would accept both the need for empirical confirmation of its objects and the irreducibility of its core theoretical statements.[219]

Reflexive theologians will not only construct the powers without, but those "within" the church and themselves. This movement overlaps with Yoder's notion of repentant historiography, but should be more critical of the social conditions of theological practice.[220] Reflexivity would allow also for the incorporation of other academic disciplines into theology, without ignoring how the presuppositions of other disciplines may conflict with theological perspectives.[221] Bourdieu's insistence that reflexivity be sociological, and not merely philosophical, is a salutary reminder here. Yoder's sociological theology would, at the very least, seem to favor the prioritization of a critical theology-sociology dialogue.

Reflexive awareness of the contingent and compromised nature of theological practice should breed a deeper theological patience and humility. As with Bourdieu's scientific city, theologians cannot obtain this level of reflexivity without help. The aim of reflexive theology is the production of the ecclesial city in which word and deed are related as intensely as possible to the life of the triune God. Each citizen of the ecclesial city has the task of receiving and constructing the divine gift of a free *polis*. Theologians' critical tools aid the church, but they should also be receptive to the entire body of Christ. Those tools should be flexible as the hands of the church, and of the triune God, reach out to shape them. Reflexive theology occurs, therefore, in the relational reciprocity between theologians and their objects of research. Intense relating to God, church, and scripture is a central, not incidental, aspect of theological science. The break from Anabaptist common sense does not lead beyond Anabaptism, but to Anabaptist science.

Conclusion

This chapter has reviewed Yoder's theological method in order to identify its major difficulties and explore revisionary resources from Bourdieu's reflexive sociology. Yoder proposes a study of the powers that identifies their moral features by way of contrast to the way of Jesus. Within his larger

219. Ibid., 49–62.

220. For theology that draws on sociological tools for reflexive purposes, see Gill, *Social Context of Theology*; Gill, *Theology and Social Structure*; Smith, "Redeeming Critique"; Tanner, *Theories of Culture*; Ward, *Cultural Transformation*.

221. Milbank, *TST*.

theological method, the theology of the principalities and powers is a type of prophetic cosmology, one of the linguistic tasks of the theologian. Other theological tasks include linguistic self-consciousness and scriptural and historical memory. Yoder emphasizes patient interaction with his various interlocutors in the face of specific issues. The theologian's goal is never to construct a master method that could suffice for all time, but to wield flexibly her constructive and critical linguistic and memory skills for the sake of the church's mission. Yoder is the first to admit that he is not the exemplar of theological patience. His critics agree, pointing to an insufficient constructive vocabulary and a memory that is too often self-serving. Bourdieu's applied rationalism gives Yoder a more critical framework for carrying out research, one in which the empirical dimensions of theological statements are subjected to rigorous confirmation. Moreover, Bourdieu's reflexivity can help Yoder's followers turn those research tools upon themselves, for the sake of a more patient, ecclesially-centered theological practice. That practice is the subject of the final two chapters.

5

Revising Yoder's Ecclesial Politics

ALONGSIDE HIS CHRISTOCENTRIC PACIFISM, Yoder is perhaps best known for posing the church as an alternative political body to the nation state. In imitation of the politics of Jesus, Christian communities are to share goods, welcome the excluded, and practice reconciliation, servant leadership, and the priesthood of believers.[1] When it does these things, the church becomes "a proclamation of the lordship of Christ to the powers from whose dominion the church has begun to be liberated."[2] Through faithfulness to its master, not compromise, the church fulfills its call "to contribute to the creation of structures more worthy of human society."[3] Because of his emphasis on the church, and on faithfulness over efficacy, many of Yoder's readers have labeled him as a sectarian. That criticism has waned somewhat in the wake of postliberalism's "eccesiological turn" and the postmodern welcome of particularity—but the criticism persists. At root is a concern that he reduces the political and moral options available to Christians due to an overly pessimistic view of the world—itself predicated on an obsession with the state—and an idealistic vision of the church. There is also worry that his ecclesiology is not animated by a robust theology of the Holy Spirit. The present chapter faces these criticisms in order to propose a revised, non-reductive ecclesiological politics based in a strong political sociology. The first section unpacks Yoder's conception of the redemption of the powers and outlines relevant criticisms. Bourdieu's sociological concepts, "circuits of legitimation," "corporatism of the universal," and "negative philosophy," are then presented in order to set up a relational theology of the concrete

1. Cf. Yoder, *BP*.
2. Yoder, *PJ*, 150.
3. Yoder, *PJ*, 155.

church. This church participates through the Holy Spirit in the coming reign of God, and its relative autonomy from other social structures births the possibility of dialogue, collaboration, and critical political legitimation.

Yoder's Ecclesial Politics

According to Yoder, the created, fallen powers participate in God's eschatological redemption of all things. Since "God is going to save his creatures *in their humanity*, the Powers cannot simply be destroyed or set aside or ignored."[4] This view would appear to be in tension with Paul's in 1 Cor 15:24–26, where he writes: "Then comes the end, when [Jesus] hands over the kingdom to God the Father, after he has destroyed [*katargēsē*] every ruler [*archēn*] and every authority [*exousian*] and power [*dynamin*]. For he must reign until he has put all his enemies under his feet. The last enemy to be destroyed [*katargeitai*] is death." If the powers are going to be destroyed, then the prospect of their redemption seems unlikely. Yoder's account of the powers, of course, follows Berkhof's, and so it is unsurprising to find exegesis in the latter's work to support an alternative interpretation of the passage. Berkhof, who is followed by Wink and others, argues that the proper translation of *katargeō* is "dethroned."[5] His case is not merely semantic, but rests on a reading of other Pauline passages on the powers that speak of Christ's redemption of "all things" (Col 1:19; Eph 1:10).[6] The redemption of all things includes the redemption of the powers, and that redemption involves freedom from their tyranny. This is Berkhof's view, and Yoder shares it. But what happens before "the end"? What are Christians to do while Jesus is reigning, putting his enemies under his feet? For Yoder, Christians participate in Jesus' victorious reign by imitating his politics. The politics of Jesus are the politics of the church, and these politics take part in the redemption of the powers.[7]

4. Yoder, *PJ*, 144.

5. Berkhof, *C&P*, 40–43. Wink, *Naming the Powers*, 51–52, suggests "neutralized." See Dawn, *Ellul*, 52–55, for an overview of the exegetical perspectives.

6. He might also have pointed out that 1 Cor 15:20–28 is about the "subjection" of Christ's enemies—destroyed powers would not be subject to Christ, as they would not exist.

7. Unlike other chapters, there is no attempt to contextualize Yoder's theology of the redemption of the powers in his broad oeuvre. Since his writings on the powers occur in two of his major writings on ecclesial politics, *Christian Witness to the State* and *The Politics of Jesus*, and there are pertinent references to the powers' redemption in a wide range of other texts, extra contextualization seems redundant. The single exception is Yoder's theology of exile, which is detailed in chapter six below.

Christ, Church, and Powers

In *The Politics of Jesus*, Yoder places Berkhof's analysis of Col 2:15 at the center of his account of the effect of Christ's death and resurrection on the powers. Berkhof focuses on the three verbs from that passage: Christ disarmed (*apekdysamenos*), made a public example of (*edeigmatisen*), and triumphed over (*thriambeusas*) the powers. According to Berkhof, the crucifixion of Christ by the powers publicly exposes their opposition to God.[8] This exposure breaks the illusion of the powers' beneficence—their primary weapon—and the resurrection shows God to be the more powerful. Once this illusion is broken, the powers become an "object of God's plan of redemption," and, therefore, "will no longer lie between man and God as a barrier, but can and shall return to their original function, as instruments of God's fellowship with His creation" (41). As Christians await the final redemption, they may observe a "limitation" now placed on the powers by Christ (43–46). This limitation is found in the way God uses the powers for God's own ends, sometimes breaking their influence completely, as when Jesus cast out demons. The existence of the church is itself a significant limitation of the powers, for, "by her very presence she breaks through that unshaken stability of life under the Powers" (44). The Holy Spirit, furthermore, "shrinks" or "de-deifies" the powers in the eyes of Christians, thereby enabling critical discernment (47–50). Christians engage the powers selectively, withdrawing when necessary, and boldly "walking through the middle of [the world's] kingdoms" when possible.[9]

The church's primary task, according to Berkhof, is to show "in her life and fellowship how men can live freed from the Powers" (51). Efforts to transform society directly are only possible when the church itself exhibits redeemed community. Ephesians 6:10–18 may instruct Christians to "put on the whole armor of God" for their struggle with the powers, but Berkhof contends that the armor listed there is for defensive purposes (52). Christ has already defeated the powers, so "our weapon is to stay close by Him and thus to remain out of reach of the drawing power of the Powers" (52). In doing so, Christians may find their influence spreading through society, even to the extent that it would be possible to speak of its "Christianization" (53–64). Christianization is not to be confused with a "restoration" of the powers to their original state, which is impossible given their ongoing

8. Berkhof, *C&P*, 38–39. Unless otherwise noted, references to *C&P* in this and the following paragraph are in the text.

9. Ibid., 50. Berkhof draws on biblical language of "strong" and "weak" Christians here: the strong walk in the midst of the powers, the weak withdrawal. Yoder does not use this distinction in his discussions of engaging the powers.

rebellion (56–57). It is instead a process through which those affected by the church's witness guide the powers in such a way that they are "oriented by and pointed toward God's dealings with men in Jesus Christ and to men's life in fellowship with this same God" (58). For instance, a Christianized state would restrict its action to "staving off chaos" rather than perpetuating ideology, and a Christianized legal system would be based on Christian morality (59). Berkhof later questioned this notion of Christianization,[10] and the anti-Constantinian Yoder unsurprisingly does not make it the center of his analysis.[11] But Yoder does agree with Berkhof that the witness of the obedient church takes part in Christ's redemptive activity, and that this witness is potentially transformative of the powers in the present age.

Yoder develops those themes throughout his *oeuvre*, beginning with his European writings. In his doctoral dissertation he contrasts sixteenth-century Anabaptist obedience with the compromises of the reformers and others from the same era. The reformers, according to Yoder, chose alignment with civic authority over scripture. Huldrych Zwingli, the reformer of Basel, is Yoder's main target: "from fear of the consequences of a consistent implementation of the Reformation, he made a pact with the powers of this world."[12] Zwingli began his reform with biblical critiques of fasting, interest, tithes, images, and the mass, but delayed introducing actual changes when the Basel town council hesitated (5–11). In October 1523 he declared that the council held ultimate control over the pace and scale of reform (11–17). The growing frustrations of some of Zwingli's closest associates now peaked, leading to a rupture in the reform movement. After a year of private debate, a final break occurred in January 1525 when some of the dissenters received believer's baptism as the only valid biblical practice (18–28). The "Anabaptists" were thus born out of refusal to let Christian practice be dictated by state power.

Within the incipient Anabaptist movement there were some who imitated Zwingli's reliance on civic authorities. Yoder is especially concerned to judge Balthasar Hubmaier "as influenced too much by the need to connect with the sociological facts" (134). More specifically, he did not

10. Berkhof wrote of "Christianization" again in his book, *Doctrine of the Holy Spirit*, 100–104, but in the preface to the second edition of *C&P* admits that "the concept of 'Christianization' . . . probably cannot be used at all anymore" (11). See Min, *Sin and Politics*, 160–64, for a recent appropriation of the language.

11. In a lecture from 1966, published in *Revolutionary Christianity*, Yoder insists that Berkhof's "Christianization" is not to be confused with Constantinianism, since Berkhof had written a critical account of Constantine elsewhere (135). He also uses "Christianization" in "Servant," 164, as a synonym for the "sobering of the powers." Otherwise he does not use the term.

12. Yoder, *ARS*, 123. Unless otherwise noted, references to *ARS* in this and the following paragraphs are in the text.

fully renounce violence and attempted to implement Anabaptist reforms through the town councils of Waldshut and Nikolsburg.[13] On the other hand, Anabaptist "pietists" such as Sebastian Pfistermeyer made no effort to institutionalize reforms.[14] Pfistermeyer "was concerned with preaching repentance, awakening, and ethical strictness, but not with the formation of a community" (100).

Yoder regards Hubmaier and Pfistermeyer as "in between figures," not fully Anabaptist (133). In contrast, those Anabaptists who both renounced civic authority and sought Christian community based on biblical teachings paradigmatically recovered the faith of the earliest followers of Jesus.[15] By making believer's baptism rather than citizenship the criteria for community membership, the Anabaptists allowed for accountability to a biblical lifestyle. This accountability took place in a community ordered by what Zwingli had initially called "the rule of Christ," discerning dialogue empowered by the Spirit and centered on the scriptures (226–28; cf. Matt 18:15–10; Gal 6:2). Unlike pietist or (Schwenckfeldian) spiritualist strands, Anabaptism thus "steps into sociological reality," focusing on the Spirit's role in forming concrete communities conducive to visible discipleship (*ARS*, 208).

A disciplined, dialogical community takes on a different character from surrounding communities in the practical integrity of its discipleship. As a distinctive community it can exist "against the world" (259–77). Yoder defines the Anabaptist understanding of "the world" in terms familiar from his theology of the powers: "'world' is the concrete form of creation's disobedience. This disobedience is not simply an attitude that invisibly hovers over all things and works unnoticed in every heart, but rather it is as visible as is the person. It is embodied in the state, worship, class, economics, and in the demonic nature of a culture that has become autonomous" (265).

13. Hubmaier was a theologian and pastor who was involved with the early Swiss Brethren in Zurich, and then ministered around Moravia. He supported radical peasants at various points, though famously clashed with the radical Anabaptist leader Hans Hut. Although he recanted his Anabaptist beliefs in 1525 to escape death, he continued his ministry until his martyrdom in Austria in 1528. Yoder, *ARS*, 43–48, 56–64; Yoder, "Balthasar Hubmaier"; Pipkin and Yoder, eds. and trans., *Balthasar Hubmaier*. See Snyder, "Swiss Anabaptism," for a recent reevaluation of Hubmaier's legacy.

14. Pfistermeyer was an Anabaptist leader in the Aargau, west of Zürich, who later recanted and sought to convert Anabaptists. See Yoder, *ARS*, 97–100, 134. A likely influence on Yoder's antipathy toward pietism was Mennonite historian Robert Friedmann, who saw it as a distraction from "radical brotherhood." See Friedmann's two-part article "Anabaptism and Pietism," its appendix, "Spiritual Changes," and his book *Mennonite Piety*. For recent criticism, see T. F. Schlabach, "Mennonites and Pietism."

15. Yoder, *ARS*, 126–30. Yoder regards Grebel, Mantz, and the movement that coalesced around Michael Sattler and the Schleitheim *Brotherly Union* as the earliest representatives of this more pure Anabaptism.

Anabaptists, unlike those reliant on state power, embark on the "greater venture of faith" represented by the proclamation of the early church that "the powers of this world . . . stood under the lordship of Christ" (271). But trust in the lordship of Christ allows Anabaptists the freedom to follow Christ and assume a "prophetic-critical" missionary stance *for* the world (281). Criticism occurs in the context of nonviolent dialogue, following the practice of those Anabaptists who sought conversation with Zwingli and other reformers until they were persecuted into sociological isolation (109–10, 120–25). It is this "inexhaustible will to dialogue," Yoder contends, that gives Anabaptism its continued viability (136). Anabaptist communities are thus internally dialogical, following the rule of Christ, and externally dialogical, engaging the powers. Internal obedience and external witness are intrinsically related as the church responds to the risen Lord.

As discussed in chapter 1 above, Yoder's major texts on the powers all emerged out of ecumenical contexts. The first of them, *Christian Witness to the State* expands the Anabaptist logic with specific reference to the state as a power. Yoder updates his opponents, however, taking aim especially at the Niebuhrs for deemphasizing Jesus as the norm of Christian witness.[16] By contrast, the early Christians exalted Christ as cosmic lord, as evidenced in the New Testament by the repeated use of Ps 110:1, and by the passages on the powers (8–9). From the perspective of the New Testament authors, the present age is intersected by another age, "the redemptive reality which entered history in an ultimate way in Christ" (9). The tension between the two ages is not temporal, but sociological. It is "a matter of direction" between those who do and those who do not do God's will. Thus the "meaning" or goal of history is seen in the work of the church as an obedient body, not the state or any other power (13). "In spite of the present visible dominion of the 'powers' of 'this present evil age,'" Yoder argues, "the triumph of Christ has already guaranteed that the ultimate meaning of history will not be found in the course of earthly empires or the development of proud cultures, but in the calling together of the 'chosen race, royal priesthood, holy nation,' which is the church of Christ" (13; cf. Eph 6:12; 1 Pet 2:9). Ecclesial faithfulness has priority in Christian witness because it shows how God is redeeming the world through Christ. Yoder therefore suggests that ordinary Christian practices such as distributing leadership throughout the community, fraternal admonition, and consensus decision-making can influence the powers (*CWS*, 18–19). For instance, human rights can be traced to Christian egalitarianism, and democratic process is related to Christian accountability.

16. Yoder, *CWS*, 7n4, 36n1, 66–68, 79–81, 89–90. References to *CWS* in this and the following two paragraphs are in the text.

Yoder develops this argument in a series of later works culminating in *Body Politics*.[17] There he focuses on the "sacramentality" of the same practices, with the addition of baptism and the Lord's Supper: each practice is a way the church responds in the power of the Spirit to Jesus, and each is a way that God acts to redeem the world.[18]

In *Christian Witness to the State*, Yoder goes on to highlight other forms of Christian proclamation. The church often serves as a "pilot," exercising "constant inventive vision" by experimenting with new institutional forms that may be taken over by others (*CWS*, 19–20). Christian individuals might have transformative influence through "conscientious participation" in various spheres, and a Christian ethos may spread through "moral osmosis" via Christian education and the church's general reputation (20–21). But in this book Yoder's focus is on more direct political witness, and he spells out in detail the conditions and form of Christian speech to rulers. Given his basic interest in obedience, it is unsurprising that he denies the possibility of meaningful Christian speech to rulers without a basic correspondence between the words used and the life of the church (21–22). The requirement of correspondence between word and work means not only that Christian speech to rulers must issue from clearly Christian concerns, but that Christians should agree on what is to be done and already be able to exhibit a significant response to the concern within their communities. A segregated church, for example, has nothing to say about integration.

These conditions being met, Christians are free to explore various linguistic formulations that will translate Christian concern into policy recommendations comprehensible to the rulers in question and apposite for the situation (*CWS*, 7n4, 36n1, 66–68, 79–81, 89–90).[19] Yoder draws from contemporary ecumenical discourse to name such formulations "middle axioms," "concepts [which] will translate into meaningful and concrete terms the general relevance of the lordship of Christ for a given social ethical issue" (32, 33n3). He lists several examples, including critiques of state violence when it exceeds the bare needs of social order, or of state power when it it threatens to overwhelm personal and cultural values (36–38, 40). Christian speech to rulers aims then not at implementing an ideal Christian social order, but at pragmatically encouraging the realization of "lesser evils" that are closer to God's will than might otherwise take place (38–40,

---

17. Yoder, *RP*, 327–29; *PK*, 22–28; *FC*; *BP*; *FTN*, 15–50.

18. See especially Yoder, *BP*, 71–80.

19. Cf. *PJ*, 239–40, where Yoder implies that the conditions for direct witness are so far from being met that Christians ought to give it up for a time.

44). Christian public speech, following the Anabaptist model, should thus be dialogical, just as dialogue is at the core of ecclesial faithfulness.

Yoder introduces *The Politics of Jesus* with a reference to the cultural upheaval that had marked the previous decade of American life, his first back from Europe. Noting the "peculiar place of Jesus in the mood and mind of many young 'rebels,'" he suggests that "there is certainly no randomness to their claim that Jesus was, like themselves, a social critic and an agitator, a drop-out from the social climb, and the spokesman of a counterculture."[20] This popular Christology may be "half-spoofing exaggeration," but it usefully raises a point made increasingly apparent by biblical scholars: Jesus was radically political, and politically radical (2). Yoder's task, as seen in preceding chapters, is to bring the relevant biblical scholarship into conversation with the many variations of "mainstream" Christian ethics that deny Jesus' political nature (4–8). The Niebuhrs are again prominent opponents, but so are pietistic spiritualism and ethical personalism. Yoder responds to them with a close reading of the gospel of Luke suggestive of Jesus' commitment to nonviolent political resistance and economic redistribution (21–75). He further shows how Jesus' political posture was anticipated by certain strands of Judaism (60–92) and elaborated by the apostolic writers, especially the authors of the Pauline literature and Revelation (93–228). The chapter on "Christ and Power" importantly connects Pauline cosmology to the politics of Jesus.

Central to "Christ and Power" is the claim that at the cross Jesus demonstrates "authentic humanity" (145). In his treatment of Luke's gospel, Yoder had argued that the cross should be understood as the natural political outcome of Jesus' politics (36–39, 48–53). Although Jesus declined violent revolutionary tactics, neither would he acquiesce to the alliance between the Jewish temple and Rome (24–27, 36).[21] He instead founded a community "marked by an alternative to accepted patterns of leadership" and "a non-conformed quality of ('secular') involvement in the life of the world" (33, 38–39). The opposition that arises to this alternative community comes in the form of the cross. By accepting the cross and persisting in obedience to God, Jesus indicates that "the cross is not a detour or a hurdle on the way to the kingdom, nor is it even the way to the kingdom; it is the kingdom come" (51). God's kingdom is brought near by Jesus' practical, obedient love that rejects violent coercion to the point of suffering and death.

---

20. Yoder, *PJ*, 1. Cf. *OR*, 7. References to *PJ* in this and the following paragraphs are in the text. With the publication in 2011 of *Revolutionary Christianity*, Yoder's 1966 South American Lectures, it is now evident that that continent's revolutionary ferment was also in Yoder's mind as he formed the material that became *PJ*.

21. See also Yoder, *OR*, 13–33. For more recent critical debate over Jesus' temptation by "Zealot" revolutionaries, see Klassen, "Jesus and the Zealots."

According to Yoder, Jesus' choice of the cross over compromise shows that he, uniquely, is free from the grasp of the powers (145). Because the social order he envisioned was greater than Rome, and the righteousness he advocated greater than the Pharisees, he was liberated from their rules. "He did not fear even death. Therefore his cross is a victory, the confirmation that he was free from the rebellious pretensions of the creaturely condition" (145). The rest of Yoder's discussion in "Christ and Power" follows Berkhof's outline explicitly. The cross exposes the rebellion of the powers, and so defeats them (146–47). The church, further, is to be a "herald of liberation" and announce Christ's victory, most significantly through the quality of its obedient community life (147–49).

As in *Christian Witness to the State*, Christian obedience is presented as a critical and generative social strategy: "The church's calling is to be the conscience and the servant within human society. The church must be sufficiently experienced to be able to discern when and where and how God is using the Powers. . . .[W]e are called to contribute to the creation of structures more worthy of human society" (155). Here an emphasis on discernment emerges that Yoder employs to position the theology of the powers and principalities as a kind of social criticism. The declaration of the lordship of Christ over the powers is "about the nature of the cosmos and the significance of history, within which both our conscientious participation and our conscientious objection find their authority and their promise" (157). Witness is therefore complex, determined as a series of overlapping responses to specific powers. But its sociological concreteness—and its visible link to Jesus' politics—are not negotiable. Christians participate in "the lamb's war," choosing "powerlessness" over the short-term efficiency calculations that justify state and revolutionary violence (228–47). "The relationship between the obedience of God's people and the triumph of God's cause is not a relationship of cause and effect but one of cross and resurrection" (232). Because the politics of Jesus "go with the grain of the cosmos," Christians can trust in their ultimate efficacy (246).[22]

In *The Politics of Jesus*, Yoder produces a novel interpretation of the apostolic "household codes" or *Haustafeln* that reads them as a call to "revolutionary subordination" (162–92). The codes specify appropriate relations between husbands and wives, parents and children, and masters and slaves (Eph 5:21—26:9; Col 3:18—14:1; 1 Pet 2:13—13:7). The second member of each pair is called to "be subject" or "submit" (*hypotassō, hypakouō, hypotagē*) to the first member, although the first has reciprocal obligations. Against those who see the codes as teaching a conservative acceptance of

22. See also Yoder, "Armaments and Eschatology"; Hauerwas, *Grain of the Universe*.

the given cultural order, Yoder points out that these codes, unlike similar codes existing in the biblical era, address the subordinate as moral agents (*PJ*, 171–72). The need to request a certain course of action from moral agents implies that these agents inhabit a context defined by some degree of choice: "the call to willing subordination is not explainable unless there has been a temptation to insubordination" (175). The reciprocity of the codes is, furthermore, "revolutionary," for it calls the dominant member to respond to the humanity of their other (177–78). For Yoder, the church is the context in which "there is no longer Jew or Greek, there is no longer slave or free, there is no longer male and female; for all of you are one in Christ Jesus" (*PJ*, 173–75, quoting Gal 3:28). Christian identity relativizes the cultural identities spoken of in the household codes; but for the very reason that they are relativized, there is no need to war against them. Christians can accept "willing servanthood in the place of domination" and enjoy "freedom from needing to smash [the structures of this world] since they are about to crumble anyway" (*PJ*, 186–87). The victory over oppressive cultural powers is realized by patient suffering—by a participation in Christ's cross made possible by faith in resurrection.[23]

Yoder extends this same logic of revolutionary subordination to the Christian relation to the state. Conventional political theologies often focus on Rom 13:1: "Let every person be subject (*hypotassesthō*) to the governing authorities (*exousiais hyperechousais*); for there is no authority (*exousia*) except from God, and those authorities have been instituted (*tetagmenai*) by God." As with subordination to cultural roles, subordination to the divinely ordained state is understood as an inherently conservative affirmation of existing states, or at least of those that "are not a terror to good conduct, but to bad" (13:3; see *PJ*, 198–201). Because God institutes the state, moreover, Christians are free to participate in it, even in its essential task of "bearing the sword" (13:4).[24]

But Yoder rejects these views, noting that Paul has just in the previous chapter called Christians to "live peaceably with all. Beloved never avenge yourselves, but leave room for the wrath of God" (12:18–19; see *PJ*, 196–98).

---

23. This chapter of *PJ* was criticized by feminist theologian Elisabeth Shüssler Fiorenza, *Bread Not Stone*, 81–83, as inviting the oppressed to simply accept their oppression. Yoder, *PJ*, 188–92, insisted that the point is simply "don't overdo your liberation"—an admonition that only makes sense if the liberation from oppression is concrete. N. Alexis-Baker, "Freedom of the Cross," 89–96, argues from a womanist perspective that Yoder's language of "subordination" is unfortunate, but his overall argument still has revolutionary potential. (She prefers his phrase "creative transformation" from *PJ*, 185).

24. On Yoder's "positivist," non-theoretical definition of the state, see *CWS*, 12, 77–79. See Bourne, *Seek the Peace*, 216–24, for a discussion of the implications of Yoder's "functional" definition for the theory of state legitimacy.

Contrasting these passages leads Yoder to surmise that Paul assigns to Christians the task of nonviolent community, and to the state the restraint of "bad conduct" through "the sword." As he put it in an earlier work, "the divine mandate of the state consists in using evil means to keep evil from getting out of hand," while "the divine mandate of the church consists in overcoming evil through the cross."[25] Neither does God's "institution" of the state permit Christian collusion with state violence. Yoder disputes the translation of *tetagmenai* as "instituted" or "ordained," as if God creates (at least some) governments and gives them an unqualified blessing (*PJ*, 201–2). The ubiquity of governmental corruption belies that translation. Rather, *tetagmenai* should be understood as the divine "ordering" of "the rebellious 'powers that be,'" just as a librarian shelves books regardless of their content. As with the other fallen powers, the Christian relation to the state is thus defined by certain critical constants derived from the politics of Jesus—the critique of state oppression, violence, idolatry and so forth—and a form of "subordination" that does not entail blind obedience (209). This potentially disobedient subordination will likely involve suffering, which "is itself a participation in God's victorious patience with the rebellious powers of creation" (209).

"Behold My Servant Shall Prosper" and "How H. Richard Niebuhr Reasoned" recapitulate Yoder's conception of ecclesial participation in Christ's victory over the powers. The first essay does so by deepening the understanding of "power" brought to bear on discussions of Christians' cultural and political engagement. Whereas in *The Politics of Jesus* "power-lessness" was exalted as the proper mode of participation in the lamb's war (237–41), here servanthood is itself portrayed as a powerful practice.[26] In a familiar list, Yoder avers that distinctive servant communities are able to be powerfully creative on an institutional level, place pressure on authorities through tactical abstention, and affect change through transformed individuals in powerful positions.[27] Christian experimentation with servanthood, further, becomes the basis for its critical and positive speech to rulers.[28] "We should," therefore, "affirm with regard to the servant role that it is powerful in reality, and with regard to the rulers' role that the ruler should become a servant."[29] In contrast to the Reformed "orders of creation" model

25. Yoder, *DPR*, 18, 21.

26. Yoder, "Servant," 151–60. This later position is adumbrated by *Revolutionary Christianity*, 94–96.

27. Ibid., 158–59.

28. Ibid., 159–60.

29. Ibid., 158.

of cultural transformation, basing the church's alternative form of power on servanthood roots its witness in the politics of Jesus and the cross. Yoder explains the significance of this christological form of politics:

> To say that the work of redemption is Christological is not a statement about logic, but about Jesus. The event that makes it possible for us to say that we are no longer the slaves of the Powers is not that we have reached a general insight into God's purpose to overcome them. It is a report of the fact that in Jesus, in his dying and his rising, they have been overcome. . . . It is a proclamation, the meaning of an event rippling out from Golgotha and needing to be reported if it is to reach anywhere. Because Christ the risen Lord rules not only over the church which is his body, but also over the world which is the terrain of his combat, this approach does yield the wherewithal for talking beyond the confines of the church. Its relevance is not limited to those who believe in Jesus or even to those who hear about Him (164).

The cosmic import of the cross and resurrection grounds the broad relevance of ecclesial witness. When Christians take up Christ's political posture of servanthood and accept the suffering it brings, they show the world that the lordship of Christ ends the tyranny of the powers.

For Yoder, the dynamic of power is between service and domination, not withdrawal and participation. Christian cultural and political activity is flexible, and proceeds through continual discernment of prospects for servanthood. Yoder names this form of participation "asymmetrical," because Christians, as a church and as individuals, are to interact with each power in different ways at different times.[30] In "How H. Richard Niebuhr Reasoned" he draws attention to Niebuhr's attempt in *Christ and Culture* to articulate a single Christian response to various cultural phenomena.[31] Yoder instead calls for "a capacity for moral discernment, in the light of which Niebuhr's ability to call all of those things 'culture' will no longer be permitted to get in the way of handling each issue in its own terms."[32] Against Niebuhr, the biblical perspective on the powers suggests that culture cannot be conceived as an autonomous, monolithic unity, but rather as variegated forms of rebellion in process of being subdued by the risen Christ (69). The church thus needs "categories of *discernment*," and not an all-encompassing typology (70). These categories help the church fulfill its vocation "to represent within society, through and in spite of withdrawal from certain of its activities, as

---

30. Ibid., 165.

31. Cf. Niebuhr's definition of "culture" in *Christ and Culture*, 29–39.

32. Yoder, "HRN," 83. Further references to "HRN" in this paragraph are in the text.

well as through and in spite of involvement in others, a real judgment upon the rebelliousness of culture and a real possibility of reconciliation for all" (71). The orientation of Christian engagement around discernment allows for a truly "conversionist" position (71)—one that "transforms [the powers] by denying their monolithic unity in favor of discerning discrimination" (76). Gathered in the Spirit around the scriptures for discerning dialogue (71–77), Christians join in God's redemption of the powers through the risen Christ (76).

Throughout Yoder's writings on the powers he emphasizes the continuity between Christian obedience and the ongoing redemption of creation initiated by the death and resurrection of Jesus Christ. By practicing the politics of Jesus, the church's body politics participate in Christ's transformation of the powers. Christian cultural participation is thus an aspect of its participation in the person of Jesus Christ, an argument Yoder sets forth in *The Politics of Jesus* and elsewhere.[33] The "gift of the Holy Spirit" makes it possible for "human being [to] correspond somehow to God's own being," namely, through following Jesus in forgiving, loving, and suffering servanthood.[34] Servanthood requires a non-defensive vulnerability to others that is expressed in dialogue, in open conversation, both within the church and between the church and others. Dialogue, established in the life of the obedient church, is a means of transformative witness. The earliest Christians and Anabaptists show that dialogical servanthood patterned after Jesus can be a powerful political and cultural force, and does not necessitate sectarian withdrawal. Yoder's own ecumenical efforts and influence reinforce his claim that the church participates in the redemption of the powers through obedient imitation empowered by the Spirit. This *imitatio Christi* is internally and externally dialogical, prioritizing responsive discernment over reactionary rigidity or servile acquiescence—it is, in other words, free from enslavement to the powers. The present chapter continues to examine issues raised by this vision of redemptive politics, and the next looks at the implications of a dialogical construal of Christian identity, particularly as Yoder conceptualizes it under the rubric of "exile."

Criticisms

Yoder's argument that ecclesial obedience is the foundation of Christian political engagement has incited vigorous debate among theologians. The critical response can be divided into questions about three issues: First, is

33. Yoder, *PJ*, 112–33. See also his *ARS*, 287; *WL*, 165–80.
34. Yoder, *PJ*, 114, 115–27.

Yoder's ecclesiology adequate? Is it idealistic, even idealist, or sectarian? Second, is Yoder's pneumatology adequate? Does Yoder think the church really needs the Spirit to follow Christ? Third, does Yoder adequately describe the socio-political context and form of Christian witness? Are his bottom-up politics naïve? Does he focus too much on witness to the state? Answers to these questions determine the viability of his understanding of the redemption of the powers.

Sectarian

The label "sectarian" has been attached to Yoder's ecclesiology from early on. In the mid-1970s, Methodist theologian J. Philip Wogaman characterized sectarianism by the conviction that Christians are called (only) to faithfulness and that God will take care of the rest of the world.[35] Wogaman finds Yoder to be more optimistic about God's redemptive action in the present than most sectarians—but his logic is still sectarian. His moral perfectionism encourages withdrawal from social responsibility, the "pure sectarian nonsense" of thinking Christians can escape the "dilemma of civilization" in which earthly rewards and punishments often motivate more than faithfulness.[36] Since Wogaman, the separatism allegedly implied by Yoder's perfectionism and church-world division has been the target of numerous theologians. Concerns center around Yoder's failure to support public institutions, especially the state and military,[37] and his interest in moral purity and interior ecclesial identity.[38] A few Mennonite theologians have traced the problem to Yoder's initial involvement with the Concern group, which supposedly embraced a theological ideal of the church rather than engaging the contingencies of ecclesial reality.[39] Yoder's "heroic pneumatology"[40] not only results in an isolated perfectionism, but it raises doubts about the possible existence of the church past and present. If these charges are accurate, then Yoder's ecclesiology is not only idealistic and sectarian, but

35. Wogaman, *Christian Method of Moral Judgment*, 191.

36. Ibid., 192.

37. Beckley, "Rawls's Idea of Justice as Fairness—Part I," 219; Mouw, *Politics and the Biblical Drama*, 110; Reimer, "Positive Theology," 245–73; G. Schlabach, "Deuteronomic or Constantinian," 449–71.

38. Gustafson, *Theology and Ethics*, 74; Hunter, *To Change the World*, 164–66, 174–75, 218–19; Mathewes, "Culture," 59; Mathewes, *Public Life*, 240–41. See also Griffin, "Dirty Hands," 36–38.

39. Nolt, "Anabaptist Visions," 288–89; G. Schlabach, "Continuity and Sacrament," 181–91; Toews, "Useable Past," 481–84.

40. G. Schlabach, "Continuity and Sacrament," 181.

idealist, in the sense of being based on a purely intellectual construct of ecclesial being.[41]

The editors of a recent collection of essays entitled *The New Yoder* celebrate the end of "old Yoder" scholarship, preoccupied as it was with the sectarianism issue. In its place they promote a new mode of scholarship philosophically oriented to find ecclesial distinctiveness unproblematic by postmodern philosophers such as Foucault and Deleuze.[42] But these editors overlook that even some "new Yoder" scholars continue to worry over Yoder's sectarianism.[43] P. Travis Kroeker and Nathan R. Kerr, for instance, are still concerned that Yoder's insistence on the visibility of the church leads, in Kroeker's words, to "a new form of 'compact collectivism' which is non-ecumenical and dogmatically closed."[44] For Kroeker, Yoder needs to be supplemented with an Augustinian theology of God's invisible reign in society, church, and individuals. Kerr, on the other hand, believes Yoder's late development of a diasporic or exilic ecclesiology already corrects for the "radical ecclesiological positivism" of his earlier "church as *polis*" model.[45] Only by embracing the radical contingency of exile, and the de-centering of identity it brings, does Yoder fully respond to the reality of God's apocalyptic inbreaking.

In the previous section, Yoder's theology of the redemption of the powers was presented in such a way as to highlight the continuities between his early and later writings, especially in regards to the dialogical nature of Christian identity. On this account Yoder's writings on exile, to be explored in the following chapter, are not a departure from his church as *polis* theology, but a more nuanced outworking of the same approach. But the persistence of the sectarian charge suggests a critical impasse. Even Yoder's friendliest critics continue to find fault with his ecclesiology. The proposed solutions, however, seem to detract significantly from Yoder's legacy. Inwardness and invisibility, radical contingency, institutional compromise with the powers, lowered standards for the church—all belie Yoder's emphasis on visible

---

41. Cf. Friesen, *Artists, Citizens, Philosophers*, 67; Layman, "Inner Ground,"; N. G. Wright, *Disavowing Constantine*, 61, 74, 158. Ochs in Yoder, *JCSR*, 179, also suggests that Yoder reduces exilic Judaism to "a few overarching principles of belief and practice" (on this see also Harink, "The Anabaptist and the Apostle, 284).

42. Dula and Huebner, "Introduction," ix–xvi.

43. For other recent theologians critical of Yoder's sectarianism, see the references to Mathewes and Hunter in note 38 above.

44. Kroeker, "Yoder's Voluntariety," 56. See also his "War of the Lamb," *NY*, 70–89.

45. N. Kerr, *Christ, History, and Apocalyptic*," 169–73, 183. See also his "*Communio Missionis.*"

discipleship modeled on the life of Jesus as a powerful stimulus to social change, even when it involves withdrawal.

Pneumatological Ecclesiology?

The charge of Yoder's "reductionism" has been examined at various points in this thesis. Critics of Yoder's ecclesial politics extend the charge to his pneumatology, specifically to his depiction of the role of the Holy Spirit in the life of the church. In short, many question whether Yoder's ecclesial politics require the Holy Spirit, or if they are a purely immanent, "secular" form of politics. Much of the criticism has focused on the potential for instrumentalization in Yoder's account of the sacraments. Are the sacraments merely tools to reach political ends that could be arrived at otherwise, or do they participate in the life of God such that they are to some extent ends in themselves?[46] Paul Martens raises these issues most acutely in his chronology of Yoder's writings on the sacraments.[47] Martens traces the process by which Yoder comes to identify church practices such as fraternal admonition and open dialogue with worship and the sacraments, and then "reduces" them to social processes. This reduction betrays "Yoder's assumption that the church is important only as a secular social community."[48] "Granted," Martens continues, "the Holy Spirit may still be functionally observable in the practices; but the force and frequency of claims that neither their substance nor pertinence depends on a particular faith seems to leave us with very little specifically Christian and very much reduced to social ethics." Yoder opens the way "for Anabaptist assimilation into a form of secular ethical discourse."[49] Martens observes a similar process at work in Yoder's transition from discussing ecclesial politics in terms of eschatological participation, to doxology, to sociological peacemaking.[50]

Martens notes that Yoder's "enthusiastic admirer" Craig Carter is likewise concerned that Yoder's account of the sacraments needs theological supplementation.[51] Yoder's biographer Mark Thiessen Nation too admits

46. Cartwright, "'Sharing the House of God,'" 606–8; Doerksen, "Share the House," 195–98.

47. Martens, "Problematic Development," 65–77.

48. Ibid., 74. Martens sees the influence of Troeltsch affecting Yoder here.

49. Ibid., 75.

50. Martens, "Universal History," 131–46. Marten's narrative complicates Cartwright's claim in "'Sharing the House of God,'" 606, that an "instrumentalist account of worship in Christian formation floats through Yoder's corpus of writing alongside other discussions of 'doxological community'" that are more promising.

51. Martens, "Problematic Development," 74. See Carter, *PC*, 199, on Yoder's

there is "some legitimacy" to the claim that works like *Body Politics* are reductive, and that more work is required in this area.[52] Martens, among others, calls for a more robust articulation of the work of the Holy Spirit in the life of the Christian community than Yoder provides.[53] Yoder does, as suggested above, see ecclesial politics as empowered by the Spirit and participative in the life of Jesus Christ. As Carter puts it, Yoder insists "on the leading of the Holy Spirit in the process of moral discernment, just as Jesus promised would happen (John 16:13)."[54] Gerald Schlabach even accuses Yoder of a "heroic pneumatology," albeit one more amenable to extraordinary individuals than ordinary congregations.[55] Nevertheless, there appears to be a need to integrate Yoder's sociological ecclesiology with a more robust account of the move of the Holy Spirit if Yoder's ecclesial politics are to remain trinitarian.

Focus on the State

The third criticism of Yoder's ecclesial politics can be stated briefly: the focus on "Christian witness to the state" limits his understanding of politics, attenuating the church's witness. James Davison Hunter raises the point forcefully when he argues that Yoder is exemplary of the American "politicization" of

---

"incomplete" theology of baptism. Carter, as Martens notes, does not argue there that Yoder is finally a reductionist, but rather that he made tactical arguments that require supplementation. Carter now repudiates Yoder as a liberal whose "influence was to train a generation of younger Evangelicals to hate and despise their own [Christendom] cultural heritage." By fighting Christendom, Yoder has paved the way for Marxism and the sexual revolution. See Carter, "Yoder and the Evangelical Left," *The Politics of the Cross Resurrected* (blog), May 2, 2011. Online: http://politicsofthecrossresurrected. blogspot.com/2011/05/yoder-and-evangelical-left.html. It will be difficult to evaluate these cursory accusations until they are developed further.

52. Nation, *John Howard Yoder*, 197, 199. Nation denies that Yoder is "really reductionistic," blaming poor word choices on the confusion. See also Dintaman, "Socio-Ecclesial Brushpile," 33–49. Finger, "Theology to Ethics," 330–331, argues that Yoder appears to be reductionistic in some areas, but not in *Body Politics*, where the Spirit plays a clear role in shaping Christian practice. N. Kerr, *Christ, History, and Apocalyptic*, 171–73, contends that Yoder's "church as *polis*" theology instrumentalizes worship for political ends and reduces the Spirit to an ordering principle, but his later exilic theology corrects for this.

53. Martens, "Discipleship," 32–40. See also Heidebrecht, "Yoder's Perspective on the Church," 118; Kroeker, "Yoder's Voluntariety," 56–58; Kroeker, "War of the Lamb," 82–83. Eller, "Review: *The Politics of Jesus*," 108, calls for more attention to the resurrection as the "enabling power" of Christian politics.

54. Carter, *Politics of the Cross*, 204.

55. Schlabach, "Continuity and Sacrament," 181.

theology.[56] Hunter does not wish for Christians to abandon state politics, but to recognize that the state is capable of only so much—society is influenced by much broader cultural forces. James K. A. Smith voices a similar complaint when he indicates that the increasing domination of the nation-state by global capitalism threatens to render Yoder's state-centric ethics "somewhat impotent."[57] Hunter, in addition, worries that Yoder's ecclesial politics are ultimately parasitic on the state, taking far too much of its (unduly harsh) rhetoric from status quo political practice.[58] The sharp church-world dichotomy present in Yoder's theology of the principalities and powers leads to the "demonization" of others.[59] Hunter instead urges Christians to a "faithful presence" that celebrates the goodness of creation as it continues to be revealed throughout culture.[60]

Yoder did, of course, engage "culture" in "How H. Richard Niebuhr Reasoned." There and in "Behold My Servant Shall Prosper" he makes it clear that he understands the multifaceted nature of social power as spread throughout the many powers. Yet as an ethicist the only contemporary issue he investigated with any depth was war and peace. His writings on economic and cultural powers offer only general biblical and theological perspectives.[61] "Impotent" may be an overstatement, but if these critics are correct, the import of Yoder's ethics may be limited. Revision of Yoder's theology of the redemption of the powers thus requires enunciating how his ecclesial politics can affect all of life, and not just state politics. This revision would complement the non-sectarian ecclesiology and non-reductive pneumatology suggested above.

Bourdieu's Sociological Politics

In light of the review of criticisms, Yoder's ecclesial politics requires a non-sectarian, concrete ecclesiology that maintains an emphasis on ecclesial

56. Hunter, *To Change the World*, 162–64. See also Martens, *Heterodox Yoder*, 54–86, on Yoder's "prioritization of politics."

57. Smith, *Introduction to Radical Orthodoxy*, 248.

58. Hunter, *To Change the World*, 164.

59. Ibid.

60. Ibid., 225–86.

61. In addition to "How H. Richard Niebuhr Reasoned," see, e.g., Yoder, *PJ*, 60–75. In his *Artists, Citizens, Philosophers*, 65–67, 155–61, Duane Friesen draws on Yoder's ethical Christology and ecclesial practices in developing his theology of culture. But Friesen's overall method is more indebted to Gordon Kaufmann, and his concrete recommendations for cultural engagement do not draw on Yoder. See also Stassen, "New Vision," 211–22.

distinctiveness; an appreciation for the work of the Holy Spirit in the church that does not deflect attention from ecclesial social process; and an ecclesial witness with a broad cultural remit, but which remains attuned to the centrality of state power. The previous two chapters suggested that Yoder's socio-political criticism is sharpened by taking on aspects of Pierre Bourdieu's reflexive sociology. The present chapter takes a further step to argue that Bourdieu's explicitly political concepts are important resources for the revision of Yoder's ecclesial politics. These concepts are "circuits of legitimation" (5.2.2), "corporatism of the universal" (5.2.3), and "negative philosophy" (5.2.3).

During the following discussion the operational nature of Bourdieu's concepts should be kept in mind. In this case, Bourdieu constructed concepts to facilitate research into political effectiveness as that research was useful for his own increasing political activity.[62] After the death of Michel Foucault in 1984, Bourdieu arguably became the leading French intellectual political activist.[63] He circulated petitions, editorialized in newspapers, and in 1995 took a well publicized stand with striking railroad workers at the Gare du Nord. Under François Mitterand's presidency he served twice as an education adviser to the government. Although some critics see Bourdieu's late political action as opportunistic attention-grabbing,[64] it is possible to see his political practice as responding to his developing sociological understanding of politics. This claim will be more comprehensible after examining the relevant concepts. The importance of Bourdieu's political activity at this point is as a reminder that the concepts are less abstract theories than tools for practical political reasoning.

Circuits of Legitimation

According to Bourdieu, authorities only maintain power over a group of subjects by having their power recognized as legitimate by other, subordinate authorities. Power is successfully legitimated when the power of the subordinate authorities is accepted by the subjects, and when it is apparent that the subordinate authorities have some measure of independence, i.e., that their words and acts of legitimation are not coerced. In modernity, the highly differentiated nature of social fields means authority can only

62. For accounts of Bourdieu's political engagement, see Heinich, *Pourquoi Bourdieu*, 68–105; Poupeau and Discepolo, "Scholarship with Commitment," 64–90; Schinkel, "Bourdieu's Political Turn?," 69–93; Swartz, "Critical Sociology," 791–823.

63. See e.g., Swartz, "Critical Sociology," 800–801.

64. E.g., Heinich, *Pourquoi Bourdieu*, 101, and especially Verdès-Leroux, *Le savant et la politique*, 54–61.

be legitimated through a number of subordinate authorities. Authority requires upkeep of increasingly lengthy "chains of legitimation."

In his essay "From the King's House to the Reason of State," Bourdieu outlines the transition in the modern period from dynastic to bureaucratic states.[65] Because the dynastic state "mingles the domestic and the political," the monarch's political power is always susceptible to familial contestation.[66] In European history, this situation led monarchs to construct and emphasize a legal basis for their authority, such that "the crown" would exceed the authority of their own person and family. Reliance on law entailed reliance on those bureaucrats entrusted with overseeing the law, and so there came about a bifurcation in the reproduction of political authority, between birth as the mode of dynastic reproduction and schooling as the mode of bureaucratic reproduction.[67] Bureaucrats began to contest the "private" basis of dynastic authority in contrast to the relatively "public," universally accessible foundation of their own authority.[68] Much early modern political theory should be seen, Bourdieu contends, as bureaucratic weapons in this struggle against the dynastic state.[69] Eventually the school-based reason of the bureaucrats proved more powerful, more legitimate in the eyes of its subjects, than the dynastic rulers.

Bourdieu suggests that this process demonstrates "how, through the lengthening of the chain of authorities and responsibilities, there came into being a veritable *public order* founded upon a degree of reciprocity within hierarchical relations themselves."[70] Bureaucrats were able to employ the autonomy granted to them by rulers for legitimation purposes to carve out a polity organized around the further distribution of power. For Bourdieu, "everything takes place as if the more a ruler's power increases, the greater his dependency on a whole network of executive relays. In one sense, the freedom and responsibility of each agent is reduced, to the point of being completely dissolved in the field. In another sense, it increases inasmuch as each agent is forced to act in a responsible manner, under the cover and

65. Bourdieu, "Reason of State," 29–54. See also his *SN*, 377–82; *PM*, 102–6. "Circuits of legitimation" has yet to become a major theme in Bourdieu scholarship. See English, "Culture Game," 111; Gartman, "Cultural Sociology," 399; McNay, "Subject, Psyche and Agency," 182; Wacquant, "Symbolic Power," 145. It would be interesting to compare Bourdieu's account with theological accounts of the emergence of the state, such as Cavanaugh, "The City."

66. Bourdieu, "Reason of State," 35–36.

67. Ibid., 40.

68. Bourdieu, *SN*, 379.

69. Bourdieu, *SN*, 380–82.

70. Bourdieu, "Reason of State," 50.

control of all the other agents engaged in the field. Indeed, as the field of power becomes more differentiated, each link in the chain becomes a point (an apex) in a field."[71]

Alongside the construction of this "public realm" in which power is relatively distributed, there is the creation of a new "public capital"—all the benefits such as salaries, titles, and honors conferred by the bureaucratic state.[72] This capital can and has been monopolized by an elite. But because its value is its "publicity" or universal accessibility, struggle for public capital can also result in its greater distribution. In *Pascalian Meditations*, Bourdieu depicts the competition for public capital as the basis for resistance to tyranny.[73] Political resistance partakes in the paradox of legitimation that requires that authorities grant autonomy to those subordinates whose legitimacy they covet, autonomy that can then be used to critique and weaken authority.[74]

What degree of autonomy is necessary for resistance? Bourdieu points to the ability of a field to "refract" the force of other fields as a measurement of its autonomy.[75] "Refraction," as one critic puts it, "is not digestion; it does not completely transform the strange into one's own according to one's internal rules. Refraction seems to imply a concern with defining the rules between different fields."[76] In other words, a field is sufficiently autonomous when the rules of its own "game"—its doxa, illusio, the forms of habitus and capital it produces—are strong enough to resist assimilation to the rules of other fields. Refraction does not imply isolation, for every field is, of course, interdependent on other fields. But it does entail that fields have relatively stable and distinct identities from one another. The existence of such fields, according to Bourdieu, is a sign of a non-tyrannical polity.[77]

Corporatism of the Universal

If field autonomy lengthens the circuits of legitimation and resists tyranny, then politics is a matter of intersecting collectives clamoring for power.

---

71. Ibid.

72. Ibid., 51.

73. Bourdieu, *PM*, 103–4.

74. Ibid., 105–6. Bourdieu, *SN*, 387, calls this paradox the *"legitimation antinomy,"* part of "the fundamental law of the economy of legitimation" (384–85; emphasis origianl).

75. Bourdieu, "Intellectual Field," 118; *Les usages sociaux de la science*, 15–16. See also his *Science of Science and Reflexivity*.

76. Fliethmann, "Bourdieu/Flaubert—Distinction?" *Practising Theory*, 45.

77. Bourdieu, *SN*, 389. Bourdieu references Pascal for this understanding of tyranny.

Bourdieu is not interested in "identity politics" as such, but rather in collectives that pursue their interests in the name of benefits that can be enjoyed by all—in the name of "the universal."[78] "The universal," on Bourdieu's reading of history, proceeds through the paradox of legitimation discussed above: since the universal is the "'spiritual point of honour' of humanity,"[79] the dominant claim that their authority benefits everyone. Subjects accept this claim, (mis)recognizing the authority as legitimate, but the gap between the claim and the realities of the distribution of goods provides them with fodder for criticism. Progress toward the universal thus does not occur through a naïve altruism that surrenders all personal interest, but through a critical struggle for the realization of a more universal distribution—which of course benefits those engaged in the struggle. Bourdieu calls this disposition for public service an "interest in disinterest," a passionate stake in a political order that benefits all.[80]

From this passionate dispassion were born truth, virtue, and reason, fragile products of history that are yet the strongest, the potentially most universal weapons against field heteronomy.[81] Truth, virtue, and reason are not, for Bourdieu, timeless essences awaiting discovery, but conquests of a critical process that subjects reality to universal questioning. They are, in other words, conquests of science. Bourdieu therefore calls for a "corporatism of the universal," a "collective intellectual" that will wield universalizing scientific reason against every force of domination.[82] A *"Realpolitik of reason"* must be practiced in which "the *institutional conditions of rational communication"* are identified through research and instantiated through activism.[83] This politics is both utopian and rationalist, as it seeks the practical implementation of ideal political arrangements. Bourdieu, however, warns against the temptation of forming an alternative political "programme" to dominant politics.[84] Because of the laws of legitimation, the effectiveness of the collective intellectual's political engagement depends on the intellectual credibility of its participants. Intellectual political power is a function of scientific autonomy, not of bending science to political demands. If political

78. See Grenfell, "Interest," 166.

79. Bourdieu, *PM*, 122–23.

80. Bourdieu, *OTP*, 216n24; *PR*, 87–89. See also Bourdieu *CD*, 45; Grenfell, "Interest," 166–67, 169; Fowler, "Autonomy, Reciprocity and Science," 103.

81. Bourdieu, "Specificity of the Scientific Field"; *PM*, 93–127. See chapter six below.

82. Bourdieu, *RA*, 339–48.

83. Bourdieu, *IRS*, 188.

84. Bourdieu, *Acts of Resistance*, 56.

authority cannot be validated by the most rigorous scientific inquiry, it loses its claim to the universal and its circuits of legitimation are broken.

Negative Philosophy

Near the beginning of *Pascalian Meditations*, Bourdieu confesses that during his research on French universities he "had never felt before the strangeness of [his] project, a kind of *negative philosophy* that was liable to appear self-destructive."[85] In the rest of the book, Bourdieu goes on to argue that, far from being self-destructive, the radical doubt of reflexive sociology exposes the barriers to reason set up by faulty scholasticism and symbolic violence. The final chapter concerns the constitutive identity that in modernity is uniquely conferred on individuals by state recognition (206–45). Humans crave a *raison d'être* or "sense of existence," and in the absence of God this is provided by the state (237, 245). State rituals of recognition confer an "ultimate" identity, from birth and death certificates, to more occasional awards and rewards. These "acts of nomination . . . lead, in a kind of infinite regress, to that realization of God on earth, the State, which guarantees, in the last resort, the infinite series of acts of authority certifying by delegation the validity of the certificates of legitimate existence" (245). Sociology is therefore "a kind of theology of the last instance," as it identifies the state's absolute creative power. The book closes with an affirmation of Durkheim's dictum that "society is God."

Loïc Wacquant separates Bourdieu from the Saint-Simonian "secular theology" in which Durkheim partook,[86] but these passages from *Pascalian Meditations* suggest otherwise. Bourdieu may have resisted direct public service for the most part, but in positioning sociology as a negative philosophy revelatory of the absolute, he casts his vocation as one of heterodoxical service to the state. In an essay entitled "The State, Economics and Sport," Bourdieu defends "the Hegelian or Durkheimian vision according to which the State, far from being reducible solely to a class-based State, is also society's self-awareness; it is society that 'thinks itself' and goes beyond its conflicts to find in the universal a compromise between opposing interests."[87] Here Bourdieu presents a utopia in which the state is the product of and means to the widest possible power distribution. The state becomes, as

85. Bourdieu, *PM*, 7. References to *PM* in this and the following paragraph are in the text.

86. Wacquant, "Social Praxeology," 50. On Saint-Simon, Comte, Durkheim, and the religion of humanity, see Hawthorn, *Enlightenment and Despair*, chapters four and six.

87. Bourdieu, "The State, Economics and Sport," 20.

he puts it elsewhere, the "universal state,"[88] the locus of critical reflection through which society reviews and revises its attempts at universality. Negative philosophy is thus key both to the achievement of the universal state and to its maintenance. Wacquant rightfully notes that "Bourdieu supplies a general principle of political engagement" that includes, on the one hand, the critical recognition that the universal is not realized and, on the other, the impetus to universalize universal values through constructive politics.[89] Reflexive sociology is a *via negativa*, but it paradoxically illuminates the necessary conditions for institutionalizing the universal state. These conditions include lengthened circuits of legitimation in which intellectual fields are granted critical autonomy.

Bourdieu is sometimes accused of setting up intellectuals as elite regulators of social life.[90] It is more accurate to say that he wishes for the rational faculties that mark intellectual life to be spread throughout the polis. When society can think itself through the rational state, society will be God omnipotent and charitable.

Revising Yoder's Ecclesial Politics

Although significant differences exist between Yoder and Bourdieu's political visions, Bourdieu's political concepts enable an interpretation of the redemption of the powers that is congenial to Yoder's theology. Yoder argues that ecclesial politics witness to the powers' dependence on God. Autonomy for Yoder is a sign of rebellion, whereas for Bourdieu it is a sign of health. Bourdieu, however, is not concerned with relations between social fields and divine reality, but with imminent social relations only. He counters the tyranny of the few over the many in ways that correspond to Yoder's opposition to Constantinian imperialism. Field autonomy is a form of social organization that promotes distinctive communal identity and intercommunal cohesiveness. It seeks a middle way between sectarian anarchy and oligarchy. From this perspective, the powers are transformed when the domination of one or two of them over the others is broken. The empowerment of many powers facilitates diverse modes of human flourishing. But this redistributive politics is not anomic. The powers hold sway only to the extent that they are oriented, in the form of personal dispositions and institutional structures, toward the service of humankind.

88. Bourdieu, *Firing Back*, 96.

89. Wacquant, "Bourdieu and Democratic Politics," 21.

90. See note 214 in chapter four above.

Bourdieu's interest in universality also appears to conflict with Yoder's emphasis on particularity. This topic will be treated in detail in the next chapter, and here it is sufficient to reiterate the conclusion of the preceding paragraph: realizing "the universal" for Bourdieu is primarily a matter of concrete public service. A more pressing issue is Bourdieu's secular, immanent approach to politics. Even a heterodoxical state servant risks idolatry, and Bourdieu's sociological "discovery" of the divinity of the state raises questions of Constantinian bondage to the powers. Nevertheless, it is arguable that Bourdieu does not see the state as the locus of history—as in Constantinianism—but rather the autonomizing fields that force the state to distribute its power throughout the polis. Although this is not yet a Christian perspective, it does sanction a sociological focus on the church as one such autonomizing field.

Sectarianism

If state authority depends on circuits of legitimation in which each node in a circuit is an autonomous field, then ecclesial distinctiveness may be seen as a contribution to the possibility of a legitimate state. Insistence on visible discipleship does not equate to withdrawal from social responsibility, but can be a concrete form of responsibility. By remaining autonomous and refracting the influence of the state, such that ecclesial politics are not assimilated to state politics, the church retains an independence through which it may criticize state tyranny and envision alternative arrangements. But further, the church recognizes, however ambivalently, state authority. If church autonomy is strong enough, and its influence broad enough, this recognition could at least partially enable state functioning. From Yoder's theological vantage, ecclesial recognition of the state is derivative of divine recognition: God grants the state authority so that it would provide a relative order in which discipleship can take place. What the church ultimately recognizes is this act of divine delegation.[91] The sociological legitimation

---

91. At this point one might suggest a rapprochement between Yoder and Barth. Barth is still wrong that the fact of divine recognition gives Christians clear standards by which to decide whether or not a state should be overthrown. But because Christians' interest is in order, and it is involved in the production of alternative political arrangements, there is nothing in principle that prohibits the church from supporting nonviolent transfers of power from one regime to another. But the church should never confuse the new regime with God's reign, should not put its primary energy into regime change, and must continue its autonomous existence. Ellul, *Violence*, 127–66, makes a similar argument, although he ambivalently accepts that Christians might use violence so long as they do not attempt to justify it theologically.

of state authority by the church is thus an aspect of its faithful response to God's redemption of the powers.

The political contribution of the church is in many ways similar to what Bourdieu envisions for the corporatism of the universal. Yoder does not describe Christian practice as "scientific," but he similarly calls for an open dialogical process in which Christians hold one another accountable for their performative responses to "the Universal," God as revealed in Christit.[92] This dialogical practice also shapes ecclesial public engagement, though with a proper adjustment to expected standards of conduct for the "world." Interestingly, Yoder too sees "legitimacy" as a key critical tool in the confrontation with state power. He regards democracy, for instance, as a preferable political arrangement mostly because democratic regimes offer very strong claims to legitimacy, claims that can be turned back on them when they fail to serve their subjects.[93] The ecclesial community thus pursues a reflexive negative philosophy—community accountability—that is useful for the transformation of the state and other powers. The autonomous church is not sectarian, but a necessary source of legitimation and a communal locus of critical creativity.

Pneumatology

Sacramental practice is not just effective, but is a response to the Holy Spirit's initiative in gathering Christians for concrete obedience to Jesus. The politics called "church" is only constituted by this special, empowering relation to the Spirit. The Spirit's labor is fully sociological and is focused on molding Christians into a visible community around a specific set of practices that correspond to the being of God as revealed in Christ.[94] The legitimacy of those practices, and of the texts that recorded them, is guaranteed by the presence of the Spirit in the church's circuit of legitimation.[95] In other words, ecclesial authority is received from the authority of the Spirit— but here the paradox of legitimacy ends. The absolute difference between the Spirit and the church's authority means the church is not engaged in a

92. Murphy, *Anglo-American Postmodernity*, 164, does draw the connection between science and ecclesial discernment.

93. Yoder, *PK*, 151–71.

94. Yoder, *Preface*, 100 (on 1 Cor 14:29): "There is a weighing process, an evaluation process, when the Spirit speaks through the prophets. What is the center of this weighing process? It is the confession that Jesus is Lord. If the Spirit makes somebody say something compatible with 'Jesus is Lord,' then it is the Holy Spirit."

95. Yoder's writings on the canon, such as in *THW*, may be a good place to begin developing such a pneumatological ecclesiology,

process of wresting power *from* the Spirit. Rather the Spirit, and the specific practices of Jesus to which it calls the church, stands as a constant refutation of all ecclesial tyranny. Christian dialogical contestation aims at recognizing the authority which the Spirit has already bestowed on every member of the body of Christ. As the Spirit facilitates this contestation in specific local socio-political settings, churches are able to realize utopian relational modes, modes which are instructive outside the church as actualized ideals.

It is also notable that Bourdieu's understanding of "interest in disinterest" would help Yoder to speak of the Spirit's formation of individual Christians to desire and participate in ecclesial politics. For Bourdieu, public virtue is a result of historical struggle toward the universal, and is inculcated through educational practices. A more truly pneumatological ecclesiology would place a like emphasis on Spirit-inspired catechism and on the virtues acquired through the body politics. Such a pneumatology supports rather than undermines a sociological, political Christian practice.

State Focus

Because state power is legitimated by a variety of autonomous fields, criticism cannot focus exclusively on the state. Bourdieu indeed only began to write explicitly on the state after years of investigating education, art, and other cultural fields—not because his sociology was apolitical, but because these are the key institutions in his context that inculcate state doxa.[96] Moreover, James Davison Hunter suggests that Christians have unrealistic expectations of the state when "there are no political solutions to the problems most people care about."[97] His proposal of "faithful witness" in all cultural realms is meant as a response to the centrality of cultural fields in shaping human practice. It thus appears that Yoder's focus on Christian witness to the state bears expansion to cultural realms. If Hunter is right that state-centrism has overdetermined the political rhetoric of Yoder's "neo-Anabaptism," then it is possible that complementary interests in "the culture of Jesus" or "body economics" are necessary.[98] Much of this work is implicit in Yoder's reflections on culture and power in "Behold My Servant Shall Prosper" and "How H. Richard Niebuhr Reasoned." *Body Politics*, furthermore, does not completely ignore economics, since the Lord's Supper is meant to

96. See Wacquant, "Foreword," in Bourdieu, *SN*, xvii–xix.

97. Hunter, *To Change the World*, 171.

98. See Carter, *Rethinking Christ and Culture*, and Friesen, *Artists, Citizens, Philosophers*, for general treatments of culture that draw on Yoder's work.

be a process of material redistribution.[99] Bourdieu's political concepts give a powerful justification, and his reflexive sociology a powerful method, for extending these nascent Yoderian cultural and economic theologies into new research areas.

Conclusion

The autonomous church is the politically engaged church. The political church is the spiritual church. The spiritual church participates in God's renewal of all of culture. These revisions to Yoder's ecclesial politics retain his focus on sociological distinctiveness through the body politics, but they more clearly demonstrate how those politics escape charges of sectarianism, secularism, and an overemphasis on the state. Bourdieu's concepts of circuits of legitimation, the corporatism of the universal, and negative philosophy aid in the articulation of a sociological ecclesiology in which the church contributes to the state's viability through its critical separation from the state. Separation is the condition of the church's public witness. Only the separated church can refract the state's influence and develop alternative political practices. Only the separated church has the authority to lengthen the state's circuits of legitimation and enable its legitimacy. Separation is, therefore, not absolute but a relative distance that is salutary for both church and state. By contrast, the church relates as intensely as possible to the Holy Spirit, who empowers its politics by directing it through discerning dialogue to the politics of Jesus. Yet the creativity of the spiritual church is not exhausted by the term "politics." The church critically interacts with a variety of political, cultural, and economic realms in order to participate in Christ's eschatological renewal of all things.

99. See also Yoder, *PJ*, 60–75, on the Jubilee. Cf. Swartley, "Smelting for Gold," and Zimmerman, "Yoder's Jesus and Economics."

6

Revising Yoder's Theology
of Christian Particularity

AT THE CENTER OF John Howard Yoder's theology of the principalities and powers is the conviction that Jesus Christ was crucified and then raised from the dead and made lord of the cosmos. Christ's lordship is universal, knowing no bounds and hindered by no opposing powers. Hence, even in their continuing rebellion, the powers are instruments of divine order. This instrumentalization of the powers denies them their autonomy, and is part of their redemptive subordination. The church participates in the redemption of the powers through intense relating to the triune God, relating that is especially empowered by the present Holy Spirit and focused on imitation of the social practices of Jesus. Christian politics are, therefore, unapologetically particular, a response to divine action that is structured by those historical structures produced through intense divine-human relations. The institutionally and personally embodied witness to Christ's universal lordship does not hesitate to affirm Israel, Jesus, scripture, and the church as guides to transformative engagement of the powers. Christianity testifies to the particular form taken by the universal, the specificities of human interaction with the divine throughout history. By recognizing the historical mediation of the universal, Yoder means to rescue universalist politics from imperialism. Or, rather, by recognizing the incarnation of God as nonviolent—and so nonpossessive, dialogical, and anti-authoritarian—he means to rescue Christianity from Constantinianism.

For the critics of Yoder's "sectarianism" discussed in the previous chapter, Yoder's construal of Christian difference is too different, too tied to a particular history to respond ably to God's relations to all of creation. The present chapter introduces a new set of critics who, while appreciative of Yoder's emphasis on communal distinctiveness, fear that he too easily assimilates non-Christian minority others to his pacifistic Christianity. According to these critics, Yoder has not fully absorbed the implications of his particular perspective on the universal. On the other hand, there is a growing number of critics—many of whom have been discussed in previous chapters—who regard Yoder as exhibiting sociologically reductive tendencies. Far from being a particular Christian, Yoder kowtows to the historicist norms of secular modernity.

Is Yoder too Christian or not Christian enough? Does he fail to see the genuine charms of secular and religious others or is he unwittingly seduced by them? The present chapter extends the perspective on Yoder's ecclesial politics developed in the previous chapter to revise his theology of Christian particularity. Bourdieu's writings on the sociological universalization of particular French Republican virtues help point Yoder's theology toward practical efforts to materialize the universal lordship of Christ. This materialized universal centers on mutually transformative encounters with particular others.

Yoder's Theology of Christian Particularity

The basis of Christian political witness, according to Yoder, is the lordship of Christ over the cosmos. Near the beginning of *Christian Witness to the State*, he observes that, "from the very earliest record of the witness and worship of the church in the first chapters of the Book of Acts to the latest portions of the New Testament canon, the affirmation is unchanging that Jesus Christ, ascended to the right hand of God, is now exercising dominion over the world."[1] The New Testament authors repeat, more than any other Old Testament passage, "The Lord [YHWH] says to my lord, 'Sit at my right hand until I make your enemies your footstool'" (Ps 110:1).[2] Yoder then suggests that the Pauline theology of the principalities and powers makes this early Christian conviction intelligible. Christ has taken the captivating powers captive and established a universal peace. The forces that long rended humanity have been rendered impotent. While the fullness of the victory tarries, Christians are fully justified in obeying their lord, precisely because he is not just "their" lord; he is lord of the powers, and imitation of Jesus' particular politics participates in universal redemption. This section examines how Yoder navigates this intersection between the particularity and universality of Christian life.

1. Yoder, *CWS*, 8.
2. See, e.g., Mark 12:36 (and parallels); Acts 2:34–35; Heb 1:3.

The Lordship of Christ over the Powers

In a brief epilogue to *Christ and the Powers*, Hendrik Berkhof suggests that Paul's references to the principalities and powers are part of "his view of life and the world" more than of his explicit theology.[3] Through his encounter with Christ, even his most basic "world view" had been transformed: "In the light of God's action Paul perceived that mankind is not composed of loose individuals, but that structures, orders, forms of existence, or whatever they be called, are given [to] us as a part of creaturely life and that these are involved, as much as men themselves, in the history of creation, fall, preservation, reconciliation, and consummation."[4] Perhaps Yoder's main innovation on Berkhof is to expand these brief comments into a coherent vision of Pauline "philosophy of history."[5] This philosophy is first articulated in *Christian Witness to the State*.

As just reviewed, the argument of that book is grounded in the New Testament vision of Christ's universal lordship. The Old Testament authors caught something of this vision, but continued to confuse God's reign with their own national political hopes. Jesus then uniquely taught that "God's true purpose was the creation of a new society, unidentifiable with any of the local, national, or ethnic solidarities of the time."[6] This new society is now the focal point of history, as the state and the other powers are allowed by God to continue insofar as they provide "'scaffolding' service" for Christian witness.[7] History, Yoder avers, is shaped around the particularities of cross and resurrection, Israel and the church.

At the heart of *The Politics of Jesus* is the argument that the lordship of Christ entails his normativeness for Christian politics and ethics.[8] The chapter "Christ and Power" presents the apostolic writings on the principalities and powers as an outworking of Christ's normativeness in the realm of social interpretation. Because Christ is Lord, Christians can discern contemporary social structures in light of his work and of the continuing existence of the church. Yoder follows Berkhof's outline to trace Christ's central role

---

3. Berkhof, *C&P*, 65.

4. Ibid., 66. Berkhof acknowledges the limitations of "worldview" terminology as a temptation to (non-Christian) philosophical systematization (65).

5. Yoder, *Preface*, 248n3. Berkhof develops a biblical "theology of history" in his *Christ the Meaning of History*. His work on principalities and powers does not feature there, though he claims it influenced the project (*C&P*, 12; *Christ the Meaning of History*, 100n1).

6. Yoder, *CWS*, 10.

7. Ibid., 10–14.

8. Yoder, *PJ*, 11, 242, 246–47.

in the creation and redemption of the world. The powers "subsist" or "hold together" in Christ (Col 1:17).[9] Jesus effects redemption on the cross because he alone escapes the powers' tyranny.[10] Yoder goes on to cite Berkhof's contention that the "resurrection manifests what was already accomplished at the cross: that in Christ God has challenged the Powers, has penetrated into their territory, and has displayed that He is stronger than they."[11] Yoder offers another quotation from Berkhof in order to affirm the novelty of the church as a unified Jewish-Gentile community. This community has an irreplaceable role in the process of redemption, for "all resistance and every attack against the gods of this age will be unfruitful, unless the church itself is resistance and attack, unless it demonstrates in its own life and fellowship how believers can live freed from the powers."[12] Even though Christian faithfulness can enable present freedom, the redemption of the powers is ultimately "Jesus Christ's own task."[13] When Christians remove their eyes from Jesus and the church, believing that "the forces which really determine the march of history are in the hands of the leaders of the armies and the markets," they give in to the "temptation of the Sadducees" that Jesus rejected.[14] The conviction that Christ is Lord concerns "the nature of the cosmos and the significance of history."[15] The church is free for discipleship because history ultimately belongs to God. In his 1994 epilogue to the chapter, Yoder reaffirms that the "proclamation of Christ's rule over the rebellious world speaks a word of grace" to the entire cosmos.[16] The universality of Christ's lordship is unhindered by the particularity of his or the church's humanity.

The rest of *The Politics of Jesus* proposes voluntary subordination and suffering as socially transformative—such activity participates in the "war of the Lamb" and goes "with the grain of the cosmos."[17] "The cross of Christ," Yoder argues, "is the model of Christian social efficacy, the power of God for those who believe."[18] His Stone Lecture "Behold My Servant Shall Prosper" expands upon this statement with its investigation of servanthood

9. Ibid., 140–41.

10. Ibid., 145 (emphasis added); cf. 187.

11. Ibid., 146, quoting Berkhof, *C&P*, 146. Berkhof later argues that the "resurrection has the ascendancy and victory over the cross" and eschatological consummation makes a "break" from the *"Gestalt"* of the cross (*Christ the Meaning of History*, 180).

12. Yoder, *PJ*, 148, quoting Berkhof, *C&P*, 51.

13. Yoder, *PJ*, 149, quoting Berkhof, *C&P*, 52.

14. Yoder, *PJ*, 153; cf. *OR*, 19–21.

15. Yoder, *PJ*, 157.

16. Ibid., 161.

17. Ibid., 246.

18. Ibid., 242.

as a practical form of deploying power.[19] Yoder then offers the theology of the principalities and powers as an analytical framework undergirding "a useable contemporary vision of social process" (162). God's creative and redemptive action—especially through the death and resurrection of Jesus Christ—provides Christians with standards for subtle social discernment (162–66). Jesus' suffering servanthood provides a powerful pattern that may be deployed in a variety of ways and situations (166–67). It works, ultimately, because it goes along with God's fatherly design and is "in conformity with the victory of the Lamb" (167).

Yoder's argument in "Behold My Servant Shall Prosper" that servanthood is efficacious is meant as an example of his thesis that ecclesial practices can be taken up in analogous forms by other communities with transformative effect (149). Because the church is fundamentally an "order of *service*," non-ecclesial groups can learn from the church and adopt servanthood patterns (151). The rationale for this thesis is set forth in the first of Yoder's Stone Lectures, published as "Why Ecclesiology is Social Ethics: Gospel Ethics Versus the Wider Wisdom."[20] In that lecture Yoder suggests that "gospel social ethics" are only possible if faith in Christ makes a difference for how people live.[21] The church is the group that tries to live by the implications of its central proclamation, Christ is Lord. It is therefore a community determined most of all by the biblical narratives about Jesus Christ (110–21). The narrative character of Christian life means it proclaims a "gospel connected with a particular name and place and time, with Jesus and the Jews and Jerusalem" (110). Liturgy and worship too affirm the church's "rootedness in the particularity of Judaism and Jesus"—whether or not that affirmation can be "verified" by supposedly more universal stories (113). Indeed, implicit in the doctrine of election is the confidence that the particularity of the Jewish and Christian stories is not a mark against their truthfulness (115). According to its central narratives, the church bears "the meaning of history" (118). Within history it is led by the Holy Spirit—"not a reasoning process but a mode of God's own working"—to faithfulness (122). God leads the church victoriously, and so its life is characterized by doxology, patterns of celebration that instill in its members a distinctive view of reality (123).

19. Yoder, "Servant," 151–60. References to "Servant" in this and the following paragraph are in the text.

20. Yoder, *RP*, 103–26. Unless otherwise noted, references to *RP* in this and the following paragraph are in the text.

21. Ibid. Yoder develops his argument in dialogue with Barth, *Against the Stream*, 15–50, and *Church Dogmatics* 4/2:719–26 (on the exemplarity of "True Church law").

This fact of a particularly contingent community gratefully guided by its victorious lord is, Yoder contends, good news for the world. The church is good news because it is how God shows where God is leading the whole world (126). Because the coming kingdom is "social in its essence," the shape of its real presence in the church can be imitated by others (104, 125–26). As Yoder argues in the second Stone Lecture, "The Scandal of the Apocalypse," the church's conviction that God is active in redeeming the world means it must challenge sociological and political assumptions about causality.[22] Yoder's point is not that causation as such should be abandoned, but that we should expect, if Christ is Lord, for his practices to be causally effective in everyday social settings. In "Behold My Servant Shall Prosper" he makes this case in regards to servanthood, and in the fourth and fifth lectures he looks at the analogical potential of various specific ecclesial practices.[23] God is bringing a "new world,"[24] and it is publicly accessible in the life of the church insofar as that is determined by the particular stories of God's inter-actions with humanity through Jesus Christ, and by particular practices that respond doxologically to God's victory over the powers.

Yoder articulates the specifically Christian basis for nonviolent prac-tice two years later in his Warsaw Lectures. His genealogy of the modern nonviolence movement from King to Gandhi to Tolstoy suggests that it cannot survive without a substantive religious cosmology that disciplines its members and gives them hope.[25] For Christians, this cosmology is pro-vided by the early church's view of the creation, fall, and redemption of the principalities and powers.[26] At the center of that cosmology is, of course, the risen Lord Christ: "to say that Christ is Lord does not mean only a declara-tion of personal allegiance but a statement about the shape and destiny of the cosmos. He must reign until all his enemies are under his feet (1 Cor 15:25): that is the significance of present history."[27] Fourteen years later, in "How H. Richard Niebuhr Reasoned," Yoder reaffirms his commitment to this cosmology by showing how it sustains a variegated and transformative Christian cultural engagement. The particularities of Christ's Jewishness

22. Published as parts of Yoder, "Armaments and Eschatology," and "Ethics and Eschatology."

23. Those lectures were published with heavy revisions as Yoder, "Sacrament as Social Process," and *RP*, 360–73.

24. The general title of Yoder's Stone Lectures was "New World on the Way" (*RP*, 126).

25. Yoder, *Nonviolence*, 17–26.

26. Ibid., 95–103.

27. Ibid., 100.

and humanity provide the baseline for cultural transformation, given that he is lord of all the cultural powers.[28]

Ecumenism and Exile

As discussed in chapter 1, Yoder was involved in ecumenical activities for the majority of his career. Many of the earliest scholars of Yoder's work found ecumenism to be definitive of his theological approach. Mark Thiessen Nation focused his doctoral dissertation on Yoder's "ecumenical patience and vocation" and his subsequent book emphasized the "catholicity" of Yoder's Anabaptist ethics.[29] Though he has recently become more critical of Yoder, in *The Politics of the Cross* Craig A. Carter represents Yoderian ethics as "a viable option for mainstream Christianity" and the rightful inheritor to classical orthodoxy.[30] Michael G. Cartwright, who wrote one of the first introductions to Yoder's thought, portrays Yoder as unifying radical reform ethics with radically catholic theology.[31] According to Cartwright, the Anabaptist practice of fraternal admonition is behind Yoder's ecumenism: "Yoder's approach to ecumenicity takes the form of admonition, and he in turn has invited 'mutual correction' from others, thereby seeking to elicit the kind of ongoing dialogue between the various communions which he would argue always characterized the church."[32] Admonitory dialogue with Christians is directed to common resources, such as scripture, but Yoder's conviction that the gospel can become intelligible in any context facilitates a variety of conversations.[33] Yoder's writings thus engage liberation theologians,[34] evangelicals,[35] Methodists,[36] various Reformed Christians,[37]

---

28. Yoder, "HRN," 87.

29. Nation, *John Howard Yoder*.

30. Carter, *Politics of the Cross*, 19, 23. See note 52 in chapter five above about recent changes to Carter's evaluation of Yoder.

31. Cartwright, "Radical Reform, Radical Catholicity," esp. 31–41.

32. Ibid., 32.

33. Ibid., 32, 35.

34. Yoder, "Exodus and Exile"; *WL*, 169–72. Yoder's *OR*, *PJ*, and "Jesus and Power" address liberation themes.

35. Yoder, "Evangelical Dualism"; "Southern Baptists."

36. Yoder, *OR*, 13–33; *PK*, 64–65, 69, 199; *BP*.

37. Besides his theology of the powers, see Yoder, "Reformed versus Anabaptist Social Strategies"; McClendon and Yoder, "Christian Identity"; Mouw and Yoder, "Anabaptist-Reformed Dialogue."

members of other "believers" and "peace" churches,[38] Roman Catholics,[39] Jews,[40] and secular intellectuals.[41] His contributions to the global ecumenical movement span the entirety of his career, a career that for many years was based in a Roman Catholic institution, the University of Notre Dame. Yoder's theology of the powers was no exception, and it was constructed for ecumenical purposes as well. For Yoder, the theology of the powers is a mode of dialogical theology, one way he seeks to engage the wider church in terms it can understand in order to move it to a practice of discipleship that is indebted to his Anabaptist tradition. It is a central means by which he proclaims his particular understanding of the universal lordship of Christ, that is, by which he proclaims the gospel.

Yoder's approach to catholicity is further outlined in an essay he composed with the "baptist" theologian James McClendon, "Christian Identity in Ecumenical Perspective: A Response to David Wayne Layman."[42] As the essay's title indicates, it was written to counter arguments against the authors by Layman, a Mennonite whose interest in Mercersburg theology puts him close to Roman Catholicism at several points.[43] Layman's criticisms are leveled at Yoder and McClendon's "restitutionist" attempt to circumvent patristic and medieval developments for a direct return to the early church.[44] For Layman, the Mercersburg theologians rightly require critical acceptance of later developments as continuous with the early church. Trinitarian ontology, high Christology, and high eucharistic theology should be central to an "Evangelical Catholicity in an Anabaptist-Mennonite Key."[45] According to McClendon and Yoder, their restitutionism does allow for identification with the great theological traditions of the church.[46] However, they suggest that "catholicity" cannot be defined as a pure theological construct. It can only be achieved in practice through the interrelations of a number

38. Yoder," "Believers' Church Conferences"; *CWS*; "'Peace Church' Perspective"; *RP*, 221–322; "Unique Role"; Gwyn, Hunsinger, Roop, and Yoder, *Declaration of Peace*.

39. Yoder, *WWIU*; *Nonviolence*, 107–46.

40. Yoder, *JCSR*; "Texts That Serve."

41. Yoder, *FTN*, 51–78; "Meaning after Babble."

42. McClendon, *Ethics*, 19–20, identifies himself with the "baptist" tradition coming out of the Radical Reformation.

43. Mercersburg theology is associated with German Reformed theologians Philip Shaff and John Nevin in nineteenth-century Pennsylvania. As described by McClendon, Yoder, and Layman, it emphasizes high church sacramental and trinitarian theology as authentic ancient Christianity.

44. Layman, "Inner Ground," 483–87.

45. Ibid., 499–502.

46. McClendon and Yoder, "Christian Identity," 571–72.

of churches striving to be faithful—and this unity is what the "baptist" emphasis on dialogue before scripture enables.[47] Such "baptist ecumenism" is to be contrasted with the "Constantinian ecumenism" that forces unity without due conversation.[48] McClendon and Yoder therefore suggest that a unified Christian identity can only be achieved through the negotiation of particular ecclesial communities as they occur in time. This achievement is a gift of the Holy Spirit, who facilitates Christian dialogue.[49] Catholicity comes through patient exploration of distinctions as a response to God's prevenient unifying activity.

Yoder's perspective on interfaith dialogue is similar. In his paper "Disavowing Constantine: An Alternative Perspective on Interfaith Dialogue," he distances Radical Protestant from Christendom models of dialogue. The latter seeks meta-frameworks for dialogue that inevitably "jettison the particular, the local, the Jewish, the specific biblical content. Jesus then matters less and agreement more. Universality will be sought at the price of specificity. Dialogue will mean the uncovering of commonality."[50] The Radical Protestant alternative is to focus on concrete encounters between local, internally dialogical congregations and other communities. These congregations engage others with a spirit of repentance for the sins of Christendom (250–51, 255–56). The present post-Christendom age may be marked by Christian "diaspora," but there is much work to be done "to get out of the way so that instead of, or beyond, us or our ancestors, us or our language system, us or our strengths or weaknesses, the people we converse with might see Jesus" (261). Repentance, in other words, opens the possibility of a form of dialogue that does not evade Christian particulars but rather places them as a real option before the interlocutor. If dialogue is to be truly dialogical, and not another means of coercion, then Christians too must see their interlocutor's faith as an option (255). It may even be possible to recognize the authentic faith of those like Gandhi who follow Jesus' way but do not invoke his name because of its negative cultural and political connotations (260–61). The question, for Yoder, is not whether Gandhi and similar persons are "anonymous Christians." "Since Constantine, it would be no compliment to Gandhi to ask the question that way. But the question is whether he was following Jesus, and if so, which Jesus?"[51]

47. Ibid., 562–65.

48. Ibid., 573. The authors examine the early Anabaptists, Particular Baptists, and Restorationists as exemplars of baptist ecumenism (576–58).

49. Ibid., 578–79.

50. Yoder, *RP*, 257. Unless otherwise noted, references to *RP* in this and the following paragraph are in the text.

51. Ibid. Karl Rahner proposed that some who do not know or reject Christ may

These comments suggest that Yoder's interests in interfaith dialogue might extend beyond the typical preoccupation with "world religions" to the encouragement of practical discipleship in a multitude of forms and under a multitude of guises. He states this capacious vision clearly in "Disavowing Constantine": "Christians have no intrinsic reason to prefer ancient interlocutors to new ones. If Marx, or Freud, or Darwin, or Adam Smith becomes the faith of a believing community, those believers, too, are potential partners for dialogue" (253). Secular interlocutors indeed began to appear in Yoder's work more frequently as his career progressed. As detailed in chapter 4, he was interested in sociology and anthropology, and he also wrote several essays on Christian knowledge and communication in a pluralistic setting.[52] Among these are two essays that engage philosopher Jeffrey Stout's book *Ethics after Babel*.[53]

The first of these, "Meaning after Babble: With Jeffrey Stout beyond Relativism," was published in the *Journal of Religious Ethics* in 1996.[54] There Yoder applauds Stout's refusal of any moral "foundation" that could somehow resolve disputes between communities without immersion into the lives of the actual communities (134). He likewise affirms Stout's insistence that this lack of foundations does not preclude the possibility of inter-communal conversation (131). However, Yoder detects a measure of nostalgia in Stout's work for a mythical time "before" rampant pluralism (126, 132). In Yoder's view no such time existed. The appearance of universal moral language has merely been imposed on pluralist reality by medieval church and Enlightenment state. The biblical story of the tower of Babel is not, furthermore, a lament over a lost monoculture (127, on Gen. 11). In the larger Genesis narrative God has just commanded that his people scatter over the earth (Gen. 9–10), so it is more likely that Babel stands as a warning against centralization and homogeneity. The reality of pluralism is thus ancient and providential, and its greatest challenge is not Babel (or foundationalism) but "babble," linguistic obfuscation that systematically renders cross-cultural communication impossible ("Meaning after Babble," 127–29).

---

in fact be "anonymous Christians," saved by Christ through their unwitting conformity to his way. See Biggar, *Behaving in Public*, 100–101, for a defense of the concept. More recent research on Gandhi significantly complicates Yoder's depiction of him as simply following Jesus in Hindu garb. For review of the relevant literature, see Anderson, "Gandhi Centre Stage."

52. Most of these essays have been gathered as Yoder, *PWK*.

53. Stout, *Ethics after Babel*.

54. Yoder, "Meaning after Babble." References to this essay in this and the following paragraph are in the text.

Stout seeks to circumvent the challenge of babble with a minimalist appeal to absolute ethics, encapsulated in the statement that slavery is an absolute moral evil.[55] Thoughtful moderns all agree on this statement, and our unenlightened ancestors may be excused by their lack of resources to question a prevalent institution. But Yoder points out a number of exceptions to the statement and, moreover, worries that by positing it Stout is still clinging to the remnants of foundationalist discourse (130–32). The alternative for Yoder "is to go through and beyond the relativity, not to try and stop just a millimeter short of it" (132). This alternative seems to be what the Genesis narrator has in mind in the Babel story. It is what Jeremiah and Ezekiel do by focusing their hearers on faithful living within Babylon, and what Peter and Paul do by using Hellenistic intellectual frameworks to preach the gospel (132–33). Relativism is not navigated by escaping it, but rather by "a vision of a coming world, a community, larger than any present community, but still finite, historically real, larger than the Corleones [i.e., traditionalists] and the Modernists, larger than the Messianic Jews and the Hellenists, *because* it was created—in the first fruits of real first-century life—out of the costly reconciliation of both of them, by means of one instance of the kind of vulnerable cross-cultural communication I have been describing" (133). Reconciliation of Jew and Greek in the early church is thus paradigmatic of the possibilities of inter-communal dialogue. For Jews and Christians such a possibility is intrinsic in their calling to organize their communities around publicly available texts in a variety of settings, employing a variety of languages. This confidence in the fruitfulness of ordinary cross-cultural encounter is rooted not in a theory of universal ethical norms, but in doxology: God "is the creator, sustainer, and ultimate savior" of the nations, so the gospel must be translatable always and everywhere (136).

Shortly before the publication of "Meaning after Babel," Yoder gave a paper titled "See How They Go with Their Face to the Sun" at a colloquium on "Communities in Exile" convened in Los Angeles.[56] Although he engages Stout in this paper too, the purpose here is to elaborate the prophet Jeremiah's understanding of "*galuth* as calling" (51). *Galuth* is a Yiddish word Yoder translates as "diaspora identity" (52). Yoder locates Jeremiah's diaspora call in his admonition to the Jews in Babylon to "seek the welfare of the city where I have sent you into exile, and pray to the Lord on its behalf, for in its welfare you will find your welfare" (Jer 29:7).[57] Diaspora was thus

---

55. Stout, *Ethics after Babel*, 82–105.

56. Yoder, *FTN*, 51–78 (also in *JCSR*, 182–202). Unless otherwise noted, references to *FTN* in this and the following paragraph are in the text.

57. Yoder, *FTN*, 53. Yoder provides his own translation of the text in a later note: "seek the salvation of the culture to which God has sent you" (76n60). Cartwright,

not a seventy-year "detour" between exile (586 BC) and the restoration of the temple, but rather "the beginning of the mission of the next millennium and a half" (53). Yoder notes how, as Babylon became the worldwide center of Judaism, its Jewish inhabitants were able to pioneer a number of sociological innovations. Chief among these innovations is the synagogue, a non-hierarchical form of local community life sustained by concrete contacts with other communities and based around practical, doxological attention to shared religious texts (58–59). Furthermore, "nothing about the self-esteem of the bearers of this new lifestyle is dependent upon or drives toward cultural homogeneity, political control, or autarchy. Jewish culture is comfortable and creative in dialogue with whatever Gentile world it lands in, as long as it is tolerated" (59).

Yoder then moves on to discuss how, contra Stout, *galuth* is a recovery of the "real mission" of God's people as indicated by the Babel story (61–65). Diaspora is in fact the sociological outworking of Jewish convictions about God's sovereignty, the coming messiah, the failure of Maccabean nationalism, and the moral value of suffering (68–69). The refusal to "take charge" is clear, and "from Jeremiah until Theodore Hertzl this was the dominant Jewish vision."[58] Jesus and his followers would have shared this vision, and from this vantage early Christian pacifism is wholly unsurprising (68–70). Jesus himself "added more and deeper authentically Jewish reasons, and reinforced and further validated the already expressed Jewish reasons, for the already well established ethos of not being in charge."[59] *Galuth* as a Jewish and Christian vocation therefore is not based on nostalgia for past glories; it is rather based on the conviction that every setting offers opportunities for demonstrating how the particular history of God's dealings with humanity can be renewed. Yoder is worth quoting at length here:

> Jeremiah does not tell his refugee brothers and sisters to try to teach the Babylonians Hebrew. The concern to learn goes in the other direction. Jews will not only learn the local languages; they will in a few generations (and for a millennium and a half) be serving the entire ancient Near Eastern world as expert translators, scribes, diplomats, sages, merchants, astronomers. They will make a virtue and a cultural advantage of their being resident aliens, not spending their substance in fighting over civil sovereignty. Their conviction that there is but one God—creator,

JCSR, 29n68, disputes this translation.

58. Yoder, *FTN*, 68. Theodore Herzl (1860–1904) was an early Jewish Zionist whose efforts later inspired the founding of the State of Israel.

59. Yoder, *FTN*, 69. Yoder cites his essay "The Political Axioms of the Sermon on the Mount," *OR*, 34–54, as explicating this argument.

sovereign, anikonic, historically active, able to speak—enhances
their cultural creativity over against the polytheistic, supersti-
tious, tribally structured, fertility-focused popular religions of
their neighbors (71).

In other words, by embracing the particularities of Jewish identity in a process
that includes dialogue with non-Jews, diaspora Jews have brought peace to
Babylon and other cities. They have "in fact contributed mightily to making
the Gentile world viable" (76). Christians are called to do likewise in their
internal, ecumenical, and interfaith dialogical engagement of the powers.

Criticisms

John Howard Yoder's writings on the principalities and powers, ecumenism, and exile suggest that the Christian proclamation of the universal lordship of Christ is unhindered by the historical particularities of Jesus, Israel,
and the church. Indeed, the universality of Christ's lordship is manifested
in his suffering service at a particular place and time in history, and it is
the redemptive potential of suffering service that is the shape and content
of Christian witness, namely, cross and resurrection. The gospel message
itself comes in the form of noncoercive dialogue, of open conversation that
structures both a congregation's doxology and its engagement of others it
meets along the diaspora way.[60]

By constantly emphasizing the church's adherence to the particularities of the universal lordship of Christ, Yoder has earned the sectarian label
discussed in the previous chapter. For opponents of sectarianism and other
critics, Yoder's vision of discipleship is *too* indebted to the particular histories of Israel, Jesus and the early church. James M. Gustafson summarizes
this objection to Yoder's overly "historicist" approach well. Yoder, as with
other historicist theologians, "rejects in principle the need to make the
particular ethics of the Christian tradition universal in its implications; the
theologian rejects the need to show that Christian ethics are applicable to
all persons. Rather, the Christian community is a particular historical community with a special vocation to follow its Lord, Jesus."[61] Gustafson's solution is a "theocentrism" that accents the universality of God rather than the
particularities of Jewish and Christian revelation. Writing in a neo-Calvinist
evangelical register, Richard J. Mouw protests Yoder's extreme historicism

60. Cf. Yoder, "Meaning after Babble," 135, on the unity between medium (dialogical community) and message (lordship of Christ) in Christian witness.

61. Gustafson, *Protestant and Roman Catholic Ethics*, 66. See Yoder's response in
"Theological Revision."

by pointing out the various ways in which Christians cannot or should not imitate Jesus' suffering servanthood: the metaphysical transaction with God and payment of ransom to the powers cannot be repeated, and the physical agony of the cross should be avoided when possible.[62] Some feminist and womanist theologians have likewise complained that making suffering servanthood paradigmatic justifies the subjugation of women and ethnic minorities.[63] On this view, the "original" meaning of the cross is negated by its later role in oppression.

Jewish philosopher Daniel J. Boyarin similarly warns against Yoder's acceptance of the language and practice of Christian mission.[64] In this case Yoder is too Christian and not Jewish enough—the Jews, according to Boyarin, are content to fulfill the commandments, trust that God is present in the world, and "leave other people alone."[65] The readings of Yoder's work on Judaism by Peter Ochs, Michael G. Cartwright, and Douglas K. Harink seem to confirm Boyarin's fears. They suggest that Yoder's zeal to vindicate his christocentric model ends in an ahistorical assimilation of Jewish history to Christian pacifism.[66] He is thereby inadvertently guilty of a kind of supersessionism[67] that denies the ambiguous realities of a Judaism which holds, from Jeremiah's time on, "religious ideals of centrality and not centrality, landedness and non-landedness, group particularity and universality."[68] Yoder reduces the complexity of his Jewish interlocutors' positions, absorbing them into his own, and so circumscribes the possibility of dialogue producing anything new.[69] In other words, he has

---

62. Mouw, *Politics and the Biblical Drama*, 113–14.

63. See note 24 in chapter five above.

64. Boyarin, "Judaism as a Free Church," 14–15.

65. Ibid.

66. Ochs in Yoder, *JCSR*, 119–20, 158–59, 179, 203–4; Cartwright in Yoder, *JCSR*, 211, 215–17, 219–20, 222–23. See also Harink, "The Anabaptist and the Apostle," 283–84; Nugent, "Biblical Warfare Revisited," 167–84.

67. Cartwright in Yoder, *JCSR*, 229, calls this a "neo-neo-supersessionism": "In no sense, does Yoder seek to replace Judaism with Christianity in the punitive sense of classical Christian supersessionism. Neither does he engage in the kind of displacement and erasure of Judaism that modernist Protestant theologicans sought in what in retrospect appears to be a form of *neo*-supersessionism. But in seeking a way for Jews and Christian to share a common witness for peace, Yoder slips into a form of *neo*-neo-supersessionism that, in effect, *erases* the covenantal basis of Jewish peoplehood even as it attempts to *redescribe* Jewish identity within the framework of the 'new covenant' of Jesus" (emphases original).

68. Ochs in Yoder, *JCSR*, 120. See also A. E. Weaver, *States of Exile*, 35–38.

69. Ochs in Yoder, *JCSR*, 158–59,

yet to learn fully the lessons of noncoercive dialogue and remains within the Constantinian imperialist project.

For secular political philosopher Romand Coles, there is a possible contradiction between Yoder's vulnerable dialogical stance and his "jealousy of Jesus as Lord."[70] At issue here is Yoder's proclamation of the universal lordship of Christ, and his concomitant suspicion of all other claims to lordship. Coles asks whether or not this jealousy "is entwined with and works in spite of itself toward the closure of the church's generous and receptive participation in historical generativity."[71] Yoder's jealousy may empower to a degree the radical politics to which "he so profoundly calls us," but "it needs to be inflected differently and reshaped, not only for the radical democratic community coalitions in which [Coles is] most invested but for the work that Yoder calls Good News."[72] Mennonite theologians Peter Dula and Alex Sider defend Yoder at this point by suggesting that the centrality of reconciliatory practice in his ecclesiology assumes "that there is no way of knowing now what kind of edges the body of Christ might finally be found to have."[73] Drawing on a quotation from Rowan Williams, they suggest that the tyrannical implications of Yoder's jealousy are mitigated by his institutionalization of "relations of 'profound and costly involvement with each other and receiving from each other' both inside and outside the church."[74]

Yet it is precisely this decentered ecclesiology that Paul Martens finds suspicious. In his essay "Universal History and a Not-Particularly-Christian Particularity: Jeremiah and John Howard Yoder's Social Gospel," Martens narrates Yoder's "gradual evolution from articulating a strong Jesus-centered ethic toward an articulation of a less-than-particularly Christian social ethic rooted in a construal of universal history."[75] At the center of this evolution is Yoder's increasing conviction that Jesus and the church stand in continuity with Jeremiah and the exilic synagogue. Martens notes how, in an essay from 1954, Yoder depicts Jeremiah as one of the prophets who correctly proclaims the eschatological nature of peace.[76] The church may be "a new people in the prophets' line," but it is

70. Coles, *Beyond Gated Politics*, 135.

71. Ibid.

72. Ibid., 136.

73. Dula and Sider, "Radical Democracy," 500. See also Hauerwas and Coles, *Christianity, Democracy, and the Radical Ordinary.*

74. Ibid., quoting Williams, *The Truce of God*, 27.

75. Martens, "Universal History," 131–32.

76. Ibid., 136, citing Yoder, *OR*, 68. Martens seems to confuse Jeremiah's "resumé" of the false prophets with Jeremiah's own message, probably because of a textual error in Yoder's essay (compare *OR*, 68, to *RP*, 153).

truly "new" insofar as it exists as a response to Jesus Christ's unique role in bringing the new aeon alongside the old.[77] By the late 1980s, Martens argues, it is difficult to discern what for Yoder is new about the church or, indeed, about Jesus Christ.[78] In his 1988 essay "To Serve Our God and to Rule the World," Yoder treats eschatological themes without using eschatological language. Christian doxology is now the primary category, for this contributes to "the progress of world history in light of the 'Rule of the Lamb.'"[79] Christians do learn their doxological stance from Jesus, but Yoder is emphatic that Jesus affirms Jeremiah's call to "seek the peace of the city"—and that this call provides the shape of doxology.[80] By the mid-1990s, in the essay "See How They Go with Their Faces to the Sun," Yoder makes no distinction between Jeremiah's call and Jesus' mission, and both are defined as a sociological stance of "not being in control."[81] "Seeking the peace of the city" now has little to do with Christ's eschatological inbreaking and much to do with a universal, "secular" socio-political struggle.[82]

Martens presents a powerful, though certainly disputable, case that Yoder moves from Christian particularity to sociological universality. The summary of Yoder's theologies of the powers, ecumenism, and exile presented above hopefully suggests significant continuity in Yoder's early and late work. This continuity is provided by his lifelong conviction that the meaning of history is defined by the death and resurrection of Jesus Christ, and by Christ's subsequent rule over the powers and the church. But Martens is right to point out the ambiguities that exist between Yoder's proclamation of the lordship of Christ and the significant overlap he finds between Christ, Jeremiah, Gandhi, and others. Is Jesus uniquely definitive of true social and political life, or is he merely an exemplar of what can be discovered from various sources? When these ambiguities are considered alongside criticisms from those who think Yoder is too tied to the particular history of Jesus, the question arises as to the coherence of Yoder's theology of Christian particularity. If Yoder can be seen as both an embodiment of extreme Christian historicism and of generic secularism, then one suspects either that his position is ill-articulated, or that it is inherently unstable.

---

77. Martens, "Universal History," 136, on Yoder, *OR*, 61.

78. Martens, "Universal History," 137–39, on Yoder, *RP*, 128–40.

79. Martens, "Universal History," 138–39.

80. Ibid., 138.

81. Ibid., 139–41.

82. Ibid., 141.

Bourdieu on the Particular and the Universal

Pierre Bourdieu's political concepts and practices are rooted in the history of the European Enlightenment, a movement he takes to have universal implications. In a similar manner to Yoder's renewal of Anabaptism, Bourdieu seeks a critical *resourcement* of Enlightenment and, more generally, modern European social and political thought with its focus on universal reason and ethics. Yet as a sociological inheritor of the Enlightenment, he is suspicious of symbolic formulations of the universal that remain detached from actual habitus and fields. He therefore calls for an *Aüfklarung of Aüfklarung*, an "Enlightenment of Enlightenment," in order to universalize "the universal" in social reality as in theory.

The irreducible specificity of social reality means, of course, that universalizing the universal also particularizes the universal. It requires negotiating concrete social spaces in order to give rise to a mode of universal distribution suited to each space and time—but for this universalization process to be effective, the universal has to remain universal and not merely another particular. This dialectical quality of the universal as both an historical product and a transhistorical norm is what makes Bourdieu's recovery of the Enlightenment an interesting model for the revision of Yoder's theology of Christian particularity.

Reason, Truth, and Virtue

In 1985 Bourdieu was interviewed about his sociological approach by three German scholars, among them the now renowned critical theorist Axel Honneth.[83] Near the end of the interview Bourdieu was asked why he, unlike Honneth's teacher Jürgen Habermas, has no place for universal norms in his work.[84] Bourdieu response was consistent with his general sociological approach: "I have a tendancy of posing the problem of reason and norms in a resolutely historicist manner."[85] He then goes on to elaborate his historicist "radical doubt," reviewed in the third chapter above.

---

83. Bourdieu, *CD*, 13–46. The other two interviewers were Hermann Kocyba, a critical theorist, and Bernd Schwibs, a sociologist of French literature.

84. Bourdieu, *CD*, 43. Jürgen Habermas argues that reason is made possible by structures inherent in language. See Habermas, "What is Universal Pragmatics"; Habermas, *Theory of Communication*, 8–42. On Habermas and Bourdieu see Crossley, "Systematically Distorted Communication"; Pilario, *Rough Ground of Praxis*, 221–22; Poupeau, "Reasons for Domination"; Vázquez García, *Pierre Bourdieu*, 220–224.

85. Bourdieu, *CD*, 43: "J'ai tendance à poser le problème de la raison ou des normes de manière résolument historiciste."

The point for Bourdieu, however, is not to wallow in doubt and relativism. Rather, he argues that "one must push historicism to its limit, by a sort of radical doubt, to see what can really be saved."[86] Chief among those things that Bourdieu believes "can be really saved" are reason and truth. He does not suggest that they have "foundations" outside of history, but rather that they can be further produced by examining the social conditions of their production. The moments within history that have been conducive to reason and truth, to an "interest in the universal," are guides to their further production. As an historical product, "truth is a stake in the struggles of every field."[87] Yet it is the scientific field that paradigmatically demonstrates how truth is produced, as the constant threat of mutual critique there leads to rigorous self-critique, to reflexivity. Bourdieu's "politics of truth" (*politique de la vérité*), the *Realpolitik* of reason discussed in the previous chapter, employs the reflexive tools of reason to protect and develop the field autonomy necessary to further the production of reason. There is no absolute or universal foundation for reason and truth, but only a continual labor of wielding the provisional instruments of reason, honed by reflexivity, "to tear oneself away, at least partially, from the relative."[88]

A few years later, in an interview with Loïc Wacquant at the University of Chicago, Bourdieu again addressed a question about reason, truth, and historicism. Wacquant frames the question broadly, suggesting that Bourdieu's approach overcomes antimonies in European philosophy between rationalism and idealism. These antinomies surface in contemporary debates involving Habermas and relativist "postmodernists," debates that have a precedent in the conflicts between followers of Kantian critique and Hegelian speculation.[89] Bourdieu's answer is similar to the one he gave to his German interlocutors, and he stresses the need for "collective reflection and action designed to bolster the *institutional conditions of rational communication* in the social sciences" in order to secure scientific autonomy.[90] These conditions are only brought about by thorough reflexivity. "*Reflexivity is a tool to produce*

86. Ibid., 43: "il faut pousser jusqu'à sa limite l'historicisme, par une sorte de doute radical, pour voir ce qui peut être réellement sauvé."

87. Ibid., 44: "La vérité est un enjeu de luttes en tout champ."

88. Ibid., 45: "pour s'arracher, au mois partiellement, au relatif."

89. Bourdieu, *IRS*, 188; see also 156n12. The "postmodernist" usually targeted by Bourdieu is Michel Foucault, though he also names Giles Deleuze, Jacques Derrida, and Richard Rorty (*Distinction*, 485–500; *PM*, 36, 110, 194n22). These thinkers tend to deny any concept of universality, and identify knowledge and power completely, e.g., Foucault, "Truth and Power." On Foucault and Bourdieu see Callewaert, "Bourdieu, Critic of Foucault"; Lash, "Modernization and Postmodernization," 237–65; Schubert, "Politics of Transgression."

90. Bourdieu, *IRS*, 188.

more science, not less," he contends, "it is not designed to discourage scientific ambition but to make it realistic." He goes on to insist that, "by helping the progress of science, and thus the growth of knowledge about the social world, reflexivity makes possible a more responsible politics, both inside and out-side of academia."[91] Practices of critical reflexivity facilitate the construction of "rational utopias," transformations of current political institutions toward reasonable ends fitted to the occasion. Such reflexive utopias include the transformation of persons, and Bourdieu speaks further of concrete, histori-cal realizations of the rational "universal subject."[92] By enabling the identifica-tion of "true sites of freedom," reflexivity helps practical reasoners construct "small-scale, modest, practical morals in keeping with the scope of human freedom."[93] Instead of the Enlightenment faith that philosophical discourse, within or without the "bounds of reason," can identify the contours of ratio-nal institutions and persons, Bourdieu offers sociological illumination of the historical conditions conducive to reason and virtue.

In lectures at the Collège de France given around the same time as his Chicago interview, Bourdieu elaborated his understanding of moral reason-ing in more detail. These lectures, published as "Is a Disinterested Act Possi-ble?," investigate whether or not self-interest and altruism are incompatible. For Bourdieu "interest" is a function of *illusio*, the "enchanted relation" that exists between habitus and field when the former has been fully immersed into the latter.[94] The resulting "feel for the game" is experienced as not only practical mastery of the dispositions, rules, and techniques needed to play well, but also as a sense that the game is important and worth playing—that the player has an interest in playing. Since social practice is always encap-sulated by and constitutive of a social field, there is no total escape from *illusio*. Self-interest predominates in every realm of human activity. Yet this admission does not, according to Bourdieu, correspond to a rejection of the possibility of disinterested actions, i.e., of actions that are not obviously directed toward one's own success in the game. The concepts of habitus and field suggest that genuine other regard is a possible disposition, even if it only exists under specific historical conditions (87, 89). The phenomenon of noblesse oblige, for instance, is a case in which generosity is definitive of nobility (87). This and other examples reinforce Bourdieu's argument that rational change occurs through the direction of personal to universal inter-est: "Without bringing in any metaphysical hypothesis . . ., one can say that

91. Ibid., 194.

92. Ibid., 190–91.

93. Ibid., 199.

94. Bourdieu, *PR*, 77. References to *PR* in this and the following paragraph are in the text.

reason has a basis in history and that if reason progresses even the slightest, it is because there are interests in universalization and because, universally, but above all in certain universes, such as the artistic or scientific field, it is better to seem disinterested rather than interested, as generous and altruistic rather than egotistical" (89). Virtue is possible when social games are set up to encourage players to revise their interests for the interests of others.

Bourdieu extended these moral reflections in a paper entitled, "A Paradoxical Foundation of Ethics." Setting aside forms of ethical analysis that begin with the "universally witnessed, metadiscursive or metapractical second-order strategies that agents employ in order to appear (in act or intention) to conform to a universal rule," Bourdieu rather focuses on practices that effectively realize the universal (141). He claims that these practices are effective because they appeal to all the members of a group and thereby affirm group identity (142). Kant's categorical imperative is based in this logic, as it insists on judging moral statements by their universalizability (144). Even "suspicion constitutes a kind of partaking of the profits of the universal," as it denounces actions that promote the interests of one part of the group over another (143). Moral persons and institutions are thus possible when they are ceaselessly scrutinized according to the criterion of universality. "It would be a question," Bourdieu avers, "of establishing social universes where, as in the Machiavellian ideal republic, agents had an interest in virtue, disinterestedness, and devotion to public service and the common good" (144). The "values of civil virtue" such as equality, fraternity, disinterest, and sincerity are universal because they foster criticism of the ways one's own and others' practices inhibit universality (145).

Bourdieu's own political activity bears witness to this interest in disinterest, as he spoke out on behalf of various marginalized groups. At the height of his engagement he was awarded the Ernst-Bloch-Preis for his outstanding scientific contributions to culture.[95] His acceptance speech, entitled "A Reasoned Utopia and Economic Fatalism," opposes a "banker's Europe" based on the fatalism that "the world cannot be any different from the way it is."[96] The dissemination of economic fatalism paralyzes alternative action, rendering Europe helpless before the non-universal self-interests of the economic elite. Against this false, imperialistic Europe he poses a rational utopia of "*a really European Europe*" in which the Enlightenment

95. Ernst Bloch, a German philosopher, is famous for his "principle of hope" (*Das Prinzip Hoffnung*) and his neo-Marxist theory of utopia. A description of the award can be found at the website of the Ernst Bloch Zentrum, last accessed August 31, 2011, http://www.bloch.de/content/view/39/57/. Bourdieu won the award in 1997.

96. Bourdieu, "Reasoned Utopia," 128.

tradition of universalization is given free reign.[97] In other speeches and occasional writings he likewise attacked contemporary journalists for serving as a vehicle for neo-liberal interests.[98] As intellectual practitioners these journalists were not only guilty of economic self-interest, but of betraying the European *intellectuel* who selflessly publishes knowledge at all costs.

The pursuit of the universal is thus for Bourdieu inseparable from the renewal of the particular histories that have promoted it, especially those of the European Enlightenment. Although the rhetoric of "globalization" is often used to promote the distribution of the benefits of European (and North American) culture globally, Bourdieu suspects that the distribution is far from universal. A truly global economic or political order would be responsive to the particular needs of all communities. The universal social order is therefore realized through care for particular others, and particular values, truths, and other forms of capital become universal when they are invested in the betterment of others.

Bourdieu treats these themes at length in the third chapter of *Pascalian Meditations*, "The Historicity of Reason."[99] There he begins by declaring historicization as "one of the most effective weapons in all the battles of the *Aufklärung* against obscurantism and absolutism and, more generally, against all the forms of absolutization or naturalization of the historical and therefore contingent and arbitrary principles of a particular social universe" (93). If reason is to escape "obscurantism and absolutism," it too must be subjected to the acids of historicization. Against suggestions that historicization dissolves reason, Bourdieu maintains that only historicization avoids relativism. That is because the history of reason displays how "the rules and regularities of social games capable of forcing egoistic drives and interests to surpass themselves in and through regulated conflict can be set up in things and in bodies" (93–94). Before reason there was only arbitrary custom,[100] that which lies behind and is hidden by every *nomos* or "common sense"

---

97. Ibid., 129.

98. Bourdieu, *Acts of Resistance*, 70–77; *Sur la télévision*.

99. Bourdieu, *PM*, 93–127. References to *PM* in this and the following paragraph are in the text.

100. Bourdieu's focus on reason as a product of the Enlightenment implies that the age "before" reason includes, not only the medieval and Reformation eras, and not only the Greco-Roman and Hebrew traditions, but also every other cultural tradition prior to the encounter with Enlightenment thought. Given his frequent citations of, for example, Plato, Aristotle, Pascal, and Berber proverbs, it is probable that he does not really view the Enlightenment as reason's lone midwife. How historicization of his view of the Enlightenment would transform his view of historicization is an open question. Presumably for reason to be truly universal it would have to be vulnerable to the insights of alternative intellectual traditions.

(94–102). Reason, as Bourdieu repeatedly emphasizes, occurs as a product of fields organized around universal capital, such as knowledge or artistic appreciation (100–101). Social scientific reflexivity now allows for systematic review of the conditions of reason's production. The existence and protection of those fields is thus justified by *"historical reason"*—not merely reason—and the reflexive sociology that justifies this reason is a "rationalist historicism" (106).

Social science thus occupies a dual position, both denying "one to move fictitiously beyond the uncrossable limits of history" and insisting that "history can be made to yield some truths irreducible to history" (109). "It is in history, and in history alone," Bourdieu suggests, "that we must seek the principle of the relative independence of reason from the history of which it is a product" (109). The history of reason is, moreover, the history of those social spaces where protection from social and especially economic demands meant survival was dependent only on the strength of one's argument (109–13). The history of reason is the history of the autonomization of scientific fields. Within that history, reflexivity is the key development (118–22). Reflexivity as a self-critical practice helps thinkers provisionally and gradually overcome the limitations imposed by history and masked by the illusion that they are "subjects" somehow existing above the historical fray. Bourdieu recognizes that his rationalist historicism denies the transcendent reason sought by Kant and Habermas under the name of Enlightenment (120–21). Yet he holds that reflexivity "radicalizes" Kant's quest "to rescue reason from history by helping to give sociological weapons to the free and generalized exercise of an epistemological critique of all by all, deriving from the field itself, in other words from the conflictual but regulated cooperation that competition imposes there" (120). Particular field struggles—fields whose struggles are for universalization—give rise to the most universal, "transcendent" of cultural products. Reason, truth, and virtue result from specific acts of reflexivity, but they are not contained by them.

Love, Beauty, and Understanding

Bourdieu likewise argues for a practice of "pure love" with Enlightenment origins and universal implications. This argument is presented with reference to romance in a short section near the end of *Masculine Domination*, but is echoed elsewhere in discussions of aesthetic experience and scientific understanding.[101] The bulk of *Masculine Domination* is devoted to showing

---

101. Contra Reader, "The State They're In," 50, and Grenfell, "Interest," 16, who see Bourdieu's writings on domestic love as novelties in his corpus.

how gender relations, in marriage as in labor, in traditional as in modern so-cieties, have been disfigured by thousands of years of male rule. One might expect Bourdieu to offer a pessimistic evaluation of romantic love,[102] and he indeed discusses two scenarios in which it serves misrecognition. The first is *amor fati*, "love of one's destiny."[103] This love is evident in the way that romantic interests can often be strongly correlated to socio-economic interests, e.g., in the limiting case of love between partners of an arranged marriage. Bourdieu is especially sensitive to the female partner's affections which, if they arise in such a situation, appear as "domination accepted, unrecognized as such and practically recognized, in happy or unhappy passion" (109). But "the mysterious grip of love can also take hold of men." As depicted in the mythological stories of Eve and Circe, the charms of women may bind "men through the magic of the attachments of passion" and so reverse domination. Yet this love too "is still a context of struggle, or war, and it excludes the very possibility of the suspension of power relations which seems constitutive of the experience of love or friendship" (110). It is for this "pure love" that Bourdieu advocates.

Bourdieu believes that gender domination can be overcome by love: through "an endless labour . . . the icy waters of calculation, violence and self-interest" may be crossed and "a world of non-violence" attained.[104] This world is an "*economy of symbolic exchanges*, of which the supreme form is the gift of self, and of one's body, a sacred object" (110–11). Reciprocal self-exchange exceeds all instrumentalization of the other; it is a truly dis-interested exchange in which self-interest is attained by seeing and meeting the other's interest. The love exchange is rooted in trust and the acceptance of the other's reason for being. Bourdieu identifies spiritual and ethical dimensions to this love, and portrays mutual recognition as a kind of mystical union in which the tension between egoism and altruism is overcome.[105] He further writes of each partner's experience of pure love as "being a quasi-

102. Especially given his earlier analyses of the function of marriage strategies in reproducing "traditional" societies: *OTP*, 39–40, 58–70; *LP*, 147–99; *Bachelor's Ball*.

103. Bourdieu, *MD*, 37, 109. Unless otherwise noted, references to *MD* in this and the following paragraph are in the text.

104. Bourdieu, *MD*, 110. Bourdieu references Sartre positively here, but Bridget Fowler, "Reading Pierre Bourdieu's *Masculine Domination*," 475, highlights the differences between their views on love.

105. Bourdieu, *MD*, 111. Bourdieu draws a distinction between recognition (*re-connaissance*) and understanding (*connaissance*) on the one hand, and misrecognition (*méconnaissance*) on the other. The ethics of recognition is a major focus for Habermas, Honneth and other critical theorists. McNay, "Trouble with Recognition," uses Bourdieu's theory of practice to resolve disagreements between Honneth and Nancy Fraser, but does not examine Bourdieu's own writings on recognition.

divine creator who makes, *ex nihilo*, the beloved, through the power that she or he grants him or her . . .; but a creator who, in return and simultaneously, unlike an egocentric and dominating Pygmalion, accepts to be the creature of his creature" (112). The loving recognition that so entwines a couple may be extremely fragile, but it also produces "an elementary social unit" that, for its total symbolic autonomy, rivals "successfully all the consecrations that are ordinarily asked of the institutions and rites of 'Society,' the secular substitute for God" (112). This divine power of love should be encouraged where possible, and Bourdieu writes elsewhere of society, and especially of the state's, ability to foster it through legal recognition of, for instance, homosexual couples and other "new families" of the modern order.[106] Pure love may match the state's symbolic power of consecration, but the state still has a unique power of consecrating love.

Bourdieu does not detail the origins of pure love, other than to say that "it is a relatively recent historical invention, as is art for art's sake, the pure love of art with which it is bound up, historically and structurally."[107] The genesis of art for art's sake is reviewed systematically in Bourdieu's 1991 book *The Rules of Art*. There he traces the nineteenth-century differentiation of the bohemian lifestyle from dominant commercial modes of life. Spurred in part by Kant's *Critique of Judgment*, where he argues for the pleasures of "pure" aesthetic contemplation, *litterateurs* such as Baudelaire and Flaubert embodied—and gradually institutionalized—the conviction that artistic production should be free from economic, political, and moral conventions.[108] Given that ten years earlier Bourdieu had launched a scathing attack on Kantian aesthetics in the postscript to *Distinction*, the bohemian ideology of pure art would seem to be an obvious critical target.[109] Yet Bourdieu here affirms the illusio that gives rise to aesthetic pleasure, denying that historicization negates it.[110] On the contrary, he insists that historicization can be a powerful aid to aesthetic pleasure.[111] Because love, even so-called crazy love (*amour fou*), includes a kind of ongoing "apologetic"

---

106. Bourdieu, *MD*, 118–24; "Des familles sans nom." See Martel, "Bourdieu et la question homosexuelle," for an appreciative critique of Bourdieu's writings on homosexuality.

107. Bourdieu, *MD*, 111.

108. Bourdieu, *RA*, 47–173; cf. 295 on the German aesthetic tradition mediated to the French *litterateurs* by the philosopher Victor Cousin.

109. Bourdieu also attacks Jacques Derrida's critique of Kantian aesthetics as failing to exceed a purely aesthetic conceptual space (*Distinction*, 485–500.) See Bennett, "Habitus Clivé," 215–20; Loesberg, "Bourdieu's Derrida's Kant."

110. Bourdieu, *RA*, 333–34.

111. Ibid., xvii–xx.

or self-justificatory commentary, sociological elucidation of the historical necessity of the artistic object can actually ground and encourage love of art. By constructing the social space of artistic production, the sociologist can enter into the point of view of the artist, effecting "a sort of *amor intellectualis rei*, the assimilation of the object to the subject and the immersion of the subject in the object, the active surrender to the singular necessity of the literary object."[112] Recognition of art's historical necessity is thus not a rejection of transcendent artistic experience, but an apprehension of the historical conditions that make it possible—of the artistic field as another of the "paradoxical worlds capable of inspiring or of imposing the most disinterested 'interests.'"[113] "The sublimated essence of the universal" emerges from, not above, the struggles and alliances of the social world.

If Bourdieu's "science of works of art" has the function of enhancing aesthetic pleasure, it does so for ethical and spiritual purposes. The passages in *The Rules of Art* defending a science of art are written against those who, failing to see the social basis of aesthetic experience, identify the love of art with the inherent spiritual superiority of the lover.[114] Bourdieu then proposes the corporatism of the universal in the book's postscript, indicating that, like the revolutionary *philosophes* and Zola, his aim is not to destroy the spiritual attainments of European intellectual culture, but to urge their concrete universalization.[115] Art for art's sake originated as "an exclusive religion . . . the last resort of those who reject submission and resignation" in the face of political and social disenchantment.[116] Far from persecuting this radical religion of art, Bourdieu hopes that the scientific illumination of its genesis will enable it to flourish and grow.[117]

Masculine Domination and *The Rules of Art* were both published in the 1990s, perhaps signaling a late "spiritual" turn. A few years earlier Bourdieu had, in fact, written explicitly of a "materialist spirituality," in an obscure

112. Ibid., xix. *Amor intellectualis rei* is Bourdieu's "secularized" version of Spinoza's *amor Dei intellectualis*, the love of God that is active assent to the determination of all things (see Spinoza, *Ethics* V). Bourdieu, who was also influenced by Leibniz, insists on the possibility of change and the limits of determinism. See Weik, "Bourdieu and Leibniz."

113. Bourdieu, *RA*, xx.

114. Ibid., xvii. See also Bourdieu and Darbel, *Love of Art*, 109–12.

115. Bourdieu, *RA*, 339–48.

116. Ibid., 59. Bourdieu is careful to point out that this evaluation does not reduce art for art's sake to politics or economics—on the contrary, only those agents endowed with artistic perception and involved in an autonomous artistic field could envision such a break from economics and politics (60).

117. The religious function of art in modern society is also invoked and affirmed in Bourdieu and Darbel, *Love of Art*, 1–4, 108–13, and Bourdieu, "Piété religieuse et dévotion artistique."

essay on the French poet Francis Ponge entitled "Nécessiter."[118] Bourdieu begins "Nécessiter" with a disavowal of any attempt to provide a commentary on Ponge's poetry. Rather, the essay is an act of recognition, a gift in exchange for that which he has received from Ponge's poetry and, at the same time, a "submission" to Ponge's legitimate authority.[119] Bourdieu goes on, lacing his prose with lines from Ponge, to write of the fight against "intellectual pharisaism" (*pharaïsme intellectuel*) to see things as they really are. This mode of seeing is connected to a way of changing things—"to kill the old man and the old world"—by changing representations of things, overcoming in particular "eschatological, fanatical, and pharisaical discourses.[120] It is not a casual mode of seeing but, in terms that adumbrate his aesthetic science, a look that lingers carefully "until it rediscovers the formula, the generative principle, the informing necessity, the reason for being of things."[121]

Yet Bourdieu sees in Ponge more than looking, an act that still implies distance from the object. Bourdieu rather moves with Ponge "toward materialism" by writing of "a consumption and a tasting of things"—things are not merely perceived from afar, but internalized.[122] Given the sensuality of taste, however, consumption requires an ethic of humility, one that leaves behind exaltation and resignation for "a form of *acquiescentia anima* [aquiescence of the soul], of an assent of the spirit to that which is and which is thus good: 'Let it be,' Ponge's pagan, *Amor intellectualis rei* [intellectual love of the thing]; assimilation of the object to the subject and immersion of the subject in the object: 'the candle that drowns itself in its food'. . . ."[123] Consumption thus enacts a spiritual unification of subject and object of the same kind that Bourdieu had written about art and love. The intensive word labor represented by Ponge's poems are further, according to Bourdieu, "like spiritual-material exercises" or "a sort of mental preparation for the *adaequatio intellectus et rei* [correspondence of the intellect and the thing] that

118. Bourdieu, "Nécessiter," 434–37.

119. Ibid., 434.

120. Ibid., 435: "tuer le vieil homme et le monde ancien" by overcoming "les discours eschatologiques, fanatiques, pharisiens."

121. Ibid.: a look that lingers "jusqu'à redécouvrir le formule, le principe générateur, la nécessité informatrice, la raison d'être des choses."

122. Ibid.: to move with Ponge "vers materialism" by writing of "une consommation et une dégustation des choses."

123. Ibid., 435: "une forme d'*acquiescentia animi*, d'adhésion de l'esprit à ce qui est et qui est bien ainsi: 'Ainsi soit-il', païen de Ponge, *Amor intellectualis rei*; assimilation de l'objet au sujet et immersion du sujet dans l'objet: la bougie qui 'se noie dans son aliment'. . . ." The internal citations are from Ponge, the ellipsis is Bourdieu's, and the Latin phrases are, again, from Spinoza.

is experienced from the necessity of the thing."[124] Apprehension of necessity is therefore "active submission to the singular necessity of the object [that] produces the text, object through which the designated object imposes itself irremediably on the reader, who learns and retains it by heart, thereby becoming capable of evoking at will the signified thing, from there to signify it purely and simply to exist. It really is magic."[125] Bourdieu draws a parallel here between Ponge's poetic identification and aesthetic pleasure, both enabling an understanding of "the unfamiliar" (*l'étranger*) that favors receptivity over judgment. This penetration of another implies a sort of violence, an intrusion, but without it understanding (*connaissance*) and recognition (*reconnaissance*) of the most strange is impossible.[126]

"Understanding," an essay written to explain the unusual ethnographic methods of *The Weight of the World*, ties in Bourdieu's reflections on love, aesthetics, and necessity with the work of reflexive science. Eschewing both non-directive interviews and questionnaires, Bourdieu and his team looked to practice a form of "*active and methodical listening*" in which systematic construction of the interviewee's social setting is combined with "a total availability to the person being questioned, submission to the singularity of a particular life history."[127] Sociological construction and interpersonal receptivity are not opposed here, as "*understanding and explanation are one*"—to grasp fully the socio-historical explanation for the genesis of a person is to be able to inhabit their mental space.[128] Bourdieu therefore insists that the sociological interview can be a "*spiritual exercise* that, through *forgetfulness of the self*, aims at a true *conversion of the way we look at* other people in the ordinary circumstances of life." This spiritual understanding is "a sort of *intellectual love*," "the capacity to take that person and understand them just as they are in their distinctive necessity."[129] Reflexivity is necessary on the part of the interviewer, in order to avoid allowing power

124. Ibid.: "comme exercices spirituels matérialistes" or "une sorte de préparation mentale à l'*adaequatio intellectus et rei* qui est expérience de la nécessité de la chose." For Spinoza, adequate knowledge is the mind's recognition of the determination of things by God, and so is bound up with the *amor Dei intellectualis* (*Ethics* 5).

125. Bourdieu, "Nécessiter," 435–36: "la soumission active à la nécessité singulière de l'objet [qui] produit le texte, objet à travers lequel l'objet désigné s'impose irrémédiablement au lecteur, qui apprend et retient par coeur, devenant ainsi capable d'évoquer *à volonté* la chose signifiée, de lui signifier purement et simplement d'exister. Il s'agit bien de magie."

126. Bourdieu, "Nécessiter," 437.

127. Bourdieu, WW, 609. This method was described more fully in chapter 3 above.

128. Ibid., 612–13. Bourdieu's language here is meant to oppose the classic hermeneutical distinctions of Wilhelm Dilthey.

129. Ibid., 614.

imbalances to distort the interview, but this "permanent control of the point of view" does not rule out mutual transformation.[130] The interview process, as an *"induced and accompanied self-analysis,"* can help interviewees gain perspective on their lives, and the transcriptions may have a similar "reve-latory" effect on readers from similar social backgrounds.[131] Interviews as spiritual exercises thus require a transformation of the self that issues in a broader social transformation.

Romantic "pure" love, aesthetic pleasure, and science are for Bour-dieu modern European practices that carry universal spiritual and ethical import, and his work is meant to spread their influence. As opposed to a universalism that ignores local variation, part of what makes these produc-tive practices universal is their sensitivity to the particular. Their wider legitimacy depends in each case on the recognition of the "necessity" of another, the specific confluence of socio-historical events productive of per-sons, works of art, and everything else. Human being exists within and as the structured, structuring practices of habitus and fields; and the specific structured, structuring products of habitus and fields are irreducible to one another, even if they are subject to regularities and family resemblances. To apprehend the universal necessity of an object is to apprehend its historicity, and thus its particularity.[132]

Revising Yoder's Theology of Christian Particularity

The cosmic lordship of the risen Christ cannot be explained by a purely immanent sociological process. Insofar as Yoder is convinced of the reality of Christ's lordship, he is committed to a broader cosmology that affirms the existence of God, Christ's special relationship to God, and thus the special relationship of Christ's followers to God. These cosmological affirmations are included in the trinitarian reading of Yoder's theology of the principali-ties and powers developed in this thesis. The triune God's practical interac-tions with humanity through creation; the election of Israel; the life, death and resurrection of Jesus Christ; and the constitutive presence of the Holy Spirit in the church entail something prior and external to history and soci-ety, namely, the divine life of the Trinity. Christianity's particularity derives its triune shape from its affirmation of the universal ultimacy of Father, Son, and Holy Spirit. Christian particularity and universality are both bound to

130. Ibid., 625–26.

131. Ibid., 615, 623.

132. Cf. Spinoza on the love of God as knowledge of things *sub specie aeternitatis* (*Ethics* 5.32).

the triune God who creates and redeems the powers, and to the structures developed in response to God's intense interactions with humanity.

The unity of Christian particularity and universality follow from Yoder's theology of the powers. His radical commitment to Christian history as uniquely revelatory can nevertheless obscure its universality; and his radical commitment to dialogical social practice as fulfilling the Jewish-Christian exilic vocation can obscure its particularity. Pierre Bourdieu's sociological resolution of the particular-universal antinomy can help clarify Yoder's position. Bourdieu's argument that social practice is constructive of the universal can be affirmed on the theological grounds that historical process is intrinsic and not incidental to God's self-revelation. Human social life occurs as a complex set of relations to God, strands of which may be more or less revelatory of God's person and purpose. The incarnation is, of course, the paradigm for this viewpoint: that the word became flesh is the heart of the gospel proclamation, not a particular add-on to a less historical, more universal truth. As Yoder put it, "what [incarnation] means is that God acted in a totally human way, and unhesitatingly entrusted his own cause to the hands of ordinary people."[133] Jesus reveals God's acceptance of the contingency and vulnerability of history. The suffering love displayed on the cross is not tangential to the incarnation, but "a revelation of the shape of what God is, and of what God does, in the total drama of history."[134] More broadly, Jesus' socio-political practices constitute the most universally significant history of divine-human interactions. Jesus' history is valid always and everywhere because it was produced through the most intense relation to God possible for a human being—that is, the unique relation of being God and human. The histories of Israel and the church have a derivative universality insofar as they exhibit high continuity with Jesus' history. Together these histories define the universal history of God's creative and redemptive relation to humanity. The story of Israel, Jesus and the church is universal history.

Universals are grounded in the objectivity of God's self-revelation, which is produced in and through social relations. Conceived without reference to God, social practices too easily appear as a collection of arbitrary occurrences without universal meaning.[135] Conceived without reference to particular social practices, God becomes a cipher for the theologian or

133. Yoder, *HCPP*, 72.

134. Ibid., 85.

135. Milbank, *Theology and Social Theory*, argues that only Christian theology can avoid Nietzschean deconstruction of the universal into the arbitrary. Whether or not Bourdieu's historicist universalism escapes this criticism is a matter for further investigation.

philosopher's preferred narrative.[136] God and the divine will are encountered through participation in a specific history and its practices. Universals are neither subject to casual revision, nor are they timeless forms to be dropped into any situation. They are, rather, being produced through the history of God's relation to God's people. Because this productive labor occurs in relation to a God who cannot be reduced to social practice, the history of the production of universals is also the history of their reception as divine gifts, i.e., as revelation. Theological science is critical participation in the church's labor of receiving revelation.

Christian particularity is universal because it entails spiritual participation in the triune God. Since spiritual participation is an intense practical mode of relating to God, Christian universality is fully particular and sociological. The choice between narrow particularism and capacious universalism is a false one. Moreover, the choice between fixed universals and relativism is false, as Christian love, reason, and virtue are produced with God in the struggle for faithfulness to God. These universals are furthered by forming institutions—i.e., churches, that foster an interest in their production. Christian interest in the universal is self-interest, a concern with the church's own purity before God. But this self-interest is also interest in the God before whom the church wishes to remain pure. True Christian self-interest is subordinate to and derivative of interest in God, that is, to worship.

But what about interest in others, and in others' interests? According to Yoder, the core of Jesus' socio-political practice was nonviolent dialogue, a will to peaceful conversation that is unmoved by threat or danger. Among Jesus' spiritual forebears and descendants, those Yoder judges as faithful are the ones that place dialogue at the center of their practice: Jeremiah, with his exilic politics, and the Anabaptists, with their suffering commitment to conversation. Dialogue is not only a means to an end, but already a realization of the universal way of being. Institutions that are not internally and externally dialogical do not participate fully in the triune life. Christian interest in faithfulness is, therefore, an interest in engaging interlocutors whose lives are likewise constituted by a relation, however intense, to God.

The church's self-interest is to be interested in God and others. In a similar manner, Christian identity is protected and consolidated insofar as it is shaped through practices that expose it to relentless questioning by God and others. The irreducible particularity of Christian identity is found in its attempt to relate intensely to the triune God, i.e., in its worship. Triune worship is exclusivist in the sense that it recognizes no God but the one God who is Father, Son, and Holy Spirit. Interaction with God is always the

136. See Martens, "Universal History," on Rauschenbusch.

church's priority. But this radical exclusivity engenders a radical inclusivity: worshipping the triune God requires receptiveness to others' witness to Christ. Worship is shaped through inclusive encounter with others; institutional purity and syncretism are not necessary opposites. Christ is lord and Christ is dialogical. His universal lordship is not an obstacle to dialogical receptivity, but its animating principle.

Conclusion

Bourdieu's sociological insight that universals such as reason, truth, love, and virtue are products of social struggles illuminates Yoder's contention that particular histories have universal significance. Particular histories can have universal significance, because universal significance only arises within them. Critics who urge Yoder to drop his historicist particularity and adopt a more universal, "theocentric" perspective are ignorant of the historicity of the universal. The historicity of the universal entails that it is not a static substance awaiting discovery and acceptance. It is in process of production. Yoder's feminist, Jewish, and secular critics who worry that his particularism binds him to unhelpful or unjust convictions participate, through their criticisms, in the production of more adequate views on gender, interreligious relations, mission, and the lordship of Christ. The interest of particularist ecclesial institutions in producing faithful convictions about these issues must be an interest in open dialogue with dissenting interlocutors.

The ongoing story of the production of universals is the particular history of God's intense interactions with Israel, Jesus, and the church. This history is sociologically objective, a product of innumerable practices of prayer and service and of habituated practices become institutions. To be Christian, those practices and institutions must be oriented toward relationship with the triune God. To be Christian, those practices must be oriented toward dialogical engagement of others. The church participates in God's redemption of the powers, the subjection of all things to the lordship of Christ.

Conclusion

THIS BOOK HAS BEEN a sustained attempt to revise John Howard Yoder's sociological theology so that it might better avoid charges of reducing theology to sociology, method to ideology, and expansive Christian witness to narrow socio-political perfectionism. Pierre Bourdieu's relational sociology has been the primary tool of revision, as it enables amendments to Yoder's social theoretical assumptions that render them more clearly non-reductive. Several of Bourdieu's key concepts were put into conversation with Yoder's theology of the principalities and powers, his broader *oeuvre*, and his critics. This conversation facilitated revisions to Yoder's thought in several areas: creation, anthropology, violence, method, politics, and Christian particularity. Yoder's understanding of the powers was placed at the center of the book, so that the revisions would have to be articulated within the horizon of the history of God's creation, preservation, and redemption of social structures. In other words, the proposed revisions are meant to be fully theological and fully sociological. They are offered as potentially faithful inheritances of Yoder's sociological theology. Insofar as the revisions help Yoder's legacy to identify more with Jesus' legacy, they are also offered as potentially faithful inheritances of the latter. Whether or not they are successful on either count, of course, is for other discerning Christians to decide.

Critics of Yoder's theology of creation suggest that it lacks a clearly stated affirmation of creation as a work of the triune God. In Yoder's hands, they charge, created society is reduced to fallen society, a wasteland barren of God's presence. This wasteland is dominated by evil social structures that the church must oppose with its nonviolent politics—leaving no room for personal spirituality. Furthermore, since he did not develop a consistent doctrine of the Trinity, he creates the problem of a nonviolent Jesus and a violent God. When this tension is combined with his unshakeable commitment to nonviolence, it is unsurprising that some critics question his belief in Christ's divinity. As in other areas, there are considerable resources within Yoder's work to counter these criticisms; but there is also sufficient ambiguity to suggest the need for significant revision.

In chapter 1, Bourdieu's basic sociological concepts were used to interpret the principalities and powers as capital-oriented habitus and fields. Because habitus and fields interpenetrate, there can be no total division between the personal and the social. Personal dispositions toward and away from specific forms of capital are formed by inhabiting social fields that are disposed toward and away from specific forms of capital. The structure of a given field, in turn, is defined by the relative amounts of capital possessed by the individuals and groups that constitute it, amounts that change over time as individuals and groups seek more capital. Society, therefore, is not a "thing" or a collection of "things," but a dynamic set of relations objectively structured by relative proximity to desired forms of capital (material, symbolic, and social). Yoder's theology of the principalities and powers suggests that God must be accounted for in the total set of relations that constitute society. God created the powers. God is not a relation among relations, but the one who brings all the other relations into being and sustains their existence. Society exists in relation to God and, since God is spirit, social relations are spiritual. Because personal dispositions are a part of society, personal relations to God are irreducible. Personal spirituality is a matter of intense participation in social practices and structures that have developed through the history of intense relationship with God. The doctrine of the two natures of Christ arises from the insistence by participants in those structures that Jesus' social practices exhibit such an intense relationship with God that he must be God. The doctrine of the Trinity is complete when those participants recognize that the Holy Spirit's work of empowering intense relationship with Jesus also indicates the Spirit's divinity. The intensity of the relations among God the Father, Jesus, and the Holy Spirit suggests a triune godhead. Their relations are real relations among persons with whom humans can relate, too. Human knowledge that relations among the divine persons are relations of identity—that is, that they are trinitarian relations—is derived from human judgments about the character of each person, judgments that result from intense relating to each person. Humans can affirm that God is triune because they have related to God—Father, Son, and Holy Spirit.

If God is God, then human knowledge about God is not simply the product of human social activity. Theological knowledge is also a gift from God that humans receive in the process of relating to God intensely. Chapter 2 developed that argument with reference to Yoder's theological anthropology. Yoder suggests that persons have the capacity to choose to relate to God. Since Yoder affirms that the powers are created and sustained by God, this capacity to choose would seem to exist only in relation to God. However, it is not always clear if he believes that genuine freedom for choice is experienced as a gift given in the encounter with God through the church, or if free choice requires individual autonomy from God and others. Bourdieu's conceptions of social reproduction and freedom are useful, at this point, because they depict capacities for change as latent within personal and institutional structures, even if those structures tend to reproduce themselves and resist change. The break from social reproduction, therefore, is not a break from society itself. From the perspective of Yoder's theology of the powers, social reproduction is not inherently oppressive, but is the gift of order that makes human life possible. The capacity to choose relationship with God is built into the structure of human being, since, again, that structure only exists in relation to the God who creates and sustains it. As a social practice, choice for God occurs in relation to God and society, as a gift from God received through social process. The structure that is continually structured through intense relating to God, the church, is the medium through which God extends the gift of freedom. The social practices of the church are the means by which anyone receives that freedom. Human freedom is a divine gift received through ecclesial practice. Baptism is the initial practice—for both converting nonbelievers and children reared in the church—that signals and enacts reception of the gift.

The existence of the church as a specific institution characterized by intense practical relating to God implies that other institutions are not so characterized—the powers are fallen. Chapter 3 examined complaints that Yoder identifies the fall with physical violence. According to some critics, the identification of fall and physical violence fails to recognize that some genuine goods must be preserved by violence from violence. On the contrary, Bourdieu's theory of symbolic violence gives strong sociological support to Yoder's contention that killing is always wrong because it takes away the victim's possibility for obedience to God. Symbolic violence works by duping the victim into recognizing the perpetrators' legitimate authority to maintain capital inequalities. Because capital bestows the power to exist in certain ways rather than others, symbolic violence reduces the being of the victim. Of course, since all being involves the possession of capital, all being is "violence" to some degree. But this admission opens up the possibility of making moral judgments among practices as more or less violent. Killing, which eliminates the victim's capital altogether, clearly is the most extreme form of violence on this scale. From a theological viewpoint, killing denies the minimum capital necessary for obedience: embodied being. In doing so, the killer refuses God's gift of freedom for obedience on behalf of the victim.

This refusal inverts Christian mission. The goods killing protects cannot be exchanged for another's freedom for obedience.

Killing is at the end of the spectrum of violences. At the other end of the spectrum are practices that encourage and restore being, practices which can be judged morally as "nonviolent." In between is a range of symbolic, physical, and structural violences, each of which, according to Bourdieu, can be converted into the other. This recognition allows for a more capacious understanding of violence than that implied by Yoder's focus on war.

Bourdieu's insight into the relations among the various types of violence is indicative of his overall methodology. He models a progressive practice of research that involves rigorous theoretical construction and empirical inquiry into the full set of relations that constitute a given object. Systematic theory denies the illusion that objects are "out there" waiting to be found, and empirical research denies the illusion that what is "in here" is all there is. This formula implies that the researcher is always involved with the object, and Bourdieu's method prizes sociological reflexivity as the primary means of social scientific progress. Chapter 4 employed this reflexive sociology to revise Yoder's theological method. Although Yoder's writings continue to command respect, many readers believe that he sometimes skewed his data to fit his theological presuppositions. Furthermore, because he was concerned mainly with communal social ethics, he left spiritual and personal classes of relations outside of his methodological purview. The revision of Yoder's methodology resulted in a proposal for a non-reductive research practice that patiently attends to all dimensions of the powers. This practice would put reflexive metaphysical construction and empirical research to work in the church's process of moral discernment.

As the church reflexively discerns the powers, it gains greater insight into how its own practices might better conform to the politics of Jesus. Chapter 5 presented Yoder's understanding of Christian politics as a form of *imitatio Christi* that participates in Christ's redemption of the powers. The fallen powers executed Jesus, but he has been raised from the dead and is now bringing all things under his cosmic lordship. When the church imitates Christ by practicing nonviolent dialogue and capital redistribution, it gives the world a glimpse of his coming reign. The body politics are the church's political witness. Although this political vision would seem to be at once public and spiritual, critics are swift to point out the ambiguities that leave it open to charges of sectarianism and sociological reductionism. At this point, Bourdieu's political concepts—the circuits of legitimation, the corporatism of the universal, and negative philosophy—are helpful for a revision that displays more clearly how only an autonomous church can give the critical legitimacy required by the state to function. Moreover, because the state exists as a node of relations to other fields, Christian politics are rightly concerned with cultural and economic issues, and not narrowly centered on the state. And because the church's politics are conducted in relation to the Holy Spirit who empowers obedient participation in Christ, Christian politics are fully spiritual as well.

The tension between the particular christocentric politics of the church and the universal lordship of Christ over the powers was the subject of the sixth chapter. Some critics contend that Yoder is so intent on locating Christian politics within the history of Christ and the church, that he ignores the universal scope of Christ's redemptive activity. Other critics suggest the opposite. Yoder, they say, was only interested in showing how Jesus presents a sociologically viable nonviolent politics, a politics that can be imitated by anyone regardless of confession or creed. Bourdieu's research into the historical production of universals is a valuable resource here, for it suggests that historicist particularity need not be opposed to the affirmation of transhistorical and universal modes of being. The particularity of Christian history is not an obstacle to its universality, but the condition of its possibility. Christian being is universal because it participates, concretely and spiritually, in God as revealed in Christ. Moreover, the particular form of Christian being is rigorously dialogical. Both the church's internal and external practices are structured by the refusal to coerce and the willingness to listen. Through its distinctively nonviolent dialogical practice, the church produces the universal freedom to know and love God and others intensely—again, a freedom that can only be produced through its reception as a gift.

The powers are created, fallen, and subject to Christ. The social is spiritual, and the inner is outer. God relentlessly relates to it all, creating it all and redeeming it all. The church participates in the life of the triune God as it learns to relate intensely to others while maintaining its autonomy.

This revision of Yoder's sociological theology, therefore, makes room for metaphysics without becoming speculative; for methodological rigor without unhinging theology from the church's mission; and for robust political engagement without losing sight of the place of the church in God's plan of redemption. The remainder of this conclusion explores the possibility that the revisionary proposal of this book satisfies at least one criterion for faithful inheritance of Yoder's legacy: it offers an integrated theological method for moral discernment of the powers.

The introduction to this book surveyed several options for inheriting Yoder's legacy faithfully. In Cramer's review of recent literature on Yoder, he discerns a philosophical option, which favors dialogue with "outsiders"; a systematic option, which surveys Yoder's writings to respond to questions about his legacy; and an ecumenical option, which puts him into conversation with specific ecclesial traditions.[1] Cramer suggests that all of these options should be pursued if Yoder's legacy is to be inherited faithfully, because Yoder's own methods sanction a plurality of approaches. Yet these options by no means exhaust the diversity that exists within Yoder's own body of work. He wrote prolifically and influentially on systematic theology, ethics, history, sociology, ecumenism, biblical exegesis, hermeneutics, epistemology, and other topics. It is unlikely that every theologian can be as well-versed as Yoder in each of these fields, but his legacy points toward an integrated theological method that might, at least, be attempted. Glen Stassen has written of the need for a "holistic method . . . that can guide [the] variety of specialties in the interdisciplinary discipline of Christian ethics, and can identify the variables that shape real existing Christian ethics as people actually do their Christian ethics."[2] Stassen sees Yoder as an exemplar of such a holistic method, and his own work combines exegesis, narrative character ethics, research on specific ethical issues, and the development of public political practices that can be engaged by Christians and others.[3]

This integrated Yoderian methodology resonates with the reflexive sociological theology proposed in this book, which is oriented toward research into specific powers met by the church in the course of its mission. Although many theologians reference Yoder's theology of the powers, none of them develop it into a framework useful for research into actual social structures.[4] That, however, was what Yoder seemed to have in mind when he referenced Jacques Ellul's works on money, law, violence, and technology as paradigmatic of a modern appropriation of the powers.[5] Ellul employs a dialectical method in which his theological and sociological assessments of various powers are split into separate books.[6] This method is meant to help Christians navigate their different responsibilities in the church and in the secular world, but Ellul admits that few readers connect the theology to the sociology or vice versa.[7] In her dissertation on Ellul, Marva Dawn argues

1. Cramer, "Inheriting Yoder," 137–41.

2. Stassen, "What I am Working on in Christian Ethics," Fuller Theological Seminary faculty page, last accessed August 31, 2011, http://www.fullerseminary.net/sot/faculty/stassen/cp_content/homepage/homepage.htm.

3. Stassen, "Concrete Christological Norms for Transformation"; Stassen, *Just Peacemaking*; Stassen and Gushee, *Kingdom Ethics*.

4. See note 59 in the introduction to this book for references to work that draws from Yoder's theology of the principalities and powers.

5. Yoder, *PJ*, 156. See note 12 in chapter 4 above for references to Ellul's works.

6. Ellul, "On Dialectic," 305–7.

7. Ibid., 307.

Conclusion

that the concept of the powers provides the conceptual link between his theology and sociology, and that some effort is needed to merge the two sides of his work.[8] An integrated or holistic sociological theology is required if the theology of the powers is to fulfill the role Yoder envisioned for it as a Christian method of social criticism.[9]

Yoder, of course, is associated with one prominent project in theological social criticism, namely, Stanley Hauerwas's attack on "liberalism." Hauerwas understands his "method" to be "a form of gossip generally known as journalism" that is "not quite theology, not quite ethics, not quite cultural criticism."[10] By "renarrating widely shared stories" in Christian language he hopes to draw people who are "captured" by liberal practices into a new, Christian world.[11] Critical theological, ethical, and cultural redescription of specific liberal practices would seem to be closer to Yoder's integrated method. Nevertheless, Hauerwas's method is subject to Bourdieu's evaluation of "journalistic" social commentary: because it evades systematic theoretical construction and empirical research, it offers few resources for combating the common sense of the dominant order.[12] Although Hauerwas's tireless polemic against war and capital can hardly be accused of willing service to the dominant, Jeffrey Stout's reading of Hauerwas adds weight to the charge that insufficient object construction weakens the critical impact of his work. Stout points out that "liberalism," for Hauerwas, represents a slim selection of egregious practices and despised philosophical texts. War, abortion, and John Rawls, however, do not equal liberalism. There may be very negative aspects of liberal democracy that must be addressed, but they cannot be addressed without some acknowledgment of the day-to-day democratic practices within liberal democracies that support the kind of traditioned communities of virtue desired by Hauerwas. Furthermore, there are many liberal theorists who celebrate tradition, virtue, and local community in terms similar to Hauerwas's own.[13] If Hauerwas's "liberalism" is a straw man, then the church he exults as an alternative is lacking similarly in

8. Dawn, *Ellul*, 375.

9. Walter Wink approaches this method but, as suggested in chapter 1 above, his melange of Jungian psychology, process theology, and quantum physics makes its validity difficult to discern. However valuable Wink's theology of the powers may be, it represents a different approach from the Yoderian sociological theology developed here.

10. Hauerwas, *Dispatches from the Front*, 9.

11. Ibid., 9–10.

12. Bourdieu, *RA*, 347; *WW*, 629. Bourdieu uses the Platonic term "doxosophes" to describe such intellectuals: their wisdom is only the wisdom of the doxa, or common sense.

13. Stout, *Democracy and Tradition*, 156–57.

concreteness.[14] Stout argues that vitriolic criticism of liberalism combined with an ethereal church only provides comfort for middle class readers who like to mock the system without lifting a finger to change it.[15] Because he prefers "journalism" over rigorous engagement with actual liberal practices and actual churches, it is difficult to see how Hauerwas's theology can aid the church in discerning how to interact with the powers.

Nigel Biggar shares some of Stout's concerns with Hauerwas's project, and offers a "Barthian Thomist" alternative. Hauerwas, Biggar acknowledges, is right to search for a theologically orthodox mode of ethics that is governed by the entire biblical narrative, including the church's embodiment of the politics of Jesus.[16] To this extent, at least, Hauerwas is a Barthian, and Biggar wishes to affirm his ethics. However, Biggar does not agree with Hauerwas that the ethical task is complete once the governing theological narrative is articulated: the task of Christian ethics is more than the squeezing of "dogmatic tenets for the juice of ethical concepts, leaving to others the task of figuring out how these generic or specific concepts should bear on concrete conduct and issue in particular judgments."[17] Biggar, accordingly, turns to the Thomistic casuistic tradition and its recognition of the dialectical relationship between ethical principles and case analysis.[18] The lack of such analysis in Hauerwas's work suggests that he leaves the task of moral discernment half finished.

If Ellul and Hauerwas do not provide integrated methods for discerning the powers, then perhaps the proposal in this book will fare better. Like Ellul, it sees theological and sociological analysis of social structures as indispensable for the church as it finds its way in a complex fallen world. It does not conflate theology and sociology, but it does bring them together in order to display the powers' full material, symbolic, and spiritual relations. Like Hauerwas, it sees the orthodox theological narrative—and its metaphysical components—as definitive for the discernment process, and accepts that Christian convictions will often lead to critical redescriptions of reality that invite persons into the freedom of the gospel. It does not assume, however, that those redescriptions can occur in the absence of significant efforts to understand the shape of the fallen powers, and it does not assume that theological discourse is sufficient for that purpose. Nor does it assume

14. Ibid., 157–60.

15. Ibid., 158. See Hauerwas and Coles, *Christianity, Democracy, and the Radical Ordinary*, for an attempt, in response to Stout, to name the democratic practices he sees as offering concrete alternatives to liberalism.

16. Biggar, *Behaving in Public*, 4–6.

17. Ibid., 22.

18. Ibid., 17–23.

that criticism of the powers is useful, or even possible, outside of involvement in concrete practices that embody an alternative.

Although these comments indicate that the proposal here may result in an integrated method for research on the powers, a proposal alone is insufficient. It must be tested through research and subjected to the exigencies of ecclesial discernment. Yoder was uninterested in theology for the sake of theology. He was interested, rather, in the church's participation in Christ's redemptive reign over the powers.

Bibliography

Accardo, Alain. *Introduction à une sociologie critique. Lire Bourdieu.* Bourdeaux: Le Mascaret, 1997.

Addi, Lahouari. *Sociologie et anthropologie chez Pierre Bourdieu. Le paradigme anthropologique kabyle et ses conséquences théoriques.* Paris: La Découverte, 2002.

Adkins, Lisa, and Beverly Skeggs, editors. *Feminism after Bourdieu.* Oxford: Blackwell, 2004.

Alexis-Baker, Andy. "Unbinding Yoder from Just Policing." In *Powers and Practices*, edited by Jermey M. Bergen and Anthony G. Siegrist, 147–66. Scottdale, PA: Herald, 2009.

Alexis-Baker, Nekeisha. "Freedom of the Cross: John Howard Yoder and Womanist Theologies in Conversation." In *Powers and Practices*, edited by Jermey M. Bergen and Anthony G. Siegrist, 83–98. Scottdale, PA: Herald, 2009.

Anderson, Gary A. "Necessarium Adae Peccatum: The Problem of Original Sin." In *Sin, Death, and the Devil*, edited by Carl E. Braaten and Robert W. Jenson, 22–44. Grand Rapids: Eerdmans, 2000.

Anderson, Perry. "Gandhi Centre Stage." *London Review of Books* 34/13 (July 5, 2012). Online: http://www.lrb.co.uk/v34/n13/perry-anderson/gandhi-centre-stage.

Anheir, Helmut K., Jürgen Gerhards, and Frank P. Romo. "Forms of Capital and Social Structure in Cultural Fields: Examining Bourdieu's Social Topography." *American Journal of Sociology* 100/4 (1995) 859–903.

Aquinas, Thomas. *The Summa Theologica of St. Thomas Aquinas.* Rev. ed. Translated by the Fathers of the English Dominican Province. Online: http://www.newadvent.org/summa.

Arner, Rob. *Consistently Pro-Life: The Ethics of Bloodshed in Ancient Christianity.* Eugene, OR: Pickwick, 2010.

Augsburger, Myron S. "Michael Sattler (d. 1527): Theological of the Swiss Brethren Movement." *Mennonite Quarterly Review* 40 (1966) 238–39.

Barber, Daniel Colucciello. *On Diaspora: Christianity, Religion, and Secularity.* Eugene, OR: Cascade, 2011.

Barth, Karl. *Against the Stream: Shorter Post-War Writings, 1946–52.* London: SCM, 1954.

———. *The Christian Life, Church Dogmatics IV/4, Lecture Fragments.* Translated by Geoffrey Bromiley. Edinburgh: T. & T. Clark, 1981.

———. *Church and State.* Translated by G. Ronald Howe. London: SCM, 1939.

———. *The Doctrine of Revelation, Church Dogmatics IV/2.* Translated by Geoffrey Bromiley. Edinburgh: T. & T. Clark, 1958.

Bibliography

Beckley, Harlan R. "A Christian Affirmation of Rawls's Idea of Justice as Fairness—Part I." *Journal of Religious Ethics* 13 (1985) 210–242.

———. "A Christian Affirmation of Rawls's Idea of Justice as Fairness—Part II." *Journal of Religious Ethics* 14 (1986) 229–46.

Belknap, Robert E. *The List: The Uses and Pleasures of Cataloguing.* New Haven: Yale University Press, 2004.

Bender, Harold S. *The Anabaptist Vision.* Scottdale, PA: Herald, 1944.

Bennett, Tony. "Habitus Clivé: Aesthetics and Politics in the Work of Pierre Bourdieu." *New Literary History* 38/1 (2007) 201–28.

———. "The Historical Universal: The Role of Cultural Value in the Historical Sociology of Pierre Bourdieu." *The British Journal of Sociology* 56/1 (2006) 142–64.

Bergen, Jeremy M. and Anthony G. Siegrist, editors. *Powers and Practices: Engaging the Work of John Howard Yoder.* Scottdale, PA: Herald, 2009.

Berkhof, Hendrik. *Christ the Meaning of History.* Translated by Lambertus Buurman. London: SCM, 1966.

———. *Christ and the Powers.* Translated by John Howard Yoder. Scottdale, PA: Herald, 1962.

———. *Doctrine of the Holy Spirit.* Atlanta: John Knox, 1964.

Biesecker-Mast, Gerald. "Anabaptist Separation and Arguments Against the Sword in the Schleitheim *Brotherly Union.*" *Mennonite Quarterly Review* 73/3 (2000) 381–402.

———. "The Persistence of Anabaptism as a Vision." *Mennonite Quarterly Review* 81/1 (2007) 21–42.

Blough, Neal. "Introduction: The Historical Roots of John Howard Yoder's Theology." In Yoder, *Anabaptism and Reformation in Switzerland: An Historical and Theological Analysis of the Dialogues between Anabaptists and Reformers,* edited by C. Arnold Snyder, translated by Snyder and David Carl Stassen, xli-lx. Kitchener, ON: Pandora, 2004.

Blum, Peter C. "Two Cheers for an Ontology of Violence: Reflections on an Im/possibility." In *Gift of Difference,* edited by Chris K Huebner and Tripp York, 7–26. Winnipeg, MB: Canadian Mennonite University Press, 2010.

———. "Yoder's Patience and/with Derrida's *Différance.*" In *The New Yoder,* edited by Peter Dula and Chris K. Huebner, 106–20. Eugene, OR: Cascade, 2010.

Boersma, Hans. *Violence, Hospitality, and the Cross: Reappropriating the Atonement Tradition.* Grand Rapids: Baker, 2004.

Bourdieu, Pierre. *Acts of Resistance: Against the New Myths of Our Time.* Translated by Richard Nice. Cambridge: Polity, 1998.

———. *The Algerians.* Translated by Alan C. M. Ross. Boston: Beacon, 1962.

———. *Algérie 60. Structures économiques et structures temporelles.* Paris: Minuit, 1977.

———. "Avenir de classe et causalité du probable." *Revue française de sociologie* 15/1 (1974) 3–42

———. *The Bachelors' Ball.* Cambridge: Polity, 2008.

———. *Le bal des célibataires. Crise de la société paysanne en Béarn.* Paris: Seuil, 2002.

———. *Ce que parler veut dire. L'économie des échanges linguistiques.* Paris: Fayard, 1982.

———. "Champ intellectuel et projet créateur." *Les temps modernes* 22/246 (1966) 865–906.

———. *Choses dites.* Paris: Minuit, 1987.

———. *Le Déracinement. La crise de l'agriculture traditionnelle en Algérie* (Paris: Minuit, 1964).

———. "Des familles sans nom." *Actes de la recherche en sciences sociales* 113 (1996) 3.

———. *Distinction: A Social Critique of the Judgement of Taste*. Translated by Richard Nice. London: Routledge, 1984.

———. *Firing Back: Against the Tyranny of the Market* 2. Translated by Loïc Wacquant. London: Verso, 2003.

———. "The Forms of Capital." Translated by Richard Nice. In *Handbook of Theory and Research for the Sociology of Education*, edited by John G. Robinson, 241–58. Westport, CT: Greenwood, 1986.

———. "From the King's House to the Reason of State: A Model of the Genesis of the Bureaucratic Field." In *Pierre Bourdieu and Democratic Politics: The Mystery of Ministry*, edited by Loïc J. D. Wacquant, 29–54. Cambridge: Polity, 2005.

———. "The Historical Genesis of a Pure Aesthetic." *Journal of Aesthetics and Art Criticism* 46 (1987) 201–10.

———. *Homo Academicus*. Translated by Peter Collier. Cambridge: Polity, 1990.

———. *Images d'Algérie: Une affinité elective*. Arles: Actes Sud, 2003.

———. "Intellectual Field and Creative Project." Translated by Sian France. *Social Science Information* 8/2 (1969) 89–119.

———. "Introduction à la socioanalyse." *Actes de la recherche en sciences sociales* 90 (1991) 3–5.

———. "Legitimation and Structured Interests in Weber's Sociology of Religion." Translated by Chris Turner. In *Max Weber, Rationality and Modernity*, edited by Scott Lash and Sam Whimster, 119–36. London: Allen & Unwin, 1987.

———. *The Logic of Practice*. Translated by Richard Nice. Stanford: Stanford University Press, 1990.

———. *Masculine Domination*. Translated by Richard Nice. Polity: Cambridge, 2001.

———. "Les modes de domination." *Actes de la recherche en sciences sociales* 2/2–3 (1976) 122–32.

———. "Nécessiter." In *Francis Ponge: Cahiers de l'Herne*, edited by Jean-Marie Gleize, 434–37. Paris: L'Herne, 1986.

———. "On the Family as a Realized Category." *Theory, Culture & Society* 13/3 (1996) 19–26.

———. *L'ontologie politique de Martin Heidegger*. Paris: Minuit, 1988.

———. *Outline of a Theory of Practice*. Translated by Richard Nice. Cambridge: Cambridge University Press, 1977.

———. "Participant Objectivation." *Journal of Royal Anthropological Institute* 9/2 (2003) 281–94.

———. *Pascalian Meditations*. Translated by Richard Nice. Cambridge: Polity, 2000.

———. "Piété religieuse et dévotion artistique. Fidèles et amateurs d'art à Santa Maria Novella." *Actes de la recherche en sciences sociales* 105 (1994) 71.

———. Postface to *Architecture gothique et pensée scholastique* by Erwin Panofsky. Paris: Minuit, 1967.

———. *Practical Reason: On the Theory of Action*. Cambridge: Polity, 1998.

———. *Propos sur le champ politique*. Lyon: Presses Universitaires de Lyon, 2000.

———. "A Reasoned Utopia and Economic Fatalism." *New Left Review* 227 (1998) 125–30.

Bibliography

————. *The Rules of Art: Genesis and Structure of the Literary Field*. Translated by Susan Emanuel. Cambridge: Polity, 1996.

————. *Science of Science and Reflexivity*. Translated by Richard Nice. Chicago: University of Chicago, 2004.

————. *Sketch for a Self-Analysis*. Translated by Richard Nice. Cambridge: Polity, 2004.

————. *Sociologie de l'Algérie*. 8th ed. Paris: Presses Universitaires de France, 1961.

————. "The Specificity of the Scientific Field and the Social Conditions of the Progress of Reason." *Social Science Information* 14/6 (1975) 19–47.

————. "The State, Economics and Sport." Translated by Hugh Dauncey and Geoffrey Hare. *Culture, Sport, Society* 1/2 (1998) 15–21.

————. "Stratégies de reproduction et modes de domination." *Actes de recherche en sciences sociales* 105 (1994) 3–12.

————. *Les structures sociales de l'économie*. Paris: Seuil, 2000.

————. "Structures sociales et structures de perception du monde social." *Actes de la recherche en sciences sociales* 1/2 (1975) 18–20.

————. "Sur l'objectivation participante. Réponse à quelques objections." *Actes de la recherche en sciences sociales* 23 (1978) 67–69.

————. "Sur le pouvoir symbolique." *Annales* 32/3 (1977) 405–11.

————. *Sur la télévision*. Paris: Liber-Raisons d'agir, 1996.

————. *Travail et travailleurs en Algérie*. Paris: Mouton-La Haye, 1963.

————. *Les usages sociaux de la science. Pour une sociologie clinic du champ scientifique*. Paris: Institut National de la Recherche Agronomique, 1997.

————. "Vive la Crise! For Heterodoxy in Social Science." *Theory and Society* 17 (1988) 773–87.

Bourdieu, Pierre, et al. *The Weight of the World: Social Suffering in Contemporary Society*. Translated by Priscilla Parkhurst Ferguson et al. Cambridge: Polity, 1999.

Bourdieu, Pierre, and Luc Boltanski. "Changes in Social Structures and Changes in the Demand for Education." In *Contemporary Europe: Social Structures and Cultural Patterns*, edited by Salvador Giner and Margaret Archer, 197–227. London: Routledge, 1978.

Bourdieu, Pierre, Jean-Claude Chamboredon, and Jean-Claude Passeron. *The Craft of Sociology: Epistemological Preliminaries*. Translated by Richard Nice. Berlin: de Gruyter, 1991.

Bourdieu, Pierre, and Alain Darbel. *The Love of Art*. Translated by Caroline Beattie and Nick Merriman. Cambridge: Polity, 1991.

Bourdieu, Pierre, and Jean-Claude Passeron. *Les Héritiers: Les étudiants et la culture*. Paris: Minuit, 1985.

————. *Reproduction in Education, Society and Culture*. 2nd ed. Translated by Richard Nice. London: Sage, 1990.

————. "Sociology and Philosophy in France since 1945: Death and Resurrection of a Philosophy without Subject." *Social Research* 34/1 (1967) 162–212.

Bourdieu, Pierre, and Monique de Saint-Martin. "La Sainte Famille." *Actes de la recherche en sciences sociales* 44/1 (1982) 2–53.

Bourdieu, Pierre, and Loïc J. D. Wacquant. "The Cunning of Imperialist Reason." In *Pierre Bourdieu and Democratic Politics: The Mystery of Ministry*, edited by Loïc J. D. Wacquant, 178–89. Cambridge: Polity, 2005.

————. *An Invitation to Reflexive Sociology*. Oxford: Polity, 1992.

Bourne, Richard. "Governmentality, Witness, and the State: Christian Social Criticism with and beyond Yoder and Foucault." In *Powers and Practices*, edited by Jermey M. Bergen and Anthony G. Siegrist, 99–116. Scottdale, PA: Herald, 2009.

———. *Seek the Peace of the City: Christian Political Criticism as Public, Realist, and Transformative*. Eugene, OR: Wipf & Stock, 2009.

Bouvaresse, Jacques, and Daniel Roche, editors. *La liberté par la connaissance. Pierre Bourdieu (1930–2002)*. Paris: Odile Jacob, 2004.

Boyarin, Daniel J. "Judaism as a Free Church: Footnotes to John Howard Yoder's *The Jewish-Christian Schism Revisited*." *CrossCurrents* 56/4 (2007) 6–21.

Brubacher Kaethler, Andrew. "The Practice of Reading the Other: John Howard Yoder's Critical and Caricatured Portrayal of Scholasticism." In *Powers and Practices*, edited by Jermey M. Bergen and Anthony G. Siegrist, 47–64. Scottdale, PA: Herald, 2009.

Burrell, David B. "An Introduction to *Theology and Social Theory*." *Modern Theology* 8/4 (1992) 319–31.

Caird, G. B. *Principalities and Powers: A Study in Pauline Theology*. Oxford: Clarendon, 1956.

Calhoun, Craig, Edward LiPuma, and Moishe Postone, editors. *Pierre Bourdieu: Critical Perspectives*. Cambridge: Polity, 1992.

Callewaert, Staf. "Bourdieu, Critic of Foucault: The Case of Empirical Social Science against Double-Game-Philosophy." *Theory, Culture & Society* 23/6 (2006) 73–98.

Callinicos, Alex. "Social Theory Put to the Test: Pierre Bourdieu and Anthony Giddens." *New Left Review* 1/236 (1999) 77–102.

Carter, Craig A. "The Liberal Reading of Yoder: The Problem of Yoder Reception and the Need for a Comprehensive Christian Witness." In *Radical Ecumenicity: Pursuing Unity and Continuity after Yoder*, edited by John C. Nugent, 85–106. Abilene, TX: Abilene Christian University Press, 2010.

———. *The Politics of the Cross: The Theology and Social Ethics of John Howard Yoder*. Grand Rapids: Brazos, 2001.

———. *Rethinking Christ and Culture: A Post-Christendom Perspective*. Grand Rapids: Brazos, 2007.

Cartwright, Michael G. "Radical Catholicity: Reflections on the Life and Work of John Howard Yoder." *Christian Century* (1998) 44–46.

———. "Radical Reform, Radical Catholicity: John Howard Yoder's Vision of the Faithful Church." In *The Royal Priesthood: Essays Ecclesiological and Ecumenical*, edited by Michael G. Cartwright, 1–49. Grand Rapids: Eerdmans, 1994.

———. "'Sharing the House of God': Learning to Read Scripture with Anabaptists." *Mennonite Quarterly Review* 74/4 (2000) 593–621.

Castel, Robert. "Entre la contrainte sociale et le volontarisme politique." In *La liberté par la connaissance. Pierre Bourdieu (1930–2002)*, edited by Jacques Bouvaresse and Daniel Roche, 303–31. Paris: Odile Jacob, 2004.

Cavanaugh, William T. "The City: Beyond Secular Parodies." In *Radical Orthodoxy: A New Theology*, edited by John Milbank, Catherine Pickstock, and Graham Ward, 182–200. London: Routledge, 1999.

Cazier, Jean-Phillipe, editor. *Abécédaire de Pierre Bourdieu*. Mons, Belgium: Sils Maria, 2006.

Certeau, Michel de. *The Practice of Everyday Life*. Translated by Steven Randall. Berkeley: University of California, 1984.

Bibliography

Champagne, Patrick, and Olivier Christin. *Mouvement d'une pensée. Pierre Bourdieu.* Paris: Bordas, 2004.

Chartier, Roger, and Patrick Champagne. *Pierre Bourdieu et les médias.* Paris: L'Harmattan, 2004.

Clayton, Philip. "God and World." In *Cambridge Companion to Postmodern Theology,* edited by Kevin J. Vanhoozer, 203–18. Cambridge: Cambridge University Press, 2003.

Coakley, Sarah. "'Persons' in the 'Social' Doctrine of the Trinity: Current Analytic Discussion and 'Cappadocian' Theology." In *Powers and Submissions: Spirituality, Philosophy and Gender,* 109–29. Oxford: Blackwell, 2002.

Colaguori, Claudio. "Symbolic Violence and the Violation of Human Rights: Continuing the Sociological Critique of Domination." *International Journal of Criminology and Sociological Theory* 3/2 (2010) 388–400.

Coles, Romand. *Beyond Gated Politics: Reflections for the Possibility of Democracy.* Minneapolis: University of Minnesota Press, 2005.

Collins, Randall. *Violence: A Micro-Sociological Theory.* Princeton: Princeton University Press, 2008.

Cramer, David C. "Inheriting Yoder Faithfully: A Review of New Yoder Scholarship." *Mennonite Quarterly Review* 85 (2011) 133–46.

Crossley, Nick. "On Systematically Distorted Communication: Bourdieu and the Socio-Analysis of Publics." In *After Habermas: New Perspectives on the Public Sphere,* edited by Crossley and John Michael Roberts, 88–112. Oxford: Blackwell, 2004.

———. *The Social Body: Habit, Identity and Desire.* London: Sage, 2001.

Cullmann, Oscar. *Christ and Time: The Primitive Christian Conception of Time and History.* Rev. ed. Translated by Floyd V. Filson. London: SCM, 1962.

———. *The Early Church.* Edited by A. J. B. Higgins. London: SCM, 1956.

———. *The State in the New Testament.* London: SCM, 1957.

Dawn, Marva. "The Concept of 'The Principalities and Powers' in the Works of Jacques Ellul." PhD diss., University of Notre Dame, 1992.

DeFerrari, Teresa M. "Review: *The Politics of Jesus* by John Howard Yoder." *Catholic Biblical Quarterly* 36 (1974) 149–50.

Derksen, Kevin. "Milbank and Violence: Against a Derridean Pacifism." In *The Gift of Difference: Radical Orthodoxy, Radical Reformation,* edited by Chris K. Huebner and Tripp York, 27–49. Winnipeg, MB: Canadian Mennonite University Press, 2010.

Dillon, Michele. "Pierre Bourdieu, Religion and Cultural Production." *Critical Studies <=> Critical Methodologies* 1/411 (2001) 411–29.

Dintaman, Stephen. "On Flushing the Confessional Rabbit Out of the Socio-Ecclesial Brushpile." *Conrad Grebel Review* 24/2 (2006) 33–49.

———. "The Spiritual Poverty of the Anabaptist Vision." *Conrad Grebel Review* 10/2 (1992) 205–8.

Doerksen, Paul G. *Beyond Suspicion: Post-Christendom Protestant Political Theology in John Howard Yoder and Oliver O'Donovan.* Eugene, OR: Wipf & Stock, 2010.

———. "Share the House: Yoder and Hauerwas among the Nations." In *A Mind Patient and Untamed: Assessing John Howard Yoder's Contributions to Theology, Ethics, and Peacemaking,* edited by Ben C Ollenburger and Gayle Gerber Koontz, 187–204. Telford, PA: Cascadia, 2004.

Donahue, John R. "Review of *The Politics of Jesus* by John Howard Yoder." *Theological Studies* 35/1 (1974) 179–80.

Dooyeweerd, Herman. *A New Critique of Theoretical Thought*. Volumes I and III. Jordan Station, ON: Paideia, 1983.

Dorrien, Gary. *Social Ethics in the Making: Interpreting an American Tradition*. Oxford: Blackwell, 2009.

Dubois, Jacques, Pascal Durand and Yves Winkin. *Le symbolique et le social. La réception internationale de la pensée de Pierre Bourdieu*. Liège, Belgium: L'Université de Liège, 2005.

Dula, Peter, and Chris K. Huebner, "Introduction." In *The New Yoder*, edited by Peter Dula and Chris K. Huebner, ix–xix. Eugene, OR: Cascade, 2010.

———, editors. *The New Yoder*. Eugene, OR: Cascade, 2010.

Dula, Peter, and Alex Sider. "Radical Democracy, Radical Ecclesiology." *CrossCurrents* 55/4 (2006) 482–504.

Durnbaugh, Donald F. "John Howard Yoder's Role in 'The Lordship of Christ over Church and State' Conferences." *Mennonite Quarterly Review* 76/3 (2003) 371–86.

Durkheim, Émile. *The Elementary Forms of Religious Life*. Translated by Karen E. Fields. New York: Free, 1995.

———. *The Rules of Sociological Method and Selected Texts on Sociology and Its Method*. Edited by Steven Lukes and translated by W. D. Halls. London: Macmillan, 1982.

Eco, Umberto. *The Infinity of Lists: From Homer to Joyce*. Translated by Alastair McEwen. London: MacLehose, 2009.

Eller, Vernard. "Review: *The Politics of Jesus* by John Howard Yoder." *Brethren Life and Thought* 18 (1973) 107–8.

Ellul, Jacques. *Apocalypse: The Book of Revelation*. New York: Seabury, 1977.

———. *The Ethics of Freedom*. Translated by Geoffrey W. Bromiley. London: Mowbrays, 1976.

———. *Money and Power*. Translated by LaVonne Neff. Hants, UK: Pickering, 1984.

———. "On Dialectic." In *Jacques Ellul: Interpretive Essays*, edited by Clifford G. Christians and Jay M. Van Hook, 291–308. Urbana, IL: University of Illinois Press, 1981.

———. *The Subversion of Christianity*. Translated by Geoffrey W. Bromiley. Grand Rapids: Eerdmans, 1986.

———. *The Technological Society*. Translated by John Wilkinson. New York: Knopf, 1967.

———. *The Theological Foundation of Law*. Translated by Marguerite Wieser. London: SCM, 1960.

———. *Violence: A Christian Perspective*. New York: Seabury, 1969.

Engler, Steven. "Modern Times: Religion, Consecration and the State in Bourdieu." *Cultural Studies* 17/3 (2003) 445–67.

English, James F. "Winning the Culture Game: Prizes, Awards, and the Rules of Art." *New Literary History* 33/1 (2002) 109–35.

Epp, Marlene, editor. "John Howard Yoder." Special Issue, *Conrad Grebel Review* 16/2 (1998).

Evens, T. M. S. "Bourdieu and the Logic of Practice: Is All Giving Indian-Giving or is 'Genetic Materialism' Not Enough?" *Sociological Theory* 17/1 (1999) 3–31.

Fasching, Darrell J. *The Thought of Jacques Ellul: A Systematic Exposition*. Lewiston, NY: Mellen, 1981.

Fernández, J. Manuel. "La noción de violence simbólica en la obra de Pierre Bourdieu. Una aproximación crítica." *Cuadernos de Trabajo Social* 18 (2005) 7–31.

Fine, Ben. *Social Capital versus Social Theory: Political Economy and Social Science at the Turn of the Millenium*. London: Routledge, 2001.

Finger, Thomas N. *A Contemporary Anabaptist Theology: Biblical, Historical, Constructive*. Downers Grove, IL: InterVarsity, 2004.

———. "Did Yoder Reduce Theology to Ethics?" In *Mind Patient and Untamed*, edited by Ollenburger and Koontz, 318–39.

Flanagan, Kieran. "Sociology into Theology: The Unacceptable Leap." *Theory, Culture & Society* 25/7–8 (2008) 236–61.

Fliethmann, Axel. "Bourdieu/Flaubert—Distinction?" In *Practising Theory: Pierre Bourdieu and the Field of Cultural Production*, edited by Jeff Browitt and Brian Nelson, 39–52. Cranbury, NJ: Associated University Press, 2004.

Flinn, Frank K. "Conversion: Up from Evangelicalism or the Pentecostal and Charismatic Experience." In *Religious Conversion: Contemporary Practices and Controversies*, edited by Christopher Lamb and M. Darrol Bryant, 51–74. London: Cassell, 1999.

Forbes, Chris. "Pauline Demonology and/or Cosmology? Principalities, Powers and the Elements of the World in their Hellenistic Context." *Journal for the Study of the New Testament* 24/3 (2002) 51–73.

———. "Paul's Principalities and Powers: Demythologizing Apocalyptic?" *Journal for the Study of the New Testament* 23/82 (2001) 61–88.

Foucault, Michel. "Truth and Power." In *The Foucault Reader*, edited by Paul Rabinow, 51–75. London: Penguin, 1984.

Fowler, Bridget. "Autonomy, Reciprocity and Science in the Thought of Pierre Bourdieu." *Theory, Culture & Society* 23/6 (2006) 98–117.

———. "An Introduction to Pierre Bourdieu's 'Understanding.'" *Theory, Culture & Society* 13/2 (1996) 1–16.

———. *Pierre Bourdieu and Cultural Theory: Critical Investigations*. London: Sage, 1997.

———. "Reading Pierre Bourdieu's *Masculine Domination*: Towards an Intersectional Analysis of Gender, Culture and Class." *Cultural Studies* 17/3–4 (2003) 468–94.

Friedmann, Robert. "Anabaptism and Pietism—Part 1." *Mennonite Quarterly Review* 14/2 (1940) 90–128.

———. "Anabaptism and Pietism—Part 2." *Mennonite Quarterly Review* 14/2 (1940) 149–69.

———. *Mennonite Piety through the Centuries: Its Genius and Literature*. Goshen, IN: Mennonite Historical Society, 1949.

———. "Spiritual Changes in European Mennonitism, 1650–1750." *Mennonite Quarterly Review* 15/1 (1941) 33–45)

Friesen, Duane K. *Artists, Citizens, Philosophers: Seeking the Peace of the City: An Anabaptist Theology of Culture*. Scottdale, PA: Herald, 2000.

Fuller, Steve. "Conatus." In *Pierre Bourdieu: Key Concepts*, edited by Michael Grenfell, 171–81. Stocksfield, UK: Acumen, 2008.

Gartman, David. "The Strength of Weak Programs in Cultural Sociology: A Critique of Alexander's Critique of Bourdieu." *Theory and Society* 36 (2007) 381–413.

Geldof, Koenraad. "Authority, Reading, Reflexivity: Pierre Bourdieu and the Aesthetic Judgment of Kant." Translated by Alex Martin. *Diacritics* 27/1 (1997): 20–43.

Gemperle, Michael. "The Double Character of the German 'Bourdieu': On the Twofold Use of Pierre Bourdieu's Work in the German-Speaking Social Sciences." *Sociologica* 1 (2009) 1–33.

Gill, Robin. *The Social Context of Theology: A Methodological Inquiry*. London: Mowbrays, 1975.

———. *Theology and Social Structure*. London: Mowbrays, 1977.

Gingerich, Ray C. "Theological Foundations for an Ethics of Nonviolence: Was Yoder's God a Warrior?" *Mennonite Quarterly Review* 77/3 (2003) 417–35.

Gingerich, Ray C. and Ted Grimsrud. *Transforming the Powers: Peace, Justice, and the Domination System*. Minneapolis: Fortress, 2006.

Girard, René. *Violence and the Sacred*. Translated by Patrick Gregory. Baltimore: Johns Hopkins University Press, 1977.

Goertz, Hans-Jürgen. "History and Theology: A Major Problem of Anabaptist Research Today." *Mennonite Quarterly Review* 53 (1979) 177–88.

Goldingay, John. *Israel's Gospel*. Downers Grove, IL: IVP, 2003.

Graber Miller, Keith. *Wise as Serpents, Innocent as Doves: American Mennonites Engage Washington*. Knoxville: University of Tennessee Press, 1996.

Grenfell, Michael. "Interest." In *Bourdieu: Key Concepts*, edited by Grenfell, chapter 9.

———. *Pierre Bourdieu: Education and Training*. London: Continuum, 2007.

———, editor. *Pierre Bourdieu: Key Concepts*. Stocksfield, UK: Acumen, 2008.

Grenfell, Michael, and David James, editors. *Bourdieu and Education: Acts of Practical Theory*. London: Falmer, 1998.

Griffin, Leslie. "The Problem of Dirty Hands." *Journal of Religious Ethics* 17/1 (1989) 31–61.

Griller, Robin. "The Return of the Subject? The Methodology of Pierre Bourdieu." *Critical Sociology* 22/1 (1996) 3–28.

Grimsrud, Ted. "Pacifism and Knowing: 'Truth' in the Theological Ethics of John Howard Yoder." *Mennonite Quarterly Review* 77/3 (2003) 403–15.

Guillory, "Bourdieu's Refusal." *Modern Language Quarterly*. 58/4 (1997) 367–98.

Gustafson, James M. *Protestant and Roman Catholic Ethics: Prospects for Rapprochement*. London: SCM, 1979.

———. *Theology and Ethics*. Oxford: Blackwell, 1981.

Gwyn, Douglas et al. *A Declaration of Peace: In God's People the World's Renewal Has Begun*. Scottdale, PA: Herald, 1991.

Habermas, Jürgen. *The Theory of Communication, Vol. 1, Reason and the Rationalization of Society*. Translated by Thomas McCarthy. Boston: Beacon, 1979.

———. "What is Universal Pragmatics." In *Communication and the Evolution of Society*, translated by Thomas McCarthy, 1–68. Boston: Beacon, 1979.

Hanchard, Michael. "Acts of Misrecognition: Transnational Black Politics, Anti-Imperialism and the Ethnocentrisms of Pierre Bourdieu and Loïc Wacquant." *Theory, Culture & Society* 20/4 (2003) 5–29.

Hanks, William F. "Bourdieu and the Practices of Language." *Annual Review of Anthropology* 34 (2005) 67–83.

Harder, Leland, editor. *The Sources of Swiss Anabaptism: The Grebel Letters and Related Documents*. Scottdale, PA: Herald, 1985.

———. "Zwingli's Reaction to the Schleitheim Confession of Faith of the Anabaptists." *The Sixteenth Century Journal* 11/4 (1980) 51–66.

Bibliography

Hardy, Cheryl. "Hysteresis." In *Pierre Bourdieu: Key Concepts*, edited by Michael Grenfell, 131–48. Stocksfield, UK: Acumen, 2008.

Harink, Douglas K. "The Anabaptist and the Apostle: John Howard Yoder as Pauline Theologian." In *A Mind Patient and Untamed: Assessing John Howard Yoder's Contributions to Theology, Ethics, and Peacemaking*, edited by Ben C. Ollenburger and Gayle Gerber Koontz, 274–87. Telford, PA: Cascadia, 2004.

———. *Paul among the Postliberals: Pauline Theology beyond Christendom and Modernity*. Grand Rapids: Brazos, 2003.

Harris, Harriet A. "Should We Say that Personhood is Relational?" *Scottish Journal of Theology* 51 (1998) 214–34.

Hauerwas, Stanley. *Christian Existence Today: Essays on Church, World, and Living in Between*. Grand Rapids: Brazos, 2001.

———. "Confessions of a Mennonite Camp Follower." *Mennonite Quarterly Review* 74/4 (2000) 511–22.

———. *Dispatches from the Front: Theological Engagements with the Secular*. Durham: Duke University Press, 1994.

———. *Hannah's Child: A Theologian's Memoir*. London: SCM, 2010.

———. *In Good Company: The Church as Polis*. Notre Dame, IN: University of Notre Dame Press, 1995.

———. *The Peaceable Kingdom: A Primer in Christian Ethics*. Rev. ed. London: SCM, 2003.

———. *Performing the Faith: Bonhoeffer and the Practice of Nonviolence*. Grand Rapids: Brazos, 2004.

———. *Sanctify them in the Truth: Holiness Exemplified*. Nashville: Abingdon, 1998.

———. *The State of the University: Academic Knowledges and the Knowledge of God*. Oxford: Blackwell, 2007.

———. *Wilderness Wanderings: Probing Twentieth-Century Theology and Philosophy*. Boulder, CO: Westview, 1997.

———. *With the Grain of the Universe: The Church's Witness and Natural Theology*. Grand Rapids: Brazos, 2001.

Hauerwas, Stanley, and Romand Coles. *Christianity, Democracy, and the Radical Ordinary: Conversations between a Radical Democrat and a Christian*. Eugene, OR: Cascade, 2008.

Hauerwas, Stanley, Chris K. Huebner, Harry J. Huebner, and Mark Thiessen Nation, editors. *The Wisdom of the Cross: Essays in Honor of John Howard Yoder*. Eugene, OR: Wipf & Stock, 2005.

Hauerwas, Stanley, and Samuel Wells, editors. *The Blackwell Companion to Christian Ethics*. Oxford: Blackwell, 2004.

Hawthorn, Geoffrey. *Enlightenment and Despair: A History of Sociology*. Cambridge: Cambridge University Press, 1970.

Hays, Richard B. *The Moral Vision of the New Testament: Community, Cross, New Creation: A Contemporary Introduction to New Testament Ethics*. San Francisco: HarperSanFrancisco, 1996.

Healy, Nicholas M. *Church, World and the Christian Life: Practical-Prophetic Ecclesiology*. Cambridge: Cambridge University Press, 2000.

Heidebrecht, Paul C. "Not Engineering, but Doxology? Reexamining Yoder's Perspective on the Church." In *Powers and Practices: Engaging the Work of John*

Howard Yoder, edited by Jeremy M. Bergen and Anthony G. Siegrist, 117–30. Scottdale, PA: Herald, 2009.

Heilke, Thomas. "Theological and Secular Meta-Narratives of Politics: Anabaptist Origins Revisited (Again)." *Modern Theology* 13/2 (1997) 228–47.

Heinich, Nathalie. *Pourquoi Bourdieu*. Paris: Gallimard, 2007.

Hershberger, Guy F., editor. *The Recovery of the Anabaptist Vision*. Scottdale, PA: Mennonite, 1957.

Hess, Cynthia. "Traumatic Violence and Christian Peacemaking." In *The New Yoder*, edited by Chris K. Huebner and Peter Dula, 196–215. Eugene, OR: Cascade, 2010.

Hillerbrand, Hans. "The 'Turning Point' of the Zwinglian Reformation: Review and Discussion." *Mennonite Quarterly Review* 39/4 (1965) 309–12.

Hobsbawm, Eric. "Sociologie critique et histoire sociale." In *La liberté par la connaissance. Pierre Bourdieu (1930–2002)*, edited by Jacques Bouvaresse and Daniel Roche, 281–92. Paris: Odile Jacob, 2004.

Holland, Ray. "Reflexivity." *Human Relations* 52/4 (1999) 463–84.

Holland, Scott, editor. "The Jewish-Christian Schism Revisited and Re-Imagined: Reflections on the Work of John Howard Yoder." Special Issue, *CrossCurrents* 56/4 (2007).

Holton, Robert. "Bourdieu and Common Sense." *SubStance* 26/3 (1997) 38–52.

Holtzen, William Curtis. "Dei Fide: A Relational Theology of the Faith of God." PhD diss., University of South Africa, 2007.

Hovey, Craig R. "The Public Ethics of John Howard Yoder and Stanley Hauerwas: Difference or Disagreement?" In *A Mind Patient and Untamed: Assessing John Howard Yoder's Contributions to Theology, Ethics, and Peacemaking*, edited by Ben C. Ollenburger and Gayle Gerber Koontz, 205–20. Telford, PA: Cascadia, 2004.

Huebner, Chris K. *A Precarious Peace: Yoderian Explorations on Theology, Knowledge, and Identity*. Scottdale, PA: Herald, 2006.

Huebner, Chris K., and Tripp York, editors. *The Gift of Difference: Radical Orthodoxy, Radical Reformation*. Winnipeg, MB: Canadian Mennonite University Press, 2010.

Huebner, Harry J. "Participation, Peace, and Forgiveness: Milbank and Yoder in Dialogue." In *The Gift of Difference: Radical Orthodoxy, Radical Reformation*, edited by Chris K. Huebner and Peter Dula, 180–204. Winnipeg, MB: Canadian Mennonite University Press, 2010.

Hunter, James Davison. *To Change the World: The Irony, Tragedy, & Possibility of Christianity in the Late Modern World*. Oxford: Oxford University Press, 2010.

Hurtado, Larry W. *God in New Testament Theology*. Nashville: Abingdon, 2010.

The Hutterian Brethren and John Howard Yoder, editors. *God's Revolution: The Witness of Eberhard Arnold*. Farmington, PA: Plough, 1984.

Jenkins, Richard. *Pierre Bourdieu*. London: Routledge, 1992.

Kauppi, Niilo. *French Intellectual Nobility: Institutional and Symbolic Changes in the Post-Sartrian Era*. Albany, NY: State University of New York, 1996.

———. "The Sociologist as *Moraliste*: Pierre Bourdieu's Practice of Theory and the French Intellectual Tradition." *SubStance* 93 (2000) 7–21.

Kerr, Fergus. *After Aquinas: Versions of Thomism*. Oxford: Blackwell, 2002.

———. *Theology after Wittgenstein*. 2nd ed. London: SPCK, 1997.

Kerr, Nathan R. *Christ, History, and Apocalyptic: The Politics of Christian Mission*. Eugene, OR: Cascade, 2009.

————. "*Communio Missionis*: Certeau, Yoder, and the Missionary Space of the Church." In *The New Yoder*, edited by Peter Dula and Chris K. Huebner, 317–36. Eugene, OR: Cascade, 2010.

Kilby, Karen. "Perichoresis and Projection: Problems with Social Doctrines of the Trinity." *New Blackfriars* 81/957 (2000) 432–45.

Kissling, Paul J. "John Howard Yoder's Reading of the Old Testament and the Stone-Campbell Tradition." In *Radical Ecumenicity: Pursuing Unity and Continuity after Yoder*, edited by John C. Nugent, 129–48. Abilene, TX: Abilene Christian University Press, 2010.

Klassen, William. "Jesus and the Zealot Option." In *The Wisdom of the Cross: Essays in Honor of John Howard Yoder*, edited by Stanley Hauerwas, Chris K. Huebner, Harry J. Huebner, and Mark Thiessen Nation, 131–49. Eugene, OR: Wipf & Stock, 2005.

————. "John Howard Yoder and the Ecumenical Church." *Conrad Grebel Review* 16/2 (1998) 77–81.

Krais, Beate. "Gender, Sociological Theory and Bourdieu's Sociology of Practice." *Theory, Culture & Society* 23/6 (2006) 119–34.

Kroeker, P. Travis. "Is a Messianic Political Ethic Possible? Recent Work by and about John Howard Yoder." *Journal of Religious Ethics* 33/1 (2005) 141–74.

————. "War of the Lamb: Postmodernity and Yoder's Eschatological Genealogy of Morals." In *The New Yoder*, edited by Peter Dula and Chris K. Huebner, 70–89. Eugene, OR: Cascade, 2010.

————. "Why O'Donovan's Christendom is not Constantinian and Yoder's Voluntariety is not Hobbesian." *Annual for the Society of Christian Ethics* 20 (2000) 41–64.

Kuhn, Thomas S. *The Structure of Scientific Revolutions*. 3rd ed. Chicago: University of Chicago Press, 1996.

Kuyper, Abraham. *Lectures on Calvinism*. Grand Rapids: Eerdmans, 1987.

————. "Sphere Sovereignty." In *Abraham Kuyper: A Centennial Reader*, edited by James D. Bratt, 461–90. Grand Rapids: Eerdmans, 1998.

Lakomski, Gabriele. "On Agency and Structure: Pierre Bourdieu and Jean-Claude Passeron's Theory of Symbolic Violence." *Curriculum Inquiry* 14/2 (1984) 151–63.

Lane, Jeremy F. "Neo-liberalism as 'Imposition' and 'Invasion': Problems in Bourdieu's Politics." *French Cultural Studies* 14/3 (2003) 323–35.

Lapeyronnie, Didier. "L'académisme radical ou le monologue sociologique. Avec qui parle les sociologues?" *Revue française de sociologie* 45/4 (2004) 621–51.

Lash, Nicholas. *Holiness, Speech and Silence: Reflections on the Question of God*. Burlington, VT: Ashgate, 2004.

Lash, Scott. "Modernization and Postmodernization in the Work of Pierre Bourdieu." In *Sociology of Postmodernism*, 237–65. London: Routledge, 1990.

Law, Alex. "Unredeemed Marxism: Political Commitment in Bourdieu and MacIntyre." *Critique* 37/4 (2009) 665–81.

Layman, David Wayne. "The Inner Ground of Christian Theology: Church, Faith, and Sectarianism." *Journal of Ecumenical Studies* 27/3 (1990) 480–503.

Lebaron, Frédéric. "Pierre Bourdieu: Economic Models against Economism." *Theory and Society* 32/5–6 (2003) 551–65.

Leithart, Peter J. *Deep Exegesis: The Mystery of Reading Scripture*. Waco, TX: Baylor University Press, 2009.

————. *Defending Constantine: The Twilight of an Empire and the Dawn of Christendom.* Downers Grove, IL: IVP, 2010.

————. *A Son to Me: An Exposition of 1 and 2 Samuel.* Moscow, ID: Canon, 2003.

Lewin, Kurt. "Constructs in Field Theory." In *Field Theory in Social Science: Selected Theoretical Papers,* edited by Dorwin Cartwright, 30–42. London: Tavistock, 1952.

Lindbeck, George A. *The Nature of Doctrine: Religion and Theology in a Postliberal Age.* Philadelphia: Westminster, 1984.

Loesberg, Jonathan. "Bourdieu's Derrida's Kant: The Aesthetics of Refusing Aesthetics." *Modern Language Quarterly* 58/4 (1997) 417–36.

Lynch, Michael. "Against Reflexivity as an Academic Virtue and Source of Privileged Knowledge." *Theory, Culture & Society* 17/3 (2000) 26–54.

MacGregor, G. H. C. "Principalities and Powers: The Cosmic Background of St. Paul's Thought." *New Testament Studies* 1 (1954–1955) 17–28.

Marginson, Simon. "Global Field and Global Imagining: Bourdieu and Worldwide Higher Education." *British Journal of Sociology of Education* 29/3 (2008) 303–15.

Martel, Frédéric. "Bourdieu et la question homosexuelle." *Magazine Littéraire* 369 (1998) 59–60.

Martens, Paul. "Discipleship Ain't Just about Jesus: or On the Importance of the Holy Spirit for Pacifists." *Conrad Grebel Review* 21/2 (2003) 32–40.

————. *The Heterodox Yoder.* Eugene, OR: Cascade, 2011.

————. "The Problematic Development of the Sacraments in the Thought of John Howard Yoder." *Conrad Grebel Review* 24/3 (2006) 65–77.

————. "Universal History and a Not-Particularly Christian Particularity: Jeremiah and John Howard Yoder's Social Gospel." In *Powers and Practices: Engaging the Work of John Howard Yoder,* edited by Jeremy M. Bergen and Anthony G. Siegrist, 131–46. Scottdale, PA: Herald, 2009.

Martens, Paul, and Jennifer L. Howell, editors. *John Howard Yoder: Spiritual Writings.* Maryknoll, NY: Orbis, 2011.

Martín-Criado, Enrique. *Les deux Algéries de Pierre Bourdieu.* Translated by Hélène Bretin. Broissieux, France: Croquant, 2008.

Mathewes, Charles. "Culture." In *The Blackwell Companion to Modern Theology,* edited by Gareth Jones, 47–64. Oxford: Blackwell, 2004.

————. *A Theology of Public Life.* Cambridge: Cambridge University Press, 2007.

Maton, Karl. "Pierre Bourdieu and the Epistemic Conditions of Social Scientific Knowledge." *Space and Culture* 6/1 (2003) 52–65.

————. "The Sacred and the Profane: The Arbitrary Legacy of Pierre Bourdieu." *European Journal of Cultural Studies* 8/1 (2005) 101–12.

Mayer, Nonna. "L'entretien selon Pierre Bourdieu. Analyse critique de *La misère du monde.*" *Revue française de sociologie* 36/2 (1995) 355–70.

McClendon, James W. *Ethics.* Nashville: Abingdon, 1986.

McClendon, James W., and John Howard Yoder. "Christian Identity in Ecumenical Perspective: A Response to David Wayne Layman." *Journal of Ecumenical Studies* 27/3 (1990) 561–80.

McNay, Lois. "Meditations on *Pascalian Meditations.*" *Economy and Society* 30/1 (2001) 139–54.

————. "Subject, Psyche and Agency: The Work of Judith Butler." *Theory, Culture & Society* 16/2 (1995) 175–93.

————. "The Trouble with Recognition: Subjectivity, Suffering, and Agency." *Sociological Theory* 26/3 (2008) 271–96.

Mehl, Roger. "The Basis of Christian Social Ethics." In *Christian Social Ethics in a Changing World: An Ecumenical Theological Inquiry*, edited by John C. Bennett, 44–58. New York: Association, 1966.

Milbank, John. *Being Reconciled: Ontology and Pardon*. London: Routledge, 2003.

————. "Materialism and Transcendence." In *Theology and the Political: The New Debate*, edited by Creston Davis, John Milbank, and Slavoj Žižek, 393–426. Durham, NC: Duke University Press, 2005.

————. "Power is Necessary for Peace: In Defence of Constantine." *ABC Religion and Ethics*, October 29, 2010. Online: http://www.abc.net.au/religion/articles/2010/10/29/3051980.htm.

————. "Radical Orthodoxy and Radical Reformation: What is Radical about Radical Orthodoxy? Forum with John Milbank." *Conrad Grebel Review* 23/2 (2005) 41–54.

————. *Theology and Social Theory: Beyond Secular Reason*. 2nd ed. Oxford: Blackwell, 2006.

Milbank, John, and Stanley Hauerwas, "Christian Peace: A Conversation between Stanley Hauerwas and John Milbank." In *Must Christianity Be Violent? Reflections on History, Practice, and Theology*, edited by Kenneth R. Chase and Alan Jacobs, 207–35. Grand Rapids: Brazos, 2003.

Milbank, John, and Catherine Pickstock. *Truth in Aquinas*. London: Routledge: 2001.

Milbank, John, Catherine Pickstock, and Graham Ward, editors. *Radical Orthodoxy: A New Theology*. London: Routledge, 1999.

Milbank, John, and Graham Ward. "Radical Orthodoxy Ten Years On: The Return of Metaphysics." In *The New Visibility of Religion: Studies in Religion and Cultural Hermeneutics*, edited by Graham Ward and Michael Hoelzl, 151–69. London: Continuum, 2008.

Miller, John W. "In the Footsteps of Marcion: Notes Toward an Understanding of John Yoder's Theology." *Conrad Grebel Review* 16/2 (1998) 82–92.

Min, Jeon Kii. *Sin and Politics: Issues in Reformed Theology*. New York: Lang, 2009.

Minear, Paul. *The Eyes of Faith: A Study in the Biblical Point of View*. Philadelphia: Westminster, 1946.

Mitrovic, Ljubisa. "Bourdieu's Criticism of the Neoliberal Philosophy of Development, the Myth of Mondalization and the New Europe (An Appeal for the Renewal of Critical Sociology)." *Philosophy, Sociology and Psychology* 4/1 (2005) 37–49.

Morrison, Clinton D. *The Powers That Be: Earthly Rulers and Demonic Powers in Romans 13:1–7*. London: SCM, 1960.

Mouw, Richard J. "Abandoning the Typology: A Reformed Assist." *TSF Bulletin* 17 (1985) 7–10.

————. *He Shines in All That's Fair: Culture and Common Grace*. Grand Rapids: Eerdmans, 2002.

————. *Politics and the Biblical Drama*. Grand Rapids: Eerdmans, 1976.

————. *When the Kings Come Marching In: Isaiah and the New Jerusalem*. Rev. ed. Grand Rapids: Eerdmans, 2002.

Mouw, Richard J., and John Howard Yoder. "Evangelical Ethics and the Anabaptist-Reformed Dialogue." *Journal of Religious Ethics* 17/2 (1989) 121–37.

Murphy, Nancey C. *Anglo-American Postmodernity: Philosophical Perspectives on Science, Religion, and Ethics*. Boulder, CO: Westview, 1997.

————. *Bodies and Souls, or Spirited Bodies?* Cambridge: Cambridge University Press, 2006.

————. "John Howard Yoder's Systematic Defense of Christian Pacifism." In *The New Yoder*, edited by Peter Dula and Chris K. Huebner, 42–69. Eugene, OR: Cascade, 2010.

Murphy, Nancey C., and George Francis Rayner Ellis. *On the Moral Nature of the Universe: Theology, Cosmology, and Ethics.* Minneapolis: Fortress, 1996.

Nation, Mark Thiessen. *John Howard Yoder: Mennonite Patience, Evangelical Witness, Catholic Convictions.* Grand Rapids: Eerdmans, 2006.

Neufeld, Justin. "Just War Theory, the Authorization of the State, and the Hermeneutics of Peoplehood: How John Howard Yoder can Save Oliver O'Donovan from Himself." *International Journal of Systematic Theology* 8/4 (2006) 411–32.

Neufeld, Mark. "Responding to Realism: Assessing Anabaptist Alternatives." *Conrad Grebel Review* 12/1 (1994) 43–62.

Niebuhr, H. Richard. *Christ and Culture.* New York: HarperCollins, 2001.

————. "The Doctrine of the Trinity and the Unity of the Church." *Theology Today* 3/3 (1946) 371–84.

Nolt, Steven M. "Anabaptist Visions of Church and Society." *Mennonite Quarterly Review* 69 (1995) 283–94.

Nugent, John C. "Biblical Warfare Revisited: Extending the Insights of John Howard Yoder." In *Powers and Practices: Engaging the Work of John Howard Yoder*, edited by Jeremy M. Bergen and Anthony G. Siegrist, 167–84. Scottdale, PA: Herald, 2009.

————. *The Politics of YAHWEH: John Howard Yoder, the Old Testament, and the People of God.* Eugene, OR: Cascade, 2011.

————, editor. *Radical Ecumenicity: Pursuing Unity and Continuity after Yoder.* Abilene, TX: Abilene Christian University Press, 2010.

————. "'Trial and Error': A Yoderian Response to Leithart's *Defending Constantine*." *Englewood Review of Books* 3/46 (2010). Online: http://http://erb.kingdomnow. org/featured-a-yoderian-rejoinder-to-leitharts-defending-constantine-vol-3-46/.

O'Donovan, Oliver. *The Desire of the Nations.* Cambridge: Cambridge University Press, 1996.

————. "A Response to James W. Skillen." In *A Royal Priesthood? The Use of the Bible Ethically and Politically: A Dialogue with Oliver O'Donovan*, edited by Craig Bartholomew, Jonathan Chaplin, Robert Song, and Al Wolters, 418–20. Carlisle, UK: Paternoster, 2002.

————. *Resurrection and Moral Order: An Outline for Evangelical Ethics.* 2nd ed. Leicester, UK: Apollos, 1994.

Ollenberger, Ben C., and Gayle Gerber Koontz, editors. *A Mind Patient and Untamed: Assessing John Howard Yoder's Contributions to Theology, Ethics, and Peacemaking.* Telford, PA: Cascadia, 2004.

Otto, Randall E. "The Use and Abuse of Perichoresis in Recent Theology." *Scottish Journal of Theology* 54 (2001) 372–77.

Outhwaite, William. "The Myth of Modernist Method." *European Journal of Social Theory* 2/1 (1999) 5–26.

Pannenberg, Wolfhart. *Anthropology in Theological Perspective.* Translated by Matthew J. O'Connell. Edinburgh: T. & T. Clark, 1985.

————. *An Introduction to Systematic Theology.* Grand Rapids: Eerdmans, 1991.

Panofsky, Erwin. *Gothic Architecture and Scholasticism: An Inquiry into the Analogy of the Arts, Philosophy, and Religion in the Middle Ages.* New York: Meridian, 1976.

Park, Joon-Sik. *Missional Ecclesiologies in Creative Tension: H. Richard Niebuhr and John Howard Yoder.* New York: Lang, 2007.

Parler, Branson. "John Howard Yoder and the Politics of Creation." In *Powers and Practices: Engaging the Work of John Howard Yoder,* edited by Jeremy M. Bergen and Anthony G. Siegrist, 65–82. Scottdale, PA: Herald, 2009.

Passeron, Jean-Claude. "Le sociologue en politique et *vice versa*: enquêtes sociologiques et réformes pédagogiques dans les années 1960." In *La liberté par la connaissance. Pierre Bourdieu (1930–2002),* edited by Jacques Bouvaresse and Daniel Roche, 15–104. Paris: Odile Jacob, 2004.

Peace, Richard V. *Conversion in the New Testament: Paul and the Twelve.* Grand Rapids: Eerdmans, 1999.

Pfeil, Margaret R. "John Howard Yoder's Pedagogical Approach: A Just War Tradition with Teeth and a Hermeneutic of Peace." *Mennonite Quarterly Review* 76/2 (2002) 181–88.

Pilario, Daniel Franklin. *Back to the Rough Grounds of Praxis: Exploring Theological Method with Pierre Bourdieu.* Leuven: Leuven University Press, 2005.

Pipkin, H. Wayne, and John Howard Yoder, editors. *Balthasar Hubmaier: Theologian of Anabaptism.* Scottdale, PA: Herald, 1989.

Poupeau, Franck. "Reasons for Domination, Bourdieu versus Habermas." In *Reading Bourdieu on Society and Culture,* edited by Bridget Fowler, 69–87. Oxford: Blackwell, 2000.

Poupeau, Franck, and Thierry Discepolo. "Scholarship with Commitment: On the Political Engagements of Pierre Bourdieu." In *Pierre Bourdieu and Democratic Politics: The Mystery of Ministry,* edited by Loïc J. D Wacquant, 64–90. Cambridge: Polity, 2005.

Rambo, Lewis R. *Understanding Religious Conversion.* London: Yale University Press, 1993.

Rambo, Lewis R., and Charles E. Farhadian. "Converting: Stages of Religious Change." In *Religious Conversion: Contemporary Practices and Controversies,* edited by Christopher Lamb and M. Darrol Bryant, 23–34. London: Cassell, 1999.

Rasmusson, Arne. "Ecclesiology and Ethics: The Difficulties of Ecclesial Moral Reflection." *Ecumenical Review* 52/2 (2000) 180–194.

———. "The Politics of Diaspora: The Post-Christendom Theologies of Karl Barth and John Howard Yoder." In *God, Truth, and Witness: Engaging Stanley Hauerwas,* edited by L. Gregory Jones, Reinhard Hütter, and C. Rosalee Velloso Ewell, 88–111. Grand Rapids: Brazos, 2005.

Reader, Keith. "The State They're In: Bourdieu, Debray and the Revival of *Engagement*." *SubStance* 29/3 (2000) 43–52.

Reed-Danahay, Deborah. *Locating Bourdieu.* Bloomington, IN: Indiana University Press, 2005.

Reimer, A. James. *Christians and War: A Brief History of the Church's Teaching and Practices.* Minneapolis: Fortress, 2010.

———. "'I came not to abolish the law but to fulfill it': A Positive Theology of Law and Civil Institutions." In *A Mind Patient and Untamed: Assessing John Howard Yoder's Contributions to Theology, Ethics, and Peacemaking,* edited by Ben C. Ollenberger and Gayle Gerber Koontz, 245–73. Telford, PA: Cascadia, 2004.

―――. *Mennonites and Classical Theology*. Kitchner, ON: Pandora, 2001.

Rey, Terry. *Bourdieu on Religion: Imposing Faith and Legitimacy*. London: Equinox, 2007.

Robbins, Derek. *Bourdieu and Culture*. London: Sage, 2000.

―――. "The Need for an Epistemological 'Break.'" In *Bourdieu and Education: Acts of Practical Theory*, edited by Michael Grenfell and David James, 27–52. London: Falmer, 1998.

―――. "The Origins, Early Development and Status of Bourdieu's Concept of 'Cultural Capital.'" *British Journal of Sociology* 56/1 (2005) 13–30.

Ross, Kristin. *May '68 and Its Afterlives*. London: University of Chicago Press, 2002.

Roth, John D., editor. Special Issue, *Mennonite Quarterly Review* 76/3 (2003).

Rouanet, Henry, Wemer Ackermann, and Brigitte Le Roux. "L'analyse géométrique des questionnaires—La leçon de *La Distinction* de Bourdieu." *Bulletin de méthodologue sociologique* 65/1 (2000) 5–18.

Rupp, E. Gordon. *Principalities and Powers: Studies in the Christian Conflict in History*. London: Epworth, 1952.

Sanders, Chris, and Karen Robson. "Introduction: Approaches to Quantifying Bourdieu." In *Quantifying Theory: Pierre Bourdieu*, edited by Robson and Sanders, 1–10. Berlin: Springer, 2009.

Sayer, Andrew. "Bourdieu, Smith and Disinterested Judgement." *The Sociological Review* 47/3 (1999) 404–31.

Schatzki, Theodore. "Practice and Actions: A Wittgensteinian Critique of Bourdieu and Giddens." *Philosophy of the Social Sciences* 27/3 (1997) 283–308.

Schinkel, Willem. *Aspects of Violence: A Critical Theory*. New York: Palgrave Macmillan, 2010.

―――. "Pierre Bourdieu's Political Turn?" *Theory, Culture & Society* 20/6 (2003) 69–93.

―――. "Sociological Discourses of the Relational: The Case of Bourdieu and Latour." *The Sociological Review* 55/4 (2007) 707–29.

Schlabach, Gerald W. "Anthology in Lieu of System: John H. Yoder's Ecumenical Conversations on Systematic Theology." *Mennonite Quarterly Review* 71 (1997) 305–9.

―――. "The Christian Witness in the Earthly City: John H. Yoder as Augustinian Interlocutor." In *A Mind Patient and Untamed: Assessing John Howard Yoder's Contributions to Theology, Ethics, and Peacemaking*, edited by Ben C. Ollenberger and Gayle Gerber Koontz, 221–44. Telford, PA: Cascadia, 2004.

―――. "Continuity and Sacrament, or Not: Hauerwas, Yoder, and Their Deep Difference." *Journal of the Society of Christian Ethics* 27/2 (2007) 171–207.

―――. "Deuteronomic or Constantinian: What Is the Most Basic Problem for Christian Social Ethics?" In *The Wisdom of the Cross: Essays in Honor of John Howard Yoder*, edited by Stanley Hauerwas, Chris K. Huebner, Harry J. Huebner, and Mark Thiessen Nation, 449–71. Eugene, OR: Wipf & Stock, 2005.

―――, editor. *Just Policing: An Alternative Response to World Violence*. Collegeville, MN: Liturgical, 2007.

Schlabach, Theron. "Mennonites and Pietism in America, 1740–1880: Some Thoughts on the Friedmann Thesis." *Mennonite Quarterly Review* 57/3 (2003) 222–40.

Schleir, Heinrich. *Principalities and Powers in the New Testament*. Edinburgh: Nelson, 1961.

Schroeder, Edward H. "The Orders of Creation—Some Reflections on the History and Place of the Term in Systematic Theology." *Concordia Theological Monthly* 43 (1972) 165–78.

Schubert, J. Daniel. "From a Politics of Transgression toward an Ethics of Reflexivity: Foucault, Bourdieu, and Academic Practice." *American Behavioral Scientist* 38/7 (1995) 1003–1017.

———. "Suffering." Chapter 11 in *Pierre Bourdieu: Key Concepts*, edited by Grenfell.

Schüssler Fiorenza, Elisabeth. *Bread Not Stone: The Challenges of Feminist Biblical Interpretation*. Boston: Beacon, 1984.

Seibel, Claude. "Les liens entre Pierre Bourdieu et les statisticians, á partir de son experience algérienne." In *La liberté par la connaissance. Pierre Bourdieu (1930–2002)*, edited by Jacques Bouvaresse and Daniel Roche, 105–19. Paris: Odile Jacob, 2004.

Shaffer, Thomas. *Moral Memoranda from John Howard Yoder: Conversations on Law, Ethics and the Church between a Mennonite Theologian and a Hoosier Lawyer*. Eugene, OR: Wipf & Stock, 2002.

Shults, F. LeRon. *Reforming the Doctrine of God*. Grand Rapids, MI: Eerdmans, 2005.

Sider, J. Alexander. *To See History Doxologically: History and Holiness in John Howard Yoder's Ecclesiology*. Grand Rapids: Eerdmans, 2011.

Skeggs, Beverley. "Exchange, Value and Affect: Bourdieu and the 'Self.'" In *Feminism after Bourdieu*, edited by Lisa Adkins and Skeggs, 75–95. Oxford: Blackwell, 2004.

Smith, James K. A. *Desiring the Kingdom: Worship, Worldview and Cultural Formation*. Grand Rapids: Baker, 2009.

———. *Introducing Radical Orthodoxy: Mapping a Post-Secular Theology*. Grand Rapids: Baker Academic, 2004.

Smith, Ted A. "Redeeming Critique: Resignations to the Cultural Turn in Christian Theology and Ethics." *Journal of the Society of Christian Ethics* 24/2 (2004) 89–113.

Smith-Christopher, Daniel L. *A Biblical Theology of Exile*. Minneapolis: Fortress, 2002.

Snyder, C. Arnold. "Beyond Polygenesis: Recovering the Unity and Diversity of Anabaptist Theology." In *Essays in Anabaptist Theology*, edited by H. Wayne Pipkin, 1–33. Elkhart, IN: Institute of Mennonite Studies, 1994.

———. "The Birth and Evolution of Swiss Anabaptism, 1520–1530." *Mennonite Quarterly Review* 80/4 (2006) 501–646.

———. "The Influence of the Schleitheim Articles on the Anabaptist Movement: An Historical Evaluation." *Mennonite Quarterly Review* 63 (1989) 323–44.

———, editor. "John Howard Yoder as Historian." Special Issue, *Conrad Grebel Review* 24/2 (2006).

———, editor. "Radical Orthodoxy and Radical Reformation." Special Issue, *Conrad Grebel Review* 23/2 (2005).

———. "The Schleitheim Articles in Light of the Revolution of the Common Man: Continuation or Departure?" *The Sixteenth Century Journal* 16/4 (1985) 419–30

Somer, Michael, editor. *La sagesse de la croix. Impulsions à partir de l'ouevre de John Howard Yoder*. Cléon d'Andron: Excelsis, 2007.

Spinoza, Benedict de. *The Ethics*. Translated by R. H. M. Elwes (1883). MTSU Philosophy WebWorks, Hypertext Edition. Online: http://frank.mtsu.edu/~rbombard/RB/Spinoza/ethica-front.html

Stackhouse, John G. *Making the Best of It: Following Christ in the Real World*. Oxford: Oxford University Press, 2008.

Stassen, Glen H. "Concrete Christological Norms for Transformation." In *Authentic Transformation: A New Vision of Christ and Culture*, by Glen H. Stassen, D. M. Yeager, and John Howard Yoder, 127–90. Nashville: Abingdon, 1996.

———. *Just Peacemaking: Transforming Initiatives for Justice and Peace*. Louisville: Westminster John Knox, 1992.

———. "A New Vision." In *Authentic Transformation: A New Vision of Christ and Culture*, by Glen H. Stassen, D. M. Yeager, and John Howard Yoder, 191–268. Nashville: Abingdon, 1996.

———. "The Politics of Jesus in the Sermon on the Plain." In *The Wisdom of the Cross: Essays in Honor of John Howard Yoder*, edited by Stanley Hauerwas, Chris K. Huebner, Harry J. Huebner, and Mark Thiessen Nation, 150–167. Eugene, OR: Wipf & Stock, 2005.

Stassen, Glen H., and David P. Gushee. *Kingdom Ethics: Following Jesus in Contemporary Context*. Downers Grove, IL: InterVarsity, 2003.

Stassen, Glen H., D. M. Yeager, and John Howard Yoder. *Authentic Transformation: A New Vision of Christ and Culture*. Nashville: Abingdon, 1996.

Stayer, James M. *Anabaptists and the Sword*. Lawrence, KS: Coronado, 1972.

———. "Reflections and Retractions on *Anabaptists and the Sword*." *Mennonite Quarterly Review* 51 (1977) 196–212.

———. "The Separatist Church of the Majority: A Response to Charles Nienkirchen." *Mennonite Quarterly Review* 57 (1983) 151–55.

Stayer, James M., Werner O. Packull, and Klaus Deppermann. "From Monogenesis to Polygenesis: The Historical Discussion of Anabaptist Origins." *Mennonite Quarterly Review* 49 (1975) 83–121.

Sterne, Jonathan. "Bourdieu, Technique and Technology." *Cultural Studies* 17/3–4 (2003) 367–89.

Stirk, Nigel. "Wittgenstein and Social Practices." *Environment and Planning D: Society and Space* 17 (1999) 35–50.

Stoltzfus, Philip E. "Nonviolent Jesus, Violent God? A Critique of John Howard Yoder's Approach to Theological Construction." In *Powers and Practices: Engaging the Work of John Howard Yoder*, edited by Jeremy M. Bergen and Anthony G. Siegrist, 29–46. Scottdale, PA: Herald, 2009.

Stott, John R. W. *The Message of Ephesians: God's New Society*. Leicester: InterVarsity, 1979.

Stout, Jeffrey. *Democracy and Tradition*. Princeton: Princeton University Press, 2004.

———. *Ethics After Babel: The Languages of Morals and their Discontents*. Princeton: Princeton University Press, 2001.

Stramara, Daniel F. "Gregory of Nyssa's Terminology for Trinitarian Perichoresis." *Vigiliae Christianae* 52/3 (1998) 257–63.

Swartley, Willard M. "Smelting for Gold: Jesus and Jubilee in John H. Yoder's *Politics of Jesus*." In *A Mind Patient and Untamed: Assessing John Howard Yoder's Contributions to Theology, Ethics, and Peacemaking*, edited by Ben C. Ollenberger and Gayle Gerber Koontz, 288–302. Telford, PA: Cascadia, 2004.

Swartz, David L. "From Critical Sociology to Public Intellectual: Pierre Bourdieu and Politics." *Theory and Society* 32/5–6 (2003) 791–823.

———. "Pierre Bourdieu and North American Political Sociology: Why He Doesn't Fit in but Should." *French Politics* 4 (2006) 84–99.

Tanner, Kathryn. *Theories of Culture: A New Agenda for Theology.* Minneapolis: Fortress, 1997.

Throop, C. Jason, and Keith M. Murphy, "Bourdieu and Phenomenology: A Critical Assessment." *Anthropological Theory* 2/2 (2002) 185–207.

Toews, Paul. "The Mennonite Search for a Useable Past: From the Declensive to the Ironic Interpretation." *Mennonite Quarterly Review* 73 (1999) 470–484.

Toole, David. *Waiting for Godot in Sarajevo: Theological Reflections on God, Nihilism, and Apocalypse.* London: SCM, 2001.

Touraine, Alain. "Le sociologue du peuple." In *Pierre Bourdieu: Son oeuvre, son héritage*, edited by Véronique Bedin, 109–11. Paris: Seuil, 2008.

Vandenbergh, Frédéric. "The Real is Relational: An Epistemological Analysis of Pierre Bourdieu's Generative Structuralism." *Sociological Theory* 17/1 (1999) 32–67.

Vázquez García, Francisco. *Pierre Bourdieu: La sociología como crítica de la razón.* Barcelona: Montesinos, 2002.

Verter, Bradford. "Spiritual Capital: Theorizing Religion with Bourdieu against Bourdieu." *Sociological Theory* 21/2 (2003) 150–174.

Visser't Hooft, W. A. *The Kingship of Christ: An Interpretation of Recent European Theology.* London: SCM, 1948.

Vogt, Virgil, editor. *Concern for Education: Essays on Christian Higher Education*, 1958–1966. Eugene, OR: Cascade, 2010.

———, editor. *The Roots of Concern: Writings on Anabaptist Renewal*, 1952–1957. Eugene, OR: Cascade, 2009.

Wacquant, Loïc J. D. "From Ruling Class to Field of Power: An Interview with Pierre Bourdieu on *La noblesse d'État.*" *Theory, Culture & Society* 10/3 (1993) 19–44.

———, editor. *Pierre Bourdieu and Democratic Politics: The Mystery of Ministry.* Cambridge: Polity, 2005.

———. "Pointers on Pierre Bourdieu and Democratic Politics." In *Pierre Bourdieu and Democratic Politics: The Mystery of Ministry*, edited by Loïc J. D. Wacquant, 10–28. Cambridge: Polity, 2005.

———. "Symbolic Power in the Rule of the 'State Nobility.'" In *Pierre Bourdieu and Democratic Politics: The Mystery of Ministry*, edited by Loïc J. D. Wacquant, 133–46. Cambridge: Polity, 2005.

———. "Toward a Social Praxeology: The Structure and Logic of Bourdieu's Sociology." In *An Invitation to Reflexive Sociology*, edited by Pierre Bourdieu and Loïc J. D. Wacquant, 1–60. Oxford: Polity, 1992.

Walton, Robert C. "Was There a Turning Point of the Zwinglian Reformation?" *Mennonite Quarterly Review* 42 (1968) 45–56.

———. *Zwingli's Theocracy.* Toronto: University of Toronto Press, 1967.

Walzer, Michael. *Exodus and Revolution.* New York: Basic, 1985.

Ward, Graham. "Between Postmodernism and Postmodernity: The Theology of Jean-Luc Marion." In *Postmodernity, Sociology and Religion*, edited by Kieran Flanagan and Peter C. Jupp, 190–205. Basingstoke, UK: Macmillan, 1996.

———. *Cities of God.* London: Routledge, 2000.

———. *Cultural Transformation and Religious Practices.* Cambridge: Cambridge University Press, 2005.

Weaver, Alain Epp. *States of Exile: Visions of Diaspora, Witness, and Return.* Scottdale, PA: Herald, 2008.

Weaver, J. Denny. "The John Howard Yoder Legacy: Whither the Second Generation." *The Mennonite Quarterly Review* 451/471 (2003) 451–71.

———. *Nonviolent Atonement*. Grand Rapids: Eerdmans, 2001.

Webb, Jenn, Tony Schirato, and Geoff Danaher. *Understanding Bourdieu*. London: Sage, 2002.

Webber, Robert E. *The Church in the World: Opposition, Tension, or Transformation?* Grand Rapids: Zondervan, 1986.

Weik, Elke. "Bourdieu and Leibniz: Mediated Dualisms." *Sociological Review* 58/3 (2010) 486–96.

Werpehowski, William. *American Protestant Ethics and the Legacy of H. Richard Niebuhr*. Washington, DC: Georgetown University Press, 2002.

Westphal, Merold. *Overcoming Onto-Theology: Toward a Postmodern Christian Faith*. New York: Fordham University Press, 2001.

Whiteley, D. E. H., and Roderick Martin, editors. *Sociology, Theology and Conflict*. Oxford: Blackwell, 1969.

Wiebe, Joseph R. "Fracturing Evangelical Recognitions of Christ: Inheriting the Radical Democracy of John Howard Yoder with the Penumbral Vision of Rowan Williams." In *The New Yoder*, edited by Peter Dula and Chris K. Huebner, 294–316. Eugene, OR: Cascade, 2010.

Wilder, Amos N. *Otherworldliness and the New Testament*. London: SCM, 1955.

Williams, Rowan. *The Truce of God*. Grand Rapids: Eerdmans, 2005.

Wink, Walter. *Cracking the Gnostic Code: The Powers in Gnosticism*. Atlanta: Scholars, 1993.

———. *Engaging the Powers: Discernment and Resistance in a World of Domination*. Minneapolis: Fortress, 1992.

———. *Naming the Powers: The Language of Power in the New Testament*. Philadelphia: Fortress, 1984.

———. *The Powers That Be: Theology for a New Millenium*. London: Doubleday, 1998.

———. *Unmasking the Powers: The Invisible Forces that Determine Human Existence*. Philadelphia: Fortress, 1986.

———. *Violence and Nonviolence in South Africa: Jesus' Third Way*. Philadelphia: New Society, 1987.

———. *When the Powers Fall: Reconciliation in the Healing of the Nations*. Minneapolis: Fortress, 1998.

Wittgenstein, Ludwig. *Philosophical Investigations*. 3rd ed. Translated by G. E. M. Anscombe. Upper Saddle River, NJ: Prentice-Hall, 1958.

Wogaman, J. Philip. *A Christian Method of Moral Judgment*. London: SCM, 1976.

———. *Christian Moral Judgment*. Louisville: Westminster John Knox, 1989.

———. *Christian Perspectives on Politics*. London: SCM, 1988.

Wright, N. T. *Jesus and the Victory of God*. Minneapolis: Fortress, 1996.

Wright, Nigel Goring. *Disavowing Constantine: Mission, Church and the Social Order in the Theologies of John Howard Yoder and Jürgen Moltmann*. Carlisle, UK: Paternoster, 2000.

Yoder, John Howard. *Anabaptism and Reformation in Switzerland: An Historical and Theological Analysis of the Dialogues between Anabaptists and Reformers*. Edited by C. Arnold Snyder. Translated by Snyder and David Carl Stassen. Kitchener, ON: Pandora, 2004.

————. "'Anabaptists and the Sword' Revisited: Systematic Historiography and Undogmatic Nonresistants." *Zeitschrift für Kirchengeschichte* 85/2 (1974) 126–39.

————. "Armaments and Eschatology." *Studies in Christian Ethics* 1/1 (1988) 43–61.

————. "Balthasar Hubmaier and the Beginnings of Swiss Anabaptism." *Mennonite Quarterly Review* 33/1 (1959) 5–17.

————. "The Believers' Church Conferences in Historical Perspective." *Mennonite Quarterly Review* 65/1 (1991) 5–19.

————. *Body Politics: Five Practices of the Christian Community before the Watching World.* Scottdale, PA: Herald, 2001.

————. *Christian Attitudes to War, Peace, and Revolution.* Edited by Theodore J. Koontz and Andy Alexis-Baker. Grand Rapids: Brazos, 2009.

————. *The Christian and Capital Punishment.* Newton, KS: Faith and Life, 1961.

————. *The Christian Witness to the State.* Scottdale, PA: Herald, 2002.

————. *Discipleship as Political Responsibility.* Scottdale, PA: Herald, 2003.

————. "Does Natural Law Provide a Basis for a Christian Witness to the State." *Brethren Life and Thought* 7/2 (1962) 18–22.

————. *The End of Sacrifice: The Capital Punishment Writings of John Howard Yoder.* Edited by John C. Nugent. Harrisonburg, VA: Herald, 2011.

————. "Ethics and Eschatology." *Ex Auditu* 6 (1990) 119–28.

————. "The Evolution of the Zwinglian Reformation." *Mennonite Quarterly Review* 43/1 (1969) 95–122.

————. "Exodus and Exile: The Two Faces of Liberation." *Cross Currents* 23/3 (1973) 297–309.

————. "The Experiential Etiology of Evangelical Dualism." *Missiology* 11/4 (1983) 449–59.

————. *For the Nations: Essays Evangelical and Public.* Grand Rapids: Eerdmans, 1997.

————. *The Fullness of Christ: Paul's Revolutionary Vision of Universal Ministry.* Elgin, IL: Brethren, 1987.

————. *He Came Preaching Peace.* Scottdale, PA: Herald, 1985.

————. "The Hermeneutics of the Anabaptists." *Mennonite Quarterly Review* 41/4 (1967) 291–308.

————. "Historiography as a Ministry to Renewal." *Brethren Life and Thought* 42/3–4 (1997) 216–28.

————. "How H. Richard Niebuhr Reasoned: A Critique of *Christ and Culture.*" In *Authentic Transformation: A New Vision of Christ and Culture*, edited by Glen H. Stassen, D. M. Yeager, and John Howard Yoder, 31–90. Nashville: Abingdon, 1996.

————. "Jesus and Power." *Ecumenical Review* 25/4 (1973) 447–54.

————. *The Jewish-Christian Schism Revisited.* Edited by Michael G. Cartwright and Peter Ochs. Grand Rapids,: Eerdmans, 2003.

————. *Karl Barth and the Problem of War & Other Essays on Barth.* Edited by Mark Thiessen Nation. Eugene, OR: Cascade, 2003. See esp. "Behold My Servant Shall Prosper," 149–68.

————, editor and translator. *The Legacy of Michael Sattler.* Scottdale, PA: Herald, 1973.

————, "Meaning after Babble: With Jeffrey Stout beyond Relativism," *Journal of Religious Ethics* 24 (Spring 1996): 125–39.

————. *Nevertheless: The Varieties and Shortcomings of Religious Pacifism.* Rev. ed. Scottdale, PA: Herald, 1992.

———. "Non-Baptists' View of Southern Baptists." *Review & Expositor* 67/2 (1970) 219–28.

———. *Nonviolence—A Brief History: The Warsaw Lectures.* Edited by Paul Martens, Matthew Porter, and Myles Werntz. Waco, TX: Baylor University Press, 2010.

———. *The Original Revolution: Essays on Christian Pacifism.* Scottdale, PA: Herald, 1972.

———. *A Pacifist Way of Knowing: John Howard Yoder's Nonviolent Epistemology.* Edited by Christian E. Early and Ted Grimsrud. Eugene, OR: Cascade, 2010.

———. "A 'Peace Church' Perspective on Covenanting." *Ecumenical Review* 38/3 (1986) 318–21.

———. *The Politics of Jesus: Vicit Agnus Noster.* 2nd ed. Grand Rapids: Eerdmans, 1994.

———. *Preface to Theology: Christology and Theological Method.* Grand Rapids: Brazos, 2002.

———. *The Priestly Kingdom: Social Ethics as Gospel.* Notre Dame, IN: University of Notre Dame Press, 1984.

———. "The Prophetic Dissent of the Anabaptists." In *The Recovery of the Anabaptist Vision,* edited by Guy F. Hershberger, 93–104. Scottdale, PA: Mennonite, 1957.

———. "Reformed versus Anabaptist Social Strategies: An Inadequate Typology." *TSF Bulletin* 17 (1985) 2–7.

———. "Reinhold Niebuhr and Christian Pacifism." *Mennonite Quarterly Review* 29/2 (1955) 101–17.

———. "Response of an Amateur Historian and a Religious Citizen." *Journal of Law & Religion* 7/2 (1989) 415–32.

———. "Review: *The Context of Decision* by Gordon D. Kaufman." *Mennonite Quarterly Review* 37 (1963) 133–38.

———. "Review: *The Scapegoat* by René Girard." *Religion & Literature* 19/3 (1987) 89–92.

———. *Revolutionary Christianity: The 1966 South American Lectures.* Edited by Paul Martens, Mark Thiessen Nation, Matthew Porter, and Myles Werntz. Eugene, OR: Cascade, 2011.

———. *The Royal Priesthood: Essays Ecclesiological and Ecumenical.* Edited by Michael G. Cartwright. Grand Rapids: Eerdmans, 1994.

———. "Sacrament as Social Process: Christ the Transformer of Culture." *Theology Today* 48/1 (1991) 33–44.

———, editor and translator. *The Schleitheim Confession.* Scottdale, PA: Herald, 1977.

———. "Texts That Serve or Texts That Summon: A Response to Michael Walzer." *Journal of Religious Ethics* 20/2 (1992) 229–34.

———. "Theological Revision and the Burden of Particular Identity." In *James M. Gustafson's Theocentric Ethics,* edited by Harlan R. Beckley and James M. Swezey, 63–89. Macon, GA: Mercer University Press, 2002.

———. *To Hear the Word.* 2nd ed. Eugene, OR: Wipf & Stock, 2010.

———. "To Serve our God and to Rule the World." *Annual of the Society of Christian Ethics* (1988) 3–14.

———. "The Turning Point in the Zwinglian Reformation." *Mennonite Quarterly Review* 32/2 (1958) 128–40.

———. "The Unique Role of the Historic Peace Churches." *Brethren Life and Thought* 14/3 (1969) 132–49.

———. *The War of the Lamb: The Ethics of Nonviolence and Peacemaking.* Edited by Glen Stassen, Mark Thiessen Nation, and Matt Hamsher. Grand Rapids: Brazos, 2009.

———. *What Would You Do? A Serious Answer to a Standard Question.* Expanded ed. Scottdale, PA: Herald, 1992.

———. *When War is Unjust: Being Honest in Just-War Thinking.* 2nd ed. Eugene, OR: Wipf & Stock, 2001.

Zanten, Angès van. "Bourdieu as Education Policy Analyst and Expert: A Rich but Ambiguous Legacy." *Journal of Education Policy* 20/6 (2005) 671–86.

Zimmerman, Earl. *Practicing the Politics of Jesus: The Origin and Significance of John Howard Yoder's Social Ethics.* Scottdale, PA: Herald, 2007.

Zimmerman, John. "Yoder's Jesus and Economics: The Economics of Jesus or the Economics of Luke?" *Mennonite Quarterly Review* 77/3 (2003) 437–50.